Concurrent
and **Real-Time**
Programming
in **Java**

Concurrent and Real-Time Programming in Java

Andy Wellings
University of York, UK

John Wiley & Sons, Ltd

Other Wiley Editorial Offices

John Wiley & Sons Inc., 111 River Street, Hoboken, NJ 07030, USA

Jossey-Bass, 989 Market Street, San Francisco, CA 94103-1741, USA

Wiley-VCH Verlag GmbH, Boschstr. 12, D-69469 Weinheim, Germany

John Wiley & Sons Australia Ltd, 33 Park Road, Milton, Queensland 4064, Australia

John Wiley & Sons (Asia) Pte Ltd, 2 Clementi Loop #02-01, Jin Xing Distripark, Singapore 129809

John Wiley & Sons Canada Ltd, 22 Worcester Road, Etobicoke, Ontario, Canada M9W 1L1

Wiley also publishes its books in a variety of electronic formats. Some content that appears in print may not be available in electronic books.

Library of Congress Cataloging-in-Publication Data

Wellings, Andrew J.
 Concurrent and real-time programming in Java / Andy Wellings.
  p. cm.
 Includes bibliographical references and index.
 ISBN 0-470-84437-X
 1. Java (Computer program language) 2. Parallel programming (Computer science)
3. Real-time programming. I. Title.
 QA76.73.J38W465 2004
 005.13'1--dc22

            2004008522

British Library Cataloguing in Publication Data

A catalogue record for this book is available from the British Library

ISBN 0-470-84437-X

Typeset in 10/12.5 pt Times by Laserwords Private Limited, Chennai, India from files produced by the author
Printed and bound in Great Britain by Biddles Ltd, King's Lynn
This book is printed on acid-free paper responsibly manufactured from sustainable forestry
in which at least two trees are planted for each one used for paper production.

Contents

Preface

Real-time systems have to respond to externally generated input stimuli within a finite and predictable time. Their correctness depends not only on the logical results of the computations, but also on the time at which those results are produced.

When Java emerged as a serious programming language in 1994, it was treated with disdain by much of the real-time community. Although the language was interesting from a number of perspectives – not least the fact that it had an integrated concurrent object-oriented programming model – the whole notion of Java as a real-time programming language was laughable. "Java and Real-time" was considered, by many, an oxymoron. What we failed to appreciate was the determination of the Java community to propagate the language into every conceivable application area.

Just over 10 years since its first conception, Java, augmented by the Real-Time Specification for Java, is one of the most exciting developments in real-time systems so far this century. The approach has been to extend the concurrency model so that it supports real-time programming abstractions and to provide a complementary approach to memory management that removes the temporal uncertainties of garbage collection.

This book is concerned with both concurrent *and* real-time programming in Java. To fully understand the facilities available for real-time programming, it is first necessary to have a good appreciation of the strengths and weaknesses of multi-threaded programming in conventional Java. Once this understanding has been achieved, the motivations for the Real-Time Specification become apparent and the full details of the real-time functionality can then be presented.

Audience

This book is aimed at final year and masters students in computer science and related disciplines. It has also been written with the professional software engineer and real-time systems engineer in mind. Readers are assumed to have knowledge of sequential programming in Java and to be familiar with the basic tenets of software engineering in general and object-oriented programming in particular. For completeness, an overview of the sequential and object-oriented components of the Java language is provided (on the web site that accompanies this book) for those programmers who have experience in languages such as C or C++.

Structure and content

The book starts with an introduction to concurrent and real-time programming. The motivations for supporting concurrency are given and some basic real-time terminology is established. The main body of the book falls into three parts.

Chapters 2 to 6 deal with concurrent programming in Java. Chapter 2 places the Java model in the context of the various concurrent programming techniques that have been developed over the last 35 years. It also considers thread creation in detail. Chapter 3 focuses on communication and synchronization. Synchronized methods and statements are covered in depth, and the new Java 1.5 Memory Model is explained. Asynchronous thread control is also covered in this chapter and the limitations of the Java thread interrupt model are discussed. Chapter 4 completes the Java concurrency model by considering the facilities for scheduling, delaying threads and providing time-outs. Thread groups are also considered in this chapter along with some concurrency-related utilities. The chapter concludes by summarizing the strengths and weaknesses of the Java model. Chapters 5 and 6 provide detailed examples using the Java model. Chapter 5 shows how the language can be used to implement various communication paradigms. Chapter 6 presents a case study of concurrent searching.

Chapters 7 to 15 provide a detailed introduction to and an examination of the Real-Time Specification for Java (RTSJ). Firstly, Chapter 7 reviews the process that led to the development of the specification and provides an overview of the main enhancements to the Java platform. Chapter 8 then tackles the new memory management facilities in detail. This is followed by consideration of the augmented clock and time facilities. Chapters 10, 11 and 12 deal with scheduling and the main schedulable entities, namely, asynchronous event handlers and real-time threads. Asynchronous transfer of control is the topic of Chapter 13. It is here that the notion of an asynchronous exception is introduced. Chapter 14 considers resource sharing between schedulable objects themselves and between non-real-time threads and schedulable objects. Chapter 15 completes the review of the RTSJ by considering access to physical and raw memory.

Chapters 16 to 18 conclude the book. Chapter 16 provides a standard real-time case study: that of an automobile cruise control system. This demonstrates many of the facilities of the RTSJ. Chapter 17 then considers the use of Java and the RTSJ for high-integrity systems programming. A profile (Ravenscar-Java) is introduced that supports a highly predictable and efficient computational model. The familiar mine control system is used as an extended example to illustrate this restrictive model. Finally, Chapter 18 draws some conclusions from this study and outlines the challenges facing Java from a concurrency and real-time perspective. An appendix summarizes the main classes and interfaces discussed in this book.

The book is consistent with the proposed 1.0.1 version of the Real-Time Specification for Java (Belliardi *et al.*, 2004). However, this version still has some limitations and inconsistencies, and work is currently under way to resolve these (in a 1.1 release). Where appropriate, the above chapters indicate the likely changes that may occur. The book is Java 1.5 compliant.

Notations and conventions

Throughout this book Java programs are presented in `Courier New` font and keywords are in **boldface** type. Classes and interfaces that are part of the packages `java.lang`, `java.util`, and `javax.realtime` are presented on a shaded background. All other programs are not shaded.

Class and object diagrams use the standard UML notation.

Teaching aids

This text is supported by further material available via the following WWW site:

    http://www.cs.york.ac.uk/rts/CRTJbook.html

Included are an introduction to sequential and object-oriented programming in Java, and powerpoint files for lecturers teaching the material.

Real-Time Systems Research at York

Andy Wellings is professor of Real-Time Systems within the Department of Computer Science at the University of York (UK). With Alan Burns, he leads the Real-Time Systems Research Group. This group undertakes research into all aspects of the design, implementation and analysis of real-time systems. The aim of the group is to undertake fundamental research and to bring into engineering practice modern techniques, methods and tools. Further information about the group's activities can be found via

    http://www.cs.york.ac.uk/rts

Acknowledgments

Writing a book is never a solo activity. I am indebted to the following people:

- Doug Locke for inviting me to join the Technical Interpretation Committee (TIC) for the Real-Time Specification for Java. This enabled me to gain invaluable insights into the motivation for and meaning of the original specification.

- Rudy Belliardi, Greg Bollella, Ben Brosgol, Peter Dibble, and David Holmes (the other members of the TIC) for helping me understand the nuances of the specification, and for the stimulating weekly conference calls and many email exchanges that led to the production of version 1.0.1 of the Real-Time Specification for Java.

- The reviewers of the first draft, and in particular David Holmes who spent many hours giving me constructive feedback. The quality of the final product has been greatly improved because of this.

- Alan Burns for being a sounding board for many of the topics covered in the book, for detailed comments on the first draft and for his general support.

- My research students and research assistants for providing me with a forum for discussing many of the topics covered in this book. In particular, Andrew Borg, Hao Cai, Yang Chang, Erik Hu, Jagun Kwon, Armando Aquilar-Soto, Pat Rogers, and Alex Zerzelidis.

- Past and present members of the Computer Science Department at York, especially Neil Audsley, Iain Bate, Ian Broster, Guillem Bernat, David Duke, Steve King, Richard Paige, and Paul Sammut for general help at various times during the writing of this book.

- The students of the 2002/2003 and 2003/2004 York Advanced MSc courses in software engineering for providing feedback on the material presented in this book during the Concurrent and Real-Time Programming module.

- Gaynor Redvers-Mutton from Wiley for her advice and guidance.

Finally, I would like to thank Sylvia Holmes for proofreading more than one draft copy of the book, suggesting many changes to improve the presentation, and for providing continuous encouragement and support.

Andy Wellings (andy@cs.york.ac.uk)
Real-Time Systems Research Group
Department of Computer Science, University of York
York, YO10 5DD, U.K.

August 2004

1 Introduction

Background and chapter structure

Java is a young programming language. It was conceived in 1991 and was originally intended for use in the consumer electronics industry. However, not until it was retargeted at the booming internet business, in 1994, did it begin to receive widespread attention from the programming community. Since that time, the popularity of Java has grown beyond all expectations. Just as the C programming language before rose to dominance with the popularity of the Unix operating system, so Java has ridden on the back of the internet tide. Of course, the language does have advantages over its competitors. They are summarized by its authors as follows (Gosling and McGilton, 1996):

- **simple, object oriented and familiar** – object-oriented programming is still the dominant programming paradigm; the Java model is simple and has many similarities with C++;
- **robust** – extensive compile-time and run-time checking ensures that programs are highly reliable;
- **distributed and secure** – a language and run-time system designed to operate in a distributed environment needs to incorporate security features;
- **interpreted, architecture neutral and portable** – the use of a virtual machine that interprets an architecture neutral byte code ensures that programs are portable from one platform to another;
- **high performance** – techniques such as just-in-time compilation allow performance-critical code to be compiled to native code, counteracting some of the overheads associated with interpreting byte codes;
- **dynamic** – linking is dynamic; classes are only loaded when needed, and new classes can be linked as the system evolves;
- **multithreaded** – language support for concurrent programming allows portable multithreaded applications to be constructed.

In recent years, proponents of Java have attempted to extend its influence into the real-time and embedded systems domains. As many of these systems are now, or will be in the future, networked, the language seems to provide an ideal basis for their implementation. Unfortunately, Java, for all its advantages, does have some serious limitations for real-time and embedded programming. This has led to the development of the *Real-Time Specification for Java* (RTSJ). This defines a set of extensions to the Java virtual machine and the class libraries that facilitate real-time programming. Given the inherently concurrent nature of real-time and embedded systems, much of the RTSJ is associated with improving the Java threading model.

This book addresses the use of Java and the RTSJ for the development of concurrent real-time systems. Many real-time systems are also embedded in a larger engineering environment, hence the facilities provided by the RTSJ are also useful in that domain.

The remainder of this chapter provides an introduction to concurrency and real-time. The book then considers, in depth, the role that Java and the RTSJ can play in the construction of real-time systems. Concurrency and real-time are advanced topics in programming, consequently the remaining chapters assume that the reader is familiar with object-oriented programming in sequential Java. The web site that accompanies this book provides an introduction to Java suitable for those programmers who know languages like C or C++ but who are unfamiliar with Java.

1.1 Concurrency

Concurrent programming is the name given to the notations that are used to express (potential) parallelism in an application program. It also encompasses the techniques for dealing with communication and synchronization between (potentially) parallel entities.

Motivations for concurrency

There are three main motivations for wanting to write concurrent programs:

- **To fully utilize the processor** – Modern processors run at speeds far in excess of the input and output devices with which they must interact. A sequential program that is waiting for I/O is unable to perform any other operation. Consider a program that wishes to perform an I/O intensive operation, for example, a graphical animation, and yet also needs to calculate the next sequence in the animation. Performing these operations sequentially would have a drastic effect on the speed at which the animation can run.

- **To allow more than one processor to solve a problem** – A sequential program can only be executed by one processor (unless the compiler has transformed the program into a concurrent one). A concurrent program is able to exploit true parallelism and obtain faster execution. In Chapter 6, a concurrent program to search a maze is given. On a multiprocessor system, this can find all paths through a large maze much more quickly than its sequential counterpart.

- **To model parallelism in the real world** – Real-time and embedded programs have to control and interface with real-world entities (robots, conveyor belts, etc.) that are inherently parallel. Reflecting the parallel nature of the system in the structures of the program makes for a more readable, maintainable and reliable application.

A major problem associated with the production of software for systems that exhibit concurrency is how to express that concurrency in the structure of the program. One approach is to leave it all up to the programmer who must construct his/her system so that it involves the cyclic execution of a program sequence to handle the various concurrent threads. There are several reasons, however, why this is inadvisable (Burns and Wellings, 2001):

- It complicates the programmer's already difficult task and involves him/her in considerations of structures that are irrelevant to the control of the threads in hand.

- The resulting program is more obscure and inelegant.

- It makes proving program correctness more difficult.

- It makes decomposition of the problem more complex.

- Parallel execution of the program on more than one processor is much more difficult to achieve.

- The placement of code to deal with faults is more problematic.

Older languages, for example, Fortran and Pascal, relied on operating system support for concurrency; C is usually associated with UNIX or POSIX. However, the more modern languages, such as C#, Ada and Java have direct support for concurrent programming.

Criticisms and new problems

One of the major criticisms of concurrent programming is that it introduces overheads and, therefore, results in slower execution when the program is running on a single processor system. However, the software engineering issues outweigh these concerns, just as the efficiency concerns of programming in a high-level sequential language are outweighed by its advantages over programming with an assembly language.

Writing concurrent programs introduces new problems that do not exist in their sequential counterparts. Concurrent activities need to coordinate their actions, if they are to work together to solve a problem. This coordination can involve intricate patterns of communication and synchronization. If not properly managed, these can add significant complexity to the programs and result in new error conditions arising. For example,

- *deadlock* may occur where each concurrent activity is waiting for another to perform an operation;

- *interference* may occur when two or more concurrent activities attempt to update the same object; this can result in the object's data becoming corrupt;

- *starvation* may happen where one or more concurrent activities are continually denied resources as a result of the actions of the others.

The desired behavior of a concurrent program is usually summarized using two properties: *safety* and *liveness*. The safety property expresses the requirement for "nothing bad to happen". In other words, the concurrent activities do not interfere with each other and cause data corruption. The liveness property expresses the requirement that "something good will happen". In other words, that all concurrent activities are able to make progress with their associated computation and do not suffer from deadlocks or starvation.

Deadlock is the most common problem in concurrent systems. There are four necessary conditions that must exist if deadlock is to occur. These are usually expressed in terms of resources allocated to a thread. In Java, for example, the lock associated with an object can be considered as a resource. The conditions are as follows:

- **Mutual exclusion** – only one concurrent activity can use a resource at once (that is, the resource is nonsharable or at least limited in its concurrent access); using locks as an example, mutual exclusion locks as opposed to read/write locks are more likely to cause deadlock.

- **Hold and wait** – there must exist concurrent activities that are holding resources while waiting for others resources to be acquired; with locks, concurrent activities must be holding locks while waiting to acquire new locks.

- **No preemption** – a resource can only be released voluntarily by a concurrent activity; the locks acquired by a concurrent activity cannot be forcibly taken away from it by another activity.

- **Circular wait** – a circular chain of concurrent activities must exist such that each activity holds resources (has locked the objects) that are being requested by the next activity in the chain.

There are three possible approaches to dealing with deadlock:

- **Deadlock prevention** – Deadlock can be prevented by ensuring that at least one of the four conditions required for deadlock never occurs. For example, by using sharable resources, never holding one resource while waiting for another, making resources preemptible, or by imposing a strict logical ordering on resource allocation requests so that all threads request resources in the same order.

- **Deadlock avoidance** – If more information on the pattern of resource usage is known, then it is possible to construct an algorithm that will allow all the four conditions necessary for deadlock to occur, but which will also ensure that the system never enters a deadlock state. A deadlock avoidance algorithm will examine dynamically the resource allocation state and take action to ensure that the system can never enter into deadlock. Any resource allocation request that is potentially unsafe is denied.

- **Deadlock detection and recovery** – In many general-purpose concurrent systems, the resource allocation usage is *a priori* unknown. Even if it is known, the cost of deadlock avoidance is often prohibitive. Consequently, many of these systems will ignore the problems of deadlock until they enter a deadlock state. They then take some corrective action (for example, by aborting a concurrent activity and preempting its resources.)

Chapters 2, 3 and 4 review the facilities that Java provides to create concurrent activities and to manage communication and synchronization, thus facilitating the safety and liveness properties of concurrent programs.

1.2 Real-time Systems

A major application area of concurrent programming is real-time systems. These are systems that have *to respond to externally generated input stimuli (including the passage of time) within a finite and specified time interval*. They are inherently concurrent because they are often embedded in a larger engineering system and have to model the parallelism that exists in the real-world objects that they are monitoring and controlling. Process control, manufacturing support, command and control are all example application areas where real-time systems have a major role. As computers become more ubiquitous and pervasive, so they will be embedded in a wide variety of common materials and components throughout the home or workplace – even in the clothes we wear. These computers will need to react with their environment in a timely fashion. The RTSJ extends the Java concurrency model to allow it to interact with external events, be they interrupts or the passage of time itself.

As well as being concurrent, real-time systems also have the following additional characteristics (Burns and Wellings, 2001):

Large and complex. Real-time systems vary from simple single-processor embedded systems (consisting of a few hundred lines of code) to multiplatform multilanguage distributed systems (consisting of millions of lines of code). The issue of engineering large and complex systems is an important topic that Java and its support environment do address. However, consideration of this area is beyond the scope of this book.

Extremely reliable and safe. Many real-time systems control some of society's critical systems such as air traffic control or chemical/power plants. The software must, therefore, be engineered to the highest integrity, and programs must attempt to tolerate faults and continue to operate (albeit perhaps providing a degraded service). In the worst case, a real-time system should make safe the environment before shutting down in a controlled manner. Unfortunately, some systems do not have easily available safe states when they are operational (for example, an unstable aircraft), consequently, continued operation in the presence of faults or damage is a necessity. Java's design goals facilitate the design of reliable and robust programs. Its exception handling facility allows error recovery mechanisms to be activated. The RTSJ extends the Java platform to allow the detection of common timing-related problems (such as missed deadlines).

Real-time facilities. Response time is crucial in any embedded system. Unfortunately, it is very difficult to design and implement systems that will guarantee that the appropriate output will be generated at the appropriate times under all possible conditions. To do this and make full use of all computing resources at all times is often impossible. For this reason, real-time systems are usually constructed using processors with considerable spare capacity, thereby ensuring that "worst-case behavior" does not produce any unwelcome delays during critical periods of the system's operation. Given adequate processing power, language and run-time support is required to enable the programmer to

- specify times at which actions are to be performed

- specify times at which actions are to be completed

- respond to situations where *all* the timing requirements cannot be met

- respond to situations where the timing requirements are changed dynamically.

These are called *real-time control facilities*. They enable the program to synchronize with time itself. For example, with digital control algorithms, it is necessary to sample readings from sensors at certain periods of the day, for example, 2 pm, 3 pm, and so on, or at regular intervals, for instance, every 5 seconds (with analog-to-digital converters, sample rates can vary from a few hundred hertz to several hundred megahertz). As a result of these readings, other actions will need to be performed. In order to meet response times, it is necessary for a system's behavior to be predictable. Providing these real-time facilities is one of the main goals of the RTSJ.

Interaction with hardware interfaces. The nature of embedded systems requires the computer components to interact with the external world. They need to monitor sensors and control actuators for a wide variety of real-world devices. These devices interface to the computer via input and output registers, and their operational requirements are device and computer dependent. Devices may also generate interrupts to signal to the processor that certain operations have been performed or that error conditions have arisen. In the past, the interfacing to devices has either been left under the control of the operating system or has required the application programmer to resort to assembly language inserts to control and manipulate the registers and interrupts. Nowadays, because of the variety of devices and the time-critical nature of their associated interactions, their control must often be direct, and not through a layer of operating system functions. Furthermore, reliability requirements argue against the use of low-level programming techniques. The augmented memory management model of the RTSJ allows memory-mapped device registers to be accessed. Support for asynchronous event handlers allows interrupts to be handled by a schedulable entity.

Efficient implementation and a predictable execution environment. Since real-time systems are time-critical, efficiency of implementation will be more important than in other systems. It is interesting that one of the main benefits of using a high-level language is that it enables the programmer to abstract away from implementation details and to concentrate on solving the problem at hand. Unfortunately, embedded computer systems programmers cannot afford this luxury. They must be constantly concerned with the cost of using particular language features. For example, if a response to some input is required within a microsecond, there is no point in using a language feature whose execution takes a millisecond! The RTSJ makes predictability a primary concern in all its design trade-offs.

Hard and soft real-time systems

It is common to distinguish between *hard* and *soft* real-time systems. Hard real-time systems are those where it is absolutely imperative that responses occur within the specified deadline. Soft real-time systems are those where response times are important, but the system will still function correctly if deadlines are occasionally missed. Soft systems can be distinguished from interactive ones in which there are no explicit deadlines. For example, the flight control system of a combat aircraft is a hard real-time system because a missed deadline could lead to a catastrophic situation and loss of the aircraft, whereas a data acquisition system for a process control application is soft, as it may be defined to sample an input sensor at regular intervals but to tolerate intermittent delays. A text editor is an example of an interactive system. Here, performance is important (a slow editor will not be used); however, the occasional poor response will not impact on the overall system's performance. Of course, many systems will have both hard and soft real-time subsystems along with some interactive components.

Java *without* the RTSJ is probably best suited for interactive systems, although with an efficient virtual machine it could be used for some soft real-time systems. The addition of a set of concurrency utilities in Java 1.5 greatly enhances its applicability in these areas. However, Java programs lack predictability and, therefore, the language is not ideal for the real-time domain. Java *with* the RTSJ allows the programmer to have much more control and, consequently, programs can be made much more predictable. Thus, this is an ideal combination for large soft real-time systems. Subsets of Java and the RTSJ are needed if the language is to be used in small embedded real-time systems or those systems that have high integrity or hard real-time requirements. This topic goes beyond the current RTSJ and is covered in Chapter 17.

1.3 Summary

This chapter has provided some necessary introductory material for the remainder of the book. The main motivations for concurrent programming have been outlined, namely, increased processor utilization, applicability to multiprocessor systems and modelling parallelism in the real world. The distinction between hard and soft real-time systems has been made. Arguably, Java as it stands is not predictable enough for reliable use in real-time systems. Java with the Real-Time Specification is probably best suited for large soft real-time systems. To use the language for hard real-time systems requires subsets (profiles) to be developed.

2 Concurrent Programming in Java

Introduction and chapter structure

Chapter 1 illustrated the need for concurrent programming. While this need is universally acknowledged, many different models of concurrent programming can be presented to the programmer. Furthermore, there is still controversy over whether the mechanisms that support a particular model should be provided by a programming language or by an operating system. Languages such as C and C++ are sequential languages and they do not explicitly support concurrent programming. Concurrent programming in these languages, therefore, requires the use of an operating system Applications Programmers' Interface (API), such as the pthread library for POSIX (Butenhof, 1997). In contrast, Java, C# and Ada are concurrent programming languages. They all explicitly support the notion of concurrency; in Java and C#, concurrent activities are called *threads*, in Ada they are called *tasks*.

The goal of this and the next four chapters is to explore concurrent programming in Java. The focus of attention is the core language facilities rather than the concurrency utilities. However, particularly utilities are covered when they address weaknesses in the language model. This chapter places the Java model in context and examines the `Thread` class. Chapter 3 deals with communication and synchronization issues, and Chapter 4 completes the Java model by discussing thread priorities, interaction with time, thread groups, and some of the concurrency-related utilities. Chapters 5 and 6 then provide detailed examples of the model in use.

2.1 Concurrency Models

Processes versus threads

Concurrent programming has a long history, and consequently the terminology has evolved over the years. The term *process* was first introduced to describe *a sequence of actions performed by executing a sequence of instructions*. Hence, a concurrent process is a sequential activity that can (potentially) be performed at the same time as (and independently of) other concurrent processes.

Important
note   The correctness of a concurrent program should not depend on the order of execution of its constituent processes by the scheduler. Any required constraints on the ordering must be explicitly programmed.

All operating systems provide facilities for creating concurrent processes. Usually, each process executes in its own virtual machine to avoid interference from other unrelated processes. Each process is, in effect, a single program. However, in recent years there has been a tendency to provide facilities for processes to be created within programs. Modern operating systems allow processes created within the same program to have unrestricted access to shared memory; such processes are called *threads* (or sometimes *tasks*). Hence, in operating systems, like those conforming to the POSIX standards, it is necessary to distinguish between the concurrency between programs (processes) and the concurrency within a program (threads). Often, there is also a distinction between threads that are visible to the operating system and those that are supported solely by application-level library routines. For example, Windows 2000 supports threads and *fibers*, the latter being invisible to the kernel. This is illustrated in Figure 2.1.

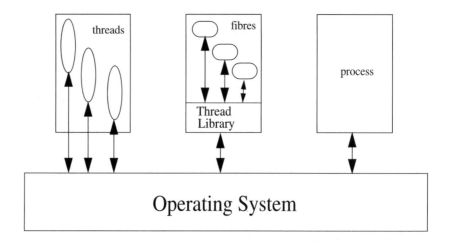

FIGURE 2.1. The Relationship between Processes, Threads and Fibers

The threads of a Java program all execute within the same Java Virtual Machine (JVM) (ignoring any distributed execution). Consequently, they can all share the same resources. A JVM will typically be executed as a single operating system process. The term *native* thread is used to describe a one-to-one mapping between a Java thread and the underlying operating system's thread abstraction. *Green* threads are threads that are implemented directly by the JVM and consequently they are invisible to the underlying operating system (comparable to fibers in Windows 2000). On multiprocessor systems, the only way to get true parallelism is to use native threads. However, the amount of parallelism obtained will depend on the implementation of the JVM and the underlying operating system. On an N processor system with native threads, N runnable threads might not simultaneously run on the N processors, even if all processors are otherwise idle.

Process and thread representation

Although all concurrent programming notations incorporate the concept of a process (or thread), the way in which processes are represented varies. In a sequential language using an operating system's API, the address of a procedure or function will often be used to identify (to the operating system) the sequence of instructions that are to form the executable code of the process. Some concurrent programming languages take a similar approach and simply provide language-defined modules (or packages) that provide procedures/functions to create threads. Procedures/functions are again used to represent the code of the thread. The main problem with this approach is that it is difficult to determine, by looking at the program source, which are the concurrent activities. Consequently, over the years there have been attempts to introduce direct language support for threads and their creation; for example, the *fork* statement of Mesa and the *PAR* construct in occam. Arguably, allowing concurrent activities to be explicitly declared in a program, in the same manner as, say, a procedure, gives the most visible representation of a thread. This is the approach taken by languages such as Ada and Modula.

Object-oriented concurrent programs

Integrating concurrent and object-oriented programming has been an active research topic since the late 1980s. There are now many mechanisms for achieving this integration (see (Briot, Guerraoui and Lohn, 1998) for a review). The majority of approaches have taken a sequential object-oriented language and made it concurrent (for example, the various versions of concurrent Eiffel (Karaorman and Bruno, 1993) (Meyer, 1993)). A few approaches have taken a concurrent language and made it object-oriented. The most important of this latter class is the Ada 95 language, which is an extension to the object-based concurrent programming language Ada 83.

Central to any concurrent object-oriented programming language is the relationship between process representation and objects. Here, the distinction is often between the concept of an *active object* and where concurrent execution is created by the use of *asynchronous method calls* (or via early returns from method calls). Active objects, by definition, will execute concurrently with other active objects. They encapsulate a thread. Asynchronous method calls return to the caller before the code in the method has completed execution. They, therefore, require implicit concurrent activities to complete the call.

Java adopts the active object model via the use of its `Thread` class.

Communica-
tion and syn-
chronization

Irrespective of how concurrent activities are represented, they need to communicate and synchronize their executions in order to cooperate effectively. Over the last 30 years, many different approaches have been explored. They may be broadly classified into those based on shared variables and those based on message passing (see (Burns and Wellings, 2001) for a detailed examination). One approach that has maintained its popularity over the years (and which has provided the inspiration for the Java model) is the *monitor*, illustrated in Figure 2.2. A monitor encapsulates a shared resource (usually some shared variables) and provides a procedural/functional interface to that resource. In essence, it is rather like an object except for the important property that the procedure/function calls are executed *atomically* with respect to each other. This means that one procedure/function call cannot interfere with the execution of another. The way this is achieved, in practice, is by ensuring that the calls are executed in *mutual exclusion*. There are several different ways of implementing this, for example, by having a lock associated with the monitor and requiring that each procedure/function acquires (sets) the lock before it can continue its execution. An alternative implementation (for a single processor system only) is to turn off all hardware interrupts and prohibit any scheduling preemptions.

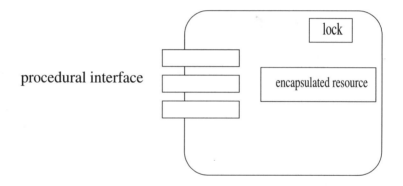

FIGURE 2.2. A Monitor Encapsulating State and a Lock

Condition
synchroniza-
tion

While providing mutually exclusive access to a shared resource will facilitate communication, it is not adequate for all forms of cooperation. Often, one process will not be able to make use of a shared resource unless another process has performed a particular operation. Consider, for example, a printer server that cannot print a file until other threads (clients) have told it what to print. A print-list resource is often used to facilitate communication between the server and the clients. Mutual exclusion is needed to ensure that the print-list remains consistent when accessed by multiple threads. However, the server must also wait when the print-list is empty; clients might need to wait when the list is full. This latter form of synchronization is often called *condition synchronization*;

it is usually supported in monitors by the introduction of *condition variables*. For every condition for which a thread wishes to wait, there is usually an associated condition variable. In the print-list resource example, two conditions listNotEmpty and listNotFull might be declared. Condition variables themselves may be considered as objects (or abstract data types) with two available operations:

- Wait – this operation will unconditionally suspend the execution of the calling thread and place it on a queue of waiting threads associated with the condition variable. For example, when the printer server waits on the listNotEmpty condition, it is immediately suspended.
- Notify (or Signal) – this operation will allow the first thread suspended on the queue associated with the condition variable to continue its execution. For example, if the printer server removes an item from the print-list so that the list is now not full, it will call the notify operation on the listNotFull condition variable, thereby waking up one client thread (if any are waiting).

A condition variable queue is usually ordered either in a *first-in-first-out* manner or according to the priority of the waiting threads. Some monitors also support a third operation called NotifyAll (or Broadcast). This operation releases all the suspended threads on the queue.

Of course, threads that have been suspended and have now been released must re-acquire the monitor lock. This is done invisibly to the programmer, and, again, the actual details vary from one implementation of a monitor to another.

Important note

It is important to realize that the Notify and NotifyAll operations have no effect if there are no suspended threads. Hence, care must be taken to avoid **race conditions**. These are situations where the correctness of a concurrent program is dependent on the order of execution of its threads.

Consider the case of an empty print-list and the situation when the printer server and a printer client are both about to access the list. The server looks to see if the list is empty, it is, however, just before it issues a wait operation on the condition listNotEmpty, the client executes. It now places an item on the list, the list is no longer empty so it calls the notify operation on the condition variable listNotEmpty. Unfortunately, no thread is waiting, so the operation has no effect. The printer server now waits even though there is an item on the list. A different ordering of executions of the threads would avoid the problem. Hence the expression *race condition*, the threads are racing to execute as fast as possible to avoid awkward interleaving. In this case, the problem can be solved by ensuring that the list is always accessed under mutual exclusion (that is, inside the monitor). However, many race conditions are much more subtle than this and are difficult to avoid. In extreme cases, they may lead to deadlock or starvation.

2.2 Overview of Java Concurrency Model

Java is one of the most interesting recent developments in concurrent object-oriented programming. As a new language, its creators were able to design a concurrency model within an object-oriented framework without worrying about backward compatibility issues. The Java model integrates concurrency into the object-oriented framework by an adaptation of the active object concept. All descendants of the predefined class `Thread` have the predefined methods `run` and `start`. A thread is created when its associated object is created. When `start` is called, the new thread begins it execution by calling the `run` method. Subclassing `Thread` and overriding the `run` method allows an application to express active objects. Alternatively, the `run` method can be passed to a `Thread` object at object creation time using the `Runnable` interface. These two ways of creating threads are illustrated in Figure 2.3.

Communication between threads is achieved by reading from and writing to shared objects. Of course, these objects need to be protected from simultaneous updates in order to avoid interference and subsequent inconsistencies developing in their encapsulated states. In Java, every class is implicitly derived from the `Object` class, which defines a mutual exclusion lock. Consequently, every object created potentially has its own lock (the locks are only created when needed). The methods of a class that are labeled as *synchronized* can only be executed when they have acquired their object's

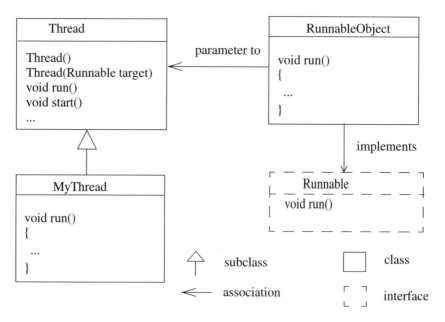

FIGURE 2.3. Thread Creation

lock. Similarly, a *synchronized statement* naming an object can only be executed when the object's lock has been obtained. The `Object` class also has methods that implement a simple form of conditional synchronization. A thread can wait for notification of a single event. When used in conjunction with synchronized methods, the language provides a functionality similar to that of a simple monitor.

2.3   Threads in Detail

As mentioned in Section 2.2, Java has a predefined class, `java.lang.Thread` that provides the mechanism by which threads (processes) are created. However, the language only supports *single inheritance*. This means that a subclass (child) can have only one super (parent) class; multiple inheritance is not supported. Consequently, to avoid the code for application threads having to be declared in child classes of `Thread`, Java also has a standard interface, called `Runnable`:

```
package java.lang;
public interface Runnable {
  public void run();
}
```

Hence, any class that wishes to express concurrent execution must implement this interface and provide the `run` method. The `Thread` class does this:

```
package java.lang;
public class Thread extends Object
            implements Runnable {
  // constructors
  public Thread();
  public Thread(String name);
  public Thread(Runnable target);
  public Thread(Runnable target, String name);
  public Thread(Runnable target, String name,
            long stackSize);
  // methods
  public static Thread currentThread();
  public void run();
  public void start();
  ...
}
```

Thread is a subclass of Object. Among other things, it provides several constructor methods and the currentThread, run and start methods.

An implementation of the Thread class may choose to implement methods like start with synchronized and/or native modifiers. These modifiers are considered part of a method's implementation, not its specification. For example, the native modifier indicates that the method is implemented in a language other than Java.

Using the constructor methods, threads can be created in two ways.

Thread creation by extending the Thread class

The first way to create a thread is to declare a class to be a subclass of Thread and override the run method. An instance of the subclass can be created, given an optional run-time string identifier and then started. For example, consider a robot that can move in three dimensions. A separate motor controls movement in each dimension, and these motors can be operated simultaneously to move the robot to the required position. The structure of the system is illustrated in Figure 2.4. It shows that a single robot (whose operations are defined by the Robot class) is driven by three motor controllers (whose operations are defined by the MotorController class). The motor controllers are governed by a user interface (defined by the UserInterface class). The Motor-Controller class is a subclass of the Thread class.

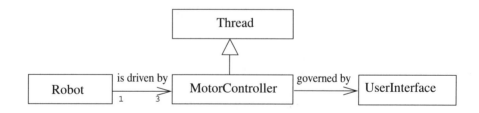

FIGURE 2.4. MotorController **as a Subclass of** Thread

Assume that the following classes and objects are available:

```java
public enum Plane {X_PLANE, Y_PLANE, Z_PLANE};
public class UserInterface {
    // Allows the next position of the robot to be
    // obtained from the operator.
    public int newSetting (Plane dim) { ... }
    ...
}
```

```
public class Robot {
  // The interface to the Robot itself.
  public void move(Plane dim, int pos) { ... }
  // Other methods, not significant here.
}
```

Given the above classes, the following will declare a class that can be used to represent the three motor controllers:

```
public class MotorController extends Thread {
  public MotorController(Plane dimension,
        UserInterface UI, Robot robo) { // constructor
    super();
    dim = dimension;
    myInterface = UI;
    myRobot = robo;
  }
  public void run() {
    int position = 0; // initial position
    int setting;

    while(true) {
      // Get new offset and update position.
      setting = myInterface.newSetting(dim);
      position = position + setting;
      myRobot.move(dim, position); // move to position
    }
  }
  private Plane dim;
  private UserInterface myInterface;
  private Robot myRobot;
}
```

Here, parameters to the MotorController constructor method indicates which dimension the motor is driving, the robot hardware and the controlling user interface. Note that it is necessary to call an appropriate constructor in the MotorController's super class (the Thread class). This is achieved by using the **super** keyword. As there are no parameters to **super**, this will result in the Thread() constructor method being called. If a string had been passed after super, for example **super**("MotorController"), then the Thread(String name) constructor method would have been called, and all threads created from this class would have the name "MotorController" associated with them.

The three motor controllers can now be created:

```
UserInterface UI = new UserInterface();
Robot robo= new Robot();

MotorController MC1 = new MotorController(
                            Plane.X_PLANE, UI, robo);
MotorController MC2 = new MotorController(
                            Plane.Y_PLANE, UI, robo);
MotorController MC3 = new MotorController(
                            Plane.Z_PLANE, UI, robo);
```

At this point, the threads have been created, any variables declared have been initialized and the constructor methods for the `MotorController` and `Thread` classes have been called (Java calls this the *new* state). However, a thread does not begin its execution until the `start` method is called.

```
MC1.start();
MC2.start();
MC3.start();
```

When a thread is started, its `run` method is called, and the thread is now executable (or runnable). When the `run` method exits, the thread is no longer executable and it can be considered terminated (Java often calls this the *dead* state). The thread remains in this state until it is garbage collected. In this example, the threads do not terminate.

Warning

Note that if the `run` method is called explicitly by the application then the code is executed sequentially not concurrently.

Thread creation using the `Runnable` interface

The second way to create a thread is to declare a class that implements the `Runnable` interface. An instance of the class can then be allocated and passed as an argument during the creation of a thread object. Remember that Java threads are not started automatically when their associated objects are created, but must be explicitly started using the `start` method. Figure 2.5 illustrates the approach.

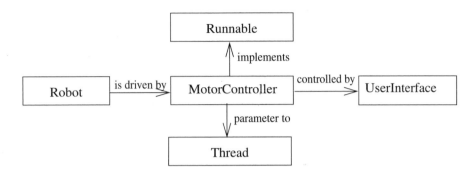

FIGURE 2.5. MotorController implementing the Runnable Interface

The following code provides the implementation.

```
public class MotorController implements Runnable {
  public MotorController(Plane dimension,
        UserInterface UI, Robot robo) { // constructor
    // No call to super() needed now.
    dim = dimension;
    myInterface = UI;
    myRobot = robo;
  }
  public void run() {
    int position = 0; // initial position
    int setting;
    while(true) {
      setting = myInterface.newSetting(dim);
      position = position + setting;
      myRobot.move(dim, position);
    }
  }
  private Plane dim;
  private UserInterface myInterface;
  private Robot myRobot;
```

The three controllers can now be created.

```
UserInterface UI = new UserInterface();
Robot robo= new Robot();
```

```
MotorController MC1 = new MotorController(
                              Plane.X_PLANE, UI, robo);
MotorController MC2 = new MotorController(
                              Plane.Y_PLANE, UI, robo);
MotorController MC3 = new MotorController(
                              Plane.Z_PLANE, UI, robo);
// No threads created yet.
```

and then associated with threads and started:

```
// Constructors passed an object (which implements
// the Runnable interface) when the threads are created.
Thread X = new Thread(MC1);
Thread Y = new Thread(MC2);
Thread Z = new Thread(MC2);

X.start(); // thread started
Y.start();
Z.start();
```

Note that when threads are constructed with a Runnable object, it is also possible to recommend to the JVM the size of the stack to be used with the thread. However, implementations are allowed to ignore this recommendation.

Warning

Passing the same Runnable object to more than one thread constructor will mean that each thread executes the same run method in the same object. This means that any variables encapsulated by the Runnable object and accessed by the run method must be protected from concurrent access by using synchronized statements (or synchronized methods provided by the Runnable object).

Current thread

Irrespective of how threads are created, the identity of the currently running thread can be found using the currentThread method. This method has a static modifier, which means that there is only one method for all instances of Thread objects. Hence, the method can always be called using the Thread class.

2.4 Thread Termination

There are several ways in which a Java thread can terminate.

- It completes execution of its run method either normally or as the result of an unhandled exception.

- Its destroy method is called (either by another thread or by itself) — destroy terminates the thread without the thread object having any chance to cleanup. Note, however, this method is not provided in many implementations of the Java virtual machine. As of Java 1.5, it has finally been deprecated.

• Its `stop` method is called (again by another thread or by itself). This is a special case of the `run` method completing with an unhandled exception. In fact, when `stop` is called, the exception `ThreadDeath` is thrown asynchronously in the target thread. This is a subclass of `Error` and, therefore, should not be caught by the program. The thread class is able to clean up (releases the locks it holds and executes any *finally* clauses) before terminating the thread. The thread object is now eligible for garbage collection. If a `Throwable` object is passed as a parameter to the `stop` method, then this exception is thrown asynchronously in the target thread. The `run` method can now exit more gracefully and clean up after itself. The `stop` methods are inherently unsafe as they release locks on objects and can leave those objects in inconsistent states. For this reason, the methods are now *deprecated* and, therefore, should not be used.

Java threads can be of two types: *user* threads or *daemon* threads. Daemon threads are those threads that provide general services and typically never terminate. Hence when all user threads have terminated, daemon threads can also be terminated, and the main program terminates. Calling the `setDaemon` method with a true parameter indicates that the thread is a daemon. By default, threads are user threads. Note the `setDaemon` method must be called before any such thread is started.

One thread can wait (with or without a timeout) for another thread (the target) to terminate by issuing the `join` method call on the target's thread object. Furthermore, the `isAlive` method allows a thread to determine if the target thread has terminated. The specifications of the above methods are shown below:

```java
package java.lang;
public class Thread extends Object implements Runnable {
  ...
  public void destroy(); // DEPRECATED
  public final boolean isAlive();
  public final boolean isDaemon();
  public final void join() throws InterruptedException;
  public final void join(long millis)
          throws InterruptedException;
  public final void join(long millis, int nanos)
          throws InterruptedException;
  public final void setDaemon(boolean on);
  public final void stop();   // DEPRECATED
  public final void stop(Throwable o); // DEPRECATED
}
```

There is one further way that a Java thread can terminate. This is by calling the `exit` method in the `System` class. However, this results in termination of the whole program. All threads, irrespective of whether they are daemon or user, are forced to terminate.

```
package java.lang;
public class System {
    ...
    public static void exit(int status);
        // By convention normal termination is
        // represented by a zero status value.
        // The method never returns.
}
```

In fact, the `System.exit` method calls the `exit` method in the `Runtime` class. This class encapsulates information concerning the current Java platform. It also provides more control over the termination of the Java program. The `addShutdownHook` and `removeShutdownHook` methods allow a programmer to specify one or more threads that should be started when the JVM has been ordered to shutdown (either internally via a call to the `exit` method or externally via an unhandled signal). The `halt` method allows the program to be terminated immediately.

```
package java.lang;
public class Runtime {
    // static methods

    public static Runtime getRuntime();
        // Get an object for the current Java platform.

    // methods

    public void addShutdownHook(Thread hook);
        // Add a thread to the list to be run on shutdown.
        // Throws IllegalThreadStateException if
        // the thread has already been started.

    public void exit(int status);
        // Shutdown the current VM after starting and
        // running the shutdown threads.

    public void halt(int status);
        // Shutdown the VM without running the shutdown threads.

    public boolean removeShutdownHook(Thread hook);
        // Remove a thread from the shutdown list.

    ...
}
```

2.5 Thread-local Data

Java provides two types of data. *Static* data declared in a class is shared between all instances of the class. *Nonstatic* data, in contrast, is replicated in all instances of the class. Consider a class that is defined as follows:

```
public class withStaticData {
  public static int shared;
  public int notShared;
}
```

If two objects of this class are created, say o1 and o2, then it will always be the case that at any point in time

$$o1.shared == o2.shared == withStatic.shared^1$$

However, there will be two notShared variables: o1.notShared and o2.not-Shared. Consequently, there is no guarantee that o1.notShared will ever equal o2.notShared.

For multithreaded applications where objects with local data may be called by more than one thread, a third type of data is often required. This is data that is shared within the same thread but that is different across threads. This is achieved by a special type of object called a *thread-local object*. If a thread-local object is declared as static, then the object holds a different value for each thread that uses the object. Thread-local objects are created from the ThreadLocal class. (This class has been made generic as of Java 1.5.)

```
package java.lang;
public class ThreadLocal<T> {
  // constructor
  public ThreadLocal();

  // methods
  public T get();
  public void set(T value);
  protected T initialValue();
  public void remove();
    // This method is a Java 1.5 addition, it clears
    // the value for the thread local.
}
```

1. This may be true in theory, however, in practice see Section 3.4.

Now the class:

```
public class withStaticData {
  ...
  public static ThreadLocal threadSharedClass;
  public ThreadLocal threadSharedObject;
}
```

will have one copy of threadSharedClass per thread that uses the class, whereas threadSharedObject will have one copy per thread per instance of the class withStaticData.

Consider, for example, a secure server that requires a client to log in before allowing it to call its methods. The login method returns a password that must be presented by the thread each time it issues a method call. Now the server could save a mapping between threads and passwords. However, this is tedious and error prone. Thread-local data provides a simple and elegant solution. First, a class is provided, which allocates a new password:

```
public class Password {
  public Password();
    // Generates a new password.
  public String getPassword();
    // Returns the password.
  public boolean match(String pass)
    // Returns true if pass is the password.
}
```

Now the server can use thread-local data to hold the password. The calls to the set and get methods are directed to the data associated with the calling thread.

```
public class SecureService {
  private ThreadLocal password = new ThreadLocal();
  public String login() {
    Password pass = new Password();
    password.set(pass);
    return pass.getPassword();
  }
  public void service(String pass) throws Exception {
    Password check = (Password) password.get();
    if(check.match(pass)) {
      // perform service
    } else throw new Exception("no access allowed");
  }
}
```

A subclass of ThreadLocal, InheritableThreadLocal allows a parent to pass on any thread-local values to its children.

```
package java.lang;
public class InheritableThreadLocal extends ThreadLocal {
  public InheritableThreadLocal();

  protected Object childValue(Object parentValue);
}
```

Usually, the values will be identical, but the childValue method allows the child value to be an arbitrary function of the parent's value.

2.6 Summary

This chapter has introduced the basic concurrency model for Java. A simple state transition diagram for a thread summarizes the model and is shown in Figure 2.6.

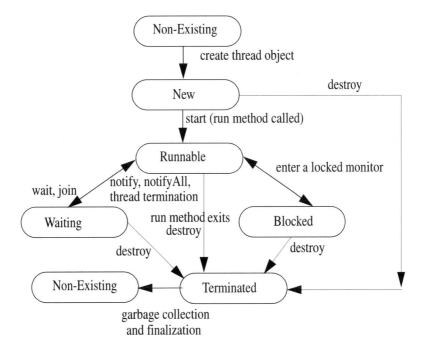

FIGURE 2.6. **Simple State Transition Diagram for a Thread**

The thread is created when an object derived from the `Thread` class is created. At this point, the thread is not runnable (executable) – Java calls this the *new* state. Once the `start` method has been called, the thread becomes eligible for execution by the scheduler. If the thread attempted to acquire a monitor lock, it may become `blocked` whilst another thread holds the lock (and, hence, no longer eligible for execution). When the lock is free, the thread becomes runnable again. If the thread calls the `wait` method in an `Object` (when holding the monitor lock), or calls the `join` method in another thread object, the thread becomes `waiting` (possibly with an associated timeout) and, again, is no longer eligible for execution. It becomes runnable as a result of an associated `notify`/`notifyAll` methods being called by another thread, or if the thread with which it has requested a join becomes terminated. A thread enters the `terminated` state either as a result of the `run` method exiting (normally or as a result of an unhandled exception) or because its `destroy` method has been called. In the latter case, the thread is abruptly moved to the `terminated` state and does not have the opportunity to execute any *finally* clauses associated with its execution. It may leave other objects locked.

A `terminated` thread becomes eligible for garbage collection during which any finalization code it has will be executed. However, this code is usually executed by another thread (in the same way that a thread's constructor is executed by a different thread); furthermore, the Java rules on finalization do not guarantee that a thread's finalization code will be run when the program exits.

A Java program terminates when all of its user threads have terminated, or the `exit` method is called in the `System` or `Runtime` classes. In the latter case, all threads are forcibly terminated.

Data associated with a thread can be static, nonstatic or thread-local. Thread-local data is created from the `ThreadLocal` class and is stored on a per thread basis.

3 Communication and Synchronization

Introduction and chapter structure Chapter 2 gave some context for the Java concurrency model and explored thread creation in detail. This chapter focuses on how threads can communicate and synchronize their activities. Communication and synchronization between Java threads is supported via a simple form of monitor. The model is explored in detail, and its strengths and limitations are discussed.

Underlying Java's communication and synchronization approach is the Java Memory Model. The criticisms that have recently been made of this model are detailed, and the changes that have occurred in Java 1.5, as a result of these criticisms, are considered. Finally, ways in which threads can interact asynchronously with each other are addressed.

3.1 Synchronized Methods and Statements

Associated with each object there is a mutual exclusion lock. This lock cannot be accessed directly by the application, but it is affected by

- the method modifier `synchronized`, and
- block synchronization.

When a method is labeled with the `synchronized` modifier, access to the method can only proceed once the lock associated with the object has been obtained. Hence, synchronized methods have mutually exclusive access to the data encapsulated by the object, *if that data is only accessed by other synchronized methods*. Nonsynchronized methods do not require the lock, and can, therefore, be called at any time. Hence, to obtain full mutual exclusion, every method that accesses encapsulated data must be labeled synchronized. A simple shared integer is, therefore, represented by

```
class SharedInteger {
  public SharedInteger(int initialValue) {
    theData = initialValue;
  }

  public synchronized int read() {
    return theData;
  }

  public synchronized void write(int newValue) {
    theData = newValue;
  }

  public synchronized void incrementBy(int by) {
   theData = theData + by;
  }

  private int theData;
}

SharedInteger myData = new SharedInteger(42);
```

Block synchronization provides a mechanism whereby a block of code can be labeled as synchronized. The synchronized keyword takes as a parameter an object whose lock it needs to obtain before it can continue. Hence, synchronized methods are effectively implementable as (using the above read method as an example)

```
public int read() {
  synchronized(this) {
    return theData;
  }
}
```

where **this** is the Java mechanism for obtaining the current object.

Warning

Used in its full generality, the synchronized block can undermine one of the advantages of monitor-like mechanisms: that of encapsulating synchronization constraints associated with an object into a single place in the program. This is because it is not possible to understand the synchronization associated with a particular object, O, by just looking at O itself. It is necessary to look at all objects that name O in a synchronized statement. However, with careful use, this facility augments the basic model and allows more expressive synchronization constraints to be programmed.

Accessing synchro- nized data

Consider a simple class that implements a two-dimensional coordinate that is to be shared between two or more threads. This class encapsulates two integers, whose values contain the x and the y components. Writing to a coordinate is simple, the write method can be labeled as synchronized. Furthermore, the constructor method cannot (by defini- tion) have any synchronization constraint:

```java
public class SharedCoordinate {
  public SharedCoordinate(int initX, int initY) {
    x = initX;
    y = initY;
  }
  public synchronized void write(int newX, int newY) {
    x = newX;
    y = newY;
  }
  . . .
  private int x, y;
}
```

The problem comes in deciding how to read the value of the coordinates. Functions in Java can return only a single value, and parameters to methods are passed by value. Consequently, it is not possible to have a single read method that returns both the x and the y components. If two synchronized functions readX and readY are used, it is pos- sible for the value of the coordinate to be updated in between the calls to readX and readY. The result will be an inconsistent value of the coordinate.

There are essentially two ways of circumventing this problem. The first is to return a new Coordinate object whose values of the x and y fields are identical to the shared coordinate. This new object can then be accessed without fear of it being changed. Of course, the returned coordinate is only a snapshot of the shared coordinate, which might be changed by another thread immediately after the read method has returned. However, the individual field values now read will be consistent.

The following class illustrates the approach.

```java
public class SharedCoordinate {
  . . .
  public synchronized SharedCoordinate read() {
    return new SharedCoordinate(x, y);
  }
  public int readX() { return x; }
  public int readY() { return y; }
}
```

Once the returned coordinate has been used, it can be discarded and made available for garbage collection.

Using syn-chronized blocks

If efficiency is a concern, unnecessary object creation and garbage collection should be avoided. In the current example, this can be achieved by ensuring that any calls to readX and readY that need to see a consistent point value are encapsulated in a synchronized block.

```
public class SharedCoordinate {
  public SharedCoordinate(int initX, int initY) {
    x = initX;
    y = initY;
  }

  public synchronized void write(int newX, int newY) {
    x = newX;
    y = newY;
  }

  public int readX() { return x; }
  public int readY() { return y; }

  private int x, y;
}
...

SharedCoordinate point1 = new SharedCoordinate(0,0);

synchronized(point1) {
  SharedCoordinate point2 = new SharedCoordinate(
             point1.readX(), point1.readY());
}
```

In this example, synchronized updates are done within the class but there is now an onus on the user of the class to provide the synchronization on reading when needed (this is termed *conditionally thread-safe access*, see Section 4.8).

Java allows a thread to acquire a lock of an object even if it has already acquired the lock. Hence, the readX and readY methods could be made synchronized for added safety, and a thread that wishes to read the two values as an atomic operation can safely enclose the reads in a synchronized statement naming the object (without fear of deadlock).

Finding the locks held by a thread and a thread's state

In general, it is not possible to determine the group of locks that a thread currently holds. However, it is possible (as of Java 1.4) for a thread to determine if it holds the lock on a particular object. This is achieved by the static method holdsLock in the Thread class.

```java
package java.lang;

public class Thread extends Object implements Runnable {
  ...
  public static boolean holdsLock(Object obj);
  ...
}
```

As of Java 1.5, it is also possible to determine the current run-time state of a thread (and, therefore, whether it is waiting for a lock) via the getState method (also in the Thread class). This returns an enumeration object where the literals correspond to the states identified in Section 2.6., with the addition of a timed waiting state (that is, a waiting state with an associated timeout).

```java
package java.lang;

public class Thread extends Object implements Runnable {
  ...

  // These are Java 1.5 extensions.
  public static final enum State{BLOCKED, NEW, RUNNABLE,
                      TERMINATED, TIMED_WAITING, WAITING);
  public State getState();


  ...
}
```

Static variables

Although synchronized methods or blocks allow mutually exclusive access to data in an object, this is not adequate if that data is static. Static data is shared between all objects created from the class. In Java, every class has an associated Class object, and it is this object's lock that must be obtained when accessing static data. The lock may be accessed either by labeling a static method with the **synchronized** modifier or by identifying the class's Class object in a synchronized block statement. In the latter case, the object associated with the class can be obtained by calling a class literal. Note that the class-wide lock is not obtained when synchronizing on an object of the class. Hence to obtain mutual exclusion over a static variable requires the following (for example):

```
class StaticSharedVariable {
  ...
  // The example shows two possible ways of acquiring
  // a lock on a Class object.
  public int Read() {
    synchronized(StaticSharedVariable.class) {
      return shared;
    }
  }
  public synchronized static void Write(int I) {
    shared = I;
  }
  private static int shared;
}
```

Obtaining the lock of a Class object does not affect the locks of any instances of the class. They are independent.

3.2 Waiting and Notifying

To obtain condition synchronization requires further support. This comes from methods provided in the predefined Object class:

```
package java.lang;
public class Object {
  ...
  // The following methods all throw the unchecked
  // IllegalMonitorStateException.
  public final void notify();
  public final void notifyAll();

  public final void wait() throws InterruptedException;
  public final void wait(long millis)
        throws InterruptedException;
  public final void wait(long millis, int nanos)
        throws InterruptedException;
  ...
}
```

These methods are designed to be used only from within methods that hold the object lock (that is, they are synchronized). If called without the lock, the exception `IllegalMonitorStateException` is thrown.

The `wait` method always blocks the calling thread *and releases the lock associated with the object*. If a thread is holding several locks (for example, in a nested monitor call), only the lock associated with the object being waited on is released. All other locks are maintained. An optional timeout can be used to stop the calling thread waiting indefinitely. However, this can be difficult to use, see Section 4.2.

Warning

The `wait(0)` or `wait(0,0)` method calls are defined to be the same as `wait()` rather than do not wait. This is slightly counterintuitive as `wait(0,1)` will timeout, whereas a `wait(0,0)` will not. Hence, care must be taken if timeout values are being calculated.

Important note

The `notify` method wakes up one waiting thread; the one woken is not defined by the Java language (however, it is defined by the RTSJ; see Section 14.2). Note that `notify` does not release the lock, and hence the woken thread must still wait until it can obtain the lock before it can continue. To wake up **all** waiting threads requires use of the `notifyAll` method; again this does not release the lock, and all the awoken threads must wait and contend for the lock when it becomes free. If no thread is waiting, then `notify` and `notifyAll` have no effect.

A waiting thread can also be awoken if it is interrupted by another thread. In this case, the `InterruptedException` is thrown.

Condition variables

Although it appears that Java provides the equivalent facilities to other languages supporting monitors, there is one important difference. There are *no* explicit condition variables. Consequently, an object cannot partition the waiting states, and, therefore, cannot have fine control over notification. When a thread is awoken, it cannot necessarily assume that a notify was associated with its wait state. For many algorithms this limitation is not a problem, as the conditions under which threads are waiting are mutually exclusive.

For example, the bounded buffer traditionally has two condition variables: `BufferNotFull` and `BufferNotEmpty` each associated with the corresponding buffer state. If a thread is waiting for one condition, no other thread can be waiting for the other condition as the buffer cannot be both full and empty at the same time. Hence, one would expect that the thread can assume that when it wakes, the buffer is in the appropriate state.

Unfortunately, this is not always the case. Java, in common with other monitor-like approaches (for example, POSIX mutexes), makes no guarantee that a thread woken from a `wait` will gain immediate access to the lock. Furthermore, a Java implementation is allowed to generate spurious wake-ups not related to the application.

Consider a thread that is woken after waiting on the `BufferNotFull` condition. Another thread could call the `put` method, find that the buffer has space and insert data into the buffer. When the woken thread eventually gains access to the lock, the buffer will again be full. Hence, it is usually essential for threads to reevaluate their conditions, as illustrated in the bounded buffer example below.

```java
public class BoundedBuffer<Data> {
  public BoundedBuffer(int length) {
    size = length;
    buffer = (Data[]) new Object[size];
    last = 0;
    first = 0;
  }
  public synchronized void put(Data item)
        throws InterruptedException {
    while (numberInBuffer == size) wait();
    last = (last + 1) % size;
    numberInBuffer++;
    buffer[last] = item;
    notifyAll();
  }
  public synchronized Data get()
        throws InterruptedException {
    while (numberInBuffer == 0) wait();
    first = (first + 1) % size;
    numberInBuffer--;
    notifyAll();
    return buffer[first];
  }
  private Data buffer[];
  private int first;
  private int last;
  private int numberInBuffer = 0;
  private int size;
}
```

Of course, if `notifyAll` is used to wake up threads, then it is more obvious that those threads must always reevaluate their conditions before proceeding.

Important note

In general, many simple synchronization errors can be avoided in Java if

- all `wait` method calls are enclosed in `while` loops that evaluate the waiting condition
- the `notifyAll` method is used to signal changes in objects' states.

This approach, while safe, is potentially inefficient as spurious wake-ups will occur. To improve performance, the `notify` method may be used when

- all threads are waiting for the same condition

- at most one waiting thread can benefit from the state change

- the JVM does not generate any wake-ups without an associated call to the `notify` and `notifyAll` methods on the corresponding object.

These first two requirements must, of course, also be met by any subclass.

The readers-writers problem

One of the standard concurrency control problems is the *readers-writers* problem. In this, many readers and many writers are attempting to access an object encapsulating a large data structure. Readers can read concurrently, as they do not alter the data; however, writers require mutual exclusion over the data, both from other writers and from readers. There are different variations on this scheme; the one considered here is where preference is always given to waiting writers. Hence, as soon as a writer is available, all new readers will be blocked until all writers have finished. Of course, in extreme situations this may lead to starvation of readers.

Important note

The key to solving most concurrency control problems is to surround each operation with an *entry* and an *exit* protocol. The entry protocol determines if the conditions for the operation to proceed are right, and if not, blocks the calling thread until they are right. The exit protocol determines whether any blocked operations can now proceed. Data may be needed to keep track of the current state of the requested operations. This data must be accessed under mutual exclusion.

The solution to the readers-writers problem using standard monitors requires four monitor methods `startRead`, `stopRead`, `startWrite` and `stopWrite`. The first two methods implement the entry and exit protocol for the readers respectively. The second two implement the writers' protocols. The readers are consequently structured as follows:

```
startRead(); // entry protocol
  // Call object to read data structure.
stopRead();  // exit protocol
```

Similarly, the writers are structured:

```
startWrite(); // entry protocol
  // Call object to write data structure.
stopWrite(); // exit protocol
```

The code inside the monitor provides the necessary synchronization using two condition variables: OkToRead and OkToWrite. In Java, this cannot be directly expressed as there are no explicit condition variables. Two approaches for solving this problem are now considered. The first approach uses a single class:

```
public class ReadersWriters {
  // Preference is given to waiting writers.
  public synchronized void startWrite()
        throws InterruptedException {
    // Wait until it is ok to write.
    while(readers > 0 || writing) {
      waitingWriters++;
      wait();
      waitingWriters--;
    }
    writing = true;
  }
  public synchronized void stopWrite() {
    writing = false;
    notifyAll();
  }
  public synchronized void startRead()
        throws InterruptedException {
    // Wait until it is ok to read.
    while(writing || waitingWriters > 0) wait();
    readers++;
  }
  public synchronized void stopRead() {
    readers--;
    if(readers == 0) notifyAll();
  }
  private int readers = 0;
  private int waitingWriters = 0;
  private boolean writing = false;
}
```

In this solution, on awaking after the wait request, a thread must reevaluate the conditions under which it can proceed. Although this approach will allow multiple readers or a single writer, arguably it is inefficient, as all threads are woken up every time the data becomes available. Many of these threads, when they finally gain access to the monitor, will find that they still cannot continue and, therefore, will have to wait again. It should also be noted that this solution is not tolerant to the InterruptedException being thrown. A waiting writer increments the waitingWriters count before waiting. If it is interrupted, the exception is propagated and the count is never decremented. One solution to this problem is to catch and propagate the exception.

```
public synchronized void startWrite()
            throws InterruptedException {
  try {
    while(readers > 0 || writing) {
      waitingWriters++;
      wait();
      waitingWriters--;
    }
    writing = true;
  } catch(InterruptedException ie) {
    waitingWriters--; throw ie;
  }
}
```

The alternative solution to the InterruptedException problem is to use the finally clause:

```
public synchronized void startWrite()
        throws InterruptedException {
  while(readers > 0 || writing) {
    waitingWriters++;
    try {
      wait();
    } finally { waitingWriters--; }
  }
  writing = true;
}
```

3.3 Implementing Condition Variables

An alternative solution to the readers-writers problem is to use another class to implement a simple condition variable. Consider

```
public class ConditionVariable {
  public boolean wantToSleep = false;
  public boolean wakeUp = false;
}
```

The general approach is to create instances of these variables (OkToRead and OkToW-rite) inside another class and to use block synchronization. To avoid waiting in a nested monitor call, the flag wantToSleep is used to indicate whether the monitor wants to wait on the condition variable. The flag wakeUp is used to control the release of the threads and to cope with spurious JVM wakeups). The following algorithm illustrates the approach (in this instance preference is given to waiting readers):

```
public class ReadersWriters2 {
  public void startWrite() throws InterruptedException {
    synchronized(OkToWrite) { // condition variable lock
      synchronized(this) { // monitor lock
        if(writing | readers > 0 | waitingReaders > 0) {
          waitingWriters++;
          OkToWrite.wantToSleep = true;
        } else {
          writing = true;
          OkToWrite.wantToSleep = false;
          OkToWrite.wakeUp = true;
          OkToRead.wakeUp = false;
        }
      } // Give up monitor lock.
      if(OkToWrite.wantToSleep) OkToWrite.wait();
      while(!OkToWrite.wakeUp) OkToWrite.wait();
      OkToWrite.wakeUp = false;
    } // Give up OkToWrite lock.
  }

  public void stopWrite() {
    synchronized(OkToRead){ // get locks in correct order
      synchronized(OkToWrite) {
        synchronized(this) {
          if(waitingReaders > 0) {
            writing = false;
            readers = waitingReaders;
            waitingReaders = 0;
            OkToRead.wakeUp = true;
            OkToRead.notifyAll();
          } else if(waitingWriters > 0) {
            waitingWriters--;
            OkToWrite.wakeUp = true;
            OkToWrite.notify();
          } else writing = false;
        } // Give up monitor lock.
      }  // Give up OkToWrite lock.
    }  // Give up OkToRead lock.
  }
}
```

```
public void startRead() throws InterruptedException {
  synchronized(OkToRead){
    synchronized(this) {
      if(writing) {
        waitingReaders++;
        OkToRead.wantToSleep = true;
      } else {
        readers++;
        OkToRead.wantToSleep = false;
        OkToRead.wakeUp = true;
      }
    } // Give up monitor lock.
    if(OkToRead.wantToSleep) OkToRead.wait();
    while(!OkToRead.wakeUp) OkToRead.wait();
  } // Give up OkToRead lock.
}

public void stopRead() {
  synchronized(OkToWrite) {
    synchronized(this) {
      readers--;
      if(readers == 0 & waitingWriters > 0) {
        waitingWriters--;
        writing = true;
        OkToRead.wakeUp = false;
        OkToWrite.wakeUp = true;
          // Transfer the lock to first waiting writer.
        OkToWrite.notify();
      }
    }
  }
}

private int readers = 0;
private int waitingReaders = 0;
private int waitingWriters = 0;
private boolean writing = false;

private ConditionVariable OkToRead =
        new ConditionVariable();
private ConditionVariable OkToWrite =
        new ConditionVariable();
}
```

Every condition variable is represented by an instance of the ConditionVariable class declared inside the class that is acting as the monitor. Conditions are evaluated while holding the monitor lock and the lock on any condition variable that will be notified or waited on inside the monitor procedure. To ensure that no deadlock occurs, these locks should always be obtained in the same order. The Java language itself ensures that the locks are released in the reverse order to the one in which they were obtained. In this case, the acquisition order is always

```
OkToRead
OkToWrite
ReadersWriters2
```

Note that in this example no while loops have been used around the testing of the conditions. This is because the conditions have explicitly been set so that if threads gain the lock for the first time ahead of those waking up, they will find that they cannot proceed and will enter the wait state. However, a while loop is still necessary to be protected against spurious JVM wake-ups.

Note also that this solution is not tolerant to the interrupted exception being thrown. As with the first readers-writers solution given in Section 3.2, the exception must be caught before being allowed to propagate. This is left as an exercise for the reader.

Java 1.5 and JSR 166 note   Within the Java Community Process there has been an activity [Java Community Process, JSR 166, 2002] that has proposed a set of concurrency-related utilities [Lea, 2004]. These have now been incorporated into java.utils in Java 1.5. One of the utilities developed is a general-purpose lock mechanism. This includes locks and condition variables that are accessed via the following interfaces.

```java
package java.util.concurrent.locks;
public interface Lock {
  public void lock();
    // Uninterruptibly wait for the lock to be acquired.
  public void lockInterruptibly()
            throws InterruptedException;
    // As above but interruptible.
  public Condition newCondition();
    // Create a new condition variable for use with the Lock.
  public boolean tryLock();
    // Returns true is lock is available immediately.
  public boolean tryLock(long time, TimeUnit unit)
                throws InterruptedException;
    // Returns true is lock is available within a timeout.
    // See Section 4.2 for information on the TimeUnit class.
  public void unlock();
}
```

```java
package java.util.concurrent.locks;
public interface Condition {
  public void await() throws InterruptedException;
  /* Atomically releases the associated lock and
   * causes the current thread to wait until
   *   1. another thread invokes the signal method
   *       and the current thread happens to be chosen
   *       as the thread to be awakened; or
   *   2. another thread invokes the signalAll method;
   *   3. another thread interrupt the thread; or
   *   4. a spurious wake-up occurs.
   * When the method returns it is guaranteed to hold the
   * associated lock.
   */
```

```java
  public boolean await(long time, TimeUnit unit)
        throws InterruptedException;
  public long awaitNanos(long nanosTimeout)
        throws InterruptedException;
  public void awaitUninterruptible();
  // As for await, but not interruptible.

  public boolean awaitUntil(java.util.Date deadline)
        throws InterruptedException;
  // As for await() but with a timeout, see Section 4.2
  // for information on TimeUnit class.

  public void signal();
  // Wake up one waiting thread.
  public void signalAll();
  // Wake up all waiting threads.
}
```

A new lock and associated condition variables can be created via the Reentrant-Lock class:

```java
package java.util.concurrent.locks;
public class ReentrantLock
        implements Lock, java.io.Serializable {
  public ReentrantLock();
```

```
  . . .
  public void lock();
  public void lockInterruptibly() throws InterruptedException;
  public ConditionObject newCondition();
    // Create a new condition variable and associated it
    // with this lock object.
  public boolean tryLock();
  public boolean tryLock(long time, TimeUnit unit)
              throws InterruptedException;
  public void unlock();
}
```

Where `ConditionObject` is an inner class definition of the `ReentrantLock` class that implements the `Condition` interface.

Using these facilities it is possible to implement the bounded buffer using the familiar algorithm:

```
import java.util.concurrent.*;
public class BoundedBuffer<Data> {
  public BoundedBuffer(int length) {
    size = length;
    buffer = (Data[]) new Object[size];
    last = 0;
    first = 0;
    numberInBuffer = 0;
  }

  public void put(Data item)
        throws InterruptedException {
   lock.lock();
   try {
     while (numberInBuffer == size) notFull.await();
     last = (last + 1) % size;
     numberInBuffer++;
     buffer[last] = item;
     notEmpty.signal();
   } finally {
      lock.unlock();
   }
  }
}
```

```
public synchronized Data get()
        throws InterruptedException {
  lock.lock();
  try {
    while (numberInBuffer == 0) notEmpty.await();
    first = (first + 1) % size ;
    numberInBuffer--;
    notFull.signal();
    return buffer[first];
  } finally {
      lock.unlock();
  }
}
private Data buffer[];
private int first;
private int last;
private int numberInBuffer;
private int size;
private Lock lock = new ReentrantLock();
private final Condition notFull =
            lock.newCondition();
private final Condition notEmpty =
            Lock.newCondition();
}
```

Here, although it is still necessary to have the while loops, threads are only awoken when the condition on which they are waiting has been signalled.

The solution to the readers/writers problem is left as an exercise for the reader.

3.4 Synchronization and the Java Memory Model

The previous sections have discussed how threads can safely communicate with each other using shared variables (and objects) encapsulated in monitors. As long as programmers ensure that all shared variables are accessed by threads only when they hold an appropriate monitor lock, they need not be concerned with issues such as multiprocessor implementations, compiler optimizations, whether processors execute instructions out-of-order, and so on. However, synchronization can be expensive, and there are times when a programmer might want to use shared variables without an associated monitor lock. One example is the so-called double-checked locking idiom [Schmidt and Harrison, 1997]. In this idiom, a singleton resource is to be created; this resource may or may not be used during a particular execution of the program. Furthermore, creating the resource is an expensive operation and should be deferred until it is required. A simple and intuitive implementation of this requirement is the following:

```
public class ResourceController {
  public static synchronized Resource getResource() {
    if(resource == null) resource = new Resource();
    return resource;
  }
  private static Resource resource = null;
}
```

The problem with this solution is that a lock is required on every access to the resource. In fact, it is only necessary to synchronize on creation of the resource, as the resource will provide its own synchronization when the threads use it. The double-checked locking idiom attempts to solve this with the following algorithm.

```
public class ResourceController {
  public static Resource getResource() {
    if(resource == null) {
      synchronized (ResourceController.class) {
        if(resource == null) resource = new Resource();
      }
    }
    return resource;
  }
  private static Resource resource = null;
}
```

Here, once the resource has been allocated, in theory, there is no need to execute the synchronized statement. In order to understand whether this program functions as intended, it is necessary to have a deeper understanding of both the relationship between Java threads and memory and the potential optimizations that a compiler or processor may perform.

The relationship between threads and memory is defined in the Java Language Specification Chapter 17 [Gosling, Joy and Steele, 1996] and is known as the Java Memory Model (JMM). Unfortunately, this model has come under much criticism over recent years because it is hard to understand [Pugh, 1999]; as a result it has been revamped in Java 1.5. In the JMM, each thread is considered to have access to its own working memory as well as the main memory that is shared between all threads. This working memory is used to hold copies of the data that resides in the shared main memory. It is an abstraction of data held in registers or data held in local caches on a multiprocessor system. The JVM transfers data between the main shared memory and a thread's local memory as and when required. It is a requirement that

- a thread's working memory is invalidated when the thread acquires an object's lock; that is, inside a synchronized method or statement any initial read of a shared variable must read the value from main memory,
- a thread's working memory is written back to the main memory when the thread releases a lock; that is, before a synchronized method or statement finishes, any variables written to during the method or statement must be written back to main memory.

Data may be written to the main memory at other times as well, however, the programmer just cannot tell when.

In order to give flexibility to compiler writers and JVM implementors, the JMM allows code to be optimized and reordered as long as it maintains "as-if-serial" semantics. That is, the result of executing the code is the same as the result that would be obtained if the code was executed sequentially. For sequential Java programs, the programmer will not be able to detect these optimizations and reordering. However, in concurrent systems, they will manifest themselves unless the program is properly synchronized.

Consider again the double-checked locking algorithm. Now suppose that a compiler implements the `resource = new Resource()` statement logically as follows:

```
tmp = create memory for the Resource class
    // tmp points to memory
Resource.construct(tmp)
    // runs the constructor to initialize
resource = tmp // set up resource
```

Now as a result of optimizations or reordering, suppose the statements are executed in the following order

```
tmp = create memory for the Resource class
    // tmp points to memory
resource = tmp
Resource.construct(tmp)
    // run the constructor to initialize
```

It is easy to see that there is a period of time when the `resource` reference has a value, but the `Resource` object has not been initialized. It is now possible to construct an interleaving of the double-checked locking algorithm, when one thread is in the process of creating the resource, a second thread sees a partially created object (outside of the synchronized block) and tries to use it. It is not possible to predict what will happen as it depends on the resource itself [Pugh 2000].

Even more insidious problems may occur if the resource is fully initialized by thread, T1, but the initialization touches other objects. Now these objects may have been written back to memory when T1 exits the synchronized statement, but another thread, T2, will see an initialized resource that potentially references objects that it already has in its local memory. Unfortunately, as it has not performed a lock operation, there is no requirement for the JVM to reload those objects, and so T2 sees stale data.

Important note

The double-checked locking algorithm illustrates that synchronized methods (and statements) in Java serve a dual purpose. Not only do they enable mutual exclusive access to a shared resource but they also ensure that data written by one thread (the writer) becomes visible to another thread (the reader). The visibility of data written by the writer is only guaranteed when it releases a lock that is subsequently acquired by the reader.

Volatile fields

Java allows fields to be defined as *volatile*. The Java Language Specification requires that a volatile field not be held in local memory and that all reads and writes go straight to main memory. Furthermore, operations on volatile fields must be performed in exactly the order that a thread requests. A further rule requires that volatile double or long variables must be read and written atomically.

Warning

Objects and arrays are accessed via references and, therefore, marking them as volatile only applies to the references, not to the fields of the objects or the components of the arrays. It is not possible to specify that elements of an array are volatile.

Visibility and synchroniza-tion points

The Java 1.5 Java Memory Model has changed as a result of a Java Specification Request (JSR 133 [Java Community Process, JSR133]). One outcome is that more attention has been paid to the point at which changes made to shared data become visible to other threads. For example, threads are synchronized in situations other than via the synchronized method (statement). In particular, the following are considered additional synchronization points [Manson and Pugh, 2004]:

- when one thread starts another - changes made by the parent thread before the start requests are visible to the child thread when it executes;

- when one thread waits for the termination of another (for example, by using the join or isAlive methods in the Thread class) - changes made by the terminating thread before it terminates are visible to the waiting thread;

- when one thread interrupts another (see Section 3.5) - changes made by the interrupting thread before the interrupt request are made visible to the interrupted thread when it next tests the interrupted flag;

- when threads read and write to the same volatile field - changes made by the writer thread to shared data (before it writes to the volatile field) are made visible to a subsequent reader of the same volatile field.

The tightening up of the definition of synchronization points have removed many of the uncertainties of the old JMM and allows more precise semantics to be given to multi-threaded Java programs.

3.5 Asynchronous Thread Control

Early versions of Java allowed one thread to affect another thread asynchronously through the following methods.

```java
package java.lang;
public class Thread extends Object implements Runnable {
    ...
    // The following methods all throw the
    // unchecked SecurityException.
    public final void suspend(); // DEPRECATED
    public final void resume(); // DEPRECATED
    public final void stop(); // DEPRECATED
    public final void stop(Throwable except);// DEPRECATED
    ...
}
```

Suspend and resume

Suspend instructs the JVM to remove the associated thread from the set of runnable threads. It is typically called by a thread that is waiting for another thread to signal an event. When the other thread has caused the event, it instructs the JVM to add the suspended thread to the set of runnable threads by calling the suspended thread's resume method. Consider, for example, simple condition synchronization using a flag. One thread, T2, sets the flag, another thread, T1, waits until the flag is set and then clears it. This would be represented in Java:

```java
boolean flag;
final boolean up = true;
final boolean down = false;
```

```
class FirstThread extends Thread {
  public void run() {
    . . .
    if(flag == down) suspend();
    flag = down;
    . . .
  }
}

class SecondThread extends Thread { // T2
  FirstThread T1;
  public SecondThread(FirstThread T) {
    super();
    T1 = T;
  }
  public void run() {
    . . .
    flag = up;
    T1.resume();
    . . .
  }
}
```

Unfortunately (even ignoring those problems outlined in Section 3.4), this approach suffers from a *race condition*. Thread T1 could test the flag and then the JVM could decide to preempt it and run T2. T2 sets the flag and resumes T1. T1 is, of course, not suspended, and so the resume has no effect. Now, when T1 next runs, it thinks the flag is down and, therefore, suspends itself.

The reason for this problem is that the flag is a shared resource that is being tested for true or false, and a subsequent action is being performed that depends on the result of that test (the thread is suspending itself). This testing and suspending is not an atomic operation and therefore interference can occur from other threads. The correct way to program this interaction is to encapsulate the variable in a class and use synchronized methods with embedded wait and notify method calls as illustrated in Section 3.1.

The use of suspend by one thread to suspend another thread is even more dangerous, as the suspended thread may be holding resources needed by other threads. The resulting anarchy may lead to the system becoming deadlocked. It is for these reasons the methods are deprecated in the current version of Java.

As already mentioned (see Section 2.4), the stop method causes the associated thread to stop its current activity and throw a ThreadDeath exception, and similarly with the stop(Throwable except) method, only this time the exception passed as a parameter is thrown. Again, use of these methods is unsafe, and they have been deprecated in the current language. Consequently, they (and suspend and resume) should not be used.

Thread interruption

Conventional Java now supports only the following methods that give a *limited* form of asynchronous thread interaction.

```
public class Thread extends Object implements Runnable {
    . . .
    public void interrupt();
        // Throws unchecked SecurityException.
        // Send an interrupt to the associated thread.
    public boolean isInterrupted();
        // Returns true if associated thread has been
        // interrupted, the interrupt status is unchanged.
    public static boolean interrupted();
        // Returns true if the current thread has been
        // interrupted and clears the interrupt status.
    . . .
}
```

One thread can signal an interrupt to another thread by calling the interrupt method. The result of this depends on the current status of the interrupted thread.

- If the interrupting thread does not have the appropriate security permissions, the SecurityException is thrown in the interrupting thread.

- If the interrupted thread is blocked in the wait, sleep or join methods, it is made runnable and has the InterruptedException thrown.

- If the interrupted thread is executing, a status flag is set, indicating that an interrupt is outstanding. *There is no immediate effect on the interrupted thread.* Instead, the called thread must periodically test to see if it has been "interrupted" using the isInterrupted or the interrupted methods. If it does not test and subsequently attempts to block in the wait, sleep or join methods, then the InterruptedException is thrown immediately.

Warning

Given that there is no guarantee that an interrupted thread will be interrupted in a timely manner, this facility is more of a synchronous notification method. It is not adequate for asynchronous notification in real-time systems. Consequently, thread interruption is one of the main areas that the RTSJ has addressed (see Chapter 7).

3.6 Summary

Communication and synchronization are fundamental to concurrent programming. Programming errors in these areas are notoriously difficult to detect. Apparently working programs can suddenly suffer from deadlock or livelock.

The Java model revolves around controlled access to shared data using a monitor-like facility. The monitor is represented as an object with synchronized methods and statements providing mutual exclusion. Condition synchronization is given by the `wait`, `notify` and `notifyAll` methods. True monitor condition variables are not directly given by the language, however, the package `java.util.concurrent.locks` provides this common locking paradigm. Therefore, they do not have to be reimplemented by the programmer.

It is important to realize that communication via nonvolatile data outside synchronized methods/statements is inherently unsafe unless the threads are synchronized by thread creation or by thread termination or by thread interruption.

Another key component of the Java communication and synchronization model is asynchronous thread control. This allows a thread to affect the progress of another thread without the threads agreeing in advance as to when that interaction will occur. There are two aspects to this: suspending and resuming a thread (or stopping it altogether), and interrupting a thread. The former are now deemed to be unsafe because of their potential to cause deadlock and race conditions. The latter is not responsive enough for real-time systems.

4 Completing the Java Concurrency Model

Introduction and chapter structure

Chapters 2 and 3 have explored the Java thread model and discussed how threads can communicate and synchronize. This chapter completes the review of the concurrency model by considering

- thread priorities and thread scheduling;
- how threads can delay themselves;
- how threads can be grouped together;
- concurrency-related utilities;
- interaction with processes outside the virtual machine;
- all the thread-related exceptions and when they occur.

The chapter finishes by summarizing the strengths and weaknesses of the Java model and by reviewing Bloch's thread safety levels.

4.1 Thread Priorities and Thread Scheduling

Although priorities can be given to Java threads via the `Thread` class, they are only used as a guide to the underlying scheduler when allocating resources. An application, once scheduled, can explicitly give up the processor resource by calling the `yield` method (again provided by the `Thread` class):

```java
package java.lang;
public class Thread extends Object implements Runnable {
  // constants
  public static final int MAX_PRIORITY  = 10;
  public static final int MIN_PRIORITY  = 1;
  public static final int NORM_PRIORITY = 5;
```

```
// methods
public final int getPriority();
public final setPriority(int newPriority);
// Throws SecurityException if the setter does not have
// the appropriate security permission.
// Throws IllegalArgumentException if newPriority
// is outside the supported range.
public static void yield();
. . .
}
```

Java allows a thread's priority to be queried and set via the getPriority and setPriority methods. The maximum, normal and minimum priorities can be found via the MAX_PRIORITY, NORM_PRIORITY and MIN_PRIORITY constants respectively. By default, a thread has the same priority as its parent. If the programmer has not allocated a priority to any thread, then all threads are given the NORM_PRIORITY (this is the priority at which the Java thread that executes the main method runs).

Warning

From a real-time perspective, Java's scheduling and priority models are weak; in particular

- no guarantee is given that the highest priority runnable thread is always executing;
- equal priority threads may or may not be time sliced; and
- where native threads are used, different Java priorities may be mapped to the same operating system priority.

Strengthening the scheduling and priority models is a key aim of the RTSJ (see Chapter 10).

4.2 Delaying Threads

Clocks and delaying a thread

Java supports the notion of a wall clock. The current time can be found by calling the static method System.currentTimeMillis in the package java.lang. This returns the number of milliseconds since midnight, January 1, 1970 GMT. The class Date in java.util uses this method as a default when constructing date objects. Further support for date and time arithmetic is provided by java.util.Calendar.

A *relative delay* allows a thread to wait for a future time rather than busy-wait on reading the `System.currentTimeMillis` method. In Java, this can be implemented by using one of the two `sleep` static methods (also defined in the `Thread` class). Although a sleep time can be given at a nanosecond granularity, very few systems will support this.

Important note

It is important to realize that `sleep` only guarantees that the thread is *released* (made executable) *after* the period has expired. The implementation of sleep in the JVM may use an interrupt timer (possibly in the underlying operating system). The granularity of the timer may affect when the interrupt occurs. The associated interrupt may also be masked for short periods. Once the thread has been made runnable, it will then have to wait to be scheduled for execution. The length of this waiting time will depend on the other runnable threads in the system and their relative priorities. The granularity of a sleep statement is illustrated in Figure 4.1.

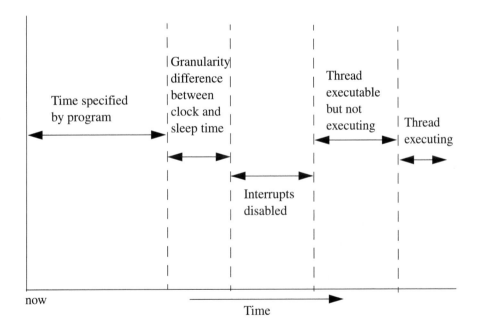

FIGURE 4.1. Sleep Granularity

The above methods are defined below.

```java
package java.lang;
public class Thread extends Object implements Runnable {
    ...
  public static void sleep(long ms)
          throws InterruptedException;

  public static void sleep(long ms, int nanoseconds)
          throws InterruptedException;

    ...
}


package java.lang;
public class System {
  public static long currentTimeMillis();
}
```

Absolute delays

Java's sleep mechanisms support relative delays, but there is no support for an *absolute delay*. It is not possible to, say, delay a thread until 2 p.m. on January 31, 2010. For example, consider a city's traffic light control system. In the morning "rush hour", say between 7 and 10 a.m., the controllers need to give more time to traffic entering the city centre than to traffic leaving the city centre. Between the 4 and 7 p.m. "rush hour", the situation is reversed. Suppose that the following class contains the appropriate duration values:

```java
public class TrafficLightTimes {
  public synchronized int getRedDurationInbound();
  public synchronized int getRedDurationOutbound();
  public synchronized int getGreenDurationInbound();
  public synchronized int getGreenDurationOutbound();

  public synchronized void setInboundTimes(
              int read, int green);
  public synchronized void setOutboundTimes(
              int read, int green);
}
```

Now consider a supervisor thread whose responsibility is to ensure that the durations are set to appropriate values at all times. The following algorithm attempts to do this using the sleep method.

```
public void run() {
  final long rushHour = 3*3600*1000;
  final long daySleep = 6*3600*1000;
  final long nightSleep = 12*3600*1000;
  TrafficLightTimes myLights = new TrafficLightTimes();

  // Initialise lights during the night and wait until 7am.

  while(true) {
    try {
      // Set morning rush hour durations.
      myLights.setInboundTimes(....);
      myLights.setOutboundTimes(....);

      Thread.sleep(rushHour);

      // Set non peak durations.
      myLights.setInboundTimes(...);
      myLights.setOutboundTimes(...);

      Thread.sleep(daySleep)

      // Set evening rush hour durations.
      myLights.setInboundTimes(...);
      myLights.setOutboundTimes(...);

      Thread.sleep(rushHour);

      // Set non peak durations.
      myLights.setInboundTimes(...);
      myLights.setOutboundTimes(...);

      Thread.sleep(nightSleep);
    } catch(InterruptedException ie) {}
  }
}
```

There are two problems with this approach:

- no attempt has been made to take into account the time taken to execute the `set-InboundTimes` and `setOutboundTimes` method calls;
- unless this is the only thread executing on the processor, it may be preempted between finishing the calls to set the durations and the call to the next `sleep` method.

These problems make it very difficult to determine the duration of any sleep. In this case, the result is that the times at which the traffic lights will change their red and green durations will drift away from the 7 a.m., 10 a.m., 4 p.m. and 7 p.m. boundaries. In this instance, the `TimeTask` Java utility can be used (see Section 4.4), but the general problem remains.

Support for absolute delays is another key extension provided by the RTSJ (see Chapter 7).

**Time-outs on
waiting**

In many situations, a thread is prepared to wait for an arbitrarily long period of time within a synchronized method (or statement) for an associated `notify` (or `notify-All`) call. However, there are occasions when the absence of the call, within a specified period of time, requires that the thread take some alternative action. Java provides two methods for this situation, both of which allows the `wait` method call to timeout (see Section 3.2). In one case, the timeout is expressed in milliseconds; in the other case, milliseconds and nanoseconds can be specified (although again, very few implementations support nanosecond delay granularity).

Important
notes

There are two important points to note about this timeout facility. The first is that, as with `sleep`, the timeout is a relative time and not an absolute time (although see later in this section). The second point is that it is not possible to know for certain if the thread has been woken by the timeout expiring or by a notify. There is no return value from the `wait` method and no timeout exception is thrown.

It is possible to read the clock and determine whether the timeout has passed. However, this is never going to indicate for certain which event woke the thread. For example, consider the following general class for implementing a wait with a timeout:

```
public class TimeoutException
              extends InterruptedException {}

public class TimedWait {
  public static void wait(Object lock, long millis)
      throws InterruptedException, TimeoutException {
    // Assumes the lock is held by the calling thread.
    long start = System.currentTimeMillis();
    lock.wait(millis);
    if(System.currentTimeMillis() >= start + millis)
      throw new TimeoutException();
  }
}
```

Unfortunately, as with absolute delays, this will sometimes fail to achieve the desired effect. Consider an arbitrary object `test` and the following code:

```
synchronized(test) {
  if(!condition) {
    try {
      TimedWait.wait(test, 1000);
      System.out.println("NO TIMEOUT");
    } catch(InterruptedException ie) {
      ...
```

```
        } catch(TimeoutException te) {
            System.out.println("TIMEOUT!");
        }
    }
}
```

Now this code may indicate that timeout occurred even though the thread executing `TimedWait.wait` was woken by a call to `test.notify` (or `test.notifyAll`). This might be because by the time the thread executing `TimedWait.wait` was scheduled for execution, the timeout time had passed. The woken thread could test to see if `condition` had indeed occurred within the `TimeoutException` handler; however, even if the condition is false, it may have been true before the thread executed and was turned false by another thread.

Java 1.5 and JSR 166 note As mentioned in Section 3.3, within the Java Community Process, there has been an activity (Java Community Process, JSR 166, 2002) that has proposed a set of concurrency-related utilities that have now been incorporated in Java 1.5. One of the issues addressed is better support for handling time granularity issues (Lea, 2004). This is achieved by the introduction of a `TimeUnit` enumeration class.

```
package java.util.concurrent;
public final enum TimeUnit {
  MICROSECONDS, MILLISECONDS, NANOSECONDS, SECONDS;

  ...

  public long convert(long duration, TimeUnit unit);
    // Convert the given duration in units to the current
    // time unit.
  public long toNanos(long duration);
    // Equivalent to NANOSECONDS.convert(duration, this).
    // Similarly for micro, milli and seconds.
  public void sleep(long timeout)
        throws InterruptedException;
    // Perform a Thread.sleep at this granularity.
  public void timedWait(Object monitor,
        long timeout) throws InterruptedException;
    // Perform a timed wait at this granularity.
  public void timedJoin(Thread thread,
        long timeout) throws InterruptedException;
    // Perform a timed join at this granularity.
}
```

Note that using this enumeration does not guarantee that any associated wait mechanism can support the requested level of time granularity in its timeout mechanism. Furthermore, it does not address the race condition associated with timeout operations.

Java 1.5 has also introduced the `nanoTime` method into the `System` class.

```
package java.lang; // This is Java 1.5 addition.
public final class System {

  ...

  public static final long nanoTime();
}
```

The `nanoTime` method returns the value of the system timer in nanoseconds. The method can only be used to measure elapsed time and is not related to calendar time in any way.

4.3   Thread Groups

Thread groups allow collections of threads to be grouped together and manipulated as a group rather than as individuals. They also provide a means of restricting who does what to which thread. Every thread in Java is a member of a thread group. There is a default group associated with the main program, and hence unless otherwise specified, all created threads are placed in this group. Thread groups are represented by the class given below.

```
package java.lang;
public class ThreadGroup implements
      UncaughtExceptionHandler {
  // The implemented interface is a Java 1.5 addition.

  // Only non deprecated methods are shown below.
  public ThreadGroup(String name);
    // Creates a new thread group.
    // The parent of this new group is the thread group
    // of the currently running thread.
  public ThreadGroup(ThreadGroup parent, String name);
    // Creates a new group with the specified parent.
    // Throws SecurityException.
```

```
public int activeCount();
  // Returns an estimate of the number of active threads.
public int activeGroupCount();
  // Returns an estimate of the number of active groups.
public final void checkAccess();
  // Determines if the currently running thread has
  // permission to modify this thread group.
  // Throws SecurityException.
public final void destroy();
  // Destroys this group and all of its subgroups.
  // Throws SecurityException and throws
  // IllegalThreadStateException if all threads in
  // the group haven't terminated.
public int enumerate(Thread[] list, boolean recurse);
  // Generates a list of all threads in the group.
  // Throws SecurityException.
public int enumerate(Thread[] list);
  // The same as enumerate(list, true).
  // Throws SecurityException.
public int enumerate(ThreadGroup[] list,
                     boolean recurse);
  // Generates a list of all thread groups in the group.
  // Throws SecurityException.
public int enumerate(ThreadGroup[] list);
  // The same as enumerate(list, true).
  // Throws SecurityException.
public final int getMaxPriority();
  // Returns the maximum priority a thread
  // in the group can have.
public final ThreadGroup getParent();
  // Returns the parent of this thread group.
public final void interrupt();
  // Interrupts all threads in the group.
public final boolean isDaemon();
  // Tests if this thread group is a daemon thread group.
public boolean isDestroyed();
  // Tests if this thread group has been destroyed.
public void list();
  // Prints information about the group on System.out.
```

```
    public final boolean parentOf(ThreadGroup g);
      // Tests if this thread group is the parent of g
      // or one of its ancestor thread groups.
    public final void setDaemon(boolean daemon);
      // Changes the daemon status of this thread group.
      //  Throws SecurityException.
    public final void setMaxPriority(int prio);
      // Sets the maximum priority a thread can have.
    public String toString();
    public void uncaughtException(Thread t, Throwable e);
      // This method is called if a thread in the group
      // terminates due to an uncaught exception.
}
```

When a thread creates a new thread group, it does so from within a thread group. Hence, the new thread group is a child of the current thread group unless a different thread group is passed as a parameter to the constructor. Using these two constructor methods allows hierarchies of thread groups to be created.

When threads are created they can be placed into explicit thread groups using the appropriate Thread class construction. Requests to destroy a thread group will (if permitted by the security manager) be applied to all threads in the group.

Warning

Setting the maximum priority of a thread group will cause the setPriority method in the Thread class to silently truncate the priorities if they are above the maximum value for the group.

Important note

The ThreadGroup class seems to have fallen from favor in recent years (Bloch, 2001). The deprecation of many of the methods means that there is little use for it. However, the interrupt mechanism is a useful way of interacting with a group of threads (an example of this will be given in Section 6.2). Also, the uncaughtException method is the only hook that Java 1.4 provides for recovering when a thread terminates unexpectedly.

Java 1.5 and JSR 166 note   To encourage the full deprecation of the ThreadGroup class, JSR 166 (Lea, 2004) proposed the introduction of the following standard interface and methods for dealing with uncaught exceptions. These have now been added to the `Thread` class (and hence the change to the `ThreadGroup` class in Java 1.5.)

```java
package java.lang; // This is a Java 1.5 addition.
public class Thread {
  ...
  public static interface UncaughtExceptionHandler {
    public void uncaughtException(Thread t,
              Throwable e);
  }
  public static UncaughtExceptionHandler
        getDefaultUncaughtExceptionHandler();
  public UncaughtExceptionHandler
         getUncaughtExceptionHandler();
  public static setDefaultUncaughtExceptionHandler(
              UncaughtExceptionHandler eh);
  public void setUncaughtExceptionHandler(
              UncaughtExceptionHandler eh);
}
```

4.4 Concurrency-related Utilities

Over the years, a vast amount of experience has been accrued in programming concurrent Java systems. This has resulted in the gradual introduction of concurrency-related utilities into the `java.util` package. For example, the `TimerTask` and `Timer` classes discussed later in this section provide support for time-triggered event handling. With Java 1.5 comes more comprehensive support for general-purpose concurrent programming. The support is partitioned into three packages:

- `java.util.concurrent` - this provides various classes to support common concurrent programming paradigms. For example, support for various queuing policies such as priority queues and blocking queues (bounded buffers). Sets and maps are also provided along with thread pools.

- `java.util.concurrent.atomic` - this provides support for lock-free thread-safe programming on simple variables such as atomic integers, atomic booleans, etc.

- `java.util.concurrent.locks` - this provides a framework for various locking algorithms that augment the Java language mechanisms. For example, read-write locks and condition variables.

It is beyond the focus of this book to cover these utilities in detail (the *next* edition of (Lea, 1999) will cover these topics in depth). Furthermore, most of the utilities have been designed without consideration to real-time issues. However, the `TimerTask` and `Timer` classes are time-related and, thus, are worthy of brief examination. Chapter 5 also considers those communication abstractions that have been found useful for real-time programming. Programming with real-time events is considered in Chapter 11.

Java event handling

In Java, threads are the entities that are scheduled by the virtual machine. However, there are occasions when it is useful to have entities scheduled for execution, which do not have the overheads associated with threads, or which have an imposed ordering. User-interface events (such as those associated with the Abstract Window Toolkit or the Swing tool kit) are good examples. Here, the events are executed by a single thread that imposes the required ordering. Events can also be time triggered. As of Java 1.3, the `Timer` and `TimerTask` classes have been added to `java.util` in order to formalize this style of programming.

Essentially, a `Timer` is an execution engine (which is implemented as a background thread) that accepts requests to schedule tasks for execution and executes these tasks sequentially in an order determined by parameters to the schedule request. Requests can be for one-off or repeated execution. A task is an instance of any subclass of the `TimerTask`:

The `TimerTask` **class**

```
package java.util;
public abstract class TimerTask implements Runnable {
    // constructors
    protected TimerTask();

    // methods

    public boolean cancel();
       // Cancel any request to schedule this task;
       // cancellation of a running task is deferred until
       // the current execution of the task is finished.
       // Returns true
       //    if the task is scheduled for repeat execution,
       //    if the task is scheduled for one-off execution
       //        and has not run.
       // Returns false otherwise.

    public abstract void run(); // the code to be run

    public long scheduledExecutionTime();
       // Returns the time (in Date.getTime() format)
       // of the most recent actual release of the task.
}
```

The Timer class

The `Timer` class itself is given below:

```
package java.util;
public class Timer {
  // constructors
  public Timer();
  public Timer(boolean isDaemon);

  // methods
  public void cancel();

  public void schedule(TimerTask task, long delay);
  public void schedule(TimerTask task,
                java.util.Data time);
  public void schedule(TimerTask task,
                java.util.Data firstTime, long period);
  public void schedule(TimerTask task, long delay,
                        long period);

  public void scheduleAtFixedRate(TimerTask task,
                java.util.Date firstTime, long period);
  public void scheduleAtFixedRate(TimerTask task,
                long delay, long period);
}
```

4.5   The `Process` and `Runtime` Classes

So far, this chapter has considered concurrency within the Java virtual machine. Threads execute within the same virtual address space and, therefore, have access to shared memory. The Java language acknowledges that the Java program might not be the only activity on the hosting computer and that the program will be executing under control of an operating system. As indicated in section 2.1, all modern operating systems support the concept of a process. Java, therefore, allows the programmer to create and interact with other processes under that host system. Of course, this interaction is heavily dependent on the actual host and consequently use of the facilities might reduce the portability of the Java program. Note also one of these other processes may be another JVM.

Java defines two classes to aid interaction with other processes: the `java.lang.Process` class and the `java.lang.Runtime` class. It assumes that all processes have connected standard input, standard output and standard error streams. That is, a process reads from standard input, writes results to standard output and produces any error messages on the standard error stream. Java also assumes that a process/operating system associates a value with the process when the process terminates. This value may be a combination of a value supplied by the process itself and a value supplied by the system. Each external process, therefore, is represented by an instance of the following `Process` class.

```
package java.lang;
public abstract class Process {

  // constructors
  public Process();

  // methods

  public abstract void destroy();
    // Forcibly destroy the external process.
  public abstract int exitValue();
    // Get the exit value associate with the process, by
    // convention 0 is normal termination;
    // Throws IllegalThreadStateException if the process
    //        has not terminated.
  public abstract java.io.InputStream getErrorStream();
  public abstract java.io.InputStream getInputStream();
  public abstract java.io.OutputStream getOutputStream();

  public abstract int waitFor()
        throws InterruptedException;
    // Wait for the process to terminate and
    // return its exit value.
}
```

The Process class is abstract, the only way to get an object that is a subclass of Process is via the Runtime class. There is only one instance of the Runtime class (available from the getRuntime method). This instance represents the currently executing Java Virtual Machine. There are various methods that duplicate the functionality in the System class (such as the method gc, which forces garbage collection); there are also methods associated with terminating the virtual machine (see Section 2.2). These are not important here. Instead, attention is focussed on those methods which allow other processes to be created (the exec methods);

```
package java.lang;
public class Runtime {
  // static methods
  public static Runtime getRuntime();

  // methods

  // The following methods allow a process to be
  // executed; a cmdarray is a command followed by
  // arguments; envp represents the environment in
  // which the process executes.
```

```
public Process exec(String[] cmdarray)
       throws IOException;
public Process exec(String command)
       throws IOException;
public Process exec(String command, String[] envp)
       throws IOException;
public Process exec(String[] cmdarray, String[] envp)
       throws IOException;
public Process exec(String cmd, String[] envp,
       java.io.File dir) throws IOException;
public Process exec(String[] command, String[] envp,
       java.io.File dir) throws IOException;
...
}
```

4.6 Thread-related Exceptions

Figure 4.2. summarizes in one place the thread-related exceptions.

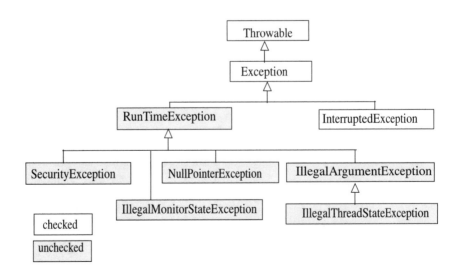

FIGURE 4.2. Thread-related Exceptions

The IllegalThreadStateException is thrown when

- the start method is called and the thread has already been started;
- the setDaemon method has been called and the thread has already been started;
- an attempt is made to destroy a nonempty thread group;
- an attempt is made to place a thread into a thread group (via the Thread constructor) and the thread group has already been destroyed.
- an attempt is made to get the exit value of a nonterminated Process.

The SecurityException is thrown by the security manager[1] when

- the Thread constructor has been called and it is requested that the thread to be created be placed into a thread group for which it has no security permission;
- a stop or destroy method has been called on a thread for which the caller does not have the correct permission for the operation requested;
- the ThreadGroup constructor has been called with a parent group parameter for which the calling group has no permission;
- a stop or destroy method has been called on a thread group for which the caller does not have the correct permission for the operation requested.

The NullPointerException is thrown when

- a null pointer is passed to the stop method;
- a null pointer is passed to the ThreadGroup constructor for the parent group.

The InterruptedException is thrown when

- a thread that has made a join method call is woken up by the thread being interrupted rather than by the target thread terminating.
- a thread that has made a wait method call is woken up by the thread being interrupted rather than by a notify or notifyAll.
- a thread that has made a waitFor method call is woken up by the thread being interrupted rather than by the target process terminating.

The IllegalMonitorStateException is thrown when

- the wait, notify, or notifyAll methods are called by a thread that has not locked the associated object.

---

1. The security manager is intended for an environment where there may be untrusted code executing (for example, where applets are being loaded across the network). This book is essentially concerned with concurrent real-time programming for single/multi processor systems. Issues of security are, consequently, not addressed.

4.7 Strengths and Limitations of the Java Concurrency Model

Strengths

The main strength of the Java concurrency model is that it is simple and it is supported directly by the language. This means that many of the errors that can occur when attempting to use an operating system interface for concurrency do not exist in Java. The language syntax and strong type checking also gives some protection against erroneous programming. For example, it is not possible to forget to end a synchronized block. Portability of programs is also enhanced because the concurrency model that the programmer uses is always the same, regardless of the operating system on which the program will finally execute.

Weaknesses

Unfortunately, the Java language model is perhaps too simple and not expressive enough to meet the demands of sometimes complex concurrent applications. Its limitations can be summarized under the following headings.

Lack of support for condition variables. Section 3.2 has already discussed the problems introduced by Java not explicitly supporting condition variables. A workaround was presented which was based on implementing a condition variable as an independent class (Section 3.3). However, there is no doubt that the use of the workaround gives more complex algorithms and more potential for deadlock situations to occur. Furthermore, coping with spurious wake-ups generated by a JVM also adds complexity.

The usual Java paradigm is to ensure that all calls to the `wait` method are enclosed in while loops that check the required conditions before allowing the threads to continue. This in conjunction with using `notifyAll` instead of `notify` allows simpler algorithms but at the cost of less efficient executions.

Poor support for absolute time and time-outs on waiting. Section 4.2 has considered the issues thrown up by Java's lack of support for delaying for an absolute time and for identifying whether a timeout has occurred. Most workarounds for both of these problems suffer from a race condition of one form or another.

No preference given to threads continuing after a `notify` over threads waiting to gain access to the monitor lock for the first time. Section 3.2 has illustrated some of the problems that occur when preferential monitor access is not given to those threads being released from waiting over those attempting to gain access for the first time. Further illustration of this problem is given in the next chapter.

Difficulties in identifying nested monitor calls and thread-safe objects. In general, the code within a synchronized method (or statement) should be kept as short as possible. Nested monitor calls should be avoided because (as noted in Section 3.2) if a thread is holding several locks, only the lock associated with the object being waited on is released. All other locks are maintained. This can lead to deadlock occurring. Unfortunately, it is not always obvious when a nested monitor call is being made, for the following reasons:

- Methods in a class not labeled as synchronized can still contain a synchronized statement.
- Methods in a class not labeled as synchronized can be overridden with a synchronized method; method calls which start off as being unsynchronized may be used with a synchronized subclass.
- Methods called via interfaces cannot be labelled as synchronized.

Poor support for priorities. While Java's priority model may be adequate for concurrent programming, it is weak from a real-time perspective (as discussed in Section 4.1). This is a major area where the RTSJ has provided added support (see Chapters 7 and 10).

Java 1.5   It is because of these problems at the language level that the Java community has developed concurrency utilities that have now been introduced into Java 1.5. In particular, the `java.util.concurrent.lock` package helps alleviate many of the above problems. However, support for real-time requires more fundamental changes.

4.8 Bloch's Thread Safety Levels

To aid the construction of concurrent Java programs, it is necessary for classes to document clearly the level of thread safety they support. Bloch (Bloch, 2001) has suggested the following levels:

Immutable. Instances of the class are constant and cannot be changed. There are, therefore, no thread safety issues. The `String` class is a good example of an immutable class.

Thread-safe. Instances of the class are mutable but they can be used safely in a concurrent environment. All methods provided by the class are properly synchronized either at the interface level or internally within the method. The `java.util.Timer` class presented in Section 4.4 is an example of a thread-safe class with internal synchronization.

Conditionally thread-safe. Instances of the class either have methods that are thread-safe or have methods that are called in sequence with the lock held by the caller. The `SharedCoordinate` class given in Section 3.1 is an example of a conditionally thread-safe class.

Thread-compatible. Instances of the class provide no synchronization. However, instances of the class can be safely used in a concurrent environment, if the caller provides the synchronization by surrounding each method (or sequence of method calls) with the appropriate lock.

Thread-hostile. Instances of the class should not be used in a concurrent environment even if the caller provides external synchronization. Ideally, classes should not be written that are thread-hostile. Typically a thread-hostile class is accessing static data or the external environment.

4.9 Summary

This chapter completes the review of the Java concurrency model by considering the following.

- How Java uses priorities to indicate to the Java Virtual Machine (JVM) where one thread should be run in preference to another.

- How threads can delay themselves by using the `sleep` and `yield` methods. The `sleep` method supports only relative time periods (intervals); it is not possible to sleep until an absolute time. Time-outs on waiting for events are also supported via the `wait` methods. However, it is not easy to determine whether the timeout has expired or the waited-for event has occurred.

- How threads can be grouped together via the `ThreadGroup` class. Hierarchies of groups can be formed and it is possible to interrupt the whole group.

- The concurrency-related utilities that allow (servers) `Timers` and (event handlers) `TimerTasks` to be created. A timer is logically a single thread that executes the timer tasks.

- The interaction with processes outside the virtual machine via the `Processes` and `RunTime` classes.

- All the thread-related exceptions and when they occur.

The chapter also summarized some of the strengths and weaknesses of the Java model and reviewed Bloch's thread safety levels. The following two chapters provide detailed examples of using the model.

5 Implementing Communication Paradigms in Java

Introduction and chapter structure

This chapter illustrates the expressive power of the Java language model by showing how it can be used to program some standard communication paradigms. There are many communication paradigms that could be chosen, the ones discussed here are those that have traditionally been used to support real-time programs. They include the following:

- *Semaphores* – A standard counting semaphore providing acquire (or wait) and release (or signal) operations. Binary and quantity semaphores are also illustrated.

- *Signals* – Allowing a thread to wait for a signal sent from another thread. There are traditionally two types of signals: transient or persistent. Transient signals that release all waiting threads are called *Pulses*.

- *Events* – Events are bivalued state variables (*up* or *down*). Threads can *set* (assign to *up*), *reset* (assign to *down*) or *toggle* an event. Any threads *waiting* for the event to become *up* (or *down*) are released by a call of *set* (or *reset*); *toggle* can also release *waiting* threads.

- *Buffers* – Supporting the standard bounded buffer abstraction.

- *Blackboards* – Blackboards are similar to events except that they allow arbitrary data to be transmitted between the signaling and the waiting thread.

- *Broadcasts* – Supporting the standard broadcast paradigm (they are pulses with data transfer).

- *Barriers* – Provide a pure synchronization mechanism; they allow a set number of threads to block until all are present. The threads are then all released.

The semantics of Java's wait and notify mechanisms mean that it is often not possible to define fully the effects of some of these communication abstractions (see Section 3.2). Some of these uncertainties can be removed by using the RTSJ facilities (see Chapter 14).

Important
note

The goal of this chapter is not to define an alternative set of Java 1.5's reusable concurrency-related utilities. Rather, the goal is to illustrate how the basic language facilities can be used to build simple communications abstractions.

5.1 Semaphores

It is often claimed that semaphores are among the most flexible low-level synchronization primitives. They can easily be implemented in Java:

```java
package communicationAbstractions;
public class Semaphore {
  public Semaphore(int initial) {
    value = initial;
  }

  public synchronized void acquire()
          throws InterruptedException {
    while(value == 0) wait();
    value--;
  }

  public synchronized void release() {
    value++;
    notify();
  }
  protected int value;
}
```

Calls to the `acquire` method are blocked until the semaphore can be decremented (a time-out could be added to this definition if the possibility of indefinite blocking needs to be avoided). Calls to `release` will increment the semaphore, and this will result in a blocked thread being released.

This Java implementation of a semaphore does not guarantee that the thread released by the call to `release` will be the one that acquires the semaphore. It is entirely possible that before the woken thread executes, another thread calling `acquire` will obtain the semaphore. Hence, in this example, the while loop in `acquire` is essential to ensure correct access.

An example of the use of a semaphore is given below. It concerns controlling access to a one-way road tunnel. For safety reasons, only a certain number of cars are allowed in the tunnel at any one time.

```java
import communicationAbstractions.Semaphore;
class RestrictedTunnelControl {
  public RestrictedTunnelControl(int maximumAllowed) {
    maxAllowed = maximumAllowed;
    tunnelControl = new Semaphore(maxAllowed);
  }

  public void enterProtocol() {
    while(true) {
      try {
        tunnelControl.acquire();
        break;
      } catch(InterruptedException ie) {
          // No action needed in this example.
      }
    }
  }

  public void exitProtocol() {
    tunnelControl.release();
  }

  private int maxAllowed;
  private Semaphore tunnelControl;
}
```

In the above example, cars wishing to enter the tunnel must first call the `enterProtocol` procedure. Potentially, this is a blocking method as it calls a method in a `Semaphore` object; only `MaximumAllowed` cars are allowed in the tunnel at any one time. The cars call `exitProtocol` as they leave the tunnel.

```java
public class Car extends Thread {

  public Car(RestrictedTunnelControl tc) {
    super();
    controller = tc;
  }
```

```
public void run() {
  // Approach tunnel.

  controller.enterProtocol();
    // Drive through tunnel.
  controller.exitProtocol();

  // Continue journey.
}
private RestrictedTunnelControl controller;
}
```

Binary
semaphores

Although semaphores can be programmed using synchronized classes, it is often more appropriate to program the actual synchronization required directly (using the monitor facility) rather than indirectly with a semaphore. For example, consider a binary semaphore:

```
package communicationAbstractions;

public class BinarySemaphore extends Semaphore {
  public BinarySemaphore(int initial) {
    super(initial);
    if(value > 1 | value < 0) throw new
        IllegalArgumentException(
      "Binary semaphore must be initialized to 0 or 1");
  }

  public synchronized void release() {
    value = 1;
    notify();
  }
}
```

To obtain mutual exclusion using this semaphore requires the following.

```
import communicationAbstractions.BinarySemaphore;
...
BinarySemaphore mutex = new BinarySemaphore(1);
// Declaration of data requiring mutually exclusive access.

try {
  mutex.acquire();
} catch (InterruptedException ie) {
    // Some recovery action.
}
```

```
    // Code to be executed in mutual exclusion.

    mutex.release();
```

However, this can often be more efficiently, safely and elegantly written as:

```
public class MutualExclusionControl {
  // Declaration of data requiring mutually
  // exclusive access.

  public synchronized void mutex_operation() {
    // Code to be executed in mutual exclusion.
  }
}
```

Quantity semaphores

Another variation on the normal definition of a semaphore is the *quantity semaphore*. With this primitive, the amount to be decremented by the `acquire` operation (and incremented by the `release` operation) is not fixed at one, but is given as a parameter to the methods.

```
public class QuantitySemaphore extends Semaphore {
  public QuantitySemaphore(int initial) {
    super(initial);
  }
  public synchronized void acquire(int num)
                          throws InterruptedException {
    while(value < num) wait();
    value = value - num;
  }
  public synchronized void release(int num) {
    value = value + num;
    notifyAll();
  }
}
```

Note that `notifyAll` is used in the `release` method as quantity semaphores may allow more than one acquirer to continue.

**Class
diagrams**

Figure 5.1 below summarizes the relationship between the semaphore classes
introduced in this section.

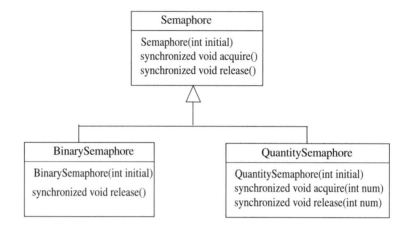

FIGURE 5.1. **Semaphore Classes**

5.2 Signals

Often a thread needs to wait for a signal from another thread before it can proceed. There
are various types of signals. A *persistent signal* (sometimes called a *latch* or a *gate*) is a
signal that remains set until a single thread has received it. A *transient signal* (or *pulse*) is
a signal that releases one or more waiting threads but is lost if no threads are waiting.

With all types of signals, it is essential to separate the sending and the waiting
interface in order to ensure that the threads are able to call only their appropriate operation (a similar approach could have been taken with semaphores if it is necessary to separate out the acquiring and releasing roles).

```
package communicationAbstractions;
public interface SignalSender {
    void send();
}
```

```
package communicationAbstractions;
public interface SignalWaiter {
    void waitS() throws InterruptedException;
}
```

As with semaphores, if indefinite waiting is to be avoided, a `waitS` operation with a
time-out can be added to the `SignalWaiter` interface. The following class implements

an abstract signal. It is structured this way because the implementation of the send operation has code common for all signals.

```java
package communicationAbstractions;

public abstract class Signal
        implements SignalSender, SignalWaiter {

  public synchronized void send() {
    arrived = true;
    notify();
  }

  public abstract void waitS() throws InterruptedException;

  protected boolean arrived = false;
}
```

Persistent signals

To illustrate Java's flexibility, a persistent signal is now defined. Here, as well as having a simple waitS operation, a watch operation is also defined. This operation returns immediately even if the signal has not been sent (rather than waiting). First, the appropriate interface must be provided:

```java
package communicationAbstractions;
public interface SignalWaiterOrWatcher
        extends SignalWaiter {
  boolean watch();
}
```

The persistent signal extends the Signal class and implements the required interface.

```java
package communicationAbstractions;
public class PersistentSignal extends Signal
            implements SignalWaiterOrWatcher {

  public synchronized void waitS()
          throws InterruptedException {
    while(!arrived) wait(); // Wait for a new signal.
    arrived = false;
  }

  public synchronized boolean watch() {
    // This method never waits.
    if(!arrived) return false;
    arrived = false;
    return true;
  }
}
```

In common with the semaphores, there is no guarantee that the thread woken by the
notify method will be the thread that receives the signal. Another thread may gain
access to the waitS method before the awoken thread can execute. Unlike semaphores,
multiple send method calls will release only one thread — no count is maintained.

For an example of the use of a persistent signal, consider the following class that
provides access to a disk. One of the functions it provides is asynchronous output. That
is, the calling thread is not blocked immediately when it requests that data be written to
the disk. Instead, the method returns a persistent signal object. When the output is complete, the controller sends the associated signal:

```java
import communicationAbstractions.PersistentSignal;
import communicationAbstractions.SignalWaiterOrWatcher;

class DiskController {
  // Various operations including:

  public SignalWaiterOrWatcher asyncWrite(
            int blockNumber, Block from) {
    reply = new PersistentSignal();

    // Set up the write operation then:
    return reply;
  }

  private PersistentSignal reply;
}
```

Inside this class, the output may be queued and actually not written to the disk for some
time.

The client of the class can proceed as soon as the asyncWrite method returns
and later check to see if the output has been written:

```java
import communicationAbstractions.SignalWaiterOrWatcher;
...
{
  DiskController controller = new DiskController();
  Block superBlock = new Block();
  SignalWaiterOrWatcher outputDone;

  ...
  outputDone = controller.asyncWrite(0, superBlock);
  // When it is time to check that the output is complete:
  try {
    outputDone.waitS();
  } catch (InterruptedException ie) {
      // Initiate recovery action.
```

```
   } // or
   if(!outputDone.watch()) {
     // Output not complete, initiate recovery action.
   }
 }
```

Remember that the persistent signal object will be garbage collected only when both the disk controller and the client have deleted their access to it.

An alternative to the disk controller object creating the persistent object is to let the client decide what type of signal to use and to pass the sender interface with the write request. The disk controller class becomes

```
import communicationAbstractions.SignalSender;

class DiskController {
  // Various operations including
  public void asyncWrite(int blockNumber,
              Block from, SignalSender done) {
    // Set up the write operation and
    whenDone = done;
  }
  // later on:
  {
    whenDone.send();
  }
  private SignalSender whenDone;
}
```

In the above, the DiskController expects the client to provide its own synchronization agent. All that the controller requires is an interface for signaling when the required operation is complete. The client body becomes:

```
import communicationAbstractions.PersistentSignal;
...
{
  DiskController controller2 = new DiskController();
  PersistentSignal outputDone2 = new PersistentSignal();
  ...
  controller2.asyncWrite(0, superBlock,outputDone2);
  // When it is time to check that the output is complete.
```

```
      try {
        outputDone2.waitS();
      } catch (InterruptedException ie) {
          // Initiate recovery action.
      }
      // Or
      if(!outputDone2.watch()) {
        // Output not complete, initiate some recovery action.
      }
  }
```

Transient signals

A transient signal is a signal that is lost if no threads are currently waiting. Two types can be recognized: one that releases a single thread, and one that releases all threads (called a *pulse*). They may be implemented as follows; first the simple transient signal that releases just one thread. This extends the abstract Signal class (that implements the SignalSender and SignalWaiter interfaces)

```
package communicationAbstractions;
public class TransientSignal extends Signal {
  public synchronized void send() {
      // Overrides send in Signal
      // and implements the SignalSender interface.
    if(waiting > 0) super.send();
  }

  public synchronized void waitS() {
          throws InterruptedException
    // Overrides waitS in Signal and
    // implements the SignalWaiter interface.
    try {
      while(!arrived) {
        waiting++;
        wait();
        waiting--;
      }
      arrived = false;
    } catch(InterruptedException ie) {
        waiting--;
        throw ie;
    }
  }
  protected int waiting = 0;
}
```

Note, in the above example, it is necessary to catch any thrown `InterruptedEx-`
`ception`. If it had not been caught, the `waiting` count would be wrong. The result
would be that eventually a transient signal would be made permanent.

Pulses

A `Pulse` allows all waiting threads to be released. Consider the following

```
package communicationAbstractions;
public class Pulse extends TransientSignal {
  public synchronized void sendAll() { // A new method.
    if(waiting > 0) {
      arrived = true;
      notifyAll();
    }
  }

  public synchronized void waitS()
          throws InterruptedException {
    // Overrides waitS in TransientSignal and
    // implements the SignalWaiter interface.
    try {
      while(!arrived) {
        waiting++;
        wait();
        waiting--;
      }
      if(waiting == 0) arrived = false;
    } catch(InterruptedException ie) {
        if(--waiting == 0) arrived = false;
        throw ie;
    }
  }
}
```

If more than one thread is waiting for the signal and `sendAll` is called, all are
released. The last one detects that there are no more threads to be released and sets the
boolean flag to false. Any threads that queue after this point will have to wait for the
next signal.

Note that with `Pulse` more than `waiting` threads might be released as new
threads might call `waitS` while the others are being released. To avoid this problem, it
is necessary ensure that those waiting inside the `waitS` method are given preferential

access to the lock over those trying to enter the `wait` method. This is difficult to ensure and is left as an exercise for the reader.

Class diagrams

Figure 5.2 below summarizes the relationship between the signal classes introduced in this section.

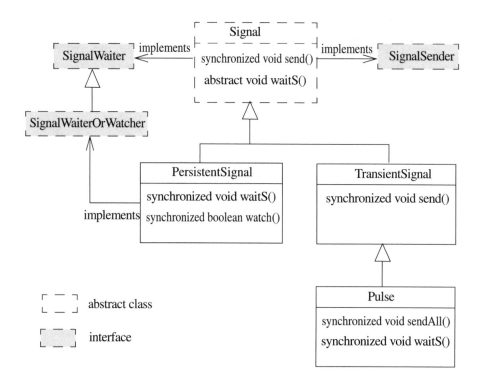

FIGURE 5.2. Signal and Related Classes and Interfaces

5.3 Events

As previously mentioned, an event is a bivalued variable (UP or DOWN). A thread can wait for an event to be set or reset. Events may be created and initialized using the class `Event`. The method `set` causes the event to go into the UP state; the method `reset` causes it to go into the DOWN state. The `toggle` procedure simply changes the state of the event from UP to DOWN, or from DOWN to UP. The function `state` returns the current state of the event. Synchronization with an event is achieved using the `await` method. This will suspend the caller until the state of the event is that required by the caller.

The implementation of an event is given below:

```
package communicationAbstractions;
public enum EventState {UP, DOWN};

package communicationAbstractions;
public class Event {
  public Event(EventState initial) {
    value = initial;
  }
  public Event() {
   value = EventState.DOWN;
  }
  public synchronized void await(int state)
          throws InterruptedException {
    while(value != state) wait();
  }
  public synchronized void set() {
    value = EventState.UP;
    notifyAll();
  }
  public synchronized void reset() {
    value = EventState.DOWN;
    notifyAll();
  }
  public synchronized void toggle() {
    if(value == EventState.DOWN) value = EventState.UP;
    else value = EventState.DOWN;
    notifyAll();
  }
  public synchronized int state() {
    return value;
  }
  protected EventState value;
}
```

Note that Java's lack of condition variables (and the possibility of JVM-generated spurious wake-ups) means it is necessary to ensure the `wait` method is called in a while loop – as it is not possible to wait for a particular condition without introducing more complexity into the algorithm (see Section 3.3).

5.4 Buffers

The basic bounded buffer has already been described in Section 3.2. It is repeated here for completeness:

```java
package communicationAbstractions;
public class BoundedBuffer<Data> {
  public BoundedBuffer(int length) {
    size = length;
    buffer = (Data[]) new Object[size];
    last = 0;
    first = 0;
  }

  public synchronized void put(Data item)
          throws InterruptedException {
    while (numberInBuffer == size) wait();
    last = (last + 1) % size ;
                // % is the integer remainder operator
    numberInBuffer++;
    buffer[last] = item;
    notifyAll();
  }

  public synchronized Data get()
          throws InterruptedException {
    while (numberInBuffer == 0) wait();
    first = (first + 1) % size ;
    numberInBuffer--;
    notifyAll();
    return buffer[first];
  }

  private Data buffer[];
  private int first;
  private int last;
  private int numberInBuffer = 0;
  private int size;
}
```

The buffer abstraction is one in which the data, once read, is destroyed. If the data is to be retained, then the blackboard abstraction is more appropriate.

5.5 Blackboard

The blackboard abstraction can be viewed either as being similar to the events abstraction with data transfer or the buffer abstraction with a nondestructive read and the facility to invalidate the data. Each notional item of the buffer is represented as a single blackboard:

```
package communicationAbstractions;
public class Blackboard<Data> {
  public Blackboard() {
    statusValid = false;
  }
  public Blackboard(Data initial) {
    theMessage = initial;
    statusValid = true;
  }
  public synchronized void write (Data message) {
    theMessage = message;
    statusValid = true;
    notifyAll();
  }
  public synchronized void clear() {
    statusValid = false;
  }
  public synchronized Data read()
          throws InterruptedException {
    while(!statusValid) wait();
    return theMessage;
  }
  public boolean dataAvailable() {
    return statusValid;
  }
  private Data theMessage;
  private boolean statusValid;
}
```

Objects are placed on a `Blackboard` by calling `write`; they are deleted by calling `clear`. The method `read` will block the caller until data on the blackboard is valid (that is, there is data present). The function `dataAvailable` indicates whether the blackboard currently has data.

A simpler form of blackboard does not have a clear operation; all data is preserved until overwritten. `Read` would then be nonblocking and hence would not throw the `InterruptedException` (assuming that the blackboard is initialized to some appropriate value).

5.6 Broadcast

A broadcast is similar in structure to a `Pulse` except that data is sent. Only those threads waiting (or attempt to receive while the broadcast is in progress) receive the data. If no threads are waiting (or a previous broadcast is in progress), the data is discarded.

```java
package communicationAbstractions;
public class Broadcast<Data> {
  public Broadcast() {
    arrived = false;
    waiting = 0;
  }
  public synchronized void send(Data message) {
    if(waiting != 0 && !arrived)   {
      theMessage = message;
      arrived = true;
      notifyAll();
    }
  }
  public synchronized Data receive()
        throws InterruptedException {
    try {
      while(!arrived) { // wait for a message to arrive
        waiting++;
        wait();
        waiting--;
      }
      if(waiting == 0) {
        // The last thread to receive the message
        // resets the boolean flag.
        arrived = false;
      }
    } catch(InterruptedException ie) {
        if(--waiting == 0)
          arrived = false;
    }
    return theMessage;
  }
  private Data theMessage;
  private boolean arrived;
  private int waiting;
}
```

5.6.1 Multicast to a group

The term *broadcast* has so far been used to indicate that the data should be sent to any thread that is waiting. Often the term broadcast (or, more correctly, *multicast*) is used to indicate that the data should be sent to a specific group of threads. In this situation, *all* threads in the group should receive the data, not just those that happen to be waiting when the data is sent. This is slightly more difficult to achieve; all potential recipients must be known (say via their thread identifiers) and only when all have received one item of data is another item allowed to be transmitted.

The following class specification defines a multicast interface. Threads that are interested in receiving from a group must join the group explicitly, and when they are no longer interested, they must leave the group:

```
package communicationAbstractions;
public class Multicast<Data> {
  public Multicast(int groupSize);
  public synchronized void join()
    throws GroupFullException, AlreadyInGroupException;
  public synchronized void leave()
    throws NotInGroupException;
  public synchronized void send(Data message)
    throws InterruptedException;
  public synchronized Data receive()
    throws NotInGroupException;
}
```

The implementation keeps track of the threads which have joined the group. Each group has a maximum size. The constructor initializes the data structures needed to keep track of threads.

```
package communicationAbstractions;
public class Multicast<Data> {
  public Multicast(int groupSize) {
    size = groupSize;
    activeThreads = new Thread[size];
    receivedMessage = new boolean[size];
    for(int i=0; i < size; i++) {
      receivedMessage[i] = true;
      activeThreads[i] = null;
    }
  }
}
  . . .
```

```
    private int size;
    private Thread[] activeThreads;
    private boolean[] receivedMessage;
    private Data theMessage;
}
```

Note that it is not possible to use ThreadGroups to capture the relationship between the multicast's recipients. Threads can only be associated with a ThreadGroup at thread creation time. They cannot be dynamically attached to a group.

The join method checks to see if the thread is already a member of the group; if it is not and the group is not at its maximum size, it adds the thread to the group. The leave methods similarly checks to see if the thread is a group member and, if so, removes it from the group.

```
    public synchronized void join()
       throws GroupFullException, AlreadyInGroupException {
       int j = size;

       for(int i=0; i < size; i++) {
         if(activeThreads[i] == null) {
           j = i;
           break;
         }
         if(activeThreads[i] == Thread.currentThread())
           throw new AlreadyInGroupException();
       }
       // j is now first free slot.
       if(j == size) throw new GroupFullException();
       activeThreads[j] = Thread.currentThread();
       receivedMessage[j] = true;
    }

    public synchronized void leave()
            throws NotInGroupException {
       int i = findThreadIndex();

       activeThreads[i] = null;
       receivedMessage[i] = true;
       notifyAll();
    }
    ...
}
```

Next the send and receive methods can be defined. The send method will be allowed to complete only if all threads have received the last message. Similarly, receive will have to wait if there is no outstanding sent message.

```
public synchronized void send(Data message)
        throws InterruptedException {
  while(!allReceived()) wait();
   // Wait for the previous multicast to terminate.
  for(int i=0; i < size; i++) {
      // Reset received flags.
      receivedMessage[i] = false;
  }
  theMessage = message;
  notifyAll();
}
public synchronized Data receive()
        throws NotInGroupException {
  while(alreadyReceived()) wait();
    // Wait for the next message.
  logReceived();
  if(allReceived()) notifyAll(); // Wakeup senders.
  return theMessage;
}
...
}
```

Finally, the protected methods can be given.

```
protected int findThreadIndex()
      throws NotInGroupException {
  int i;
  for(i=0; i < size; i++) {
    if(activeThreads[i] == Thread.currentThread())
      break;
  }
  if(i == size) throw new NotInGroupException();
  return i;
}
protected boolean alreadyReceived()
          throws NotInGroupException {
 return(receivedMessage[findThreadIndex()]);
}
```

```
protected void logReceived()
  throws NotInGroupException {
  receivedMessage[findThreadIndex()] = true;
}

protected boolean allReceived() {
  boolean done = true;
  for(int i=0; i < size; i++) {
    if(activeThreads[i] != null && !receivedMessage[i]) {
      done = false;
      break;
    }
  }
  return done;
}
```

5.7 Barriers

A barrier simply blocks several threads until all have arrived at the barrier. In this case, no data is passed, but a form of multicast could be programmed, which passes data as well. Threads wishing to block at a barrier call the waitB method. If the barrier is in the process of releasing threads (from the previous batch), the threads are held. Otherwise, a count is incremented and when the last thread arrives, all threads are released.

```
public class Barrier {
  public Barrier(int number) {
    need = number; // Number of threads to block.
    arrived = 0;
    releasing = false;
  }

  public synchronized void waitB()
        throws InterruptedException {
    while(releasing) wait();
      // Wait for previous batch to depart.
    try {
      arrived++;
      While(arrived !=needed) && !releasing) wait();
      if(arrived == need){ // When all present.
        releasing = true;
        notifyAll();
      }
```

```
      } finally {
         arrived--;
         if (arrived == 0) { // Last thread to leave.
           releasing = false;
           notifyAll();  // Allow new batch to arrive.
         }
      }
   }
   public synchronized int value() {
     return arrived;
   }
   public int capacity() {
     return need;
   }
   private int need;
   private int arrived;
   private boolean releasing;
}
```

5.8 Summary

In concurrent programming, there are many different communication and synchronization paradigms. This chapter has focused on those that have been found useful in real-
time systems over the years. The chapter has also illustrated the results of two of the
main limitations of the Java monitor model.

Lack of preferential access to the monitor lock. This has resulted in either

- nonpredictability of the communications paradigm, as in the case of semaphores,
  and signals or
- more complex implementation models, as in the case of pulses, broadcasts and barriers.
- The presence of spurious JVM wakeups further complicate the algorithm designs.

Lack of condition variables. This has resulted in the introduction of inefficiency where
threads are woken up more often then they need be, as in the implementation of events.

  Java 1.5 now has its own set of concurrency utilities, which should ease the programmer's burden when more complex communication patterns, than that supported by
the core Java language, are required. However, for simple communication abstractions,
it is often more efficient to implement the mechanisms directly as illustrated in this
Chapter.

6 Case Study: Concurrent Maze Search

Introduction and chapter structure

This chapter presents a case study that exploits the facilities of Java. The example involves a common problem in Computer Science – that of searching a problem space for a particular solution. In this case, the problem space is a maze, and the requirement is to find paths through the maze. This could represent, for example, finding all the routes from a starting point to a destination in a city.

A maze can be defined as an arrangement of intricate paths (usually between hedges) in which it is difficult to find a way out. A very simple maze is illustrated below, with two unique paths through it.

FIGURE 6.1. A Simple Maze

There are two main motivations for using concurrency to find all the paths through the maze, rather than using a sequential approach with backtracking:

- a concurrent solution is easier to design because conceptually it is easy to imagine creating a new thread to explore each branch in the maze rather than having to remember which branches have yet to be explored;

- a concurrent solution will be quicker for large mazes when the program is executed on a multiprocessor system, as each thread really will execute in parallel (assuming that the JVM is fully able to exploit the multiple processors).

The case study comes in three parts:

- Firstly, a multithreaded Java program is presented that searches through a maze to find all the unique solutions. A new thread is created for every potential path found, and the threads perform their searches concurrently. The solution illustrates the general concurrency facilities of Java and shows how many of the resource control issues can be left to the JVM to manage. The details of the maze are given in an input file. Each unique solution is given an integer identifier (between 1 and the maximum number of unique paths in the maze). When the search is complete, the program prints the number of unique paths and then offers the user the option of illustrating any of the unique paths. If the user types an integer between 1 and the number of unique paths, then that path is illustrated on the screen.

- The first part finds all possible solutions, the second part requires that as soon as one searcher thread finds a solution, all other active searcher thread are immediately informed of the fact and they stop their searches. This solution illustrates the use of thread groups and the thread interrupt mechanism.

- For some applications, allowing the JVM to manage all resources is inefficient. The third part of the case study, therefore, limits the number of concurrent searches and requires that the searcher threads are reused.

6.1 Concurrent Maze Searching

In the first solution, a single searcher thread is created, which starts its search from the maze entrance. As the searcher proceeds, it encounters a branch in the path. It chooses one branch to follow and creates one or more new searcher threads to explore the other branches. Each new searcher is initialized with the details of the path that its parent has explored so far. Figure 6.2 illustrates the creation of some of the threads for the simple maze given in Figure 6.1.

Note that the threads illustrated in Figure 6.2 are not the only threads that will be created. At the square marked ** two new threads will be created: one by the first searcher thread that will explore to the left, and one by the fourth searcher that will explore upwards. These, in turn, will create other threads but they all will eventually terminate as they detect cycles in their search paths or they hit dead ends.

The solution consists of several objects. Here, attention is focused on the objects that are needed to represents the maze and the searcher threads.

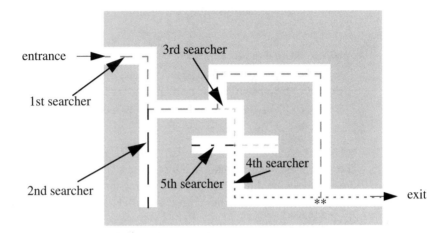

FIGURE 6.2. Searcher Threads

The first object represents the maze itself. It is responsible for reading the maze description from a file and maintaining the program's internal representation of the maze and its user interface. The maze is modeled as a two-dimensional array. Each position in the maze is represented by the class MazePosition, which encapsulates a row and column number as illustrated below:

```
public class MazePosition {
  public int getRow();
  public int getColumn();
  public void setRow(int R);
  public void setColumn(int C);
  public boolean equals(MazePosition mp);
}
```

The SearchableMaze class, shown below, extends the Maze class and provides methods to navigate the maze. The next method returns the coordinates of all the valid maze positions that are adjacent to the given position.

```
public class SearchableMaze {
  public MazePosition entrance();
  public boolean atExit(MazePosition mp);
  public MazePosition[] next(MazePosition from);
}
```

A path through the maze is called a trail and is represented by the `Trail` class.

```
public class Trail {
  public Trail clone();
  public boolean visited(MazePosition mp);
  public MazePosition[] mark(MazePosition mp);
}
```

The `visited` method takes a `MazePosition` and returns true if that position is already present in the trail, thereby indicating that the position has already been visited. The `mark` method adds a maze position to the trail and returns all the valid moves from that position.

A complete trail through the maze will start at the maze entrance, end at the maze exit and have no cycles in it. When a searcher thread finds a complete trail, it will invoke the method `trailFound` in the `Tracker` class.

```
public class Tracker {
  public synchronized Trail giveTrail(int n);
  public synchronized void newSearcher();
  public synchronized int numberOfSolutions();
  public synchronized void searcherFinished();
  public synchronized void trailFound(Trail t);
  public synchronized int waitAllFinished();
}
```

The `Tracker` class keeps track of all the complete trails through the maze. It also keeps track of the number of active searcher threads. The `newSearcher` method is called by a searcher thread when it is created; the `searcherFinished` is called just before the searcher terminates, and the `waitAllFinished` method is called by the main program. The other methods are used by the main program to control the user interface.

Finally, the Searcher class is presented below:

```
public class Searcher {
  public void run();
  static void main(String[] args);
}
```

Class relationships

The relationships between the above classes are illustrated in Figure 6.3. Each searcher thread follows only a single trail; however, for every searchable maze there are many searcher threads (indicated by the * in the figure).

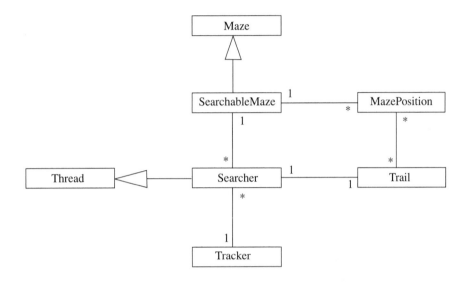

FIGURE 6.3. Relationship between Classes in the Maze Case Study

Object collabora- tions

Figure 6.4 illustrates the main collaboration between the objects. When a potential new path is identified, a parent searcher thread creates a new (child) searcher thread and passes details of the objects it needs to interact with (labeled 1 in the diagram). The child informs the tracker object that it has been created (2) and then takes a clone of the trail the parent was following (3). It marks the current position on the new trail (4). This results in the trail object determining the next valid moves that can be made (5). These are returned to the searcher. The next operation of the searcher depends on the available moves. If the searcher is at the exit, it calls the tracker object to indicate that it is termi- nating with a found solution. If there are no valid moves, it again calls the tracker object to indicate that it is terminating without a found solution. If there is only a single path, it iterates through collaborations 4 and 5. If there is more than one path, it creates a new searcher (6b) for all but one path, and then explores the chosen path.

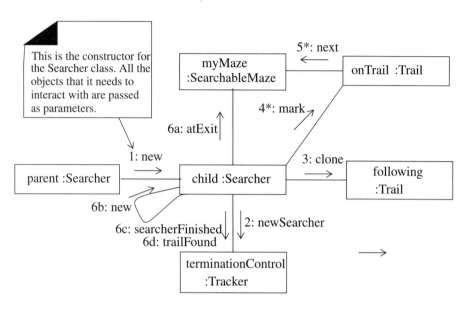

FIGURE 6.4. Collaboration between Objects

The Searcher thread

The Searcher class is a subclass of the Thread class. It also contains the main method that initializes the system and creates the first searcher thread. First consider the code associated with the thread constructor. When a new searcher is created, it needs to know which maze it is searching, which trail it is currently following, where in the maze it currently is, and which tracker to use for termination control of the whole program. The constructor takes a clone of the Trail. Because the constructors are called sequentially before the newly created thread is started, this method does *not* need to be synchronized; there is no concurrent access. Note also that as Searcher is a subclass of Thread, the constructor needs to invoke the superclass' constructor. Here, it is indicating that the textual name "Searcher Thread" can be used to identify the thread. Note that in the program fragments given below, all details of the user interface have been removed.

```
public class Searcher extends Thread {
  public Searcher (SearchableMaze m, MazePosition from,
                   Trail following, Tracker tr) {
    super("Searcher Thread");
    myMaze = m;
    currentPosition = from;
    onTrail = following.clone();
    tr.newSearcher();
    terminationControl = tr;
  }
```

```
  . . .
  private SearchableMaze myMaze;
  private MazePosition currentPosition, previous;
  private Trail onTrail;
  private Tracker terminationControl;
}
```

Next the run method is presented. This gives the main functionality of the thread.

```
public void run() {
  MazePosition[] moves;
  int count;
  Searcher s;
  do { // Loop until no more moves.
    count = -1;
    // Get the next valid moves.
    moves = onTrail.mark(currentPosition);

    for (int index = 0; index < moves.length; index++) {
      // For each valid move.
      if(moves[index] != null)
        if(!moves[index].equals(previous))
          if(!onTrail.visited(moves[index])) {
            // Have not visited here before.
            if(count == -1) count = index;
            else {
              // More than one path, so create a new thread.
              s = new Searcher(myMaze, moves[index],
                      onTrail, terminationControl);
              s.start();
            }
          }
    }
    if(count != -1) {
      previous = currentPosition;
      currentPosition = moves[count];
    }
  } while(count != -1);
  if(myMaze.atExit(currentPosition))
    terminationControl.trailFound(onTrail);
  else
    terminationControl.searcherFinished();
} // end run
```

The search algorithm takes its current position and adds this to the trail it is following (by calling onTrail.mark). This returns an array of MazePosition, where each element in the array is a valid move from the current position. As the maze paths only go at 90 degrees, the length of the array can be from 1 to 4. An array of length 1 would indicate that the only valid position is to return on the path that the searcher is following. Hence, the searcher has reached the edge of the maze. Position A in Figure 6.5 has only one valid move, Position B, two, position C, three and Position D, four.

Once the searcher has determined the valid moves, it must decide which move to take. Here, it decides to take the first valid move (first ensuring that it is not where it came from and that it has not already visited that position on the current trail). For all other new valid moves, it creates a new searcher thread and passes the current state of the trail to them. The searcher continues on its trail until either it reaches a dead end or it finds the maze exit. Before terminating, it calls the tracker to indicate that it is finishing and whether it has found a valid path through the maze.

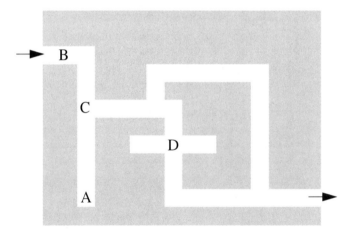

FIGURE 6.5. **Positions in the Maze**

The main program

The main program is responsible for creating the required objects and starting the first searcher thread. It then waits for all the threads to terminate before interacting with the user to display the solutions.

```java
public static void main(String[] args) {
    Tracker tr = new Tracker();
    SearchableMaze sm = new SearchableMaze(tr);
    Trail t = new Trail(sm);
    Searcher s = new Searcher(sm, sm.Entrance(), t, tr);
    s.start();
    int numberOfSolutions = tr.waitAllFinished();
    // Call user interface classes to display solutions.
}
```

In the course of searching a maze, many hundreds of threads may be created. They do not directly communicate with each other except when one searcher creates a new searcher. Furthermore, although they all access the `SearchableMaze`, there is no contention as they are only reading the state not modifying it.

The
Tracker
class

The only real contention is via the `Tracker` class. An object of this class (`terminationControl`) is used to keep track of how many active searchers there are and what solutions have been found so far. Consequently, this object needs to be synchronized. Also, as the main program needs to wait until all the searchers have been created and terminated, the wait and notify facility is used.

```
public class Tracker {
  public synchronized void newSearcher() {
    alive++;
  }
  public synchronized void searcherFinished() {
    alive--;
    if(alive == 0) notify();
  }
  public synchronized void trailFound(Trail t) {
    alive--;
    solutions[count++] = t;
    if(alive == 0) notify();
  }
  public synchronized int waitAllFinished() {
    while(alive != 0)
      try {
        wait();
      } catch(InterruptedException e) {// ignore}
    return count;
  }
  public synchronized Trail giveTrail(int n) {
    if(n < count) return solutions[n];
    else return solutions[0];
  }
  public synchronized int numberOfSolutions () {
   return count;
  }

  private int alive = 0;
  private Trail[] solutions= new Trail[100];
    // Initial size (code not shown to grow the array).
  private int count = 0;
}
```

6.2   Stopping the Search when a Solution is Found

The above solution exploits the maximum amount of concurrency in order to find all the paths through the maze (it could easily be extended to find the shortest route). Its main advantages over a sequential solution are its simplicity and its potential to exploit any parallel processing facility available. However, if the goal of the search is to find just one path, then with a sequential solution the program can simply stop when it has found a solution. With the concurrent solution, it is necessary to inform all the threads that they can stop their searches. One way of doing this is simply to force termination of the whole program. However, this is clumsy and does not cater for the situation where the program wants to continue so that it can display the solution.

Java provides two facilities that help solve this termination problem. They are the interrupt mechanism and thread groups. By creating all the searcher threads in the same group, it is possible to interrupt them all via the group interrupt mechanism, without the programmer having to know the identity of all the searchers. Only changes to the searcher thread are required to implement this approach.

```java
public class Searcher extends Thread {
  ... // as before

  static final ThreadGroup allSearchers = new
                    ThreadGroup("All Searchers");
  public Searcher (SearchableMaze m, MazePosition from,
                    Trail following, Tracker t) {
    super(allSearchers, "Searcher Thread");
    ... // as before
  }

  public void run() {
    ... // As before.
    do {
      ... // As before.
    } while(count != -1 & !isInterrupted());

    if(myMaze.atExit(currentPosition) & !isInterrupted()) {
      terminationControl.trailFound(onTrail);
      allSearchers.interrupt();
    } else terminationControl.searcherFinished();
  } // end run
}
```

In this solution, there is a static thread group (`allSearchers`), which is used to link all the searcher threads. When a searcher finds a solution, it calls the `interrupt` method on this group. This results in all the threads currently in the group having their interrupt status set. There are two main disadvantages of this approach.

- The searcher threads have to poll for the interrupt. Here, they test the interrupt status every time they make a new move.
- There is a race condition between the searcher threads being informed of the interrupt and the creation of new searchers that have yet to join the group. It is possible for new searchers to be created after the group has been interrupted. The result will be that they continue the search. However, once one of them finds a solution, the others will be interrupted.

An alternative approach to using thread groups and the interrupt mechanism, is to have all threads poll the tracker to determine the number of solutions. When this returns greater than 0, they can terminate.

6.3 Limiting the Concurrency by Reusing Threads

One of the attractions of the previous solutions is that they let the JVM manage the resources needed by the threads. Threads are created dynamically and the JVM has the responsibility of reclaiming their resources when the threads terminate. This can be expensive. Also most multiprocessor systems only have a handful of processors, not hundreds. Consequently, it is not possible to obtain increased speed from the extra threads. A compromise solution is, therefore, sought – one which can exploit the actual parallelism, but without the cost of unrestricted dynamic thread creation and destruction.

The goal is to have a pool of worker threads. These threads get their work from a buffer. When the searchers find new paths to explore, instead of creating a new thread, they place the paths into the buffer. Worker threads, once they have finished with a path (either because they reach the exit or reach a dead end), request new paths from the buffer. The workers terminate when they are all waiting on the buffer empty condition (that is, there are no more paths to explore). The bounded buffer class is shown below; it is based on that given in Chapter 5.

```
public class BoundedBufferData<Data> {
  public synchronized int getCurrentSize();
  public synchronized boolean isFull();
  public synchronized void put(Data obj);
  public synchronized Data get();
}
```

Unfortunately, the standard bounded buffer has no way of knowing when all its producers have finished and all its consumers are waiting. It is, therefore, necessary to extend this class to produce a signaling bounded buffer.

```
public class SignallingBuffer<Data>
            extends BoundedBuffer<Data> {
  public SignallingBuffer(int size, int maxConsumers,
                          ThreadGroup group);
  public synchronized void put(Data o);
  public synchronized Data get();
}
```

The thread pool class contains a private array of threads. These threads take their work from a signalling buffer. The only interface into the thread pool is a method to allocate work.

```
public class ThreadPool {
  public void allocateWork(Runnable r);
}
```

As the threads are now supplied by the thread pool, the searcher class no longer needs to be a thread. Hence, now it simply implements the `Runnable` interface.

Class relationships   The relationship between the new set of classes is given by Figure 6.6.

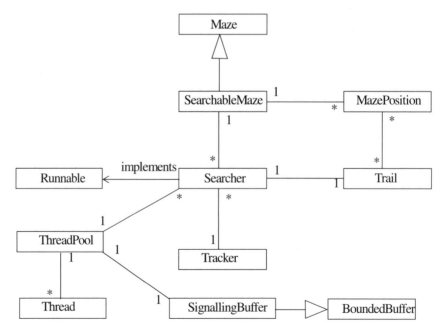

FIGURE 6.6. New Relationships between Classes

**The Sig-
nalling-
Buffer
class**

The goal of the signalling buffer is to be able to determine when all its clients can be released because there is no more data to be had from the buffer. In this instance, the clients are also the producers (as the workers are performing the searches, which both produce the new paths and consume the paths). Consequently, when all workers are waiting for new paths to explore, no new paths can be produced and the workers can be terminated. Termination is achieved by interrupting the workers (which all belong to the same thread group). The kickOff flag is required because the first item of work is allocated from outside the workers (by the main program).

```java
public class SignallingBuffer<Data>
        extends BoundedBuffer<Data> {
  public SignallingBuffer(int size, int maxConsumers,
                          ThreadGroup group) {
    // Assert size > maxConsumers.
    super(size);
    this.maxConsumers = maxConsumers;
    consumers = 0;
    this.group = group;
    kickOff = false;
  }
  public synchronized void put(Data o)
        throws InterruptedException {
    if(!kickOff) kickOff = true;
    super.put(o);
  }
  public synchronized Data get()
        throws InterruptedException {
    try {
      consumers++;
      if(kickOff & consumers == maxConsumers &
          getCurrentSize() == 0 ) {
        group.interrupt(); // Time to terminate.
        throw new InterruptedException();
      } else {
        Object o = super.get();
        return o;
      }
    } finally { consumers--; }
  }
  private int maxConsumers;
  private int consumers;
  private ThreadGroup group;
  private boolean kickOff;
}
```

The
Thread-
Pool class

The `ThreadPool` class can now be presented

```java
public class ThreadPool {
  public ThreadPool(int poolSize) {
    // Assert check poolSize > 0.
    workPool = new SignallingBuffer<Runnable>(
                    workBufferSize, poolSize, workersGroup);
    workers = new Worker[poolSize];
    for (int i = 0; i < poolSize; i++) {
      workers[i] = new Worker();
      workers[i].start();
    }
  }
}
```

The constructor creates a new signalling buffer indicating its size, how many workers will be consuming from the buffer and their group identity. It also creates an array of worker threads and starts each worker. The `allocateWork` method takes as a parameter any object which implements the `Runnable` interface. It puts this object into the signalling buffer. The worker threads simply call the signalling buffer to get an item of work. When an item is available, an object implementing the `Runnable` interface is returned. The worker thread then calls the associated `run` method. If the `Interrupt-edException` is thrown, the worker threads terminate.

```java
  public void allocateWork(Runnable r) {
    while(true) {
      try {
        workPool.put(r);
        break;
      } catch(InterruptedException IE) {
        // No action needed.
      }
    }
  }

  private class Worker extends Thread {
    public Worker() {
     super(workersGroup, "worker");
    }
```

```
public void run() {
  while (true) {
    try {
      Runnable r = workPool.get();
      r.run();
    } catch(InterruptedException E) {
      break; // No other action needed.
    }
  }
}
private Worker workers[];
private SignallingBuffer<Runnable> workPool;
private final int workBufferSize = 500; // say

private final static ThreadGroup workersGroup =
       new ThreadGroup("Workers");
}
```

The Searcher class

The modified Searcher object is given below. The only real difference is that when the new Searcher object is created, it is passed to the thread pool as an item of work to be allocated. The main program now creates the thread pool and passes it to the first searcher it creates. This is then assigned to a static attribute of the class so that it is available to all searchers. The size of the thread pool is given by a parameter to the main program.

```
public class Searcher implements Runnable {
  public Searcher (..., ThreadPool tp) {
    . . .
    myThreadPool = tp;
  }
  public void run() {
    . . .
    do {
      . . .
      for (int index = 0; index < moves.length; index++) {
        . . .
        if(count == -1) count = index;
```

```
      else {
        s = new Searcher(myMaze, moves[index],
                onTrail, terminationControl);
        myThreadPool.allocateWork(s);
      }
    }
    ...
  } while(count != -1);
  ...
} // end run

public static void main(String[] args){
  int poolSize = 5;
  if (args.length > 0) poolSize =
        Integer.parseInt(args[0]);
  ...
  ThreadPool tp = new ThreadPool(poolSize);
  Searcher s = new Searcher(sm, t, tr,tp);
  tp.allocateWork(s);
  ...
}
...
private static ThreadPool myThreadPool;
}
```

6.4 Summary

The solutions to the maze problem have illustrated the main features of Java's concurrency model. The model is simple but reasonably expressive. The JVM handles much of the resource allocation. In particular, garbage collection of terminated threads and their associated memory removes many burdens from the application programmer.

7 The Real-time Specification for Java

Introduction and chapter structure

Since its inception in the early 1990s, there is little doubt that Java has been a great success. However, the language does have weaknesses both in its overall model of concurrency and in its support for real-time systems. Section 4.7 has summarized some of the main problems in the concurrency area. This chapter considers real-time systems.

First, the chapter reviews the activities from which the original motivation for the RTSJ developed and examines the National Institute of Standards and Technology (NIST) requirements for "real-time Java". Then the main enhancements to the Java platform are introduced. These take the form of an additional package `javax.realtime`, which defines various classes and interfaces that provide extra functionality for the Java programmer and that require modification to the semantics of the Java virtual machine. The chapter presents an overview of these classes and interfaces in each of the main enhanced areas.

7.1 Background and NIST Requirements

Java's success has led to several attempts to extend the language so that it is more appropriate for a wide range of real-time systems. Much of the early work in this area was fragmented and lacked clear direction. In the late 1990s, under the auspices of the US National Institute of Standards and Technology (NIST), approximately 50 companies and organizations pooled their resources and generated several guiding principles and a set of requirements for real-time extensions to the Java platform (Carnahan and Ruark, 1999). Among the guiding principles was that Real-Time Java (RTJ) should take into account current real-time practices and facilitate advances in the state of the art of real-time systems implementation technology. The following facilities were deemed necessary to support the current state of real-time practice (Carnahan and Ruark, 1999).

- Fixed priority and round-robin scheduling.

- Mutual exclusion locking (avoiding priority inversion).

- Inter-thread communication (e.g. semaphores).

- User-defined interrupt handlers and device drivers – including the ability to manage interrupts (e.g. enabling and disabling).
- Timeouts and aborts on running threads.

These facilities will be described in detail in the remaining chapters of this book.

The NIST group recognized that profiles (subsets) of RTJ were necessary in order to cope with the wide variety of possible applications. These included safety critical, no dynamic loading and distributed real-time profiles.

There was also an agreement that any implementation of RTJ should provide the following.

- A framework for finding available profiles.
- Bounded preemption latency on any garbage collection.
- A well-defined model for real-time Java threads.
- Communication and synchronization between real-time and non-real-time threads.
- Mechanisms for handling internal and external asynchronous events.
- Asynchronous thread termination.
- Mutual exclusion without blocking.
- The ability to determine whether the running thread is real-time or non-real-time.
- A well-defined relationship between real-time and non-real-time threads.

Following on from the NIST requirements, there were two main efforts to define a "real-time" Java (J-Consortium, 2000; Bollella *et al.*, 2000). Perhaps the most high-profile attempt is the one backed by Sun and produced by The Real-Time for Java Expert Group (Bollella *et al.*, 2000). It is this that is the focus of the remaining chapters of this book.

The RTSJ in its defining document makes only a passing reference to the NIST requirements and instead defines its own "guiding principles". These include requirements to

- be backward compatible with non-real-time Java programs,
- support the principle of "Write Once, Run Anywhere" but not at the expense of predictability,
- address current real-time system practices and allow future implementations to include advanced features,
- give priority to predictable execution in all design trade-offs,
- require *no* syntactic extensions to the Java language,
- allow implementers flexibility.

Warning

The requirement for no syntactic enhancements to Java has had a strong impact on the manner in which the real-time facilities can be provided. In particular, all facilities have to be provided by a library of classes and interfaces. In places, this has had a marked effect on the readability of real-time applications.

7.2 Overview of Enhancements

The RTSJ enhances Java in the following areas:

- memory management
- time values and clocks
- schedulable objects and scheduling
- real-time threads
- asynchronous event handling and timers
- asynchronous transfer of control
- synchronization and resource sharing
- physical and raw memory access.

Important
note

It should be stressed that the RTSJ is only intended to address the execution of real-time Java programs on single-processor systems. It attempts not to preclude execution on shared-memory multiprocessor systems, but it has no facilities directly to control, for example, allocation of threads to processors.

The remainder of this chapter will present an overview of the RTSJ and introduce the various classes and interfaces. Later chapters will consider each of the above enhancements in detail.

7.3 Memory Management

Many real-time systems (particularly those that form part of an embedded system) have only a limited amount of memory available; this is either because of the cost or because of other constraints associated with the surrounding system (for example, size, power or weight constraints). It may, therefore, be necessary to control how this memory is allocated so that it can be used effectively. Furthermore, where there is more than one type of memory (with different access characteristics) within the system, it may be necessary to instruct the compiler to place certain data types at certain locations. By doing this, the program is able to increase performance and predictability as well as interact more effectively with the outside world.

Heap memory

The run-time implementations of most programming languages provide a large amount of memory (called the *heap*) so that the programmer can make dynamic requests for chunks to be allocated (for example, to contain an array whose bounds are not known at compile time). An allocator (the *new* operator in Java) is used for this purpose. It returns a reference to memory within the heap of adequate size for the program's data structures (classes). The run-time system (JVM) is responsible for managing the heap. Key problems are deciding how much space is required and deciding when allocated space can be released and reused. The first of these problems requires application knowledge (the SizeEstimator class in RTSJ helps here). The second can be handled in several ways, requiring

- the programmer to return the memory explicitly – this is error prone but is easy to implement;

- the run-time support system (JVM) to monitor the memory and determine when it can logically no longer be accessed – the scope rules of a language allows its implementation to adopt this approach; when a reference type goes out of scope, all the memory associated with that reference type can be freed;

- the run-time support system (JVM) to monitor the memory and release chunks that are no longer being used (*garbage collection*) – this is, perhaps, the most general approach as it allows memory to be freed even though its associated reference type is still in scope.

From a real-time perspective, the above approaches have an increasing impact on the ability to analyze the timing properties of the program. In particular, garbage collection may be performed either when the heap is full (there is no free space left) or incrementally (either by an asynchronous activity or on each allocation request). In either case, running the garbage collector may have a significant impact on the response time of a time-critical thread.

All objects in Java are allocated on the heap, and the language requires garbage collection for an effective implementation. The garbage collector runs as part of the JVM. Although there has been much work on real-time garbage collection and progress continues to be made, there is still a reluctance to rely on these techniques in time-critical systems.

Memory areas

The RTSJ recognizes that it is necessary to allow memory management, which is not affected by the vagaries of garbage collection. To this end, it introduces the notion of *memory areas*, some of which exist outside the traditional Java heap and never suffer garbage collection. It also requires that the garbage collector can be preempted by real-time threads and that the time between a real-time thread wishing to preempt and the time it is allowed to preempt is bounded (there should be a bounded latency for preemption to take place).

The MemoryArea class is an abstract class from which all RTSJ memory areas are derived. When a particular memory area is entered, all object allocation is performed within that area. Using this abstract class, the RTSJ defines various kinds of memory including the following:

- HeapMemory – Heap memory allows objects to be allocated in the standard Java heap.

- ImmortalMemory – Immortal memory is shared among all threads in an application. Objects created in immortal memory are never subject to garbage collection delays and behave as if they are freed by the system only when the program terminates.

- ScopedMemory – Scoped memory is a memory area where objects with a well-defined lifetime can be allocated. A scoped memory may be entered explicitly or implicitly by attaching it to a real-time entity (a real-time thread or an asynchronous event handler) at its creation time. Associated with each scoped memory is a reference count. This keeps track of how many real-time entities are currently using the area. When the reference count reaches 0, all objects resident in the scoped memory have their finalization method executed, and the memory is available for reuse. The ScopedMemory class is an abstract class that has several subclasses.

- VTMemory – A subclass of ScopedMemory where allocations may take variable amounts of time.

- LTMemory – A subclass of ScopedMemory where allocations occur in linear time (that is, the time taken to allocate the object is directly proportional to the size of the object).

Memory parameters can be given when real-time threads and asynchronous event handlers are created. They can also be set or changed while the real-time threads and asynchronous event handlers are active. Memory parameters specify

- the maximum amount of memory a thread/handler can consume in its default memory area,

- the maximum amount of memory that can be consumed in immortal memory,

- a limit on the rate of allocation from the heap (in bytes per second),

and can be used by the scheduler as part of an admission control policy and/or for the purpose of ensuring adequate garbage collection.

Figure 7.1 illustrates the various RTSJ classes that support memory management.

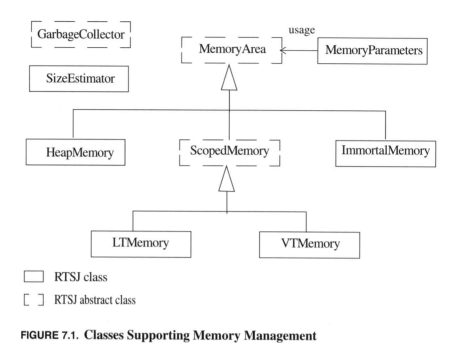

FIGURE 7.1. Classes Supporting Memory Management

Further control over the allocation of memory, in particular, specifying memory of a particular type (for example, flash memory) or specifying the actual machine address where memory is to be allocated, is given by the physical and raw memory access facility, which is considered in Section 7.10.

7.4 Time Values and Clocks

As mentioned in Section 4.2, Java supports the notion of a wall clock (calendar time). The Date class is intended to reflect UTC (Coordinated Universal Time), however, accuracy depends on the host system [Gosling, Joy and Steele, 1996].

The RTSJ introduces clocks with high-resolution time types. The associated classes are illustrated in Figure 7.2.

HighResolutionTime encapsulates time values with nanosecond granularity and an associated clock. A value is represented by a 64-bits millisecond and a 32-bits nanosecond component. There are methods to read, write and compare time values, as well as methods to get and set the clock. The class is an abstract class that has three subclasses: one that represents relative time, one that represents absolute time, and one that represents "rational'" time. Relative time is a duration measured by a particular clock. Absolute time is actually expressed as a time relative to some epoch. This epoch depends on the associated clock. It might be January 1, 1970, GMT for the wall clock or

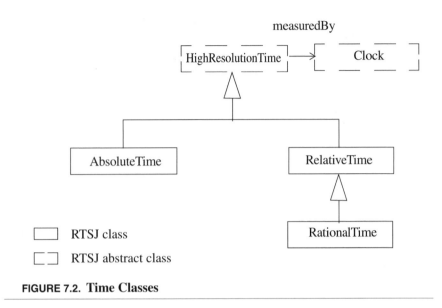

FIGURE 7.2. **Time Classes**

system start-up time for a monotonic (nondecreasing and no added leap seconds) clock. Rational time is a relative-time type, which has an associated frequency. It is used to represent the rate at which certain events occur (for example, periodic thread execution).

The RTSJ Clock class defines the abstract class from which all clocks are derived. The specification allows many different types of clocks; for example, there could be a CPU execution-time clock (although this is not required by the RTSJ). There is always one real-time clock that advances monotonically. A static method getRealtimeClock allows this clock to be obtained.

Countdown clocks are called *timers* by the RTSJ. They will be considered in Section 7.7.

7.5 **Schedulable Objects and Scheduling**

Scheduling of threads is a key aspect for all real-time systems. Java allows each thread to have a priority that can be used by the JVM when allocating processing resources. However, as discussed in Section 4.1, Java offers no guarantees that the highest priority runnable thread will be the one executing at any point in time. This is because a JVM may be relying on a host operating system to support its threads. Some of these systems may not support preemptive priority-based scheduling. Furthermore, Java only defines 10 priority levels, and an implementation is free to map these priorities onto a more restricted host operating system's priority range if necessary.

The weak definition of scheduling and the restricted range of priorities means that Java programs lack predictability and, hence, Java's use for real-time systems' implementation is severely limited. Consequently, this is a major area that needs to be addressed. The RTSJ attacks these problems on several fronts. Firstly, it generalizes the entities that can be scheduled away from threads toward the notion of *schedulable objects*. A schedulable object is one that implements the `Schedulable` interface. Each schedulable object must also indicate its specific

- release requirement (that is, when it should become runnable),
- memory requirements (for example, the rate at which it will allocate memory on the heap),
- scheduling requirements (for example, the priority at which it should be scheduled).

Parameters affecting scheduling

Release requirements are specified via the `ReleaseParameters` class hierarchy. Scheduling theories often identify three types of releases: periodic (released on a regular basis), aperiodic (released at random) and sporadic (released irregularly, but with a minimum time between each release). These are represented by the `PeriodicParameters`, `AperiodicParameters` and `SporadicParameters` classes respectively. All release parameter classes encapsulate a `cost` and a `deadline` (relative time) value. The `cost` is the maximum amount of CPU time (execution time) needed to execute the associated schedulable object every time it is released. The `deadline` is the time at which the object must have finished executing the current release; it is specified relative to the time the object was released. `PeriodicParameters` also include the `start` time for the first release and the time interval (`period`) between releases. `SporadicParameters` include the minimum inter-arrival time between releases.

For aperiodic schedulable objects, it is possible to limit the amount of time the scheduler gives them in a particular period. This is achieved by `ProcessingGroupParameters` that have associated start, period and cost times. Where the same `ProcessingGroupParameters` class is associated with more than one schedulable object, the limitations apply to the group as a whole.

Scheduling parameters are used by a scheduler to determine which object is currently the most eligible for execution. The abstract class `SchedulingParameters` provides the root class from which a range of possible scheduling criteria can be expressed. The RTSJ defines only one criterion that is based on priority (as would be expected, it is silent on how those priorities should be assigned). In common with most other languages and operating systems, high numerical values for priority represent high execution eligibilities. `ImportanceParameters` allow an additional numerical scheduling metric to be assigned; it is a subclass of the `PriorityParameters` class.

Schedulers

The scheduler is responsible for scheduling its associated schedulable objects. The RTSJ is silent on how many schedulers might exist within a single real-time JVM but typically only a single scheduler will be present. Although RTSJ explicitly supports priority-based scheduling via the `PriorityScheduler` (a fixed preemptive priority-based scheduler with 28 unique priority levels), it acknowledges that an implementation might provide other schedulers. Consequently, `Scheduler` is an abstract class with `PriorityScheduler` a defined subclass. This allows an implementation to provide, say, an Earliest-Deadline-First scheduler. Any attempt by the application to set the scheduler for its threads has to be checked to ensure that it has the appropriate security permissions.

The relationship between the above classes is illustrated in Figure 7.3.

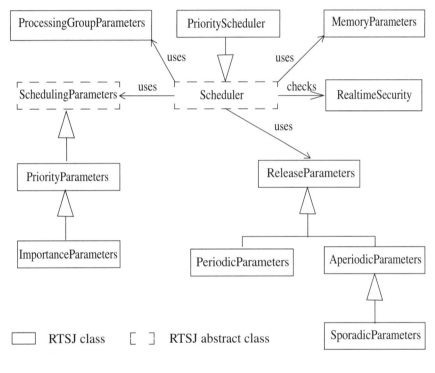

FIGURE 7.3. Scheduling and its Parameter Classes

Meeting deadlines

Once a system accepts that schedulable objects have deadlines and a cost associated with their execution, there is an obligation on the system to undertake the following activities (Burns and Wellings, 2001):

- provide a means by which it is possible to predict whether a set of application objects will meet their deadlines, and

- provide mechanisms whereby the system can report that an application object has missed its deadline, consumed more resources than indicated by the cost value or has been released more often than indicated by its minimum inter-arrival time.

For some systems it is possible to predict offline whether the application will meet its deadline – for example, via a form of schedulability analysis (see Burns and Wellings, 2001). For other systems, some form of on-line analysis is required. The RTSJ does not require that an implementation support on-line analysis, but it does provide the hooks that can be used if needed.

Irrespective of whether or how prediction has been performed, it is necessary to report overruns, etc. The RTSJ provides an asynchronous event-handling mechanism for this purpose. All release parameters also specify which event handlers should be released as a consequence of a deadline miss or a cost overrun[1]. Of course, a program can indicate that it is not concerned with a missed deadline, etc., by setting a null handler.

7.6 Real-time Threads

One type of schedulable object is a real-time thread represented by the `Realtime-Thread` class. This is an extension of the Java `Thread` class, which also implements the `Schedulable` interface. A real-time thread's parameters are illustrated in Figure 7.4.

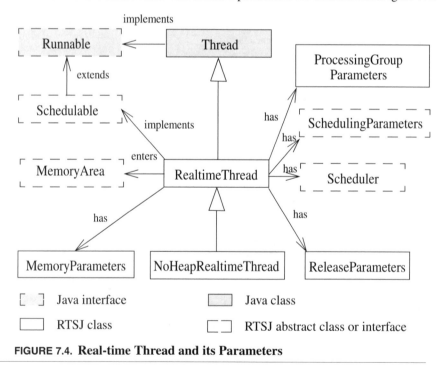

FIGURE 7.4. **Real-time Thread and its Parameters**

---

1. However, the RTSJ does not require an implementation to support execution-time monitoring.

A periodic real-time thread is a real-time thread that has periodic release parameters. Similarly, an aperiodic (or sporadic) real-time thread is one that has aperiodic (or sporadic) release parameters. A `NoHeapRealtimeThread` is one that guarantees not to create or reference any objects on the heap. Hence, its execution is totally independent of the garbage collector.

7.7 Asynchronous Event Handling and Timers

Threads and real-time threads are the appropriate abstractions to use when representing concurrent activities that have a significant life history. However, it is also often necessary to respond to events that happen asynchronously to a thread's activity. These events may be happenings in the environment of an embedded system or notifications received from internal activities within the program. It is always possible to have extra threads that wait for these events, but this is inefficient and may result in an explosion of the number of threads in a program.

In Java, standard classes can be programmed that multiplex events onto a single thread that handles them in a particular order. For example, the Abstract Windows Toolkit has an event-handling thread for interacting with user interface windowing events. The Java `Timer` and `TimerTask` (see Section 4.4) classes provide similar functionality for time-triggered events.

From a real-time perspective, events may require their handlers to respond within deadlines. Hence, more control is needed over the order in which events are handled. The RTSJ, therefore, generalizes Java event handlers to be schedulable entities. Like real-time threads, they have a variety of parameters (as illustrated in Figure 7.5).

In practice, the real-time JVM will (usually) dynamically associate an event handler with a real-time thread when the handler is released for execution (some may even delay the association until the handler has the highest execution eligibility). To avoid this overhead, it is possible to specify that the handler must be permanently bound to a real-time thread. Each `AsyncEvent` can have one or more handlers, and the same handler can be associated with more than one event. When the event occurs, all the handlers associated with the event are released for execution according to their `Scheduling-Parameters`.

Asynchronous events can be associated with interrupts or POSIX signals (if supported by the underlying operating system) or they can be linked to a timer. The timer will cause the event to fire when a specified time (relative to a particular clock) expires. This can be a one-shot firing or a periodic firing. Figure 7.6 illustrates the classes associated with events and their handlers.

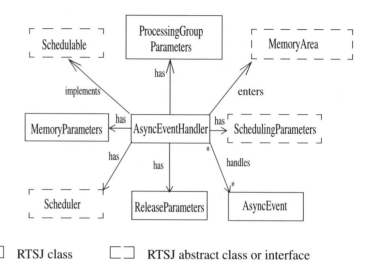

RTSJ class   RTSJ abstract class or interface

FIGURE 7.5. **Asynchronous Event Handler Parameters**

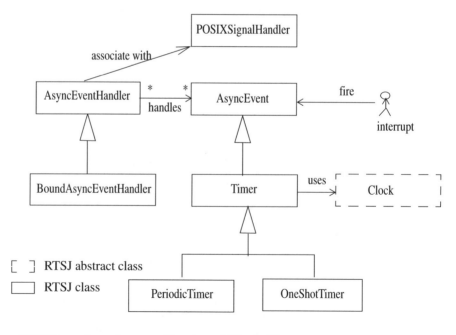

RTSJ abstract class

RTSJ class

FIGURE 7.6. **Asynchronous Events and Timer Classes**

7.8 Asynchronous Transfer of Control

Asynchronous events allow the program to respond in a timely fashion to a condition that has been detected by the program or the environment. However, they do not allow a particular schedulable object to be directly informed. In many applications, the only form of asynchronous notification that a real-time thread needs is a request for it to terminate itself. Consequently, languages and operating systems typically provide a kill or abort facility. Unfortunately, for real-time systems this approach is too heavy-handed; instead what is required is for the schedulable object to stop what it is currently doing and begin executing an alternative algorithm.

In Java, it is the interrupt mechanism (see Section 3.5) that attempts to provide a limited form of asynchronous notification. Lamentably, the mechanism is synchronous and does not support timely response to the "interrupt". Instead, a running thread has to poll for notification. This delay is deemed unacceptable for real-time systems. For these reasons, the RTSJ provides an alternative approach for interrupting a schedulable object, using asynchronous transfer of control (ATC). The ATC model is based on the following principles (Bollella *et al.*, 2000).

- A schedulable object (real-time thread or event handler) must explicitly indicate that it is prepared to allow an ATC to be delivered. By default, a schedulable object will have ATCs deferred. The rationale for this approach is that the schedulable object may be executing a method inside an object that is unaware that an ATC may be delivered. If the schedulable object is forced to abandon execution of the method, it might compromise the integrity of the object's state.

- The execution of synchronized methods and statements always defers the delivery of an ATC.

- ATCs have termination semantics; this means that the real-time thread (or event handler) does not resume execution at the point in its code where the ATC was delivered. An ATC is a nonreturnable transfer of control (it is, therefore, more analogous to a goto statement than a procedure call).

The RTSJ ATC model is integrated with the Java exception handling facility. An `AsynchronouslyInterruptedException` (AIE) class defines the ATC event. Every method that is prepared to allow the delivery of an AIE must indicate so via a `throws AsynchronouslyInterruptedException` in its declaration. ATCs are deferred until the thread is executing within such a method. The `Interruptible` interface provides the link between the AIE class and the object executing an interruptible method. A subclass of AIE, called `Timed`, allows an ATC to be generated at a point in time (absolute or relative). The relationship between the classes is illustrated in Figure 7.7.

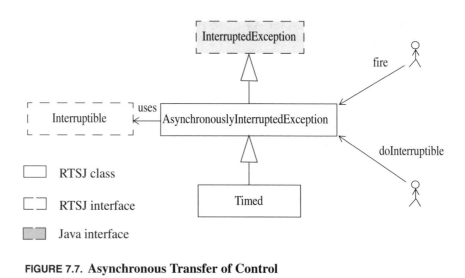

FIGURE 7.7. Asynchronous Transfer of Control

The ATC facilities (possibly used in conjunction with the asynchronous event-handling mechanisms) also allow real-time threads to be terminated in a controlled and safe manner.

7.9 Synchronization and Resource Sharing

The key to predicting the behavior of multithreaded real-time programs is understanding how threads (and other schedulable objects) communicate and synchronize with each other. Java provides a mechanism that is based on mutually exclusive access to shared data via a monitor-like construct (see Chapter 3). Unfortunately, all synchronization mechanisms that are based on mutual exclusion suffer from *priority inversion*.

The problem of priority inversion and its solution *priority inheritance* is now a well-researched area of real-time systems (see (Burns and Wellings, 2001)). There are a variety of priority inheritance algorithms; the RTSJ explicitly supports two: *simple priority inheritance* and *priority ceiling emulation inheritance* (sometimes called i*mmediate ceiling priority inheritance, priority protect inheritance protocol* or the *highest locker protocol*).

The RTSJ and priority inheritance

The way in which the RTSJ supports priority inheritance algorithms is through the MonitorControl class hierarchy. The abstract root class has several static methods that allow

- the default inheritance property for all monitor locks to be set and queried
- a specific object's inheritance property to be set.

The actual policies are defined by subclasses as illustrated in Figure 7.8.

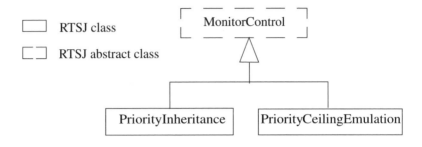

FIGURE 7.8. Priority Inheritance Classes

Priority inheritance and garbage collection

Priority inheritance algorithms allow the blocking suffered by schedulable objects to be bounded. However, if schedulable objects want to communicate with non-real-time threads, then interaction with garbage collection must be considered. It is necessary to try to avoid the situation where a non-real-time thread has entered into a mutual exclusion zone shared with a schedulable object. The actions of the non-real-time thread results in garbage collection being performed. The schedulable object then preempts the garbage collector, but is unable to enter the mutual exclusion zone. It must now wait for the garbage collection to finish and the non-real-time thread to leave the zone.

Wait-free communication

One way of avoiding unpredictable interactions with the garbage collector is to provide a nonblocking communication mechanism for use between non-real-time threads and schedulable objects. The RTSJ provides three wait-free nonblocking classes to help facilitate this communication:

- `WaitFreeWriteQueue` – This is a bounded buffer intended for the case where the schedulable object wishes to send an object to the non-real-time thread. The read operation on the buffer is synchronized and blocks if the buffer is empty. The write operation is not synchronized and indicates whether it has succeeded in writing to the buffer.

- `WaitFreeReadQueue` – This is a bounded buffer intended for the case where the non-real-time thread wishes to send an object to the schedulable object. The write operation on the buffer is synchronized. The read operation is not, and returns either an object or null if the buffer is empty. The reader can request to be notified when data arrives.

- `WaitFreeDequeue` – This is a bounded buffer, which allows both blocking and nonblocking read and write operations.

The RTSJ classes are illustrated in Figure 7.9.

FIGURE 7.9. Wait-free Communication Classes

7.10 Physical and Raw Memory Access

As mentioned in Section 7.3, embedded real-time systems may support more than one type of memory (with different access characteristics); furthermore, devices may have their interface registers mapped into the virtual memory address space. There are, therefore, two main mechanisms that must be provided by the RTSJ.

1. Mechanisms that allow objects to be placed into areas of memory that have particular properties or access requirements; for example Direct Memory Access (DMA) memory, or shared memory.

2. Mechanisms that allow the programmer to access raw memory locations that are being used to interface to the outside world; for example memory-mapped input and output device registers.

Figure 7.10 summarizes the various classes.

To support the first requirement, the RTSJ provides extensions of the Scoped-Memory areas discussed in Section 7.3. These extensions provide the physical memory counterparts to the linear-time and variable-time scoped memory classes. They enable the programmer to specify that objects should be created in memory with a particular characteristic (for example, shared memory) as well as the usual requirements for linear time allocation etc. Immortal physical memory is also provided.

To support the second requirement, the RTSJ provides classes which can access raw memory in terms of reading and writing Java variables or arrays of primitive data types (int, long, float etc.). The implementation of both these physical and raw memory classes can assume the existence of a PhysicalMemoryManager class, which must be provided by the real-time Java virtual machine. This class can also make use of implementation-dependent classes, called *filters*, which help support and police the various memory categories. All these classes must support the PhysicalMemoryType-Filter interface. The memory manager can also check that the program has the necessary security permissions before allowing access to physical and raw memory.

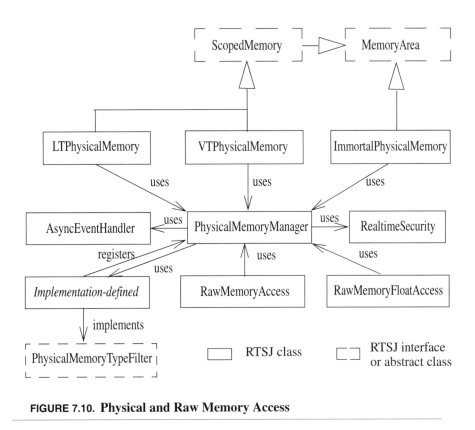

FIGURE 7.10. Physical and Raw Memory Access

7.11 System-wide Properties

The overall properties of an RTSJ virtual machine can be acquired via the `Realtime-System` class. Operations on this class also allow the system's performance to be tuned. For example, the total number of concurrent object locks can be specified. The byte ordering of the machine can also be determined.

7.12 Synchronization and the RTSJ

Most of the classes provided by the RTSJ will be used in a concurrent environment. However, in some cases there will be no concurrent use of a particular object. For example, consider the `AsyncEvent` class. In general, an asynchronous event may be fired by more than one real-time thread. In practice, only one firer will exist for many events. There is, therefore, a dilemma for the RTSJ designers of whether to make the `fire` method synchronized or not. Indeed, the initial version of the RTSJ has `fire` as synchronized (Bollella *et al.*, 2000). Version 1.0 has it nonsynchronized!

The advantage of making a method synchronized is that the class designer is forced to consider the use of the class in a concurrent environment (making it "thread safe" or "thread conditionally safe", using Bloch's terminology – see Section 4.8). The disadvantage is that the program incurs a run-time overhead in calling synchronized methods irrespective of whether the actual object is subject to concurrent calls.

The alternative approach is to declare the class as being "thread compatible". This means that the class has paid no considerations to concurrent calls of its methods but does guarantee that it is not completely "thread hostile". It is, therefore, up to the programmer to provide the required synchronization if an object is called concurrently. This is a burden to the programmer, but the run-time overhead is only incurred when it is really needed. It is this latter approach that is generally (but not universally) taken by the RTSJ. Methods are only made synchronized when absolutely necessary; for instance, because there is some condition synchronization required. On occasions, the synchronization is hidden in the class.

There are many ways to make a "thread compatible" class "thread safe". The simplest is to create a subclass and override the methods that can be called concurrently (directly or indirectly). The overridden methods can then be made synchronized. The subclass can be used in all places where the superclass can be used, and run-time dispatching will ensure the correct method is called.

If this approach is not appropriate (perhaps because the methods are `final` methods), an alternative is to lock the object when an unsynchronized method is called. However, this is more error prone, as it requires all users of the object to first obtain the lock.

7.13 Summary

This chapter has introduced the majority of classes and interfaces that can be found in the Real-Time Specification for Java and has attempted to illustrate the overall motivation for their inclusion. The details of the semantic model behind these classes and full descriptions of their methods (and how they can be used) are given in the following chapters.

At the beginning of this chapter, the NIST core requirements for real-time Java extensions were identified. It is now possible to review these requirements and see how closely the RTSJ has met them. Firstly, the facilities needed to support the current state of real-time practice:

- Fixed priority and round-robin scheduling – the RTSJ supports a fixed priority scheduler and allows implementations to provide other schedulers.

- Mutual exclusion locking (avoiding priority inversion) – the RTSJ supports priority inheritance algorithms of synchronized objects and requires that all RTSJ implementations avoid unbounded priority inversion.

- Inter-thread communication (e.g. semaphores) – schedulable objects can communicate using the conventional Java mechanisms augmented with priority queues and priority inversion avoidance algorithms.

- User-defined interrupt handlers and device drivers (including the ability to manage interrupts; e.g. enabling and disabling) – the RTSJ allows interrupts to be associated with asynchronous events. Memory-mapped device registers can be accessed by the raw memory facilities.

- Timeouts and aborts on running threads – the RTSJ allows asynchronous transfers of control via asynchronous exceptions; they can be event-triggered or time-triggered.

In terms of implementation requirements:

- A framework for finding available profiles – the RTSJ does not explicitly address the issues of profiles other than by allowing an implementation to provide alternative scheduling algorithms (e.g. EDF) and allowing the application to locate the scheduling algorithms. There is no identification of, say, a safety critical systems profile or a profile that prohibits dynamic loading of classes. Distributed real-time systems are not addressed, but there is another Java Expert Group that is considering this issue (Wellings, Clark, Jenson, and Wells, 2002).

- Bounded preemption latency on any garbage collection – supported by the `GarbageCollector` class.

- A well-defined model for real-time Java threads – supported by the `RealtimeThread` and `NoHeapRealtimeThread` classes.

- Communication and synchronization between real-time and non-real-time threads – supported by the wait-free communication classes.

- Mechanisms for handling internal and external asynchronous events – supported by the `AsyncEvent`, `AsyncEventHandler` and `POSIXSignalHandler` classes.

- Asynchronous thread termination – supported by the `AsynchronouslyInterruptedException` class and the `Interruptible` interface.

- Mutual exclusion without blocking – supported by the wait-free communication classes.

- The ability to determine whether the running thread is real-time or non-real-time – supported by the `RealtimeThread` class.

- A well-defined relationship between real-time and non-real-time threads – supported by the real-time thread, the scheduling and memory management models.

Overall, it can be seen that the RTSJ addresses all the NIST top level requirements in some form or other. It is, however, a little weak in its support for profiles.

8 Memory Management

**Introduction
and chapter
structure**

One of the main advantages of using a high-level language is that it relieves the programmer of the burden of dealing with many low-level resource allocation issues. Activities such as assigning variables to registers or memory locations, allocating and freeing memory for dynamic data structures, etc., all distract the programmer from the task at hand. The adage "can't see the wood for the trees" sums up the programmer's dilemma. Languages like Java remove many of these distractions and provide high-level abstract models that the programmer can use. Unfortunately, for real-time and embedded systems programming there is a conflict. On the one hand, the use of high-level abstractions aid in the software engineering of the application. On the other hand, embedded and real-time systems often have only limited resources (time and space) and these must be carefully managed. Nowhere is this conflict more apparent than in the area of memory management.

Embedded systems usually have a limited amount of memory available; this is because of cost, size, power, weight or other constraints imposed by the overall system requirements. It may, therefore, be necessary to control how this memory is allocated so that it can be used effectively.

The run-time implementations of most programming languages provide two essential data structures to help manage the dynamic memory of the program: the *stack* and the *heap*. In Java, the stack is typically used for storing variables of basic data types (such as `int`, `boolean` and reference variables) that are local to a method. All objects that are created from class definitions are stored on the heap, and the language requires garbage collection for an effective implementation. The garbage collector runs as part of the JVM. Although there has been much work on real-time garbage collection, there is still a reluctance to rely on these techniques in time-critical systems. This is because garbage collection may be performed either when the heap is full or incrementally (either by an asynchronous activity or on each allocation request). In either case, running the garbage collector may have a significant impact on the response time of a time-critical thread. Consider, for example, a time-critical periodic thread that has had all its objects preallocated. Even though it may have a higher priority than a non-time-critical thread and will not require any new memory, it may still be delayed if it preempts the non-time-critical thread when garbage collection has been initiated by an action of that thread. In this instance, it is not safe for the time-critical thread to execute until garbage collection has finished (particularly if memory compaction is taking place).

For the above reasons, the RTSJ recognizes that it is necessary to allow memory management that is not affected by the vagaries of garbage collection. It does this via the introduction of immortal and scoped memory areas. These are areas of memory that are logically outside of the heap and, therefore, are not subject to garbage collection. Issues concerned with raw and physical memory allocation are deferred until Chapter 15. Memory areas and their relationship to heap memory is the topic of this chapter. The chapter is structured as follows:

- The basic model is presented and the main memory area types are introduced. How to estimate the size of memory required is also covered.

- The object assignment rules for the different memory areas are detailed. In order to enforce these rules, the JVM must keep track of active memory areas; logically this is performed using a memory area stack. Programmers need to understand the underlying model so that they can construct error-free object structures. The single parent rule for memory areas is described.

- Memory areas can be shared between schedulable objects. The support mechanisms for both competitive and cooperative sharing are considered.

- Using scoped memory areas with prewritten classes is fraught with difficulties in the RTSJ. Guidelines are presented to help the programmer manage these problems.

- Finally the chapter briefly reviews some of the real-time issues. These include a discussion of the timing properties of scoped memory areas, the role of memory parameters and modern approaches to real-time garbage collection that attempt to avoid some of the problems mentioned above.

8.1 The Basic Model

The RTSJ provides two alternatives to using the heap memory area; they are called *immortal* memory and *scoped* memory.

Important note

The memory associated with objects allocated in immortal memory is never subject to garbage collection delays and behaves as if it is never released during the lifetime of the application creating the objects. Class objects and their associated static memories, along with objects created by static initialisation and interned strings (the list of program-defined constant strings that is maintained by the String class) are allocated in immortal memory.

Hence, once space has been allocated from immortal memory, it can never be automatically reclaimed. The programmer must reuse the memory by other means (for example, a pool of reusable objects). In contrast, objects allocated in scoped memory have a well-defined lifetime. Schedulable objects may enter and leave a scoped memory area. While they are executing within that area, all memory allocations (resulting from creating new objects) are performed from the scoped memory. When there are no schedulable objects active inside a scoped memory area, the allocated memory is reclaimed.

Important note

In general, schedulable objects must explicitly indicate whether memory is to be allocated from immortal or scoped memory. The default memory area is the heap.

Fine detail note

The RTSJ allows an implementation to detect if an object in immortal memory is no longer reachable. If it can do this, it may execute any associated finalizers and even return the allocated space. *However, this activity must not be part of general garbage collection and must not cause preemption delays to high priority no-heap schedulable objects.* On the other hand, an implementation may not even run finalizers when the application terminates. The remainder of this book assumes that immortal memory is never collected.

Memory areas

All memory areas in the RTSJ are represented by subclasses of the abstract `Memory-Area` class, an abridged version of which is shown below. (Note parameters to some of the methods in the classes defined in this chapter represent the size of memory in bytes. The type is given as a long. All the classes throw `IllegalArgumentExceptions` if negative values are passed –similarly, if an object is expected and a null value is passed.)

```
package javax.realtime;
public abstract class MemoryArea {
  // constructors
  protected MemoryArea(long size); // In bytes.
  protected MemoryArea(long size, Runnable logic);
  ...

  // methods
  public void enter();
    // Throws IllegalArgumentException,
    //        IllegalStateException.
    // Associate this memory area to the current schedulable
    // object for the duration of the logic.run method
    // passed as a parameter to the constructor.
    // IllegalArgumentException is thrown if no Runnable
    // object was passed as a parameter to the constructor.
```

```
public void enter(Runnable logic);
   // Throws IllegalArgumentException,
   //        IllegalStateException.
   // Associate this memory area to the current
   // schedulable object for the duration of the
   // logic.run method passed as a parameter.
public static MemoryArea getMemoryArea(Object object);
   // Get the memory area associated with the object.
public long memoryConsumed();
   // Get the number of bytes consumed in this area.
public long memoryRemaining();
   // Get the number of bytes remaining in this area.
public long size();
   // Get the current size of this area.

   ...
}
```

**Important
note**

Only a schedulable object (real-time threads or asynchronous event handlers) can enter into a memory area. If a Java thread calls one of the enter methods, the IllegalStateException is thrown. A Java thread has too much context established on the heap, and consequently if it were allowed to enter a memory area, this would inevitably lead to the memory assignment rules being broken.

**Immortal
memory**

Consider the ImmortalMemory class:

```
package javax.realtime;
public final class ImmortalMemory extends MemoryArea {
   public static ImmortalMemory instance();
}
```

There is only one ImmortalMemory area, hence the class is defined as final and has only one additional method (instance) that, when called, will return a reference to the immortal memory area. Immortal memory is shared among all threads and schedulable objects in an application. Note, there is no public constructor for this class. Hence, the size of the immortal memory is fixed by the real-time JVM.

Unlike scoped memory, there is no indication of whether the time taken to allocate immortal objects is linear with respect to object sizes. This is because it is anticipated that objects will usually be created in immortal memory during initialization of the program.

The simplest method for allocating objects in immortal memory is to use the `enter` method in the `MemoryArea` class and to pass an object implementing the `Runnable` interface:

```
ImmortalMemory.instance().enter(new Runnable()
    {
      public void run() {
        // Any memory allocation performed here
        // using the allocator will occur in
        // immortal memory.
      }
    } );
```

Important note

It should be stressed that although all memory allocated by the above `run` method will come from immortal memory, any memory needed by the object implementing the `run` method will be allocated from the current memory area at the time of the call to `enter`. In this instance, it looks as if there will be no memory needed by the anonymous class implementing the `Runnable` interface. However, all classes are implicitly subclasses of the `Object` class; fortunately that class usually does not have any instance variables. Nevertheless, some small amount of memory will still be allocated by the virtual machine in order to implement the object (see scoped memory example below).

Also note any call to the version of the parameterless `enter` method on the `ImmortalMemory` area will result in the `IllegalArgumentException` being thrown, as it is not possible to create an `ImmortalMemory` area with an initial `Runnable` object.

Heap Memory Area

Once schedulable objects are allowed to enter memory areas, a mechanism is needed to allow them to start using the heap again. Hence, the Java heap is also represented as a memory area.

```
package javax.realtime;
public final class HeapMemory extends MemoryArea {
  public static HeapMemory instance();
}
```

Scoped memory areas

Scoped memory is a memory area where objects with a well-defined lifetime can be allocated. They can be created as and when needed by an application. There are two types: one that requires the allocation time to be directly proportional to the size of the object being allocated (linear time memory – `LTMemory`), and one where the allocation can occur in a variable time (variable time memory – VTMemory). The ScopedMemory class itself is, therefore, abstract – an abridged version is presented below:

```
package javax.realtime;
public abstract class ScopedMemory extends MemoryArea {
  // constructors
  public ScopedMemory(long size); // in bytes
  public ScopedMemory(long size, Runnable logic);

  ...

  // methods
  public void enter();
    // Throws ScopedCycleException (see Section 8.5),
    // ThrowBoundaryError (see important note below),
    // IllegalArgumentException, IllegalStateException.
    // Associate this memory area to the current
    // schedulable object for the duration of the
    // logic.run method passed as a parameter to the
    // constructor.
  public void enter(Runnable logic);
    // Throws ScopedCycleException (see Section 8.5),
    // ThrowBoundaryError (see important note below),
    // IllegalArgumentException, IllegalStateException.
    // Associate this memory area to the current
    // schedulable object for the duration of
    // the logic.run method passed as a parameter.

  public long getMaximumSize();
  public String toString();
    // Returns a string identifying the memory area.

  ...
}
```

Important notes

1. The memory used for allocated objects when a scoped memory area is active is called the scoped memory's **backing store**. It resides in a part of memory that is otherwise invisible to the application. It is separate from the memory required for the scoped memory object itself (which is allocated from the current memory area when the object is created). The backing store is usually assigned to the scoped memory object when the object is created, and it is freed when the object is finalized. When assigned, memory within the backing store used for allocated objects can be reclaimed when the scoped memory becomes inactive (see the discussion on reference counts below).

2. Unchecked exceptions which are thrown during the execution of the `Runnable` called by the `enter` method may be allocated in the current memory area. Hence, if they are allowed to propagate through the `enter` method, they will be no longer be accessible to the application. It this situation, the exception will be lost and the real-time VM will throw a `ThrowBoundaryError` exception. To avoid this problem, some real-time JVM may pre-define some standard run-time and error exceptions in immortal memory.

The two subclasses are abridged below:

```
package javax.realtime;
public class LTMemory extends ScopedMemory {
  // constructors
  public LTMemory(long initial, long maximum);
  public LTMemory(long initial, long maximum,
                  Runnable logic);
  public LTMemory(long size); // in bytes
  public LTMemory(long size, Runnable logic);

  . . .

  // methods
  public String toString();
}

package javax.realtime;
public class VTMemory extends ScopedMemory {
  // constructors
  public VTMemory(long initial, long maximum);
  public VTMemory(long initial, long maximum,
                  Runnable logic);
  public VTMemory(long size); // in bytes
  public VTMemory(long size, Runnable logic);
  . . .

  // methods
  public String toString();
}
```

The expectation is that allocation time for objects in `VTMemory` will be faster but less predictable than allocation in `LTMemory`.

Important note

Object creation in Java requires both allocating the space needed for the object and running its constructor. Linear-time memory refers to the time needed for allocating the space (and the setting of any default values to fields), not the time needed to run the constructor (which can contain arbitrary code).

For scoped memory objects, a minimum and maximum size can be given. This allows extra flexibility in the implementation, although it is quite acceptable for an implementation to allocate the maximum size immediately.

Reference counts

Each scoped memory object has a reference count that indicates the number of times the scope has been entered and not exited. When that reference count goes from 1 to 0, the memory allocated in the scoped memory area is reclaimed (after running any finalization code associated with the allocated objects).

Fine detail note

Java finalizers consist of user-written code, and executing them can result in the enclosing memory area becoming reactivated again (for example, if a finalizer creates a schedulable object). Java semantics require that once the memory area becomes inactive again, the memory is freed without reexecuting the previously executed finalizers. Any newly created objects will be finalized.

8.2 An Example of Scoped Memory Usage

Consider the example given below. Here, a class encapsulates a large table that contains (two by two) matrices. The match method takes a two-by-two matrix and performs the dot product of this with every entry in the table. It then counts the number of results for which the dot product is the unity matrix.

```java
public class MatrixExample {
  public MatrixExample(int Size) {
    table = new int[Size][2][2];
    // Initialize table here.
  }
  public int match(final int with[][]) {
    int found = 0;
    for(int i=0; i < table.length; i++) {
      int[][] product = dotProduct(table[i], with);
      if(equals(product, unity)) found++;
    }
    return found;
  }
```

```
private int[][] dotProduct(int[][] a, int[][] b) {
  int [][] result = new int[2][2];
  // Calculate dot product.
  return result;
}

private boolean equals(int[] [] a, int[] [] b) {
  // Returns true if the matrices are equal.
}

private int [][][] table; // A table of 2 by 2 matrices.
private int [][] unity = {{1,0},{0,1}};
}
```

Note that the match method has a loop, and each time around that loop a call to dot-Product is made that creates and returns a new matrix object. This object is then compared to the unity matrix. After this comparison, the matrix object is available for garbage collection.

Now consider how this example can be rewritten so that it can reclaim the space for the temporary matrix without garbage collection. First, a scope memory area is needed; here LTMemory is used. Next, the code that is going to create and use the temporary matrix has to be constructed into a class that implements the Runnable interface; then that class has to be passed as a parameter to enter. To avoid creating a named class, an anonymous inner class can be used. Hence:

```
public int match(final int with[][]) { // first attempt
  LTMemory myMem = new LTMemory(1000, 5000);
  int found = 0;
  for(int i=0; i < table.length; i++) {
    myMem.enter(new Runnable() // start restructured code
      {
        public void run() {
          int[][] product = dotProduct(table[i], with);
          if(equals(product, unity)) found++;
        }
      });                        // end restructured code
  }
  return found;
}
```

Unfortunately, there are several problems with using inner classes that require this code to be modified. The first concerns the accessibility of the for loop parameter i. The only local parameters that can be accessed from within a class nested within a method are those that are final. Here, the `with` parameter is final, but the integer `i` is not. Furthermore, `found` is not final. To solve this problem, it is necessary to create a new final variable, `j`, inside the loop, which contains the current value of `i`. The variable `found` must be moved to be local to the class and initialized to 0 on each call of `match`.

The next problem is that the anonymous class is a subclass of `Object`, not the outer class `MatrixExample`. Consequently, the default `equals` method is the one in `Object` and a compilation error occurs. This can be circumvented by naming the method explicitly. The `myMem` object can also be moved to be local to the object in order to avoid recreating the object on every call to `match`. Hence, the new class is:

```java
import javax.realtime.*;
public class MatrixExample { // second attempt
  public MatrixExample(int Size) {
    table = new int[Size][2][2];
    // initialize table
    myMem = new LTMemory(1000, 5000); // say
  }

  public int match(final int with[][]) {
    found = 0;
    for(int i=0; i < table.length; i++) {
      final int j = i;
      myMem.enter(new Runnable() {
          public void run(){
            int[][] product = dotProduct(table[j], with);
            if(MatrixExample.this.equals(product, unity))
              found++;
          }
      });
    }
    return found;
  }

  private int[][] dotProduct(int[][] a, int [][] b) {
    int [][] result = new int[2][2];
    // Calculate dot product.
    return result;
  }

  private boolean equals(int[] [] a, int[] [] b) {
    // Returns true if the matrices are equal.
  }
```

```
   private int [] [] [] table; // A table of 2 by 2 matrices.
   private int [] [] unity = {{1,1},{1,1}};
   public int found;
   private LTMemory myMem;
}
```

This approach now reclaims the temporary memory every time the `enter` method terminates. However, as mentioned above, the creating of the anonymous class will still use memory in the surrounding memory area. In this case, there will be memory for a private copy of the `j` variable and a private reference to the `with` array (this is how the compiler implements the access to the method's data). As well as these, there will be some other memory allocated for implementing the object. Although this memory cannot be entirely eliminated, it can be significantly reduced by creating an object from a named inner class and reusing that object. The approach is illustrated below:

```
import javax.realtime.*;  // final attempt
public class MatrixExample {

  public MatrixExample() {
    table = new int[10][2][2];
    // Initialize the table here.
    produce = new Product();
    myMem = new LTMemory(1000, 5000);
  }

  public int match(final int with[][]) {
    produce.found = 0;
    for(int i=0; i < table.length; i++) {
      produce.j = i;
      produce.withMatrix = with;
      myMem.enter(produce);
    }
    return produce.found;
  }

  private class Product implements Runnable {
    int j;
    int withMatrix[][];
    int found = 0;

    public void run() {
      int[][] product = dotProduct(table[j], withMatrix);
      if(MatrixExample.this.equals(product, unity))
         found++;
    }
  }
}
```

```
private int[][] dotProduct(int[][] a, int [][] b) {
  // Calculate dot product and return result.
}

private boolean equals(int[] [] a, int[] [] b) {
  // Returns true if the matrices are equal.
}

private int [] [] [] table;
private int [] [] unity = {{1,1},{1,1}};
private Product produce;
private LTMemory myMem;
}
```

With this solution, there is just the initial cost of creating the produce object. Note that the only way to pass parameters to the run method is by setting attributes of the object (in this case directly).

8.3 Estimating the Size of Scoped Memory Areas

In order to use scoped memory areas effectively, it is necessary to be able to estimate the amount of memory required to hold the objects being allocated there. If the programmer underestimates the memory required, then the unchecked exception OutOfMemoryError will be thrown when space is exhausted. Vast overestimates might have equally serious consequences, in terms of overall memory size requirements and the resulting power consumption or heat production in the embedded processor.

To help the programmer estimate the size of memory required for a particular object, the RTSJ provides the SizeEstimator class given below.

```
package javax.realtime;
public final class SizeEstimator {

  // constructor
  public SizeEstimator();

  // methods
  public long getEstimate();
  public void reserve(Class c, int number);
  public void reserve(SizeEstimator s);
```

```
public void reserve(SizeEstimator s, int number);
public void reserveArray(int dimension);
   // For arrays of non primitive types.
public void reserveArray(int dimension, Class type);
   // For arrays of primitive types.
   // Throws IllegalArgumentException if type is not
   // a primitive type.
}
```

Objects of class `SizeEstimator` can be used to collect the size information about various classes. A call to one of the `reserve` methods adds the size of the parameter to the current estimate. For example, the following will calculate the size of a single `PriorityParameters` object and add it to the current estimate:

```
{
   SizeEstimator s = new SizeEstimator();
   ...
   s.reserve(javax.realtime.PriorityParameters.class, 1);
   System.out.println("size of PriorityParameters is "
                      +s.getEstimate());
}
```

Warning
The estimate given by these facilities is only a guide to the amount of memory that will be allocated. For example, it may or may not include any monitor lock that the system may need to create in support of synchronized methods and statements.

The current estimate in one `SizeEstimator` object can be used to reserve space in another `SizeEstimator` by using one of the overloaded reserve methods with a `SizeEstimator` parameter.

Consider now the following class.

```
public class Anonymous implements Runnable {
   final int j;
   final int with[][];

   public void run() {
   }
}
```

The value that a `SizeEstimator` gives for this object on a particular implementation of the RTSJ is 16 bytes. Indeed, the overheads associated with a null object is 8 bytes. This also represents the minimum cost of creating an anonymous `Runnable` object.

There are constructors for the various memory area classes, which take `SizeEstimator` objects:

```
package javax.realtime;
public abstract class MemoryArea {
  // constructors
  ...

  protected MemoryArea(SizeEstimator size);
  protected MemoryArea(SizeEstimator size,
                       Runnable logic);

  ...
}
```

```
package javax.realtime;
public abstract class ScopedMemory extends MemoryArea {
  // constructors
  ...

  public ScopedMemory(SizeEstimator size);
  public ScopedMemory(SizeEstimator size,
                       Runnable logic);

  ...
}
```

```
package javax.realtime;
public class LTMemory extends ScopedMemory {
  // constructors
  ...
  public LTMemory(SizeEstimator initial,
                      SizeEstimator maximum);
  public LTMemory(SizeEstimator initial,
                      SizeEstimator maximum,
                      Runnable logic);
  public LTMemory(SizeEstimator size);
  public LTMemory(SizeEstimator size, Runnable logic);
  ...
}
```

```
package javax.realtime;
public class VTMemory extends ScopedMemory {
  // constructors
  ...
  public VTMemory(SizeEstimator initial,
                    SizeEstimator maximum);
  public VTMemory(SizeEstimator initial,
                    SizeEstimator maximum,
                    Runnable logic);
  public VTMemory(SizeEstimator size);
  public VTMemory(SizeEstimator size, Runnable logic);
  ...
}
```

Important
note

A size estimator returns only the size of the created object. It does not take into account any objects that might be created by the object either as a result of initialization or from running the constructor.

8.4 Assignment Rules

To recap, in the RTSJ there are four types of memory:

- heap memory – collected by the garbage collector;

- local variables (stack memory) – collected automatically when methods exit;

- immortal memory – never collected;

- scoped memory – available for collection when the associated reference count goes from one to zero.

Given that the collection mechanism for scoped memory is different from the collection of heap memory and local variables, it is necessary to impose some restrictions on assignments between the different types of memory. Otherwise, dangling references may occur. A dangling reference is a reference to an object that has been collected when scoped memory is reclaimed. Consider, for example, the scenario depicted in Figure 8.1.

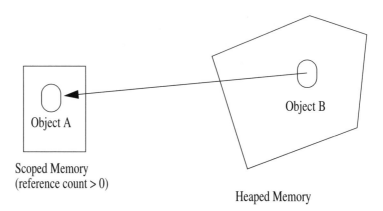

FIGURE 8.1. An Illegal Potential Dangling Reference to Scoped Memory

Here, object A has been created in a scoped memory region. A reference to that object has been stored in object B, which resides in the heap. The lifetime of a scoped memory is controlled by its reference count.

Warning

> The reference count of a scoped memory area is the count of the number of active calls (explicit or implicit) to its `enter` method (or the `executeInArea` method—see Section 8.5). It is *not* a count of the number of objects that have references to the objects allocated in the scoped memory.

Consequently, unless forbidden, the scenario depicted in Figure 8.1 would result in the reference to object A, from object B, becoming invalid (dangling) when object A's memory area is reclaimed. There would be no way to detect this invalid reference, and the safety of the Java program would be compromised.

To avoid dangling references, the RTSJ requires that the assignment rules, given in Figure 8.2, be enforced.

Important
note

> Local variables (including method parameters) are not held in any memory area but reside on the stack of the calling thread. They can, therefore, hold references to objects stored anywhere. A local variable will always go out of scope before any scoped memory area containing the object to which it can point. The only exception to this rule is references to portal objects (see Section 8.7.)

If the program violates the assignment rules, the unchecked exception `Illegal-AssignmentError` is thrown.

From Memory Area	Reference to Heap Memory	Reference to Immortal Memory	Reference to Scope Memory
Heap Memory	Allowed	Allowed	Forbidden
Immortal Memory	Allowed	Allowed	Forbidden
Scoped Memory	Allowed	Allowed	Allowed: if to the same scope or to a less deeply nested scope. Forbidden: if to a more deeply nested scope.
Local variable	Allowed	Allowed	Allowed

FIGURE 8.2. **Memory Assignment Rules**

Implementation note

Given that one of the requirements for the RTSJ is that there should be no changes to the Java language and that existing compilers can be used to compile RTSJ programs, these rules must be enforced on most assignment statements at run-time by the real-time JVM. Of course, an RTSJ-aware compiler may be able to undertake some static analysis in order to reduce this burden. However, it is not clear whether a real-time JVM can assume that these checks have been made as they have no direct representation in the Java byte code (if checks can be omitted for the whole class, the class file can indicate this). Alternatively, checks may be performed at class loading time.

The success of the RTSJ may well hinge on the ability of vendors to produce an efficient implementation of the RTSJ memory assignment rules.

8.5 Nested Memory Areas and the Single Parent Rule

To appreciate the full implications of the memory assignment rules, it is necessary to consider in more detail the nesting of memory areas. The real-time JVM will need to keep track of the currently active memory areas of each schedulable object. One way this can be achieved is via a stack. Every time a schedulable object enters a memory area, the identity of that area is pushed onto the stack. When it leaves the memory area, the identity is popped off the stack. Consider, for example, the stack of a schedulable object illustrated in Figure 8.3 (the stack grows upwards). Here, all active memory areas are shown, however, it is only the scoped memory areas that are important for checking illegal memory references.

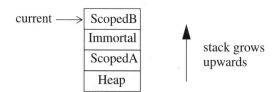

FIGURE 8.3. The Memory Stack of a Schedulable Object

In this example, the schedulable object began its execution with the heap as its active memory area. It first entered a scoped memory area (`ScopedA`) and then, while active in that area, it entered into the immortal memory, and then into a second scoped memory area (`ScopedB`). The stack can be used to check for invalid memory assignment to and from scoped memory areas.

*   A reference from an object in one scoped memory area to another object in another scoped memory area *below* the first area in the stack is *allowed*.

*   A reference from an object in one scoped memory area to another object in another scoped memory area *above* the first area in the stack is *forbidden*.

Hence, if O1 is created in ScopedB and O2 is created in ScopedA then

*   `O1.O2Ref = O2` is allowed as `O1` will be reclaimed before `O2` and hence there will be no dangling pointer

*   `O2.O1Ref = O1` is disallowed as it will result in a dangling pointer in `O2` when `O1` is reclaimed.

The memory assignment rules by themselves still do not prevent the dangling reference problem. Consider the case where a schedulable object wishes to enter a memory area that it already has active. If this were allowed, then the stack illustrated in Figure 8.4 might develop.

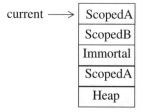

FIGURE 8.4. An Illegal Memory Area Stack

Here, an object could be created in ScopedA, which references an object in ScopedB (as ScopedB is below it in the stack). However, when the current ScopedA memory is exited, the reference count for that area is still greater than zero and so its objects are not reclaimed. Now when ScopedB is exited, its objects are reclaimed and consequently, the object in ScopedA is left with a dangling reference. To avoid this problem, the RTSJ requires that each scoped memory area has a single parent. The parent of an active scoped memory area is (in the single stack case) as follows.

- If the memory is the first scoped area on the stack, its parent is termed the *primordial* scoped area.
- For all other scoped memory areas, the parent is the first *scoped area* below it on the stack.

In the example in Figure 8.3, the parent of ScopedA is the primordial scoped area and the parent of ScopedB is ScopedA. In the example in Figure 8.4, ScopedA has two parents, the primordial scoped area and ScopedB. This violates the single-parent rule and, therefore, the unchecked ScopedCycleException is thrown.

Moving between memory areas

Given that it is therefore not possible to enter a scoped memory area that is already active, it is necessary to provide alternative mechanisms for moving between active memory areas and allocating memory from an active memory area that is not the current memory area. The MemoryArea class provides the following methods for this purpose.

```
package javax.realtime;
public abstract class MemoryArea {

  ...
  // methods
  public void executeInArea(Runnable logic);
    // Throws IlegalArgumentException,
    // InaccessibleAreaException;
    // Execute the logic.run method in the context of an
    // active memory area.

  public Object newArray(Class type, int number);
    // Throws a variety of unchecked exception including
    // InaccessibleAreaException and OutOfMemoryError.
    // Allocate an array.

  public Object newInstance(Class type) throws
          IllegalAccessException,InstantiationException;
    // Throws a variety of unchecked exception including
    // InaccessibleAreaException and OutOfMemoryError.
```

```
    // Allocate an object where the constructor has
    // no parameters.
public Object newInstance(reflect.Constructor c,
            Object[] args) throws
        IllegalAccessException,InstantiationException
        InvocationTargetException;
    // Throws a variety of unchecked exception including
    // InaccessibleAreaException and OutOfMemoryError.
    // Allocate an object where the constructor does
    // have parameters.

    ...
}
```

The `executeInArea` allows the current allocation area to be moved to a memory area on the stack for the duration of the execution of a `Runnable` object. The unchecked `InaccessibleAreaException` is thrown if the area is not active.

If a schedulable object executing with the stack given in Figure 8.3 wanted to start allocating objects from the scoped memory `ScopedA`, it could use the following:

```
ScopedA.executeInArea(new Runnable() {
    public void run() {
        // Memory now allocated from ScopedA.
    }
});
```

The result of using `executeInArea` and then entering a new memory area means that a simple stack is no longer adequate for keeping track of the active scopes. Instead, a *cactus* stack (or tree) must be used. Consider the example given in Figure 8.5. Here, a schedulable object stack is initially illustrated in (a). It then uses `executeInArea` to make `ScopedA` the current memory area – as illustrated in (b). After this, it enters into

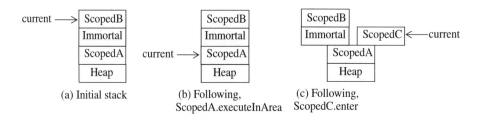

FIGURE 8.5. **Using** `executeInArea`

a new scoped memory area, ScopedC. This results in the formation of a cactus stack illustrated in (c).

Of course, although complex cactus stacks (as illustrated in Figure 8.6) can be created, they must not violate the single-parent rule.

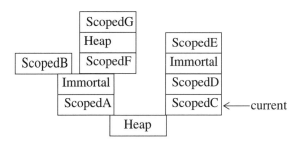

FIGURE 8.6. A Cactus Stack of Memory Areas

Important note

A call to executeInArea with a parameter of the heap (or immortal) memory results in a new memory stack being created, with the heap (or immortal) memory area at its base.

If it is just one object that needs to be created in a particular memory area, then the newArray or newInstance methods can be used. For example, to create a new copy of the current object on the heap

```
Object o = HeapMemory.instance().newInstance(
        this.getClass());
```

The above assumes that the object does not require any parameters to its constructor. If it does, then the alternative version of newInstance must be used. To create an array of objects, the newArray method should be used. Of course, when the constructor is called, it could itself change the current memory area to create other objects.

Java threads and memory areas

In general, a Java thread is not allowed to enter into a memory area. However, it is allowed to call executeInArea with immortal memory or the heap as a parameter. Furthermore, it is allowed to creates objects in those areas via the newArray and newInstance methods.

8.6   Sharing Memory Areas between Schedulable Objects

Multiple schedulable objects can access the same memory areas. Consequently, the cactus stacks for each schedulable object are linked together. Consider the example presented in Figure 8.7. Here, two real-time threads (ThreadA and ThreadB) have active memory stacks. Now suppose that ThreadA wishes to enter ScopedE. It cannot do so directly because ScopedE is already active and has a parent ScopedD. If ThreadA were to try and enter ScopedE, a ScopedCycleException would be thrown (as ScopedE would have two parents if the operation were allowed).

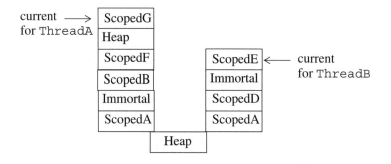

FIGURE 8.7.   Multiple Stacks

To gain access to ScopedE, ThreadA must first move to ScopedA (using executeInArea), then enter ScopedD followed by ScopedE. The resulting cactus stack would be

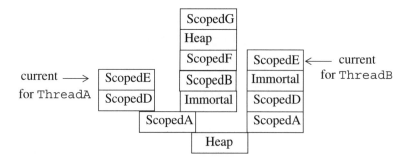

FIGURE 8.8.   Cactus Stack for Two Threads

Inheritance of the scoped memory area stack

When a schedulable object is created, its initial memory area can be set. This is done via a parameter to one of the constructors. For example, the RealtimeThread class (see Chapter 12) has the following constructor.

```
package javax.realtime;
public class RealtimeThread extends Thread
      implements Schedulable{
  // constructors
  public RealtimeThread(SchedulingParameters scheduling,
    ReleaseParameters release, MemoryParameters memory,
    MemoryArea area, ProcessingGroupParameters group,
    Runnable logic);
  ...

  // methods

  ...

}
```

The initial stack of a created schedulable object is determined by the value of the initial memory area (the area parameter) and the currently active memory area as follows:

If current area is the heap and

- the initial memory area is the heap, then the new stack contains only the heap memory area;
- the initial memory area is not the heap, then the new stack contains the heap and the initial memory area.

If current area is the immortal memory area and

- the initial memory area is the immortal memory area, then the new stack contains only the immortal memory area;
- the initial memory area is not the immortal memory area, then the new stack contains the immortal memory area and the initial memory area.

If the current area is a scoped memory area and the initial memory area is the currently active memory area (or null), then

- the new stack is the parent's stack up to and including the current memory area.

If the current area is a scoped memory area and the initial memory area is not the currently active memory area, then

- the new stack is the parent's stack up to and including the current memory area, plus the initial memory area.

Important
note

All scoped memory areas that are present on the newly created stack have their reference counts incremented. For a real-time thread, this occurs when the thread is started; the counts are decremented when the thread terminates. For an asynchronous event handler, the counts are effectively incremented when the handler is first capable of being released and decremented when its last release has finished. In other words, the memory associated with a scoped memory area containing an asynchronous event handler cannot be reclaimed until that event handler is waiting for a new release and no further releases are possible.

**Manipulating
the memory
area stack**

There are a group of static methods and one instance method available in the `RealtimeThread` class that enable the memory area stack to be manipulated. They are self-explanatory and are defined below. Note that the `getMemoryArea` method returns the default memory area for the real-time thread. This is the active memory area for the real-time thread at its creation time. This is the only memory area that another schedulable object can acquire from a real-time thread (as it is the only one that does not change dynamically).

```
package javax.realtime;
public class RealtimeThread extends Thread
      implements Schedulable {
  ...

  // methods
  public static MemoryArea getCurrentMemoryArea();
  public static MemoryArea getOuterMemoryArea(int index);

  public static int getInitialMemoryAreaIndex();
  public static int getMemoryAreaStackDepth();

  public MemoryArea getMemoryArea();
    // Get the initial (default) memory area for this.
  ...
}
```

The static methods can also be called from event handlers as well as real-time threads. The `getMemoryArea` method is also declared in the `AsyncEventHandler` class.

```
package javax.realtime;
public class AsyncEventHandler implements Schedulable {
  ...

  public MemoryArea getMemoryArea();
  // Returns the initial (default) memory area for this.
}
```

Entering and joining scoped memories

Scoped memory areas can be used by schedulable objects in one of two modes of operation. They can be used *cooperatively* or *competitively*. In cooperative use, the schedulable objects aim to be active in a scoped memory area simultaneously. They use the area to communicate via shared objects. When they leave, the memory is reclaimed. An example of cooperative behavior is given in Section 8.7. Of course, two groups of schedulable objects might use a scoped memory area in competitive mode, but within each group, the schedulable objects use the memory in cooperative mode.

Where the schedulable objects cannot guarantee to be simultaneously active in the scoped memory area (but nevertheless wish to communicate through it), it will be necessary to keep the area alive. This can be achieved by creating a real-time thread within the area. The last schedulable object to use the area can then inform the thread that it is time to terminate.

When schedulable objects are using a scoped memory area competitively, the goal is to make the most efficient use of memory. Consequently, the schedulable objects are trying to take their memory from the same area but are not using the area for communication via shared objects. In this mode of operation, it is usually required for only one schedulable object to be active in the memory area at one time. The intention is that the memory can be reclaimed when each of the schedulable objects leave the area (the reference count should become zero in this case). However, it may be difficult for the programmer to ensure that the area does becomes inactive. There are two ways that this problem can be solved. The first is that the programmer has to use the current synchronizing mechanisms of Java to coordinate access to the memory. The alternative is for the RTSJ to provide mechanisms that facilitate the competitive sharing of scoped memory areas. Usually, the RTSJ has shied away from providing synchronization, preferring to require programmers to provide their own. However, in this instance it does provide some help in the `ScopedMemory` class.

```java
package javax.realtime;
public abstract class ScopedMemory extends MemoryArea {

  ...

  // methods

  public int getReferenceCount();

  public void join() throws InterruptedException;
  public void join(HighResolutionTime time)
    throws InterruptedException;

  public void joinAndEnter() throws InterruptedException;
    // Throws IllegalArgumentException,
    //        ScopedCycleException.
```

```
public void joinAndEnter(HighResolutionTime time)
  throws InterruptedException;
  // Throws IlegalArgumentException,
  //        ScopedCycleException.

public void joinAndEnter(Runnable logic)
  throws InterruptedException;
  // Throws ScopedCycleException.
public void joinAndEnter(Runnable logic,
                          HighResolutionTime time)
  throws InterruptedException;
  // Throws ScopedCycleException.
  ...
}
```

The join method simply waits for the reference count to become zero (with or without a timeout). Note that it is difficult to determine whether the timeout has expired or not (see also the comment on timeouts with Java in Section 4.2), as by the time the thread actually executes on return from join

1. the timeout may have passed, and
2. the reference count may have been incremented or decremented (by another thread) between the time the first thread was scheduled and when it actually executed.

The joinAndEnter methods (with and without timeouts) provide the ability to wait for the reference count to become zero (and any object finalization to complete) and for the memory area to be entered as an indivisible action. As with enter, a Runnable object can be provided, or the one given when the memory object was created can be used. If no Runnable has been given, joinAndEnter throws IllegalArgumentException immediately.

Warning   If a timeout is given with joinAndEnter and the timeout expires, the memory area is entered irrespective of whether the reference count went to zero or not.

8.7 Portals

When schedulable objects are using scoped memory in a cooperative manner and there is no other relationship between the schedulable objects, it becomes difficult to see how they can effectively share objects created in the scoped memory area. To share an object requires each schedulable object to have a reference to that object. A reference to an object can only be stored in an object in the same scoped area or in an object in a nested scoped area. It cannot be stored in the immortal or heaped memory areas. Consequently, unless there is some relationship between the schedulable objects, one schedulable object cannot pass a reference to an object it has just created to another schedulable object. The RTSJ provides *portals* to solve this problem. Each scoped memory area can have one object that can act as a gateway into that memory area. Schedulable objects can use this mechanism to facilitate communication. The interface is shown below.

```
package javax.realtime;
public abstract class ScopedMemory extends MemoryArea {
   ...
  public Object getPortal();
    // Throws MemoryAccessError - if the portal is a heap
    // reference and the caller is a no-heap schedulable
    // object, IllegalAssignmentError - if the returned
    // cannot be legally stored in the caller's
    // allocation context.
  public void setPortal(Object o);
    // Throws IllegalAssignmentError - if the object
    // is not allocated in the scoped instance.
}
```

Important note

Portal objects are intended to be objects that are created in the associated scoped memory area. To avoid `IllegalAssignmentError` being thrown, `getPortal` should only be called on a scoped memory, S, if S is the current active allocation context or S is below the current active memory context in the schedulable object's scoped memory stack. This applies even if the portal object's reference is being assigned to a local variable in a method.

Example of the use of portals

To illustrate how portals can be used, consider the example of an object that controls the firing of a missile. For the missile to be launched, two independent real-time threads must call its `fire` method, each with its own authorization code (here, all problems associated with the timing of the calls are ignored). The interface is shown below:

```
import javax.realtime.*;
public class FireMissile {
   public FireMissile();
   public boolean fire1(final String authorizationCode);
   public boolean fire2(final String authorizationCode);
}
```

The two real-time threads call `fire1` and `fire2` respectively. Whichever calls in first has its authorization code checked and is held until the other real-time thread calls its fire method. If both threads have valid authorization codes, the missile is fired and the methods return `true`. If either of the two thread's authorization code fails, the missile is not fired and the fire methods return `false`.

Now, in order to implement the fire methods, assume that objects need to be created in order to check the authorization. Let the following class implement the required algorithm:

```
public class Decrypt {
  public boolean confirm(String code) {
    // Check authorization.
  }
}
```

Furthermore, to obtain the required synchronization, the two real-time threads must communicate. Assume that the following class is used for this purpose (based on the `Barrier` class given in Section 5.7). The threads call `waitB` indicating whether they wish to fire. If both pass `true`, `wait` returns `true`.

```
public class BarrierWithParameter {

  public BarrierWithParameter(int participants) {
    requiredParticipants = participants;
    arrived = 0;
    confirmed = true;
  }

  public synchronized boolean waitB(boolean go) {
    arrived++;
    if(!go) confirmed = false;
    try {
      while(arrived != requiredParticipants) wait();
      else notifyAll();
    } catch(InterruptedException ie){confirmed = false;}
    return confirmed;
  }

  private final int requiredParticipants;
  private int arrived;
  private boolean confirmed;
}
```

Now the goal is to implement the `FireMissile` class without using extra memory other than that required to instantiate the class. All memory needed by the fire methods should be created in scoped memory, which can be reclaimed when the fire methods are inactive.

In order to implement the required firing algorithm, the class needs two `Decrypt` objects and one `BarrierWithParameter` object. Hence, the constructor for the `FireMissile` class undertakes the following actions:

```
import javax.realtime.*;
public class FireMissile {

  public FireMissile() {
    ...
    SizeEstimator s = new SizeEstimator();
    s.reserve(Decrypt.class, 2);
    s.reserve(BarrierWithParameter.class, 1);
    shared = new LTMemory(s.getEstimate());
  }

  private LTMemory shared;
  ...
}
```

A `SizeEstimator` object is used to calculate the memory for the three objects. A new `LTMemory` is then created. Now the fire methods can be presented. Given that both the calling threads will need to access the `BarrierWithParameter` object, they must both enter into the same scoped memory area. However, care is needed because the `shared` memory area must only have a single parent. As this class is unaware of the scoped stacks of the calling threads, it needs to create new scoped memory stacks. It does this by using the `executeInArea` method to enter into immortal memory. The associate `run` method can now enter into the scoped memory area. Once again, to avoid having to create dynamically anonymous classes, named internal classes are used. In this instance, two are needed; one to enter into immortal memory and another to enter into the scoped memory.

```
import javax.realtime.*;
public class FireMissile {

  public FireMissile() {
    fireController1 = new FireAction();
    fireController2 = new FireAction();
    immortalController1 = new ImmortalAction();
    immortalController2 = new ImmortalAction();
```

```
      SizeEstimator s = new SizeEstimator();
      s.reserve(Decrypt.class,2);
      s.reserve(BarrierWithParameter.class, 1);
      shared = new LTMemory(s.getEstimate());
    }
  class FireAction implements Runnable {
    String authorization;
    boolean result;
    public void run() {
      // Coordinate the firing of the missile.
    }
  }

  class ImmortalAction implements Runnable {
    FireAction fireController;
    public void run() {
      shared.enter(fireController);
        // Enter the shared scoped memory.
    }
  }

  public boolean fire1(String authorizationCode) {
    immortalController1.fireController =
                        fireController1;
    fireController1.authorization = authorizationCode;
    ImmortalMemory.instance().executeInArea(
                    immortalController1);
    return fireController1.result;
  }
  // Similarly for fire2.

  private LTMemory shared;
  private FireAction fireController1, fireController2;
  private ImmortalAction immortalController1,
                        immortalController2;
}
```

Once inside the scoped memory area, the required objects can be created. However, a problem occurs with the shared BarrierWithParameter object. In order for both threads to access the BarrierWithParameter method they both must have a reference to it. Usually, the reference would be stored in a private reference declared at the class level. However, this is not possible in this case, as it would break the RTSJ assignment rules because the BarrierWithParameter object is in an inner (more deeply nested) scope. This is where the notion of a portal can be used. The first thread to arrive attempts to obtain the portal object for the `shared` memory region. This is null, so it creates the `BarrierWithParameter` object and sets it up as the portal object. The next thread to arrive can then obtain the required reference. When both threads leave the `shared` memory area, all the memory is reclaimed. However, even here, things are not quite that simple as there is a race condition between checking for the existence of the portal object and setting a newly created one. Consequently, a lock is needed. The only locks available at this stage are those associated with static objects, those associated with `Class` objects, and the lock associated with the scoped memory object itself! The latter is used here. The complete `fireAction` class is given below.

```
class FireAction implements Runnable {
  String authorization;
  boolean result;

  public void run() {
    BarrierWithParameter sync;
    Decrypt check = new Decrypt();
    boolean confirmed = check.confirm(authorization);

    synchronized(RealtimeThread.getCurrentMemoryArea()) {
      sync = (BarrierWithParameter)shared.getPortal();
      if(sync == null) {
        sync = new BarrierWithParameter(2);
        shared.setPortal(sync);
      }
    }
    result = sync.waitB(confirmed);
  }
}
```

Figure 8.9 illustrates the main interactions between the objects. Each real-time thread calls its appropriate fire method. The figure illustrates a real-time thread calling `fire1`. The `fire1` method calls `executeInArea` to enter immortal memory and runs the `immortalController1`, which then enters into the `Shared` (scope) memory area. This then runs the `fireController1` object, which confirms that the correct authorization has been given. Once confirmed, it tries to get the portal object. If the portal object is null, it is the first to arrive. It then creates the `sync` object (step 8a) and sets it as the portal object (step 8b). If it is not the first, `getPortal` returns `sync`. The `waitB` method is then called to determine if the missile should be fired.

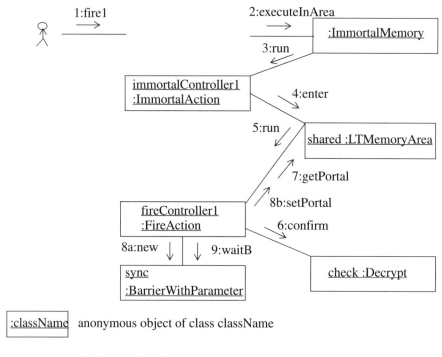

FIGURE 8.9. **Collaboration between Objects**

8.8 Using Scoped Memory

The difficulties mentioned in the previous section are indicative of the problems that will be encountered when programmers attempt to use the RTSJ model. This section attempts to give some guidelines on when scoped memory areas can be safely used. This is particularly relevant when designing for reuse.

Class versus thread-based use of scoped memory

One of the main programming decisions to take when using the RTSJ memory area facilities is deciding where the responsibility should lie for using scoped memory. For example, when a class is written, which needs some temporary memory space, should it take responsibility for creating and entering a scoped memory area? At first sight, the answer to this question is "yes, of course". But the issue is not quite as straightforward as it seems. It is necessary to determine if the class may be used concurrently. Often a programmer may decide that controlling concurrent access to a class is the responsibility of the user of the class, not the class itself[1]. This is an approach often taken in the

---

1. The class is Thread Compatible using Bloch's thread safety levels presented in Section 4.8.

RTSJ, for example. It is a more efficient approach as locks are not acquired unless they are needed. However, it is more dangerous as the result may be that data is accessed without the appropriate locks in place. In the case of using scoped memory, the following issues need to be addressed:

1. If the class targets sequential access and enters into a scoped memory area, then if it is used concurrently from schedulable objects with active memory areas, a `ScopedCycleException` will be thrown when the entered scoped memory area has more than one parent. The client schedulable objects must, therefore, either ensure that the scoped memory stack is empty before using the class or ensure that all clients call the object with the same stack. Consequently clients need to have details of when a class is using scoped memory areas.

2. If the class targets concurrent access, it must either assume the calling schedulable objects have the same (or empty) scoped memory stacks, or it must "execute in" a heap or an immortal area first (to create new stacks). This is necessary for ensuring no cycles occur. If it chooses the heap, the class cannot be used by a no-heap schedulable object; if it chooses the immortal memory, named inner classes must be used – otherwise every time it creates an object from an anonymous class, some memory will be created in immortal memory and this will not be reclaimed.

Given that many of the problems of using scoped memory area are related to threads (schedulable objects), it is perhaps easier to manage the problems at the thread level rather than the object level. Executing object constructors are perhaps the only real occasion when a thread can guarantee that the code is called sequentially.

As more experience with using scoped memory is acquired, software design patterns will be developed to ease the programming burden (these are already beginning to emerge, for example, see (Benowitz and Niessner, 2003; Pizlo, Fox, Holmes and Vitek, 2004)).

Using prewritten classes

The RTSJ has been carefully designed so that RTSJ programs can use prewritten Java software with the minimum of surprises (for example, the ATC model presented in Chapter 13 ensures that software written without knowledge of ATC will not be broken when ATCs occur). The assignment rules for RTSJ given in Section 8.4 make the use of prewritten classes problematic. In general, if the active memory area is the heap or immortal memory, then it is safe to call a method in the object as long as it does not return an object in scoped memory (which it will not do, if the object has never been used in a scoped memory context). Otherwise, it is necessary to have detailed knowledge of the class' implementation.

If an object is either created in scoped memory or its methods are called from an active scoped area, then care must be taken. Firstly, even if the object has been created in scoped memory, any static variables or static references it owns are stored in the immortal memory. Figure 8.10 illustrates some of the potential problems if a method is called when there is an active scoped memory area.

	Server Object in Heap Memory	Server Object in Immortal Memory	Server Object in Scoped Memory
no reference parameters	Problems if the method creates objects and saves them in local references	Problems if the method creates objects and saves them in local references	OK, if the server's scope is the same or less deeply nested than the active scope, otherwise problems if the method creates objects and saves them in local references
reference parameters to scoped memory objects	As for no reference parameters case, plus problems if the method saves parameters in local references	As for no reference parameters case, plus problems if the method saves parameters in local references	As for no reference parameters case, plus problems if parameters are in a more deeply nested scope compared to the server, and the method saves parameters in local references
returned reference to a created object	As for reference parameters case, plus returned reference must be assigned to the same scope or more deeply nested scope of the current active scope	As for reference parameters case, plus returned reference must be assigned to the same scope or more deeply nested scope of the current active scope	As for reference parameters case, plus returned reference must be assigned to the same scope or more deeply nested scope of the current active scope

FIGURE 8.10. **Using Prewritten Classes with an Active Scoped Memory Area**

Further problems occur with static fields, which are stored in immortal memory.

The maze example revisited

As an example of when it is safe and appropriate to use scoped memory consider the maze example given in Chapter 6. Here, a description of the Maze has to be read from a file. An example of the format of the file is shown in Figure 8.11. The first line contains the size of the maze, the second line the entrance position and the third line the exit position. The maze itself is then given with the 'F' character indicating a wall, and a space character indicating a passage.

```
20  78   // actual rows, actual columns
2  1     // start
11 69    // finish
FFFFFFFFFFFFFFFFFFFFFFFFFFFFFFFFFFFFFFFFFFFFFFFFFFFFFFFFFFFFFFFFFFFFFFFFFFFFFFFF
                                   F                          F             F
F FFFFF FFFFFFFFFFFFFFF FFFFFFFFFFFFFFFFFFF FFFFFFFFFFFFFFF FFFFFFFFFFFFFFFFF F
F F        F                  F                    F                    F F
F F FFFFFFFFFFFFFFFFFFFFFFFFFFFF FFFFFFFFFFFFFFFFFFFFF FFFFFFFFFFFFFF FFFFFFFF  F
F F F          F                 F                       F          F FFF
F F F FFFF FFFFFFFF FFFFFFFFFFFF FFFFFFFF FFFFFFFFFFFFFFFFFFFFFFFFFFFFF  F   F
F FFF F      F          F              F               F FF F
F   F F FFFF FFFF FFFFFFFFFFFFFFFFFFFFFFFFFFFFFFFF FFFFFFFFFFFFFFFF F FFF F
FFF FFF FF F    F    F   F   F   F   F   F   F   F   F   F   F    FFF   F   F
F F F F FF   F   F   F   F   F   F   F   F   F   F   F   F    F  FF FF FFF
F    F FFFFFFFFFFFFFFFFFFFFFFFFFFFFFFFFFFFFFFFFFFFFFFFFFF FFFFF F    F
F FFF F          F                    F                 F    F FFF F
F   F FFFFFFFFFF FFFFFFFFF FFFFFFFFFFFFFFFFFFF FFFFFFF FFFFF FFFFFFF F   F
FFF F       F            F            F           F      F FFF
F    FFFFFFF FFFFFFFF FFFFFFFF FFFFFFFFF FFFFF FFFFFFFFFFFFFFFF FFFFFFFF     F
F F    F          F              F              F           F F
F FFFFFFFFFFFFFFFFFFFF FFFFFFFFFFFFFFFFFFFFFFFF FFFFFFFFFFFFFFFFF FFFFFFFFF F
F          F             F                      F               F  F
FFFFFFFFFFFFFFFFFFFFFFFFFFFFFFFFFFFFFFFFFFFFFFFFFFFFFFFFFFFFFFFFFFFFFFFFFFFFFFFF
```

FIGURE 8.11. An Example Maze File

In order to read the maze details from file, various predefined classes can be used. These all require memory to be allocated, all of which can be reclaimed once the details have been processed. The maze is modeled in the program as a `Maze` class, the constructor of which reads in the maze details. This constructor is called sequentially and, therefore, can use scoped memory for the temporary objects created. The approach is illustrated below.

```java
import java.io.*; import java.util.*;
import javax.realtime.*;

public class Maze {
  public char [][]board;
  public int startX, startY;
  public int finishX, finishY;
  public int mazeRows, mazeColumns;

  // constructor
  public Maze() {
    LTMemory myMem = new LTMemory(100000); // say
    myMem.enter(
      new Runnable() {
        public void run()
        {
          // Read in and process maze information.
```

```
                    . . .
               // Now create board in immortal memory.
               ImmortalMemory im = ImmortalMemory.instance();
               im.enter(new Runnable() {
                  public void run()
                  {
                     board = new char[mazeRows][mazeColumns];
                  }
               } );
               // Now read in maze itself.
            }
         } );
   } // end of constructor method

   . . .

} // end of class Maze
```

Note that the board reference variable and the integers startX, startY, finishX, finishY, mazeRows and mazeColumns are all stored in the memory area in which an object of the class will be created (here it is assumed that the maze will be placed in immortal memory). Care must be taken when the values are assigned. Given that integers are primitive values, this should not be a problem. However, the board will refer to an object. Consequently, when the object is to be created, the memory area must be switched to the immortal memory.

The full details of reading the maze file are now presented.

```
public class Maze {
   . . .
   // constructor
   public Maze() {
      . . .
      myMem.enter(new Runnable() {
         public void run() {
            BufferedReader din = new BufferedReader(
                 new InputStreamReader(System.in));
            System.out.print("where is the maze file? ");
            try {
               String fileName= din.readLine().trim();
               File mazeFile = new File(fileName);
               if (!mazeFile.exists())
                  System.out.println(fileName + " not found");
```

```
        else {
          FileReader mazeReader =
                  new FileReader(mazeFile);
          BufferedReader mReader =
                  new BufferedReader(mazeReader);
          String line = mReader.readLine();
          StringTokenizer st = new
                  StringTokenizer(line);
          mazeRows = Integer.parseInt(st.nextToken());
          mazeColumns = Integer.parseInt(
                      st.nextToken());
          line = mReader.readLine();
          st = new StringTokenizer(line);
          startX = Integer.parseInt(
                  st.nextToken()) - 1;
         startY = Integer.parseInt(st.nextToken()) -1;
          line = mReader.readLine();
          st = new StringTokenizer(line);
          finishX = Integer.parseInt(
                  st.nextToken()) - 1;
          finishY = Integer.parseInt(
                  st.nextToken()) - 1;
          ImmortalMemory im =
                  ImmortalMemory.instance();
          im.enter(new Runnable() {
            public void run()
            {  /* as before */}
          } );
          for (int row = 0; row < mazeRows; row++) {
            line =mReader.readLine();
            for (int col = 0; col < mazeColumns;
                col++) {
              board[row][col] = line.charAt(col);
            }
          }
        } // end else
      } catch (java.io.IOException E) {... }
    } // end run
  } );

  } // end of constructor method
  ...
} // end of class Maze
```

Note that the values assigned to `startX`, `startY`, `finishX`, `finishY`, `mazeRows` and `mazeColumns` are all returned on the stack as a result of the function calls. They can, therefore, be copied into the object's memory without problems. Also note that, *in this case*, the objects created from the standard Java libraries could be used without problems.

Utilities and scoped memory

Scoped memory works best when an application wants space to store some temporary objects. As long as these objects can be grouped together so that they follow a stacking algorithm (last-in-first-out—or in this case, last created-first destroyed), the model works well. However, many algorithms require a first-in-first-out or some other order. For example, consider a simple `List` (as found in `java.util`). Now suppose objects are created and placed in the list. At a later time, they are removed from the list (say one at a time and in the order in which they were placed) and processed. Once processed, they are no longer required. Programming this using scoped memory areas (so that objects are automatically reclaimed) is far from straightforward and requires detailed knowledge of both the list structure and the lifetime of the object when it is added to the list. If this is available, then a combination of scoped memory areas and the use of the `enter` and `executeInArea` methods can usually achieve the desired result (Borg, 2004). However, the algorithms are difficult and not very elegant. Again, this is an area where design patterns will, in time, emerge. Furthermore, just as with Java, it has been found necessary to allow interactions between the program and the garbage collector (via weak references), so it is also necessary to allow interactions between the program and the implementation of scoped memory areas (Borg and Wellings, 2003).

8.9 Real-time Issues

The timing properties of scoped memory

One of the overriding goals of the RTSJ is to facilitate predictable implementation. The use of scoped memory has some interesting impacts on the execution of schedulable objects. These impacts must be fully understood if programmers are going to be able to analyze their systems. They can be broken down into the following four components:

1. *Entry to scoped memory* – on entry into a scoped memory region, a schedulable object may be blocked if it uses one of the `join` or `joinAndEnter` methods. The duration of this blocking may be difficult to bound (unless timeouts are used, but these have their own problems, see Section 8.6). If the schedulable objects using the scoped memory do not themselves block after they have entered the scoped memory region, the blocking time will be the maximum time that lower-priority schedulable objects take to execute the associated run method. When a schedulable object

attempts to enter into a previously active scoped memory area, it may also have to wait for the memory to be reclaimed (see 3 below).

2. *Predictable scoped memory allocation* – memory allocation in a scoped memory should be predictable from the details of the implementation and the objects being created. It will consist of two components: the time taken to allocate the space for the objects (which will be proportional to their sizes, for LTMemory), and the time taken to execute the constructors for the objects created.

3. *Exit from scoped memory* – the RTSJ gives a great deal of freedom on when the memory used in a scoped memory area is reclaimed. An implementation might decide to reclaim the memory immediately when the reference count becomes zero or sometime after it becomes zero, but no later than when a new schedulable object wishes to enter it. Hence, a schedulable object on one occasion may leave the scoped memory and suffer no impact; on another occasion, it is the last object to leave and reclamation occurs immediately; alternatively it may suffer when it first enters the scope (see 1).

4. *Object finalization* – whenever scoped memory is reclaimed, the objects that have been created must have their finalization code executed before reclamation. The time for this to occur must be accounted for in any analysis.

5. *Garbage collector scans* – the impact, if any, of the garbage collector scanning the scoped memory area looking for heap references when those memory areas are being reclaimed concurrently.

Memory Parameters

Given that memory is an important resource in real-time and embedded systems, it is important to be able to capture the amount of memory a schedulable object needs in order that

- it can be taken into account during any feasibility analysis performed by the on-line scheduler as part of its admission protocol (see Chapter 10);
- it can be used to pace any incremental garbage collector to ensure that there is always adequate free memory available.

The above information is represented by the MemoryParameters class given below.

```
package javax.realtime;
public class MemoryParameters implement Cloneable {
  // fields
  public static final long NO_MAX;

  // constructors
  public MemoryParameters(long maxMemoryArea,
                          long maxImmortal);
    // Throws IllegalArgumentException.
```

```
public MemoryParameters(long maxMemoryArea,
                 long maxImmortal, long allocationRate);
  // Throws IllegalArgumentException.

// methods
public Object clone();
public long getAllocationRate();
public long getMaxImmortal();
public long getMaxMemoryArea();
public void setAllocationRate(long allocationRate);
public void setAllocationRateIfFeasible(
        long allocationRate);
public boolean setMaxImmortalIfFeasible(long maximum);
public boolean setMaxMemoryAreaIfFeasible(
        long maximum);
}
```

Each schedulable object has access to three types of memory area: scoped memory, immortal memory and heap memory. It can be created with a default memory. The MemoryParameters class allows the following information to be specified (the NO_MAX value indicates that there is no limit):

- the maximum amount of memory that will be consumed in the default memory area

- the maximum amount of memory that will be consumed in the immortal memory area

- the maximum number of bytes per second that will be allocated on the heap.

An instance of the MemoryParameters class can be associated with a schedulable object and this defines the requirements of that object. The requirements can be changed by calling the "set" methods. However, if the schedulable object has been guaranteed by the scheduler, the scheduler will need to undertake a new feasibility analysis.

Important notes

1. There is an obligation on an RTSJ implementation to check for violations of the memory usage and to throw appropriate exceptions.

2. Cloning a memory parameter object does not copy any association that is being maintained with a schedulable object.

Garbage Collection and the RTSJ

As mentioned in Section 8.1, the RTSJ does not rely on the presence of an efficient and predictable real-time garbage collector. However, it does not rule out that one might be present and consequently defines how the programmer might interact with it. The `MemoryParameters` class, just given, is one example of this. The other main example is via the abstract `GarbageCollector` class, which allows the maximum time between the collector's preemption-safe points to be obtained. This is the time that a schedulable object (which uses the heap) might have to wait before it can preempt any active garbage collection. The class definition is given below.

```
package javax.realtime;
public abstract class GarbageCollector {
  // methods
  public abstract RelativeTime getPreemptionLatency();
}
```

The current garbage collector can be obtained via the `RealtimeSystem` class:

```
package javax.realtime;
public final class RealtimeSystem {

  ...
  // methods
  public static GarbageCollector currentGC();

}
```

In general, garbage collectors for real-time systems are incremental and can be classified as *work-based* or *time-based* (Bacon, Cheng and Rajan, 2003). In a work-based collector, every application request, to allocate an object or assign a reference, performs a small amount of garbage collection work. The amount is determined by the required allocation rate. Here, the worst-case execution time of each application memory request includes a component for garbage collection. With a time-based collector, a real-time thread is scheduled to run at a given priority and with a given CPU budget in a given period. It performs as much garbage collection as it can and competes with other real-time threads for the processor. An feasibility analysis performed by the on-line or off-line scheduler must take into account this collector real-time thread. It is beyond the scope of this book to discuss individual strategies for real-time garbage collection (they do not affect the applications programmer other than as discussed in this section). See (Henriksson, 1998; Kim *et al.*, 1999; Siebert, 1999 and Bacon, Cheng and Rajan, 2003; Siebert, 2004) for possible approaches.

8.10 Summary

The lack of confidence in real-time garbage collection is one of the main inhibitors to the widespread use of Java in real-time and embedded systems. The RTSJ has introduced an alternative (additional) memory management facility based on the concept of memory areas. There are two types of nonheap memory areas. The first is a singleton immortal memory that is never subject to garbage collection delays. Once an object is created in immortal memory, it remains there. Programmers have to reuse the space explicitly themselves.

The second type of memory area is scoped memory, which schedulable objects can enter and leave. When there are no schedulable objects active in a scoped memory area, all the objects are destroyed and their memory reclaimed.

Because of the variety of memory areas, the RTSJ has strict assignment rules between them in order to ensure that dangling references do not occur. These rules are complicated by the presence of concurrent activities. They are summarized below:

- Objects in the heap or the immortal memory area cannot reference objects in scoped memory areas.

- Objects in one scoped memory area cannot reference objects in another more deeply nested scoped memory area.

- A memory area can only have a single parent.

There is little doubt that nonheap memory management is one of the most complicated areas of the RTSJ, and one that has a major impact on the overheads of the virtual machine and on the structure of application code. This chapter has reviewed many of the problems and has given some guidelines on safe usage. In the long-term, real-time garbage collection algorithms will mature and become trusted in time-critical applications. In the meantime, the RTSJ provides alternative mechanisms for memory management.

9 Clocks and Time

In Section 4.2, it was noted that Java supports the notion of a wall clock (calendar time) only and that for many applications, a clock based on UTC (Coordinated Universal Time) is sufficient. However, real-time systems often require additional functionality. In particular, they may need access to the following (OMG, 2002).

1. A monotonic clock that progresses at a constant rate and is not subject to the insertion of extra ticks to reflect leap seconds (as UTC clocks are). A constant rate is required for control algorithms that need to execute on a regular basis. Many monotonic clocks are also relative to system startup and can be used only to measure the passage of time, not calendar time. A monotonic clock is also useful for delaying a thread for a period of time, for example, while it waits for a device to respond. In addition, it may be used to provide timeouts so that the nonoccurrence of some event (for example an interrupt) can be detected.

2. A countdown clock that can be paused, continued or reset (for example, the clock that counts down to the launch of a space shuttle).

3. A CPU execution time clock that measures the amount of CPU time that is being consumed by a particular thread or object.

All of the above clocks also need a resolution that is potentially finer than the millisecond level. They may all be based on the same underlying physical clock, or be supported by separate clocks. Where more than one clock is provided, the relationship between them may be important – in particular, whether their values can drift apart. Even with a single clock, drift in relation to the external time frame will be important.

This chapter considers the additional clock and time classes that are provided by the RTSJ to augment the Java facilities. The concept of relative time, absolute time and rational time values are introduced along with the operations that can be performed on them. The notions of a real-time clock and a wall clock are also presented along with some examples of their use.

9.1 The Basic Model

The RTSJ defines a hierarchy of time classes rooted in the abstract `HighResolutionTime` class. This abstract class has three subclasses: one that represents absolute time, one that represents relative time, and one that represents rational time. The intention is to allow support for time values down to nanosecond accuracy. A range of clocks are supported via the abstract `Clock` class.

Version 1.0 notes

Version 1.0 of the RTSJ was a little underspecified in the relationship between high resolution time objects and clocks. Version 1.0.1 explicitly requires that all high resolution time objects have an associated clock and that operations that take more than one high resolution time objects must have compatible clocks or `IllegalArgumentExceptions` will be thrown.

High-resolution time values

First, consider the `HighResolutionTime` class. As with all classes that are essentially abstract data types, there are methods to read, write, compare and clone time values, all of which are self-explanatory. Some methods, however, do need further consideration. The method `compareTo`, which takes an arbitrary object, is provided so that the class can implement the `java.lang.Comparable` interface. If an object passed to this method is not a `HighResolutionTime` type, the method will throw `ClassCastException`. In contrast, the `equals` method that overrides its counterpart in the `Object` class will return -1. Note, that two high-resolution `time` objects must have the same clock if they are to be compared (otherwise, an `IllegalArgumentException` is thrown). As `equals` is overridden, the corresponding `hashCode` method must be provided.

```
package javax.realtime;
public abstract class HighResolutionTime
      implements Comparable, Cloneable {
  // methods
  public abstract AbsoluteTime absolute(Clock clock);
  public abstract AbsoluteTime absolute(
      Clock clock, AbsoluteTime destination);
  public Object clone();
  public int compareTo(HighResolutionTime time);
    // Throws ClassCastException, IllegalArgumentException.
  public int compareTo(Object object);
    // Throws ClassCastException, IllegalArgumentException.
  public boolean equals(HighResolutionTime time);
  public boolean equals(Object object);
  public Clock getClock();
  public final long getMilliseconds();
```

```
    public final int getNanoseconds();
    public int hashCode();
    public abstract RelativeTime relative(Clock clock);
    public abstract RelativeTime relative(
            Clock clock, RelativeTime time);
    public void set(HighResolutionTime time);
      // Throws ClassCastException.
    public void set(long millis);
    public void set(long millis, int nanos);
      // Throws IllegalArgumentException.
    public static void waitForObject(
            Object target, HighResolutionTime time)
      throws InterruptedException;
      // Throws IllegalArgumentException,
      // IllegalThreadStateException.
}
```

The abstract methods (`absolute` and `relative`) allow time types that are relative to be re-expressed as absolute time values and vice versa. The methods also allow the clocks associated with the values to be changed. The concrete implementation of these methods will be provided by the subclasses. The role of these methods is to convert the encapsulated time (be it absolute, relative or rational) to an absolute time relative to some clock (or vice versa) according to the following:

absolute to absolute. The value returned has the same millisecond and nanosecond components as the encapsulated time value. The returned object is associated with the given clock.

absolute to relative. The value returned is the value of the encapsulated absolute time minus the current time as measured from the given clock parameter. The returned object is associated with the given clock.

relative to relative. The value returned has the same millisecond and nanosecond components as the encapsulated time value. The returned object is associated with the given clock.

relative to absolute. The value returned is the value of current time as measured from the given clock parameter plus the encapsulated relative time. The returned object is associated with the given clock.

In the above, if a null `Clock` value is given as a parameter, the real-time clock is assumed.

Also consider, for example, the method `absolute`, which takes a destination parameter. If an `AbsoluteTime` object is passed as a parameter, that object is over-written to reflect the encapsulated time value. Furthermore, the same object is also returned by the function. If a null object is passed as a parameter, a new object is created and returned. This approach also gives the caller full control over the memory allocated for the returned object. If a different clock parameter is passed (to that of the encapsu-lated clock), the return value is associated with the given clock.

Warning

Changing the clock associated with a time value is potentially unsafe, particularly for absolute time values. This is because absolute time values are represented as a num-ber of milliseconds and nanoseconds since an epoch. Different clocks may have dif-ferent epochs.

It should also be noted that when setting the millisecond and nanosecond compo-nent of a high-resolution time type, the nanosecond component can be greater than one millisecond, however, all values held internally in the object are normalized, The `IllegalArgumentException` is thrown if this normalization results in the milli-seconds component overflowing.

Finally, the `waitForObject` static method is introduced to enable a schedula-ble object to have a high-resolution timeout while waiting for a condition to be signaled inside a monitor. This is needed because the `wait` method in the `Object` class is defined to be final. Of course, the calling schedulable object must hold the lock on the `target` object when this method is called.

Warning

The `waitForObject` does not resolve the problem of determining if the schedula-ble object was woken by a `notify` method call or by a timeout (see Section 4.2). It does, however, allow both relative and absolute time values to be specified. As with the Java `wait` method, `waitForObject` throws `IllegalArgumentExcep-tion` if a negative (relative) time value is given and `IllegalThreadStateEx-ception` if the calling thread has not already locked the target object.

Absolute time values

The `AbsoluteTime` class is given below. Again the methods are self-explanatory. An absolute time is actually expressed as a time relative to a given epoch. Note that an absolute time can have either a positive or a negative value and that, by default, it is rel-ative to the epoch of the real-time clock (with the millisecond and nanosecond compo-nents set to zero). Further, any attempt to add or subtract time values from different clocks will result in an exception (`IllegalArgumentException`) being thrown.

For example, it makes no sense to subtract an absolute time value measured by one clock from an absolute time value measured by another.

```java
package javax.realtime;
public class AbsoluteTime extends HighResolutionTime {
  // constructors
  // The following assume the real-time clock.
  public AbsoluteTime();
  public AbsoluteTime(AbsoluteTime time);
  public AbsoluteTime(java.util.Date date);
  public AbsoluteTime(long millis, int nanos);
    // Throws IllegalArgumentException.

  // Version 1.0.1 has added the following constructors.
  public AbsoluteTime(Clock clock);
  public AbsoluteTime(AbsoluteTime time, Clock clock);
  public AbsoluteTime(java.util.Date date, Clock clock);
  public AbsoluteTime(long millis, int nanos, Clock clock);
    // Throws IllegalArgumentException.

  // methods
  public AbsoluteTime absolute(Clock clock);
  public AbsoluteTime absolute(Clock clock,
                               AbsoluteTime destination);

  // The following add methods all throw
  // ArithmeticException if there is an overflow.
  public AbsoluteTime add(long millis, int nanos);
  public AbsoluteTime add(long millis, int nanos,
                          AbsoluteTime destination);
  public AbsoluteTime add(RelativeTime time);
  public AbsoluteTime add(RelativeTime time,
                          AbsoluteTime destination);

  public java.util.Date getDate();
    // Throws UnsupportedOperationException.

  public RelativeTime relative(Clock clock);
  public RelativeTime relative(Clock clock,
                               AbsoluteTime destination);

  public void set(java.util.Date date);
    // Throws UnsupportedOperationException.
```

```
    // The following subtract methods all throw
    // ArithmeticException if there is an overflow.
    public RelativeTime subtract(AbsoluteTime time);
    public RelativeTime subtract(AbsoluteTime time,
                                        RelativeTime destination);
    public AbsoluteTime subtract(RelativeTime time);
    public AbsoluteTime subtract(RelativeTime time,
                                        AbsoluteTime destination);
    public String toString();
}
```

Warning   Some clocks have no external synchronization. Hence, to request that the absolute time be set from, or converted to, the java.util.Date format will result in an exception (UnsupportedOperationException) being thrown. A good example of such a clock is one which measures the CPU time consumed by a thread.

Relative time   A relative time value is an interval of time measured by some clock; for example, 20 milliseconds measured by the real-time clock.

```
package javax.realtime;
public class RelativeTime extends HighResolutionTime {
  // constructors
  // The following assume the real-time clock.
  public RelativeTime();
  public RelativeTime(long millis, int nanos);
    // Throws IllegalArgumentException.
  public RelativeTime(RelativeTime time);

  // Version 1.0.1 has added the following constructors.
  public RelativeTime(Clock clock);
  public RelativeTime(long millis, int nanos,
                      Clock clock);
    // Throws IllegalArgumentException.
  public RelativeTime(RelativeTime time, Clock clock);

  // methods
  public AbsoluteTime absolute(Clock clock);
  public AbsoluteTime absolute(Clock clock,
                                        AbsoluteTime destination);
```

```
// The following add methods all throw
// ArithmeticException if there is an overflow.
public RelativeTime add(long millis, int nanos);
public RelativeTime add(long millis, int nanos,
                        RelativeTime destination);
public RelativeTime add(RelativeTime time);
public RelativeTime add(RelativeTime time,
                        RelativeTime destination);
public RelativeTime relative(Clock clock);
public RelativeTime relative(Clock clock,
                             RelativeTime destination);

// The following subtract methods all throw
// ArithmeticException if there is an overflow.

public RelativeTime subtract(RelativeTime time);
public RelativeTime subtract(RelativeTime time,
                             RelativeTime destination);
public String toString();

// The following methods have been deprecated at
// Version 1.0.1 as the RationalTime class has been
// deprecated.
public void addInterarrivalTo(
        AbsoluteTime destination);
public RelativeTime getInterarrivalTime();
public RelativeTime getInterarrivalTime(
                    RelativeTime destination);
}
```

The set of deprecated methods are associated with the RationalTime class discussed below.

Rational time   Rational time is a relative time type, which has an associated frequency. It is used to represent the rate at which certain events occur (for example, periodic thread execution). Hence, a RationalTime value with, say, an interval of 1 second and a frequency of 100, has a inter-arrival time of 10 milliseconds. If no interval is given, the frequency is deemed to be in cycles per second and, hence is equivalent to an interval of 1000 milliseconds with the given frequency.

```
package javax.realtime;
public class RationalTime extends RelativeTime {
    // This class has been deprecated at Version 1.0.1
```

```
// constructors
// The following constructors throw
// IllegalArgumentException if the parameters
// are less than zero or cannot be normalized.
public RationalTime(int frequency);
public RationalTime(int frequency, long millis,
    int nanos);
public RationalTime(int frequency,
    RelativeTime interval);

// methods
public AbsoluteTime absolute(Clock clock,
                                 AbsoluteTime destination);
public void addInterarrivalTo(
        AbsoluteTime destination);
public int getFrequency();
public RelativeTime getInterarrivalTime();
public RelativeTime getInterarrivalTime(
                    RelativeTime destination);
public void set(long millis, int nanos);
  // Throws IllegalArgumentException.
public void setFrequency(int frequency);
  // Throws ArithmeticException.
}
```

Important note

When a rational time is used to represent the frequency of a periodic activity, then the system only has to guarantee that the activity occurs at the frequency requested. There is no requirement for the releases of the activity to be equally spaced within time. Indeed, the granularity of the associated clock may be such that it cannot have equally spaced releases.

Warning and version 1.0 note

RationalTime was a controversial class in version 1.0 of the RTSJ. The reasons for making RationalTime a subclass of HighResolutionTime were not clear and caused problems elsewhere in the specification (for example, the idea of passing a RationalTime to, say, the waitForObject method is very strange; an implementation will use the interval divided by the frequency in these circumstances — or millis/nanos or one second if the other constructors are used). For these reasons, the class has been deprecated in version 1.0.1 of the RTSJ and alternative approaches to meeting the original requirements will be provided in version 1.1.

Clocks   The RTSJ Clock class defines the abstract class from which all clocks are derived. The specification allows many different types of clocks; for example, there could be an execution-time clock which measures the amount of execution time being consumed. There is always one real-time clock which advances monotonically. This means that the clock can never go backwards. The RTSJ also recommends that the real-time clock should progress uniformly, not stall and not be subject to the insertion of leap ticks. The method getRealtimeClock allows this clock to be obtained; note that this is a static method and, therefore, it can be called directly without knowledge of any subclasses. Other methods are provided to get the resolution of a clock and, if the hardware permits, to set the resolution of a clock. If the epoch of the clock is synchronized with the external time frame, getEpochOffset will return a value consistent with java.util.Date. If not, the exception UnsupportedOperationException will be thrown.

```
package javax.realtime;
public abstract class Clock {
  // constructor
  public Clock();

  // methods
  public static Clock getRealtimeClock();
  public abstract RelativeTime getResolution();
  public abstract AbsoluteTime getTime();
  public abstract AbsoluteTime getTime(
                  AbsoluteTime time);
  public abstract void setResolution(
                          RelativeTime resolution);
  // The following method has been added at version 1.0.1
  public abstract RelativeTime getEpochOffset();
    // Throws UnsupportedOperationException.
}
```

Version 1.1 note   Version 1.1 of the specification is likely to provide better integration between the Java wall clock and the Clock class. It is likely that a new static method will be added to the Clock class, which will allow the Java wall clock to be obtained. New clocks may also be introduced to measure the CPU time consumed by a schedulable object.

Version 1.0 note

Version 1.0 of the RTSJ was a little too restrictive in defining the epoch of all clocks to be January 1, 1970, GMT. The epoch should be clock dependent. For example, the epoch for a monotonic clock might be system start-up time. Version 1.1 is likely to make some further changes in this area.

Note also, the `getTime(AbsoluteTime time)` method returned void in version 1.0.

Warning

Other standards defines the notion of a real-time clock, for example, both POSIX and Ada. All these clocks have slightly different semantics. For example, in POSIX the real-time clock is not monotonic and in Ada it does not have a defined epoch.

9.2 Examples

Measuring the passage of time

First, consider a simple example where the elapsed time taken to perform a computation is measured:

```
{
    AbsoluteTime oldTime, newTime;
    RelativeTime interval;
    Clock clock = Clock.getRealtimeClock();
    oldTime = clock.getTime();
    // Other computations.
    newTime = clock.getTime();
    interval = newTime.subtract(oldTime);
}
```

Of course, this approach would only measure the approximate elapsed time, as the schedulable object executing the code may be preempted after it has finished the computation and before it reads the new time.

A launch clock

As further illustration of the use of some of the classes defined in this chapter, consider a launch clock, such as that used by the Space Shuttle. A launch clock is clock that is initiated with a relative time value and an absolute time value. The absolute time value is the time at which the clock is to start ticking. The relative time value is the duration of the countdown. The countdown can be stopped, restarted, or reset.

Although the launch clock is more like an RTSJ `Timer` (see Section 7.7) than a RTSJ `Clock`, it can be created from just the facilities used in this chapter and Java threads. Its implementation is given below. The class extends the `Thread` class. The constructor saves the start time and the duration. The resolution of the countdown is one second, and a function allows the current launch time to be queried (assuming it is not stopped). Note, the thread will run at the default priority. This will affect the accuracy of the countdown process. To increase the accuracy, a real-time thread should be used and run at a high priority. The example assumes that all high resolution time objects are associated with the real-time clock.

```
import javax.realtime.*;
public class LaunchClock extends Thread {
  public LaunchClock(AbsoluteTime at,
        RelativeTime countDown) {
    super();
    if(at == null | countDown == null) throw
       new IllegalArgumentException();
    startTime = at;
    remainingTime = countDown;
    myClock = Clock.getRealtimeClock();
    counting = true;
    go = false;
    tick = new RelativeTime(1000,0);
  }
  public RelativeTime getResolution() {
    return tick;
  }
  public synchronized AbsoluteTime getCurrentLaunchTime() {
    if(myClock.getTime().compareTo(startTime) < 0)
      return new AbsolutTime(
         startTime.add(remainingTime));
    else
      return new AbsoluteTime(
         myClock.geTime().add(remainingTime));
  }
  ...
  private AbsoluteTime startTime;
  private RelativeTime remainingTime;
  private RelativeTime tick;
  private Clock myClock;
  private boolean counting;
  private boolean go;
}
```

Next, there are various methods which control the countdown process. The `counting` variable is used to indicate whether the countdown is in progress or whether it has been stopped. A change in its status results in the `notifyAll` method being called.

```java
import javax.realtime.*;
public class LaunchClock extends Thread {
  ...

  public synchronized void stopCountDown() {
    counting = false;
    notifyAll();
  }

  public synchronized void restartCountDown() {
    counting = true;
    notifyAll();
  }

  public synchronized void resetCountDown(
               RelativeTime to) {
    remainingTime = to;
  }

  ...
}
```

Finally, the `launch` and `run` methods can be presented. The `launch` method simply waits until the launch is go.

```java
import javax.realtime.*;
public class LaunchClock extends Thread {
  ...

  public synchronized void launch() throws Exception {
    while(!go) {
      try {
        wait();
      } catch(InterruptedException ie) {
        throw new Exception("Launch failed: waiting");
      }
    }
    // Launch is go.
  }
```

The run method first uses the waitForObject method to wait until the countdown should start (note that it uses the default real-time clock). It then loops around counting down one second at a time (again using the waitForObject method). If the count is stopped, the wait is immediately terminated (the timing is only approximate here, to a granularity of one second).

```
public void run() {
  synchronized(this) {
    try {
      while(myClock.getTime().compareTo(startTime) < 0)
          HighResolutionTime.waitForObject(
                  this, startTime);
      while(remainingTime.getMilliseconds() > 0) {
        while(!counting) wait();
        HighResolutionTime.waitForObject(this, tick);
        remainingTime.set(
            remainingTime.getMilliseconds() -
            tick.getMilliseconds());
      }
    } catch(InterruptedException ie) {
      ...
    }
    go = true;
    notifyAll();
  }
}
```

9.3 Summary

Clocks and time are fundamental to any real-time system. The RTSJ has augmented the Java facilities with high resolution time types (both relative and absolute) and a framework for supporting various clocks. A real-time clock is guaranteed to be supported by any compliant RTSJ implementation. This is a monotonically non-decreasing clock that progresses at a uniform rate.

The facilities of clock and times were underspecified in version 1.0 of the RTSJ and there have been some significant changes in version 1.0.1. of the specification. Further changes are likely in version 1.1.

10 Scheduling and Schedulable Objects

Introduction and chapter structure

Real-time systems differ from traditional information processing systems in that they must be able to interact with their environments in a timely and predictable manner. The days when *real-time* simply meant *fast* have long gone. It is no longer acceptable to build systems and hope that they meet their timing requirements. Instead, designers must engineer analyzable systems whose timing properties can be predicted and mathematically proven to be correct (possibly from within a probabilistic framework). This change in practice has been brought about by advances in scheduling.

> *Scheduling is the ordering of thread/process executions so that the underlying hardware resources (processors, networks, etc.) and software resources (shared data objects) are efficiently and predictably used.*

Scheduling consists of three components:

- an algorithm for ordering access to resources (scheduling policy)
- an algorithm for allocating the resources (scheduling mechanism)
- a means of predicting the worst-case behavior of the system when the policy and mechanism are applied (schedulability analysis – called feasibility analysis by the RTSJ).

Once the worst-case behavior of the system has been predicted, it can be compared with the system's timing requirements to ensure that all deadlines will be met.

This chapter considers scheduling and the support for it provided by the RTSJ. First, an introduction to fixed priority scheduling is given, followed by an overview of the RTSJ's basic model. The various parameters needed for scheduling are then considered in detail. This is followed by an example of how simple Earliest-Deadline-First (EDF) scheduling can be implemented from within a priority-based framework.

10.1 Scheduling and Fixed Priority Scheduling

Although there have been many different scheduling approaches developed over the last 10 to 15 years, one coherent approach, based around the use of fixed priorities, has become popular. Fixed priority scheduling (FPS) can be defined in terms of its scheduling policy, its scheduling mechanism and its associated feasibility analysis techniques.

Scheduling policy. FPS requires that

- schedulable objects are statically allocated to processors – this means that the same processor is always responsible for executing a particular schedulable object; this approach is more predictable than, say, allowing an arbitrary processor (in a multiprocessor system) to execute a schedulable object as and when required;

- the execution of schedulable objects on a single processor are ordered according to a priority;

- priorities are assigned to schedulable objects at their creation time – although no particular priority assignment algorithm is mandated by FPS, it is usual to assign priorities according to the relative deadline of the schedulable object (relative to the object's release time); the shorter the deadline, the higher the priority (this is known as *deadline monotonic priority ordering*);

- priority inheritance be implemented when accessing resources (this topic is covered in Chapter 14).

Scheduling mechanism. FPS requires preemptive priority-based dispatching of schedulable objects – the processing resource is always given to the highest-priority runnable schedulable object allocated to that processor.

Feasibility analysis. There are many different techniques for analyzing whether a fixed priority-based system will meet its deadlines. Perhaps the most flexible is *response time analysis.*

There are, of course, other approaches to scheduling, such as that based on earliest deadline first (EDF). Here, the execution of schedulable objects is ordered according to the closest absolute deadline. See (Burns and Wellings, 2001) and (Stankovic *et al*, 1998) for a detailed discussion on fixed priority (with response time analysis) and earliest deadline scheduling respectively. It is beyond the scope of this book to discuss the details of schedulability analysis. However, it is important to understand what basic information about the system must be known in order to undertake the analysis. Most approaches view the system as consisting of a number of schedulable objects. Each schedulable object is characterized by the following:

Release profile. Typically after a schedulable object is *started*, it waits to be *released* (or may be released immediately); when released, it performs some computation and then waits to be released again (the time at which it waits is often called its *completion time*). The release profile defines the frequency with which the releases occur; they may be *time triggered* or *event triggered*. Time-triggered releases usually occur on a regular basis, they are called *periodic* releases. Event-triggered releases are typically classified into *sporadic* (meaning that they are irregular but with a minimum inter-arrival time) or *aperiodic* (meaning that no minimum inter-arrival assumptions can be made, although other information may be available, such as the distribution of releases). Once a schedulable object has been released, it is eligible for execution. During its execution, it may be blocked waiting for a resource. When the resource becomes available, the schedulable object is again eligible for execution.

Processing cost per release. This is some measure of how much of the processor's time is required to execute the computation associated with the schedulable object's release (that is, after it has been released and until it has completed). This may be a worst-case value or an average value depending on the feasibility analysis being used.

Other hardware resources required per release. This is some measure of the hardware resources needed (other than the processor). For networks, it is usually the time needed (or bandwidth required) to send the schedulable object's messages across the network. For memory, it is the amount of memory required by the schedulable object (and if appropriate, the types of memory).

Software resources required per release. This is a list of the nonshareable resources that are required for each release of the schedulable object and the processing cost of using each resource. Access to nonshareable resources is a critical factor when performing schedulability analysis. This is because nonshareable resources are usually nonpreemptible. Consequently, when a schedulable object tries to acquire a resource, it may be blocked if that resource is already in use. This blocking time has to be taken into account in any analysis. If the list of software resources is not available then a maximum blocking time must be provided.

Deadline. The time that the schedulable object has to complete the computation associated with each release. As usually only a single deadline is given, the time is a relative value rather than an absolute value. Where the deadline of a schedulable object is greater than its minimum period between releases (or it has overrun its deadline and the application has decided to let it continue), the schedulable object may be released even though the execution associated with the previous release has not completed. In this case, when the schedulable object does complete, it is immediately rescheduled for execution.

Value. A metric that indicates the schedulable object's contribution to the overall functionality of the application. It may be

- a very coarse indication (such as safety critical, mission critical, non critical),
- a numeric value giving a measure for a successful meeting of a deadline, or

- a time-valued function that takes the time at which the schedulable object completes and returns a measure of the value (for those systems where there is no fixed deadline or where quality of service is the main issue).

The information needed for the above characteristics comes from a variety of sources. It may be specified as part of the application's requirements (for example, the value parameter), derived during the system design (for example, the deadline parameters), or result from static or dynamic analysis of the final code (for example, the cost and blocking time parameters).

Off-line and on-line analysis

One of the key characteristics of schedulability (feasibility) analysis is whether the analysis is performed off-line or on-line. For safety critical systems, where the deadlines associated with schedulable objects must always be met (so-called *hard* real-time systems), off-line analysis is essential, as the system must not enter service if there is a possibility of deadlines being missed. Other systems do not have such stringent timing requirements or do not have a predictable worst-case behavior. In these cases, on-line analysis may be appropriate or, indeed, the only option available. These systems must be able to tolerate schedulable objects not being feasible (that is, failing the schedulability analysis) and offer degraded services. Furthermore, they must be able to handle deadlines being missed or situations where the assumed worst-case loading scenario has been violated.

Mode changes

The essence of fixed priority systems is that the priorities of the schedulable objects do not change except on a temporary basis as a result of priority inheritance (see Chapter 14). However, in many applications, not all the schedulable objects are needed at all times during the lifetime of the system. For example, a fly-by-wire civil aircraft may have many different components that control take-off, cruising and landing. The component used to lower the undercarriage is not needed during cruising. Furthermore, although some components are used in more than one phase of the flight, their scheduling-related characteristics may change. For example, a component responsible for monitoring wind shear needs to be more responsive on landing than when cruising.

These characteristics present a problem for fixed priority systems. To assume that all components are active all the time (and with their most demanding resource requirements) leads to very pessimistic analysis and an overengineered system. To avoid this, real-time systems are considered to have several *modes of operation*. Changes between modes are usually well planned. The schedulability analysis is performed on a per mode basis and on the intervals during which mode changes occur. Within each mode of operation, schedulable objects have fixed priority (other than when subjected to priority inheritance). However, a schedulable object's priority may be different in different modes. Consequently, the programmer may need to change its priority at run-time. Hence, although priorities may change as a result of both priority inheritance and mode changes, the system is still viewed as being fixed priority.

10.2 The Basic Model

The RTSJ provides a framework from within which on-line feasibility analysis of priority-based systems can be performed for single-processor systems. The specification also allows the real-time JVM to monitor the resources being used and to release asynchronous event handlers if this use of resources goes beyond that specified by the programmer.

As mentioned in Section 7.5, the RTSJ introduces the notion of a *schedulable object* rather than considering only threads. A schedulable object is any object that implements the Schedulable interface (although the priority scheduler only supports real-time threads and asynchronous event handlers). This allows the following attributes to be associated with each schedulable object.

- ReleaseParameters – Giving the processing cost for each release of the object and its deadline; if the object is released periodically or sporadically, then subclasses allow an interval to be given. Event handlers can be specified for the situation where the deadline is missed or the processing resource consumed becomes greater than the cost specified. *However, note that there is no requirement for a real-time JVM to monitor the processing time consumed by a schedulable object. If it does, then there is a requirement that a schedulable object be given no more than cost processing units each release (see Section 10.4.1).*

- SchedulingParameters – The SchedulingParameters class is empty; however, subclasses allow the priority of the object to be specified along with its importance to the overall functioning of the application. Although the RTSJ specifies a minimum range of real-time priorities (28), it makes no statement on the allowed values of the importance parameter.

- MemoryParameters – Giving the maximum amount of memory used by the object in its default memory area, the maximum amount of memory used in immortal memory, and a maximum allocation rate of heap memory. Where memory parameters are given by an application, it is required that the real-time JVM monitor the memory consumed and report any violation.

- ProcessingGroupParameters – This allows several schedulable objects to be treated as a group and to have an associated period, cost and deadline (see Section 10.4.5).

Version 1.1 note

It should be noted that version 1.0.1 of the RTSJ makes no mention of blocking time in any of the parameters associated with schedulable objects. The assumption is that a particular implementation will subclass ReleaseParameters to bring in this data. Typically, this will be a RelativeTime set by the programmer as a result of off-line analysis of the code.

It is likely that version 1.1 will formally introduce blocking time into the ReleaseParameters class.

**The
Schedulable
interface**

The methods in the Schedulable interface can be divided into three groups.

- Methods that will communicate with the scheduler and will result in the scheduler either adding or removing the schedulable object from the list of objects it manages (called its *feasibility set*), or changing the parameters associated with the schedulable object (but only if the resulting system is feasible). The scheduler performs a feasibility test on the objects it manages and the methods return true if the system is feasible, false otherwise. Note that changing the parameters of a schedulable object that is not in the current feasibility set is equivalent to "adding and changing" the parameters if feasible.

- Methods that get or set the parameter classes associated with the schedulable object. If the parameter object set is different from the one currently associated with the schedulable object, the previous value is lost and the new one will be used in any future feasibility analysis performed by the scheduler. Note these methods do not result in feasibility analysis being performed and the parameters are changed even if the resulting system is not feasible.

- Methods that get or set the scheduler. For systems that support more than one scheduler, these methods allow the scheduler associated with the schedulable object to be manipulated. Note the second setScheduler method, as well as setting the scheduler, also informs the scheduler of the parameter classes for the schedulable object.

The RTSJ defines two classes that implement the Schedulable interface: AsyncEventHandler and RealtimeThread. The details of these are discussed in Chapters 11 and 12 respectively. The specification of the parameter classes are given later in this chapter.

The full definition of the Schedulable interface is given below.

```java
package javax.realtime;
public interface Schedulable extends Runnable {

    // Methods which result in feasibility being tested.
    public boolean addIfFeasible();
    public boolean addToFeasibility();
    public boolean removeFromFeasibility();

    // The remaining methods throw one or more of the
    // following unchecked exceptions:
    //    IllegalArgumentException - if the parameter
    //       values are not compatible with the scheduler.
    //    IllegalAssignmentError - if this object cannot hold
    //       references to all the parameter objects or the
    //       parameters cannot hold references to this object.
```

```
//    IllegalThreadStateException - if the new release
//      parameters change the schedulable object from
//      periodic scheduling to some other protocol and
//      the schedulable object is currently waiting for
//      the next release, or if the sched parameter is
//      not compatible with the scheduler associated
//      this schedulable object.


public boolean setIfFeasible(
   ReleaseParameters release, MemoryParameters memory);
public boolean setIfFeasible(
   ReleaseParameters release, MemoryParameters memory,
   ProcessingGroupParameters groupParameters);
public boolean setIfFeasible(
   ReleaseParameters release,
   ProcessingGroupParameters groupParameters);
public boolean setIfFeasible(
   SchedulingParameters sched,
   ReleaseParameters release, MemoryParameters memory);
public boolean setIfFeasible(
   SchedulingParameters sched,
   ReleaseParameters release, MemoryParameters memory,
   ProcessingGroupParameters groupParameters);

public boolean setMemoryParametersIfFeasible(
   MemoryParameters memory);
public boolean setProcessingGroupParametersIfFeasible(
   ProcessingGroupParameters groupParameters);
public boolean setReleaseParametersIfFeasible(
   ReleaseParameters release);
public boolean setSchedulingParametersIfFeasible(
   SchedulingParameters sched);

// Methods which get/set the various parameter classes.
// No feasibility analysis is performed.
public MemoryParameters getMemoryParameters();
public void setMemoryParameters(MemoryParameters memory);
public ProcessingGroupParameters
      getProcessingGroupParameters();
```

```
    public void setProcessingGroupParameters(
            ProcessingGroupParameters groupParameters);
    public ReleaseParameters getReleaseParameters();
    public void setReleaseParameters(
      ReleaseParameters release);
    public SchedulingParameters getSchedulingParameters();
    public void setSchedulingParameters(
      SchedulingParameters sched);

    // Methods which get or set the scheduler.
    public Scheduler getScheduler();
    public void setScheduler(Scheduler scheduler);
    public void setScheduler(Scheduler scheduler,
        SchedulingParameters scheduling,
        ReleaseParameters release, MemoryParameters memory,
        ProcessingGroupParameters processing);
}
```

Important note

Changing the parameters of a schedulable object while it is executing can potentially undermine any feasibility analysis that has been performed and cause deadlines to be missed. Consequently, the RTSJ provides methods that allow changes of parameters to occur only if the new set of schedulable objects is feasible. In these situations, the new parameters may not have an impact on a schedulable object's executions *until the end of its current release* (it depends on the current scheduler). Some applications will need the changes to take place *unconditionally* (and to affect the current release). These unconditional changes are supported by the RTSJ through the methods that do not test for feasibility. In both cases, the scheduler's feasibility set is updated.

Version 1.1 note

The Schedulable interface is likely to change in version of 1.1 of the RTSJ to allow for a better handling of cost enforcement (see Section 10.4.1).

10.2.1 Schedulers

As well as generalizing threads to schedulable objects, the RTSJ also generalizes the notion of priority to one of *execution eligibility*. This is so that it can leave the door open for implementations to provide other schedulers (say value-based schedulers or earliest-deadline-first schedulers). All schedulers, however, must follow the framework specified by the abstract Scheduler class.

```
package javax.realtime;
public abstract class Scheduler {
  // constructors
  protected Scheduler();

  // methods
  // The methods throw IllegalArgumentException if null
  // release or schedulable parameters are passed, and
  // IllegalAssignmentError if the scheduler cannot hold
  // a reference to the schedulable object.
  protected abstract boolean addToFeasibility(
      Schedulable schedulable);
  protected abstract boolean removeFromFeasibility(
      Schedulable schedulable);

  public abstract boolean isFeasible();

  public abstract boolean setIfFeasible(
      Schedulable schedulable, ReleaseParameters release,
      MemoryParameters memory);
  public abstract boolean setIfFeasible(
      Schedulable schedulable, ReleaseParameters release,
      MemoryParameters memory,
      ProcessingGroupParameters group);

  public abstract void fireSchedulable(
      Schedulable schedulable);
    // Throws UnsupportedOperationException if the scheduler
    // does not support this type of schedulable object.
  public static Scheduler getDefaultScheduler();
  public abstract String getPolicyName();
  public static void setDefaultScheduler(
          Scheduler scheduler);
}
```

Each scheduler maintains a set of schedulable objects that it manages. It may perform some form of feasibility analysis on that set to determine if the objects will meet their deadlines. The protected methods are called from schedulable objects and enable those objects to be unconditionally added to or removed from the list, the boolean return values indicate whether the resulting system is feasible. The setIfFeasible methods provides an atomic operation that allows the parameters of a schedulable object to be changed only if it does not affect the feasibility of the whole set of objects being managed by the scheduler. The isFeasible method can be called to determine if the current set of objects can be scheduled to meet their deadlines.

Important
note

Even if a scheduler indicates that a set of schedulable objects is infeasible, there might still be some merit in allowing those objects to execute. In particular, the cost the scheduler is given may represent the worst-case estimates and it may be extremely unlikely that all schedulable objects consume their worst-case cost at the same time. Furthermore, worst-case blocking may not occur and sporadic objects may not be released at their worst-case frequency.

The fireSchedulable method, when called, informs the scheduler that a new schedulable object is ready for release. Typically, this method would only be called by an application if an RTSJ vendor implements its own schedulable object type (rather than using the predefined real-time thread or asynchronous event handler abstractions). However, it is far from clear how such implementer-defined schedulable objects can indicate that they have completed their release.

There are two static methods in the Scheduler class, which allow the default scheduler to be set and obtained. The method getPolicyName allows a scheduler to return a string that characterizes its policy. For example, an EDF scheduler might return "EdfScheduler".

Important
notes

It should be stressed that the RTSJ does not insist that feasibility analysis should be performed, it simply demands that if it is then it should follow the framework given by the Scheduler class. It is acceptable for an implementation to simply return true when asked if the set of objects is feasible. This would indicate that the scheduler assumes that it has access to an adequately fast computer. Arguably, it would be better for a scheduler to return false when asked about feasibility. After all, it cannot verify that the system is schedulable.

Where a scheduler does provide feasibility analysis, it is important for the implementation to document the assumptions that the analysis makes. For example, a scheduler that simply calculates the processor utilization and returns true if it is less that 100% is probably assuming that the schedulable objects do not share any resources and, therefore, are not subject to blocking.

10.3 The Priority Scheduler

The only scheduler that the RTSJ fully defines is a priority scheduler, which can be summarized as follows.

Scheduling policy. The PriorityScheduler

- supports the notion of *base* and *active* priority;

- orders the execution of schedulable objects on a single processor according to the active priority;

- supports a real-time priority range of at least 28 unique priorities (the larger the value, the higher the priority);

- requires the programmer to assign the base priorities (say, according to the relative deadline of the schedulable object);

- requires the deadline of a schedulable object with periodic release parameters to be less than or equal to the period;

- allows base priorities to be changed by the programmer at run-time;

- supports priority inheritance or priority ceiling emulation inheritance for synchronized objects (see Chapter 14);

- assigns the active priority of a schedulable object to be the higher of its base priority and any priority it has inherited.

Scheduling mechanism. The `PriorityScheduler`

- supports preemptive priority-based dispatching of schedulable objects – the processor resource is always given to the highest-priority runnable schedulable object;

- does not define where in the run queue (associated with the priority level) a preempted object is placed; however, a particular implementation is required to document its approach and the RTSJ recommends that it be placed at the front of the queue;

- places a blocked schedulable object that becomes runnable, or has its base priority changed, at the back of the run queue associated with its (new) active priority;

- places a schedulable object that performs a `Thread.yield` method call at the back of the run queue associated with its priority;

- does not define whether schedulable objects of the same priority are scheduled in FIFO, round-robin order or any other order.

Schedulability (feasibility) analysis. The `PriorityScheduler`

- requires no particular analysis to be supported.

The specification of the `PriorityScheduler` class is given below:

```
package javax.realtime;
public class PriorityScheduler extends Scheduler {
  // fields — these have been deprecated at version 1.0.1
  public static final int MAX_PRIORITY;
  public static final int MIN_PRIORITY;

  // constructors
  protected PriorityScheduler();
```

```
// The methods throw IllegalArgumentException if null
// release or schedulable parameters are passed, and
// IllegalAssignmentError if the scheduler cannot hold
// a reference to the schedulable object.

 // methods which test feasibility
protected boolean addToFeasibility(
   Schedulable schedulable);
public boolean isFeasible();
protected boolean removeFromFeasibility(
   Schedulable schedulable);
public boolean setIfFeasible(Schedulable schedulable,
   ReleaseParameters release, MemoryParameters memory);
public boolean setIfFeasible(Schedulable schedulable,
   ReleaseParameters release, MemoryParameters memory,
   ProcessingGroupParameters group);

// The following method is likely to be added in version
// 1.1 of the RTSJ
public boolean setIfFeasible(Schedulable schedulable,
   PriorityParameters priority,
   ReleaseParameters release, MemoryParameters memory,
   ProcessingGroupParameters group);

 // other methods

public void fireSchedulable(Schedulable schedulable);
  // This method always throws UnsupportedOperationException

public int getMaxPriority();
public static int getMaxPriority(Thread thread);
  // Throws IllegalArgumentExeption if thread is not
  // being scheduled by the priority scheduler.
public int getMinPriority();
public static int getMinPriority(Thread thread);
  // Throws IllegalArgumentException if thread is not
  // being scheduled by the priority scheduler.
public int getNormPriority();
public static int getNormPriority(Thread thread);
  // Throws IllegalArgumentExeption if thread is not
  // being scheduled by the priority scheduler.

public String getPolicyName();

public static PriorityScheduler instance();
}
```

As well as overriding the nonstatic methods of the Scheduler class (thereby providing the methods needed by objects implementing the Schedulable interface), the PriorityScheduler also adds three new methods to query the maximum, normal and minimum priority levels supported by the scheduler. The normal priority is defined to be

$$\text{getMinimumPriority() + (getMaximumPriority() -}$$
$$\text{getMinimumPriority())/3}$$

The associated static methods allow Java threads to determine their priority range. If they are being scheduled by the PriorityScheduler this is the Priority-Scheduler's priority range, otherwise it is the standard Java thread priority range.

Note that the MAX_PRIORITY and MIN_PRIORITY fields have been deprecated in version 1.0.1 of the RTSJ as they allowed the values to be statically represented in a Java class file. This reduced portability. Note also that the PriorityScheduler only supports real-time threads and asynchronous event handlers as schedulable objects.

10.4 The Parameter Classes

Each schedulable object has several associated parameters. These parameters are tightly bound to the schedulable object and any changes to the parameters' attributes can have an immediate impact on the scheduling of the objects or any subsequent feasibility analysis performed by its scheduler (see Section 10.5).

Each schedulable object can have only one set of parameters associated with it. However, a particular parameter object can be associated with more than one schedulable object. In this case, any changes to the parameter objects affects all the schedulable objects bound to those parameters.

Details of the MemoryParameters class were given in Section 8.9. The full definition of the remaining parameter classes are given in this section.

10.4.1 Release parameters

Release parameters characterize how often a schedulable object is released and provide an estimate of the worst-case processor time needed for each release, and a relative deadline by which each release must have completed.

Version 1.1 note   An estimate of the blocking time (called blockingTerm below) that will be suffered on each release is likely to be added in version 1.1 of the RTSJ.

There is a close relationship between the actions that a schedulable object can perform and its release parameters. For example, the RealtimeThread class has a method called waitForNextPeriod; however, a real-time thread object can only call this method if it has PeriodicParameters associated with it. This may seem a little counter-intuitive and indeed early versions of the RTSJ had subclasses of RealtimeThread representing periodic activity. The main advantage of the current approach is that it allows a real-time thread to change its release characteristics and hence adapt its behavior.

The root of the ReleaseParameters class hierarchy is given below. The RTSJ takes the view that the minimum information that a scheduler will need for feasibility analysis is the cost, (blockingTerm) and deadline associated with each release of a schedulable object.

Warning   Typically the cost (and blockingTerm) is set by the application and is a measure of how much processor time the scheduler should assume that the associated scheduling object will require for each release (and for how much time it will be blocked waiting for resources). These are clearly dependent on the processor on which the schedulable object is being executed. Consequently, any programmer-defined values will not be portable.

The deadline is the time from a release that the schedulable object has to complete its execution. The overrunHandler is an asynchronous event handler that should be released if the schedulable object overruns its cost value on a particular release. Similarly, the missHandler is released if the schedulable object is still executing when its deadline arrives.

The ReleaseParameters class defines methods for getting and setting the cost (and blockingTerm), deadline and their associated handlers. It also provides a method setIfFeasible that will change the cost and deadline but only if the set of objects managed by the associated scheduler is still feasible. Unconditional changes to the cost, blockingTerm and deadline attributes take place immediately. However, with the default priority scheduler, changes to the deadline will not be acted upon until the next release.

The clone method copies only the public data, not any association that are maintained with schedulable objects.

```
package javax.realtime;
public class ReleaseParameters implements Cloneable{
    // constructors
    protected ReleaseParameters();
    protected ReleaseParameters(RelativeTime cost,
                RelativeTime deadline,
                AsyncEventHandler overrunHandler,
                AsyncEventHandler missHandler);
    // Throws IlegalArgumentException if cost is less than
```

```
     // zero or deadline is less than or equal to 0.
     // The following constructor is likely to be added in
     // Version 1.1 of the RTSJ.
     protected ReleaseParameters(RelativeTime cost,
             RelativeTime deadline,
             RelativeTime blockingTerm,
             AsyncEventHandler overrunHandler,
             AsyncEventHandler missHandler);
     // methods
     public Object clone();
     public RelativeTime getCost();
     public AsyncEventHandler getCostOverrunHandler();
     public RelativeTime getDeadline();
     public AsyncEventHandler getDeadlineMissHandler()
     public void setCost(RelativeTime cost);
     // Throws IlegalArgumentException if cost is less than
     // zero.
     public void setCostOverrunHandler(
               AsyncEventHandler handler);
     public void setDeadline(RelativeTime deadline);
     // Throws IlegalArgumentException if deadline is less
     // than or equal to 0.
     public void setDeadlineMissHandler(
               AsyncEventHandler handler);

     public boolean setIfFeasible(RelativeTime cost,
                                  RelativeTime deadline);

     // The following methods are likely to be added in
     // Version 1.1 of the RTSJ.
     public RelativeTime getBlockingTerm();
     public void setBlockingTerm(RelativeTime blockingTerm);
     public boolean setIfFeasible(RelativeTime cost,
         RelativeTime deadline, RelativeTime blockingTerm);
}
```

Null values for cost (and blockingTerm) parameters result in new RelativeTime objects being created with zero millisecond and nanosecond components. A null deadline results in a new RelativeTime object being created with Long.MAX_VALUE milliseconds and 999999 nanoseconds components. Null missHandler or overrunHandler values indicate that no handlers should be released when the deadline is missed or the cost overruns.

Cost enforcement

The RTSJ does not require that an implementation monitor the processing time consumed by schedulable objects, as this requires support from the underlying operating system. Many operating systems do not currently provide this support. However, it is likely that they will in the future as the POSIX standards now define such a facility.

If cost monitoring is supported, the RTSJ requires that the priority scheduler gives a schedulable object a CPU budget of no more than its cost value on each release. Hence, if a schedulable object overruns its cost budget, it is automatically descheduled (made not eligible for execution) *immediately. It will not be rescheduled until either its next release occurs (in which case its budget is replenished) or its associated cost value is increased.* The facilities to support the handling of cost overruns depend on whether the schedulable object is an asynchronous event handler or a real-time thread. They are not uniformly very well defined in version 1.0.1. of the RTSJ. It is likely version 1.1 will enhance these facilities and that the following methods will be provided in the Schedulable interface.

```
package javax.realtime;
public interface Schedulable extends Runnable
{
  ...
  // The following methods are likely to be added in
  // version 1.1 of the RTSJ.
  public void deschedule();
  public void schedule();
}
```

The deschedule method informs the associated scheduler that the schedulable object should be made not eligible for execution *at the end of its current release*. The schedule method informs the associated scheduler that the schedulable object should be made eligible for execution when its *next* release event occurs.

Further details of cost monitoring are given in the sections 11.3 and 12.1 for asynchronous event handlers and real-time threads respectively.

10.4.2 Periodic and aperiodic parameters

Subclasses of the ReleaseParameters class allow more information to be provided to the scheduler. The RTSJ defines three such subclasses. The PeriodicParameters class is for those schedulable objects that are released on a regular basis. It has two extra components: a start time and a period. The start time can be an

AbsoluteTime or a RelativeTime and indicates that the schedulable object should be first released at this time. If the schedulable object is a real-time thread then the actual first release time is given by

- if start is a RelativeTime value then
  first release = time of the start() method call + start

- if start is an AbsoluteTime value then
  first release = Maximum of the time of the start() method call and start

- if start is null then
  first release = time of the start() method call

The period parameter defines the interval between successive releases of the associated schedulable object.

Important note

The deadline for a schedulable object with periodic parameters is measured from the time that it is released, not when it is started. Its default value is the same value as the period.

The full definition of the PeriodicParameters class is given below.

```
package javax.realtime;
public class PeriodicParameters
      extends ReleaseParameters {
  // Constructors: throw IllegalArgumentException if
  // period is null.
  public PeriodicParameters(RelativeTime Period);
  public PeriodicParameters(HighResolutionTime start,
      RelativeTime period);
  public PeriodicParameters(
      HighResolutionTime start, RelativeTime period,
      RelativeTime cost, RelativeTime deadline,
      AsyncEventHandler overrunHandler,
      AsyncEventHandler missHandler);

  // The following constructor is likely to be added in
  // Version 1.1 of the RTSJ.
  public PeriodicParameters(
      HighResolutionTime start, RelativeTime period,
      RelativeTime cost, RelativeTime deadline,
      RelativeTime blockingTerm,
      AsyncEventHandler overrunHandler,
      AsyncEventHandler missHandler);
```

```
        // methods
        public RelativeTime getPeriod();
        public HighResolutionTime getStart();
        public void setPeriod(RelativeTime period);
          // Throws IllegalArgumentException if period is null.
        public void setStart(HighResolutionTime start);

        public boolean setIfFeasible(RelativeTime period,
                RelativeTime cost, RelativeTime deadline);
          // Throws IllegalArgumentException if period is null.
}
```

Warning   The getStart method returns the value passed in the constructor or the last value
set by a call of the setStart method. It does *not* return the time the schedulable
object was first released. Such a facility is not available in the current RTSJ. However, it is likely to be added in a future release.

Note also that changing the start time of an already started schedulable object
has no effect.

Aperiodic   In contrast to periodic activity, aperiodic activity can occur at any time. Hence a sched-
activity   ulable object with AperiodicParameters can give no added information to its
release characteristics over that supplied by ReleaseParameters. However, as it is
likely that a release will occur before the previous release has completed, an implementation will maintain an internal queue of outstanding invocation requests for aperiodic
schedulable objects. Consequently, the RTSJ provides facilities to define the size of the
queue and what happens if the queue overflows. The class definition is given below.

```
package javax.realtime;
public class AperiodicParameters
        extends ReleaseParameters {
  // fields
  public static final String arrivalTimeQueueOverflowExcept;
  public static final String arrivalTimeQueueOverflowIgnore;
  public static final String arrivalTimeQueueOverflowReplace;
  public static final String arrivalTimeQueueOverflowSave;

  // constructors

  public AperiodicParameters();
  public AperiodicParameters(
          RelativeTime cost, RelativeTime deadline,
          AsyncEventHandler overrunHandler,
          AsyncEventHandler missHandler);
```

```
// The following constructor is likely to be added in
// Version 1.1 of the RTSJ
public AperiodicParameters(
        RelativeTime cost, RelativeTime deadline,
        RelativeTime blockingTerm,
        AsyncEventHandler overrunHandler,
        AsyncEventHandler missHandler);
// methods
public String getArrivalTimeQueueOverflowBehavior();
public void setArrivalTimeQueueOverflowBehavior(
        String behavior);

public int getInitialArrivalTimeQueueLength();
public void setInitialArrivalTimeQueueLength(
        int initial);

public boolean setIfFeasible(RelativeTime cost,
                             RelativeTime deadline);
}
```

Consider, for example, an event handler that is released by a call to the `fire` method of its associated asynchronous event. Suppose that the maximum length of the queue is 3 and the implementation is simply keeping track of the time of the arrival of the fire request (that is, there are no other parameters associated with the fire event and deadline overrun is not being tested for). At some point in time the queue is

X	X+4	X+7

where X is an absolute time and the increments are measures in, say, seconds.

Queue overflow

Now consider a new release event occurring at X+12 that will result in the queue overflowing if no action is taken. The available actions are

- *throw an exception* – the exception `ResourceLimitError` is thrown on the offending call of the `fire` method; note that even if more than one handler is associated with the event, the exception is thrown if one or more of them suffer a queue overflow;

- *ignore the* `fire` – the call to fire the asynchronous event is ignored for that handler; if more than one handler is associated with the event, then the `fire` is ignored *only* for those handlers that would suffer a queue overflow;

- *replace the last release* – the last release event is overwritten with the new release event. Hence, in the above example, the queue would now be

X	X+4	X+12

- *save the request* – the queue is lengthened.

The above range of options are specified via string parameters to the `setArrival-TimeQueueOverflowBehavior`

Important note and warning

The deadline of an aperiodic schedulable object can never be guaranteed as there is no limit on how often it can be released. Hence, the deadline attribute should be interpreted as a *target completion time* rather than as a strict deadline. Furthermore, the `setIfFeasible` method should always return false as aperiodic parameters indicate a potentially unbounded demand on the processor's time. However, the `PriorityScheduler`'s default feasibility algorithm assumes an adequately fast computer and, consequently, always return true!

Version 1.0 note

In version 1.0, the arrival time queue was only specified for sporadic release parameters. This was an error in the specification, which has now been corrected.

10.4.3 Sporadic parameters

Schedulable objects that have sporadic parameters are released at irregular intervals but the scheduler can assume (for its feasibility analysis) that the time between any two releases will always be greater than or equal to a minimum inter-arrival time (MIT). At run-time, the scheduler must check for violation of this constraint and take some corrective action.

MIT violation

The available actions on violation of the minimum inter-arrival time are similar to those for the arrival queue overflow presented in the previous section. Assume again that the maximum length of the arrival queue is 3 and that the queue contains the following:

Assume that the minimum inter-arrival time is 2 seconds. Now a new request arrives at time X+5, the following actions can be specified

- *throw an exception* – the exception MITViolationException is thrown on the offending call of the fire method; note that even if more than one handler is associated with the event, the exception is thrown if one of more of them suffer a minimum inter-arrival time violation;

- *ignore the* fire – the call to fire the asynchronous event is ignored; if more than one handler is associated with the event, then the fire is ignored *only* for those handlers that would suffer a minimum inter-arrival time violation;

- *replace the last request* – the last request is overwritten with the new request. In the above example the queue would now be

X+5	

If the last release is already active (or has already completed), the new request is ignored.

- *save the request* – the request is saved, but the time between the request and the last request is set to the minimum inter-arrival time; in the above example the new queue would be

X+4	X+6	

Note although X+6 is the effective release time of the sporadic handler, any deadline requirement will be measured relative to the actual arrival time (X+5).

The above range of options are specified via string parameters defined in the SporadicParameters class. The full class definition is given below. There are methods to get and set the minimum inter-arrival time, along with methods to get and set the actions to be taken on minimum inter-arrival time violation. The setIfFeasible method changes the cost, deadline and minimum inter-arrival time parameters but only if the set of objects managed by the associated scheduler is still feasible.

Important note

Where an asynchronous event is associated with an external happening, the throwing of any exception is suppressed if it is caused by the happening.

The full definition of the SporadicParameters class is given below:

```
package javax.realtime;
public class SporadicParameters
        extends AperiodicParameters {
  // fields
  public static final String mitViolationExcept;
  public static final String mitViolationIgnore;
  public static final String mitViolationReplace;
  public static final String mitViolationSave;
```

```
        // Constructors throw IllegalArgumentException if
        // interarrival is null, zero or negative.
        public SporadicParameters(RelativeTime minInterarrival);
        public SporadicParameters(RelativeTime minInterarrival,
          RelativeTime cost, RelativeTime deadline,
          AsyncEventHandler overrunHandler,
          AsyncEventHandler missHandler);

        // The following constructor is likely to be added in
        // Version 1.1 of the RTSJ.
        public SporadicParameters(RelativeTime minInterarrival,
          RelativeTime cost, RelativeTime deadline,
          RelativeTime blockingTerm,
          AsyncEventHandler overrunHandler,
          AsyncEventHandler missHandler);

        // methods
        public String getMitViolationBehavior();
        public void setMitViolationBehavior(String behavior);

        public RelativeTime getMinimumInterarrival();
        public void setMinimumInterarrival(
          RelativeTime interarrival);
          // Throws IllegalArgumentException if interarrival
          // is null, zero or negative.

        public boolean setIfFeasible(RelativeTime interarrival,
              RelativeTime cost, RelativeTime deadline);
          // Throws IllegalArgumentException if
          // interarrival is null, zero or negative.

        // The following method is likely to be added at version 1.1
        public boolean setIfFeasible(RelativeTime interarrival,
              RelativeTime cost, RelativeTime deadline,
              RelativeTime blockingTerm);

}
```

10.4.4 Scheduling Parameters

Typically, scheduling parameters are set by the programmer. In order to be fully extensible, the root of the class hierarchy is defined to be empty.

```
package javax.realtime;
public abstract class SchedulingParameters
        implement Cloneable {
  // constructors
  public SchedulingParameters();

  // methods
  public void clone();
}
```

The two subclasses defined by the RTSJ are given below:

```
package javax.realtime;
public class PriorityParameters
        extends SchedulingParameters {
  // constructors
  public PriorityParameters(int priority);
      // Throws IllegalArgumentException if priority
      // is outside the supported range.

  // methods
  public int getPriority();
  public void setPriority(int priority)
      // Throws IllegalArgumentException if priority
      // is outside the supported range.
  public String toString();
}
package javax.realtime;
public class ImportanceParameters
              extends PriorityParameters {
  // constructors
  public ImportanceParameters(int priority, int importance);
      // Throws IllegalArgumentException if priority or
      // importance is outside the supported range.

  // methods
  public int getImportance();
  public void setImportance(int importance);
      // Throws IllegalArgumentException if importance
      // is outside the supported range.
  public String toString();
}
```

Priorities are used by the priority scheduler. Importance parameters are typically used when a system enters into a transient overload situation where it is unable to meet all its deadlines. In these situations, the scheduler may decide to deschedule one or more schedulable objects. The importance parameters can be used to inform the scheduler which objects are critical to the system. Their use is not required by the RTSJ default priority scheduler.

10.4.5 The `ProcessingGroupParameters` class

In any system where guarantees are required, aperiodic schedulable objects present a problem. As they have no well-defined release characteristics, they can impose an unbounded demand on the processor's time. If not handled properly, they can result in periodic or sporadic schedulable objects missing their deadlines, even though those schedulable objects have been "guaranteed".

One simple way of scheduling aperiodic activities, within a preemptive priority-based scheme, is to run them at a priority below the priorities assigned to periodic and sporadic schedulable objects. In effect, the aperiodic schedulable objects run as background activities and, therefore, cannot preempt the other schedulable objects. Although a safe scheme, this does not provide adequate support to aperiodic schedulable objects that will often miss their target completion times if they only run as background activities. To improve the situation, a *server* can be employed. Servers protect the processing resources needed by periodic and sporadic schedulable objects but otherwise allow aperiodic schedulable objects to run as soon as possible.

Several types of servers have been defined by the real-time community. The one that is most relevant to the RTSJ is a *deferrable server* (Lehoczky, Sha and Strosnider, 1987). With the deferrable server, an analysis is undertaken that enables a new logical thread to be introduced at a particular priority level. This thread, the server, has a period and a capacity. These values can be chosen so that all the periodic and sporadic schedulable objects in the system remain schedulable even if the server executes periodically and consumes its capacity. At run-time, whenever an aperiodic thread is released, and there is capacity available, it starts executing at the server's priority level until either it finishes or the capacity is exhausted. In the latter case, the aperiodic thread is suspended (or transferred to a background priority). With the deferrable server model, the capacity is replenished every period.

The RTSJ provides support for aperiodic server technologies via processing group parameters. When processing group parameters are assigned to one or more aperiodic schedulable objects, a server is effectively created. The server's start time, cost (capacity) and period is defined by the particular instance of the parameters. These collectively define the points in time when the server's capacity is replenished.

Any aperiodic schedulable object that belongs to a processing group is executed at its defined priority. However, it only executes if the server still has capacity. As it executes, each unit of CPU time consumed is subtracted from the server's capacity. When capacity is exhausted, the aperiodic schedulable objects are not allowed to execute until the start of the next replenishment period. If the application only assigns aperiodic schedulable objects of the same priority level to a single ProcessingGroupParameters object, then the functionality of a deferrable server can be obtained.

The RTSJ is, however, a little more general. It allows

- schedulable objects of different priorities to be assigned to the same group,

- the inclusion of sporadic and periodic schedulable objects,

- the "servers" to be given a deadline, and cost overrun and deadline miss handlers[1].

The latter may be useful if the programmer has more information about the pattern of arrivals of the aperiodic activities and wants to detect variations from that pattern.

The ProcessingGroupParameters class is given below.

```
package javax.realtime;
public class ProcessingGroupParameters
            implement Cloneable{
// Constructors throw IllegalArgumentException if
// cost or period is null.
public ProcessingGroupParameters(
        HighResolutionTime start, RelativeTime period,
        RelativeTime cost, RelativeTime deadline,
        AsyncEventHandler overrunHandler,
        AsyncEventHandler missHandler);
// The following constructor is likely to be added in
// Version 1.1 of the RTSJ, see Section 10.4.1.
public ProcessingGroupParameters(
        HighResolutionTime start, RelativeTime period,
        RelativeTime cost, RelativeTime deadline,
        RelativeTime blockingTerm,
        AsyncEventHandler overrunHandler,
        AsyncEventHandler missHandler);
```

---

1. For a deferrable server, the deadline would equal the period and there would be no overrun or miss handlers.

```
// methods
public Object clone();
public RelativeTime getCost();
public AsyncEventHandler getCostOverrunHandler();
public RelativeTime getDeadline();
public AsyncEventHandler getDeadlineMissHandler();
public RelativeTime getPeriod();
public HighResolutionTime getStart();
public void setCost(RelativeTime cost);
    // Throws IllegalArgumentException if cost is null.
public void setCostOverrunHandler(
        AsyncEventHandler handler);
public void setDeadline(RelativeTime deadline);
public void setDeadlineMissHandler(
        AsyncEventHandler handler);
public void setPeriod(RelativeTime period);
    // Throws IllegalArgumentException if period is null.
public void setStart(HighResolutionTime start);
public boolean setIfFeasible(RelativeTime period,
        RelativeTime cost, RelativeTime deadline);
    // Throws IllegalArgumentException if period or
    // cost is null.

// The following methods are likely to be added in
// Version 1.1 of the RTSJ, see Section 10.4.1.
public RelativeTime getBlockingTerm();
public void setBlockingTerm(RelativeTime blockingTerm);
public boolean setIfFeasible(RelativeTime period,
        RelativeTime cost, RelativeTime blockingTerm,
        RelativeTime deadline);
    // Throws IllegalArgumentException if period
    // or cost is null.
}
```

Important notes

To get full predictability, it may be necessary for an implementation to restrict the generality of processing group parameters so that they support one (or more) of the well-known server technologies, such as deferrable servers (Burns and Wellings, 2003).

Also note each schedulable object may still have its own deadline and cost constraints.

10.5 Parameters Classes and the Priority Scheduler

**Default
parameters**

The priority scheduler uses the following default parameters when presented with null values:

- `PriorityParameters` – a new object is created with a priority set to the normal priority (see Section 10.3)

- `ReleaseParameters` – a new `AperiodicParameters` object is created with

  cost: a `RelativeTime` object with cost set to 0

  blocking time (if added to Version 1.1): a `RelativeTime` object with the blocking time set to 0

  deadline: a `RelativeTime` object with the deadline set to `Long.MAX_VALUE` milliseconds and 999999 nanoseconds

  cost overrun handler: set to null

  deadline miss handler: set to null

- `ProcessingGroupParameters` – set to null

- `MemoryParameters` – set to null.

**Parameter
changes**

Under the priority scheduler, changes to scheduling, release, memory, and processing group parameters take effect as follows:

- Changes to scheduling parameters take effect immediately; that is, the *base* priority is changed immediately (the default priority scheduler does not use important parameters). Whether this change will affect the *active* priority will depend on whether any priority avoidance algorithms are currently in progress.

- Changes to release parameters take effect as follows:

  deadline – at the start of the next release

  cost – immediately

  deadline miss handler – at the start of the next release

  overrun handler – at the start of the next release

  period – at the start of the next release

  minimum interarrival time – at the start of the next release

  the type of release parameters object – at the start of the next release.

- Changes to memory parameters take effect immediately.

- Changes to a processing group's parameters attributed (period, deadline, or handlers) take effect at the start of the next replenishment period.

| Warning | The priority scheduler only notices that parameters have changed if the complete parameter objects are replaced by new parameter objects. Changes to the fields of parameter objects via setter methods are not acted upon until the next release. |

10.6 Alternative Schedulers and EDF Scheduling

The vast majority of real-time operating systems support fixed priority preemptive scheduling with no on-line feasibility analysis. However, as more and more computers are being embedded in engineering (and other) applications, there is need for more flexible scheduling. Broadly speaking, there are three ways to achieve flexible scheduling:

1. Pluggable schedulers – in this approach the system provides a framework into which different schedulers can be plugged. The CORBA Dynamic Scheduling (OMG, 2003) specification is an example of this approach. Kernel loadable schedulers also fall into this category.

2. Application-defined schedulers – in this approach, the system notifies the application every time an event occurs that requires a scheduling decision to be taken. The application then informs the system which thread should execute next. The proposed extensions to real-time POSIX support this approach (Aldea Rivas and González Harbour, 2002).

3. Implementation-defined schedulers – in this approach, an implementation is allowed to define alternative schedulers. Typically this would require the underlying operating system (virtual machine, in the case of Java) to be modified.

The RTSJ adopts the implementation-defined schedulers approach (although it also tries to provide a framework for the implementation to follow) and allows for applications to determine dynamically whether the real-time JVM on which it is executing has a particular scheduler. Unfortunately, this is the least portable approach, as an application cannot rely on any particular implementation-defined scheduler being supported. The only scheduler an application can rely on being present is the `PriorityScheduler`. Furthermore, no assumption can be made on whether a particular `PriorityScheduler` supports on-line feasibility analysis.

| Version 1.1 note | Version 1.0.1 of the RTSJ is weak in its support for implementation-defined schedulers. It is likely that Version 1.1 will enhance its support in this area and, possibly, also address pluggable and user-defined schedulers. |

Fortunately, priority-based scheduling is very flexible if schedulable objects can change their priority (as they can in the RTSJ). Consequently, much can be done that is portable by allowing the application to implement its own scheduling policy on top of the `PriorityScheduler`. This section discusses how a simple earliest-deadline-first (EDF) scheduler can be implemented. Figure 10.1 illustrates the approach; it is based on that given for EDF scheduling in the Ada 95 programming language (Burns and Wellings, 1998):

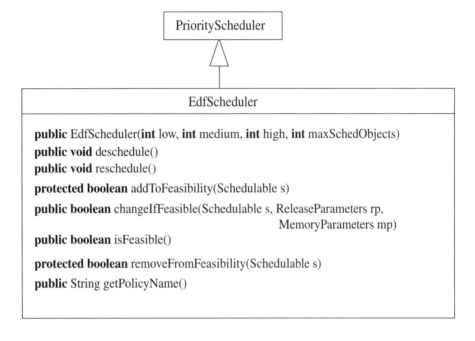

FIGURE 10.1. **An EDF Scheduler**

The `EdfScheduler` extends the `PriorityScheduler` and overrides the methods associated with feasibility analysis. It also introduces some new methods that are used by applications. The implementation approach is as follows.

- All objects that are to be scheduled by the `EdfScheduler` run at one of three priority levels. These are called *low*, *medium* and *high*.

- When schedulable objects are released, they are released at the *high* priority level. They immediately call the `reschedule` method to announce themselves to the `EdfScheduler`.

- The `EdfScheduler` keeps track of the schedulable object with the closest absolute deadline. This object has its priority set to the *medium* level.

- When a call is made to `reschedule`, the `EdfScheduler` compares the deadline of the calling object with that of its closest deadline. If the caller has a closer deadline, the object with the current closest deadline has its priority set to *low* and the caller has its priority set to *medium*.

- After the end of each release, a schedulable object calls `deschedule`. The `EdfScheduler` sets the caller's priority to `high` (ready for the next release), and then scans its list of schedulable objects to find the one with the closest deadline. It sets the priority of this object to *medium*.

- The constructor for the class gives the appropriate priority values for *low*, *medium* and *high*. It also contains the maximum number of schedulable objects to be scheduled by the scheduler.

Consider the execution of three real-time threads (T1, T2 and T3) that are released at times t1, t2, and t3 respectively (where t1 < t2 < t3). T2 has the closest deadline, followed by T3 and T1. Figure 10.2 shows how the priorities change over time and the resulting execution schedule.

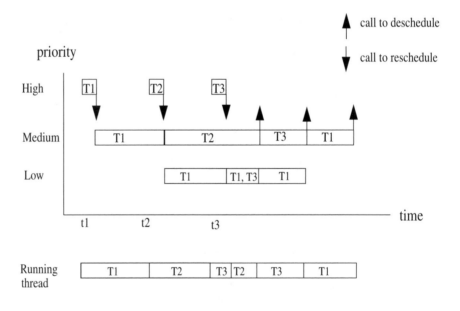

FIGURE 10.2. EDF Scheduling via Parameters

With this approach, a thread with a longer deadline will execute in preference to a shorter deadline thread but only for a limited time when it is released. This can be ensured by encapsulating the calls to `reschedule` and `deschedule`. Consider, for example, periodic threads

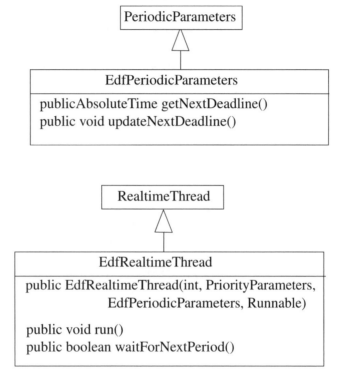

FIGURE 10.3. **EDF real-time threads**

Here, calls to `waitForNextPeriod` etc., will call the appropriate methods in the EDF scheduler.

10.7 Summary

Scheduling is the ordering of thread/process executions so that the underlying hardware resources (processors, networks, etc.) and software resources (shared data objects) are efficiently and predictably used. In general, scheduling consists of three components

- an algorithm for ordering access to resources (scheduling policy)
- an algorithm for allocating the resources (scheduling mechanism)

- a means of predicting the worst-case behavior of the system when the policy and mechanism are applied (schedulability or feasibility analysis).

The RTSJ has two types of schedulable objects: real-time threads and asynchronous event handlers. The only scheduler guaranteed to be provided by a RTSJ implementation is a fixed priority scheduler which has the following characteristics.

Scheduling policy. Fixed priority scheduling (FPS) requires that

- the execution of schedulable objects on a single processor be ordered according to an active priority;
- priorities are assigned to schedulable objects at their creation time – although no particular priority assignment algorithm is required by FPS, it is usual to assign base priorities according to the relative deadline of the schedulable object;
- priority inheritance is implemented when accessing resources.

Scheduling mechanism. FPS requires preemptive priority-based dispatching of schedulable objects – the processing resource is always given to the highest-priority runnable schedulable object (allocated to that processor).

Feasibility analysis. The RTSJ does not require any particular schedulability analysis technique.

11 Asynchronous Events and their Handlers

Introduction and chapter structure

One of the main incentives for supporting concurrency in a real-time programming language is to facilitate the modeling of parallelism in the real world (Burns and Wellings, 2001). For example, within embedded system design, the controllers for real-world objects (such as conveyor belts, engines and robots) are represented as threads in the program. The interaction between the real-world objects and their controllers can be either time triggered or event triggered. In a time-triggered system, the controller is activated periodically. It samples the environment in order to determine the status of the real-time objects it is controlling. On the basis of its findings, it writes to actuators that are able to affect the behavior of the objects. For example, a robot controller may determine the position of a robot via a sensor and decide that it must cut the power to a motor, thereby bringing the robot to a halt. In an event-triggered system, sensors in the environment are activated when the real-world object enters into certain states. The events are signaled to the controller via interrupts. For example, a robot may trip a switch when it reaches a certain position. This is a signal to the controller that the power to the motor should be turned off, thereby bringing the robot to a halt.

The system designer often has a choice whether to implement the control algorithm as time-triggered or event-triggered. Event-triggered systems are often more flexible, whereas time-triggered systems are more predictable (Burns, 2002; Kopetz, 1997). In either case, the controller is usually represented as a thread. However, there are situations where this is not appropriate. These include (Ousterhout, 1996; van Renesse, 1998) when

- the external objects are many and their control algorithms are simple and nonblocking, and
- the external objects are interrelated, and their collective control requires significant communication and synchronization between the controllers.

In the former case, using a thread per controller leads to a proliferation of threads along with the associated per thread overhead. In the latter case, complex communication and synchronization protocols are needed that can be difficult to design correctly and may lead to deadlock or unbounded blocking.

An alternative to thread-based programming is event-based programming. Each event has an associated handler. When events occur, they are queued and one or more server threads take events from the queue and execute their associated handlers. When a server has finished executing a handler, it takes another event from the queue, executes the handler, and so on. The execution of the handlers may generate further events. With this model, there are only server threads. Furthermore, if the mapping of event handler to server is under program control, it is possible to ensure there is no need for explicit communication between the handlers (as they can simply read and write from shared objects without contention). The disadvantages of controlling all external objects by event handlers is that it is difficult to have tight deadlines associated with event handlers. This is because a newly arrived high-priority handler with a short deadline must wait for potentially long-lived and nonblocking handlers to terminate before a server can be freed up.

One of the main examples often quoted as requiring an event-handling system is the implementation of a graphical user interface. For example, Java supports threads but its Swing and Abstract Windows Toolkits are event-based. Here, only one server thread is required. As noted in Section 4.4, there is also a utility for timer-based events. Here, the number of servers and the mapping of handlers to servers is defined in the program.

In an attempt to provide the flexibility of threads and the efficiency of event handling, the RTSJ has introduced the notion of *real-time* asynchronous events and their associated handlers. However, the specification is silent on how these events can be implemented and how their timing requirements can be guaranteed.

This chapter discusses the RTSJ event-handling facilities in detail; real-time threads are considered in the next chapter. The topics are considered in this order as an understanding of events and event handlers is needed in order to appreciate the full facilities associated with real-time thread execution.

The basic event model is presented first, followed by details of the time-triggered event-handling mechanisms. RTSJ events are parameterless. The chapter illustrates how they can contain data. Examples of using the event-handling facilities are also given.

In order to understand the full real-time implications of using the event-handling facilities, it is necessary to appreciate how they may be implemented. This is discussed along with issues of event handling and program termination.

11.1 The Basic Model

The RTSJ views asynchronous events as dataless occurrences that are either fired (by the program) or associated with the triggering of interrupts (or signals) in the environment. One or more handlers can be associated with (attached to) a single event, and a single handler can be associated with one or more events. The association between handlers and events is dynamic. Each handler has a count (called `fireCount`) of the number of outstanding occurrences. When an event occurs (is fired by the application or is triggered by an interrupt), the count is atomically incremented. The attached handlers are then released for execution (once any minimum inter-arrival time constraint has been obeyed—see Section 10.4.3). Recall from Section 10.1, a schedulable object can be released even though it has not completed the execution associated with its previous releases. The fire count caters for this situation, allowing the implementation to start the execution associated with the new release as soon as the old releases have finished.

Asynchronous events

The AsyncEvent class is given below:

```
package javax.realtime;
public class AsyncEvent {
  // constructors
  public AsyncEvent();

  // methods

  // The methods that take parameters all throw
  // IllegalArgumentException if null is passed.

  public void addHandler(AsyncEventHandler handler);
  public void removeHandler(AsyncEventHandler handler);
  public void setHandler(AsyncEventHandler handler);
  public boolean handledBy(AsyncEventHandler target);

  public void bindTo(String happening);
    // Throws UnknownHappeningException;
  public void unBindTo(String happening);
    // Throws UnknownHappeningException.

  public ReleaseParameters createReleaseParameters();
  public void fire();
    // Throws MITViolationException(see Section 10.4.3) and
    // ArrivalTimeQueueOverflowException (see Section 10.4.2).
}
```

The addHandler and removeHandler methods are self-explanatory. Note that the same handler can only be associated with a particular event once (that is, the addHandler operation can be repeated several times but the result is the same as executing it once). The adding and removing of event handlers is atomic with respect to the releasing of any attached handlers. That is, they cannot be added or removed while the event is releasing the current set of associated handlers.

The handledBy method allows the programmer to determine if a handler has already been associated with the event. The setHandler method removes all the handlers currently associated with the event and installs the parameter as the sole handler. If a null handler is passed, the result of the method call is to remove all handlers associated with the event. Of course, adding and removing handlers will affect the feasibility of the system.

Important notes

The above methods *do not* check whether the system is feasible with the new settings.

The `bindTo`/`unBindTo` method associates/disassociates an external "happening" (an interrupt or an operating system signal) with a particular event. An event can be bound to more than one external happening. The values of `happening` are implementation defined.

An event that is created in scoped memory and then subsequently bound to an external happening has the effect of increasing the reference count associated with that scoped memory area. The reference count is decremented when the happening is unbound. This is to ensure that the scoped memory area is active when interrupts occur.

When setting up a handler (which is a schedulable entity) for an event, it is necessary to set up the release parameters for the handler. Some of the information needed for the release parameters may be unknown to the code setting up the handler. The `createReleaseParameters` method returns the release parameters associated with the event. In most cases, the event itself will not know its release frequency (unless it is a periodic timer) so it will return aperiodic release parameters. If the event is to be associated with an interrupt and the programmer is aware of the frequency at which interrupts can occur, the `AsyncEvent` class can be subclassed and the `createRelease-Parameters` method can be overridden to return the appropriate parameter class.

Warning

An implementation is not required to check that an event that claims to fire periodically actually does fire periodically.

Finally, the `fire` method is called to increment the count of outstanding fire requests (for each associated handler) and to release the event handlers. Note the RTSJ allows the software firing of an event even if the event has been associated with an external happening. To signal this as an error requires the programmer to subclass `AsyncEvent`, override the `fire` method and throw an unchecked exception.

Event handlers

Event handlers are defined using the `AsyncEventHandler` class hierarchy (which implements the `Schedulable` interface). Application-defined handlers are created either by subclassing this base class and overriding the `handleAsyncEvent` method or by passing an object that implements the `Runnable` interface to one of the constructors. Once attached to an event, in the former case, the overridden `handleAsync-Event` method is called whenever the event's fire count is greater than zero. In the latter case, the `run` method of the `Runnable` object is called by the `handler-AsyncEvent` method.

The `AsyncEventHandler` class has several constructor methods that allow the passing of various parameter classes associated with a schedulable object (scheduling, release, memory and processing group parameters; whether the schedulable object is a no-heap object and any memory area that should be set up as the default memory area) along with the optional Runnable object. The full set of constructors are given below. Where no parameter (or null) is given, the defaults are

- SchedulingParameters – inherited from the current schedulable object (or the default values for the current scheduler if the creator is a Java thread); a new object is created,

- ReleaseParameters – the default values for the current scheduler (a new object is created),

- MemoryParameters – null,

- MemoryArea – the current MemoryArea,

- ProcessingGroupParameters – null.

```java
package javax.realtime;
public class AsyncEventHandler implements Schedulable {
  // constructors

  // Those constructors that have the nonheap parameter
  // throw IllegalParameterException if nonheap is true
  // and any parameter, or the AsyncEventHandler instance
  // is in heap memory or the initial memory area is heap.
  public AsyncEventHandler();
  public AsyncEventHandler(Runnable logic);
  public AsyncEventHandler(boolean nonheap);
  public AsyncEventHandler(boolean nonheap,
                           Runnable logic);
  public AsyncEventHandler(SchedulingParameters scheduling,
    ReleaseParameters release, MemoryParameters memory,
    MemoryArea area, ProcessingGroupParameters group,
    Runnable logic);
  public AsyncEventHandler(SchedulingParameters scheduling,
    ReleaseParameters release, MemoryParameters memory,
    MemoryArea area, ProcessingGroupParameters group,
    boolean nonheap);
  public AsyncEventHandler(SchedulingParameters scheduling,
    ReleaseParameters release, MemoryParameters memory,
    MemoryArea area, ProcessingGroupParameters group,
    boolean nonheap, Runnable logic);
  ... // methods to follow
}
```

By default, an asynchronous event handler can access the heap. This may be changed by calling an appropriate constructor with the `noheap` boolean parameter set to true.

The methods defined by the `AsyncEventHandler` class can be divided into three categories. Those that manipulate the parameters necessary for a schedulable object, those that are directly associated with the handling of the event and those that are needed to support a handler's use of memory areas (and its daemon status). The methods needed to support the `Schedulable` interface are given below; they have been fully described in Section 10.2.

```
package javax.realtime;
public class AsyncEventHandler implements Schedulable {
    ...
    // Methods needed to support the Schedulable interface,
    // see Section 10.2. for full details.

    // Methods which result in feasibility being tested.
    public boolean addIfFeasible();
    public boolean addToFeasibility();
    public boolean removeFromFeasibility();
    public boolean setIfFeasible(ReleaseParameters release,
                MemoryParameters memory);
    public boolean setIfFeasible(ReleaseParameters release,
                MemoryParameters memory,
                ProcessingGroupParameters group);
    public boolean setIfFeasible(ReleaseParameters release,
                ProcessingGroupParameters group);
    public boolean setIfFeasible(SchedulingParameters sched,
                ReleaseParameters release,
                MemoryParameters memory);
    public boolean setIfFeasible(SchedulingParameters
                ReleaseParameters release,
                MemoryParameters memory,
                ProcessingGroupParameters group);
    public boolean setMemoryParametersIfFeasible(
                MemoryParameters memory);
    public boolean setProcessingGroupParametersIfFeasible(
                ProcessingGroupParameters group);
    public boolean setReleaseParametersIfFeasible(
                ReleaseParameters release);
    public boolean setSchedulingParametersIfFeasible(
                SchedulingParameters scheduling);
```

```
// Methods which get or set the various
// parameter classes.

public MemoryParameters getMemoryParameters();
public void setMemoryParameters(MemoryParameters memory);
public ProcessingGroupParameters
            getProcessingGroupParameters();
public void setProcessingGroupParameters(
        ProcessingGroupParameters groupParameters);
public ReleaseParameters getReleaseParameters();
public void setReleaseParameters(
        ReleaseParameters release);
public SchedulingParameters getSchedulingParameters();
public void setSchedulingParameters(
        SchedulingParameters scheduling);

   // Methods which get or set the scheduler.
public Scheduler getScheduler();
public void setScheduler(Scheduler scheduler);
        // Throws IllegalThreadStateException.
public void setScheduler(Scheduler scheduler,
  SchedulingParameters scheduling,
  ReleaseParameters release, MemoryParameters memory,
  ProcessingGroupParameters processing);
...
}
```

The next set of methods are for handling the occurrences of the associated event(s). A set of protected methods allow the fire count to be manipulated; their visibility is restricted to classes in the `javax.realtime` package and subclasses of the `AsyncEventHandler` class. Consequently, they can only be called by the application programmer by creating a subclass and overriding the `handleAsyncEvent` method. The default code for `handleAsyncEvent` is null unless a `Runnable` object has been supplied with the constructor. If this is the case, the method calls the `run` method of the supplied `Runnable` object. Finally, the `run` method of the `AsyncEventHandler` class itself is the method that will be called by the underlying system when the object is released (and the `fireCount` has changed from zero to one). It will call `handleAsyncEvent` repeatedly whenever the `fireCount` is greater than zero. The method is final and, therefore, cannot be overridden.

```
package javax.realtime;
public class AsyncEventHandler implements Schedulable {
   ...

   // methods needed for handling the associated event
   protected int getAndClearPendingFireCount();
   protected int getAndDecrementPendingFireCount();
   protected int getAndIncrementPendingFireCount();
   protected int getPendingFireCount();
   public void handleAsyncEvent();
   public final void run();

   ...

}
```

Important notes

The CPU budget and deadline allocated to the asynchronous event handler are not affected by changes to fireCount. Their use by the programmer is to allow event handling to be optimized. Note also that the goal of getAndIncrementPend-ingFireCount is to simulate an extra firing of the associated event for this handler only.

The final methods defined by the AsyncEventHandler class is given below:

```
package javax.realtime;
public class AsyncEventHandler implements Schedulable {
   ...

   public MemoryArea getMemoryArea();
      // Returns the initial memory area. See Section 8.6

   // Methods to manipulate the daemon status,
   // see Section 11.5.
}
```

11.2 Bound Event Handlers

In the RTSJ, both event handlers and real-time threads are schedulable objects. However, in practice, threads provide the vehicles for execution of event handlers. Therefore, it is necessary to bind an event handler to a server real-time thread (see Section 11.9). For

AsyncEventHandler objects this binding is done dynamically. There is, therefore, inevitably some latency between the event occurring and the handler being assigned to a server thread. BoundAsyncEventHandler objects are supplied to eliminate this latency. Bound event handlers are permanently associated with a server real-time thread. The server can only be dedicated to a single bound event handler at any one time.

```
package javax.realtime;
public class BoundAsyncEventHandler
                extends AsyncEventHandler {
  // constructors
  public BoundAsyncEventHandler();
  public BoundAsyncEventHandler(
    SchedulingParameters scheduling,
    ReleaseParameters release, MemoryParameters memory,
    MemoryArea area, ProcessingGroupParameters group,
    boolean nonheap, Runnable logic);
}
```

11.3 Cost Enforcement and Deadline Monitoring

As mentioned in Section 10.4.1, if an asynchronous event handler overruns its cost budget and the implementation of the RTSJ is supporting cost enforcement, the handler is descheduled (made not eligible for execution) *immediately*. Version 1.0.1 of the RTSJ is clear that it will be rescheduled either when its next release occurs or the cost value is increased. However, the specifications lacks the facilities to give the same level of control as that given to real-time threads (with periodic release parameters – see Section 12.1). Version 1.1 of the RTSJ is likely to have more comprehensive facilities and include the schedule and deschedule methods defined in Section 10.4.1 and also to include a method to be executed in the advent of a deadline miss.

```
package javax.realtime;
public class AsyncEventHandler implements Schedulable {
  ...
  // The following methods may be added in
  // Version 1.1 of the RTSJ
  public void deschedule();
  public void schedule();
  public void deadlineMissCondition();
}
```

With these, the cost enforcement and deadline monitoring model is likely to be defined as follows (for an event handler, h, with a cost value of c):

1. Every call of the `handleAsyncEvent` method by the real-time virtual machine results in the CPU budget for the handler being replenished by c units.

2. If cost overrun is detected

    • any overrun handler is released

    • handler h is descheduled immediately

3. h remains descheduled until either

    • c is increased (via h.`getReleaseParameters()`.`setcost()`) (usually by the overrun handler); or

    • h is re-released

4. If a deadline is missed

    • any associated deadline miss handler is released at the moment the deadline has passed, the condition is cleared by calling h.`schedule()`

5. At the end of the current release where a deadline has been missed (a return from `handleAsyncEvent`),

    • if there were handlers released, h is descheduled until (or unless) any deadline miss condition has been cleared

    • if there were no deadline miss handler released, h.`deadlineMissCondition()` is immediately called by the `run` method and the conditions is cleared.

It should be stressed that this is only one potential approach that Version 1.1 of the RTSJ might take.

11.4 Timers

Event handlers can also be time triggered. The abstract `Timer` class defines the base class from which timer events can be generated. All timers are based on a clock; a null clock value indicates that the real-time clock should be used. A timer has a time at which it should fire, that is, release its associated handlers. This time may be an absolute or relative time value. If no handlers have been associated with the timer, nothing will happen when the timer fires. The appropriate release parameters associated with the timer can be created by the `createReleaseParameters` method (this overrides the method in the `AsyncEvent` class).

Once created, a timer can be

- started and stopped – indicating whether the timer should count or not
- enabled and disabled – indicating whether the timer should fire or not
- rescheduled – indicating that the timer should not fire (or not fire again) until the rescheduled time
- destroyed – indicating that the resources used by the timer should be returned to the system; the timer cannot be used again.

If a disabled timer is enabled after its firing time has passed, the firing is lost.

The getClock and getFireTime methods are self-explanatory, although it should be noted that the value returned from the getFireTime method may return null if the timer was created with a relative start time and has yet to be started. The start methods start the timer running (trying to start an already started timer results in an IllegalStateException being thrown). By default, a timer is enabled when it is started. The overloaded start method (added at version 1.0.1.) allows a timer to be started but disabled. Any relative time given in the constructor to a timer is converted to an absolute time at the point the start method is called; if an absolute time is given in the constructor, and the time has passed, the timer fires as soon as it is started (assuming is not started disabled). Finally, the isRunning method returns true as the timer is both started and enabled.

```
package javax.realtime;
public abstract class Timer extends AsyncEvent {
  // constructors
  protected Timer(HighResolutionTime time, Clock clock,
                  AsyncEventHandler handler);
    // Throws IllegalArgumentException if time is a
    // negative RelativeTime value.

  // methods
  // All methods called on a destroyed timer result in the
  // IllegalStateException being thrown.

  public ReleaseParameters createReleaseParameters();
  public void destroy();
  public void disable();
  public void enable();
  public Clock getClock();
  public AbsoluteTime getFireTime();
  public boolean isRunning();
  public void reschedule(HighResolutionTime time);
  public void start();
```

```
public boolean stop();
  // Returns true if the timer was started,
  // false otherwise.
  // The following methods were added at version 1.0.1
public void fire();
  // Always throws UnsupportedOperationException.
public void start (boolean disabled);
}
```

There are two subclasses of the Timer class. The OneShotTimer class and the PeriodicTimer class. A one shot timer is a timer that will only fire once (unless it is restarted). However, before it has fired, its fire time can be rescheduled. Any relative time given when the timer is rescheduled is interpreted as follows:

- if the timer is active, the relative time value is interpreted to be relative to the time at which the reschedule method call was made,

- if the timer has not started, the relative time value is interpreted to be relative to the time at which the timer will be started.

```
package javax.realtime;
public class OneShotTimer extends Timer {
  // constructors
  public OneShotTimer(HighResolutionTime fireTime,
                      AsyncEventHandler handler);
    // Assumes the default real-time clock.
  public OneShotTimer(HighResolutionTime fireTime,
        Clock clock, AsyncEventHandler handler);
    // FireTime is based on the clock parameter.
}
```

Note that if a one-shot timer is rescheduled after the timer has already fired, then there will be no further firing unless the timer is restarted (by calling start again). Furthermore, a call to start will have no effect if the timer is already counting down.

A periodic timer, once started by a call to the start method, will fire on the first occasion at the time indicated by the start parameter in its constructor method (assuming that it has not been disabled or destroyed) according to the following rules, which are similar to those associated with ReleaseParameters (see Section 10.4.1):

- if start is a RelativeTime value then
  first fire time = time of invocation of the start method + start

- if start is an AbsoluteTime value then
  first fire time = Maximum of (the time of start method call, start)

It then fires periodically according to the time indicated by the interval parameter in the constructor. Hence, if the start time is an absolute time of say 10 time units, and the interval is 5 time units, then the fire times of the timer would be approximately at times (assuming it is started before time 10) 10, 15, 20, and so on. If the start time is a relative time of 10 time units, and the start method is called at time 0, then again the timer would fire approximately at times 10, 15, 20, and so on. A periodic timer that is rescheduled does not fire again until the rescheduled time, it then fires periodically.

The word 'approximately' has been used here to indicate that the actual firing times may vary because of clock granularity issues (see Section 4.2). For example, the actual times of firing the event might be 11, 15, 21, 27, 30, and so on. This is usually called *local drift*. However, there will be no *cumulative drift* with a periodic timer. So for example, the last firing of the timer will not be used as the start time for the next interval.

The PeriodicTimer class overrides the createReleaseParameters and returns PeriodicReleaseParameters. Finally, there are some methods that allow the next fire time and current interval to be obtained, and the interval to be set.

Important note

The start time and interval can be measured by different clocks.

```
package javax.realtime;
public class PeriodicTimer extends Timer {
  // constructors
  public PeriodicTimer(HighResolutionTime start,
        RelativeTime interval, AsyncEventHandler handler);
  public PeriodicTimer(HighResolutionTime start,
        RelativeTime interval, Clock clock,
        AsyncEventHandler handler);

  // methods
  public ReleaseParameters createReleaseParameters();
  public AbsoluteTime getFireTime();
  public RelativeTime getInterval();
  public void setInterval(RelativeTime interval);
}
```

Figure 11.1 illustrates the main states that a timer can hold and the possible state transitions. Attempts to start an already started timer, or to start, enable, disable, destroy or reschedule a destroyed timer have no effect.

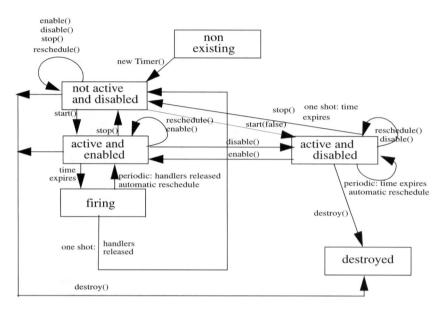

FIGURE 11.1. **Simplified State Transition Diagram for a Timer**

Important
note

A timer that is created in scoped memory has the effect of increasing the reference count associated with that scoped memory area. The reference count is decremented when the timer is destroyed. This is to ensure that the scoped memory area is active when timer interrupts occur.

11.5 Program Termination and Asynchronous Event Handlers

Many real-time systems do not terminate. However, on occasion they may, and so it is necessary to define under what conditions a program terminates. In Java, threads are classified as being daemon or user threads. The program terminates when all user threads have terminated; the daemon threads are destroyed at this point.

Warning

Version 1.0 of the RTSJ assumes all asynchronous event handlers are executed by daemons threads. This means that when all user (Java and real-time) threads are terminated, the program will terminate. Consequently, where events are bound to happenings in the environment or to timers, the program may not execute as the programmer intended.

For example, consider the spacecraft thruster system given in Section 11.7. Here, two timers are used to control the firing of an engine. The firing of these timers can be considered as external happenings. The resulting handlers are executed by daemon threads. Consequently when there are no other threads in the system, the program will terminate even though it may be in the middle of controlling the thruster engine. Of course, in this case, there will be other threads in the system so premature termination will not occur. However, the programmer does need to be aware that if a periodic activity is implemented by a periodic event handler, instead of a real-time thread with periodic release parameters, that activity will be deemed by the system to be a daemon and, therefore, will not be included when considering program termination.

Version 1.0.1 of the RTSJ has formally introduced the notion of daemon and user asynchronous event handlers:

```
package javax.realtime;
public class AsyncEventHandler implements Schedulable {
  ...

  // The following methods have been added in
  // Version 1.0.1 of the RTSJ.
  public final boolean isDaemon();
  public final void setDaemon(boolean on);
    // Throws:
    //     IllegalThreadStateException if the handler
    //     is attached to an event;
    //     SecurityException if the caller does not have
    //     the required security permissions.
}
```

By default the AsyncEventHandler class constructors set the handler to be a daemon. The status can be changed by calling the setDaemon method after the handler has been created *but before it has been attached*. A non-daemon event handler is termed a *user event handler*.

With this change, a program will terminate when

1. all non-daemon Java threads have terminated,

2. all non-daemon real-time threads have terminated,

3. the fireCount of all nondaemon asynchronous event handlers (bound or not bound) equals zero and all current releases have completed, and

4. there are no nondaemon asynchronous event handlers (bound or not bound) attached to external events or timers.

Hence, an RTSJ 1.0.1 program will not terminate while it has nondaemon event handlers attached to events, even if their `fireCounts` are zero. This allows true event-triggered systems to be implemented without having to introduce redundant user threads. Of course, careful consideration needs to be given to which handlers should be giving non-daemon status, otherwise the program will not terminate when the programmer requires.

11.6 POSIX Signals

For the case where the RTSJ is being implemented on top of a POSIX-compliant operating system, the class `POSIXSignalHandler` allows application programs to associate asynchronous event handlers with the occurrence of a POSIX signal. An abridged specification is given below (see Appendix A.38. for the full list).

```
package javax.realtime;
public final class POSIXSignalHandler {
  public static final int SIGABRT;
  public static final int SIGALRM;
  public static final int SIGBUS
  ... // Similar definitions for all POSIX signals.

  public static void addHandler(int signal,
              AsyncEventHandler handler);
  public static void removeHandler(int signal,
              AsyncEventHandler handler);
  public static void setHandler(int signal,
              AsyncEventHandler handler);
}
```

In practice, it may not be possible to handle all signals. For example, those which indicate that the program should be killed or that it has violated its memory protection boundaries may make it difficult for the whole program to remain viable.

11.7 Examples

A panic button in an intensive care unit

Most application-defined events will not need to subclass the `AsyncEvent` class. They simply need to create an event and if necessary bind it to an external happening. For example, consider a computerized hospital Intensive Care Unit. A patient's vital signs are automatically monitored and if there is cause for concern, a duty doctor is paged automatically. There is also a bedside "panic" button that can be pushed by the patient or a visitor should they feel it is necessary. However, the "panic" button is mainly for the patient/visitor's benefit; if the patient's life is really in danger, other sensors will have detected the problem. To be on the safe side, the system responds to a press of the panic button in the following ways:

- if there has been no paging of the doctor in the last five minutes, test to see if the patient's vital signs are strong, if they are weak, the duty doctor is paged immediately;

- if the vital signs are strong and a nurse has been paged in the last ten minutes, the button is ignored;

- if the vital signs are strong and a nurse has not been paged in the last ten minutes, the duty nurse is paged.

The press of the "panic" button is an external happening to the RTSJ system. It is identified by the string "PanicButton". A pager is represented by an asynchronous event; dutyDoctor and dutyNurse are the events for the doctor's and nurse's pagers respectively. The occurrence of the appropriate event results in the associated handler initiating the paging phone call.

First, the event handler for the "panic button" can be defined. The constructor attaches itself to the "panic button" event. This is a common paradigm for event handlers, the event is passed as a parameter and the constructor performs the attachment. Note also that the handler clears the fire count as it is possible that the patient/visitor has pressed the "panic button" multiple times.

```java
import javax.realtime.*;
public class PanicButtonHandler
        extends AsyncEventHandler {

  public PanicButtonHandler(AsyncEvent button,
          AsyncEvent nPager, AsyncEvent dPager,
          PatientVitalSignsMonitor signs) {
    super();
    lastPageTime = new AbsoluteTime(0,0);
    myClock = Clock.getRealtimeClock();
    nursePager = nPager;
    doctorPager = dPager;
    patient = signs;
    button.addHandler(this);
      // Add this handler to the panic button.
  }
  public void handleAsyncEvent() {
    RelativeTime lastCall =
            myClock.getTime().subtract(lastPageTime);
```

```
      if(lastCall.getMilliseconds() > doctorPagesGap) {
        if(!patient.vitalSignsGood()) {
          lastPageTime = myClock.getTime();
          doctorePager.fire();
        } else {
          if(lastCall.getMilliseconds() > nursePagesGap) {
            lastPageTime = myClock.getTime();
            nursePager.fire();
          }
        }
      }
    int throwAway = getAndClearPendingFireCount();
      // Clear multiple presses and throw away result.
  }
  private AbsoluteTime lastPageTime;
  private Clock myClock;
  private final long nursePagesGap = 600000; // 10 mins
  private final long doctorPagesGap = 300000;// 5 mins
  private AsyncEvent nursePager;
  private AsyncEvent doctorPager;
  private PatientVitalSignsMonitor patient;
}
```

The following shows the code required to set up the "panic button". Given that the handler is a Schedulable object, its scheduling and release parameters must be defined. The release parameters will be aperiodic in this case.

```
// Assume the nursePager and doctorPager have been
// defined and are in an appropriate memory area.
AsyncEvent nursePager = new AsyncEvent();
AsyncEvent doctorPager = new AsyncEvent();

// Assume also a class for monitoring the
// patient's vital signs
PatientVitalSignsMonitor signs = new ... ;

// and appropriate scheduling parameters for the handler.
PriorityParameters appropriatePriority = new ...;

...

AsyncEvent panicButton = new AsyncEvent();

// Create handler.
```

```
AsyncEventHandler handler = new PanicButtonHandler(
        panicButton, nursePager,doctorPager, signs);

// Assign scheduling parameters.
handler.setSchedulingParameters(appropriatePriority);
handler.setReleaseParameters(
            panicButton.createReleaseParameters());
if(!handler.addToFeasibility()) {
  // Output warning.
}
panicButton.bindTo("PanicButton");
// Start monitoring.
```

Spacecraft thruster control system

Consider a spacecraft that is orbiting the Earth. In order to change its orbit, it needs to "burn" (fire) a thruster engine for a finite period of time. The duration of the engine "burn" is set by the astronaut via a dial. To initiate the thruster, the astronaut presses a thruster button. Control of the engine requires a 100-millisecond periodic activity to adjust the valve settings to avoid mechanical drift and, therefore, obtain an even fuel flow. The RTSJ-based control of the thruster system consists of the following components:

- an asynchronous event bound to the thruster button; a pressing of the button results in the event being fired;
- an asynchronous event handler that is scheduled for execution as a result of the thruster event firing; to cater for "bounce" of the button, the event handler ignores multiple presses;
- a periodic timer that when started will generate events every 100 milliseconds;
- a handler for the periodic timer that will provide the engine control algorithm;
- a one-shot timer that will be used to control the duration of the engine "burn";
- a handler for the one-shot timer that will destroy the periodic timer, thereby turning off the engine.

The following class defines the interface to the thruster dial; the details of this class are of no concern here.

```
import javax.realtime.RelativeTime;
public class ThrusterDial {
  public ThrusterDial();
  public RelativeTime getSetting();
}
```

Engine control is performed by the `EngineControl` class. This implements a `Runnable` interface. The `start` and `stop` methods start and stop the engine respectively. The `run` method provides the control algorithm needed every 100 milliseconds. Again the details of these methods are of no concern here. Note, however, the `EngineControl` class will eventually be tied to an event handler that will be used in conjunction with a periodic timer. As the `run` method does not need access to any of the protected methods of the `AsyncEventHandler` class, the `EngineControl` class can be independent from it. Contrast this with the `ThrusterButtonHandler` class given later.

```
public class EngineControl implements Runnable {
  public EngineControl();
  public void start();
  public void stop();

  public void run();
    // Adjusts valve to ensure no mechanical drift
    // and, thereby, achieve a steady fuel flow.
}
```

The `EngineStop` class is similar in structure. It also implements the `Runnable` interface. However, it will be tied to a one-shot timer. Its goal is to turn off the engine and to destroy the periodic timer that implements the engine control algorithm.

```
public class EngineStop implements Runnable {
  public EngineStop(PeriodicTimer engine,
                    EngineControl control) {
    myEngine = engine;
    myControl = control;
  }

  public void run() {
    myControl.stop(); // turn off engine
    myEngine.destroy(); // destroy timer
  }
  private PeriodicTimer myEngine;
  private EngineControl myControl;
}
```

The `ThrusterButtonHandler` class is the event handler that responds to the button being pressed. It must get the duration of the engine "burn", start the engine, create and start a periodic timer for the engine control, and create and start a one-shot timer for turning off the engine. It also deals with any bounce or multiple pressing of the button. To do this, it must access the protected methods of the `AsyncEventHandler` class. It is, therefore, a subclass of that class.

```
import javax.realtime.*;
public class ThrusterButtonHandler
                extends AsyncEventHandler {

  public ThrusterButtonHandler(AsyncEvent button,
        ThrusterDial dial, EngineControl control) {
    super();
    myDial = dial;
    myControl = control;
    button.addHandler(this);
  }

  public void handleAsyncEvent() {
    // Look to see when last button press was, if recent,
    // ignore it, otherwise perform the following.
    RelativeTime thrusterDuration = myDial.getSetting();
    myEngineTimer = new PeriodicTimer(null,
        new RelativeTime(100,0),
        new AsyncEventHandler(myControl));
    engineOff = new OneShotTimer(thrusterDuration,
        new AsyncEventHandler(
            new EngineStop(myEngineTimer, myControl)) );
    myControl.start(); // start the engine
    myEngineTimer.start();  // start the periodic timer
    engineOff.start();// start the one shot timer
    int throwAway = getAndClearPendingFireCount());
  }
  private PeriodicTimer myEngineTimer;
  private OneShotTimer engineOff;
  private EngineControl myControl
  private ThrusterDial myDial;
}
```

Finally, the thruster event and its handler must be created along with the thruster dial and engine controller. The event must also be bound to the environment.

```
AsyncEvent thrusterButton  = new AsyncEvent();
ThrusterButtonHandler handler =
    new ThrusterButtonHandler(thrusterButton,
      new ThrusterDial(), new EngineControl() );
thrusterButton.bindTo("ThrusterButton");
```

Object collaborations

Figure 11.2 illustrates the collaborations between the various objects. When the thruster button is pushed, the thruster button event handler is called, this reads the required duration of the burn from the thruster dial and sets up the two timers. The engine is started along with the timers. The periodic timer is scheduled for execution every 100 milliseconds and calls the engine controller. The one-shot timer fires after the burn time, stops the engine and destroys the periodic timer.

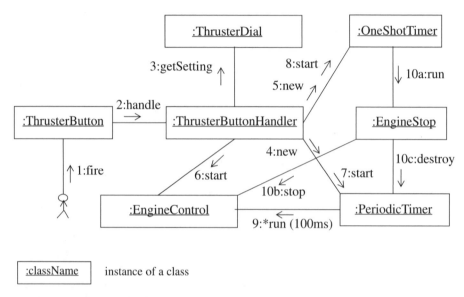

FIGURE 11.2. **Object Collaboration Diagram for the Thruster Control System**

Note that in this example, for simplicity of representation, no consideration has been given to the scheduling and release parameters of the event handlers. In particular, it has been assumed that the handler for the thruster button runs at a high priority and will not be preempted.

11.8 Asynchronous Events with Parameters

Asynchronous events are parameterless. It is possible to provide a class that builds upon the RTSJ class and provides a parameter-passing mechanism. One way of doing this is illustrated below. It extends the `AsyncEvent` class and provides a new `fire` method. This `fire` method places the object passed as a parameter into a bounded buffer (defined in Section 5.4). The `lastParam` method allows the parameter associated with the last event to be obtained. The `bindTo` method is overridden and always raises an exception, as external happenings cannot have parameters.

```
import javax.realtime.*;
import communicationAbstractions.BoundedBuffer;
public class ParameterizedAsyncEvent<Data>
              extends AsyncEvent {
  public ParameterizedAsyncEvent(int bufferSize) {
    super();
    buf = new BoundedBuffer<Data>(bufferSize);
  }
  public void fire(Data o) throws InterruptedException {
    buf.put(o);
    super.fire();
  }
  public Data lastParam() throws InterruptedException {
    return buf.get();
  }
  public void bindTo(String happening) {
    throw new UnknownHappeningException(
            happening +" cannot have parameters");
  }
  public void fire() {
    throw new IllegalArgumentException("No parameter");
  }
  protected BoundedBuffer<Data> buf;
}
```

Warning

In practice, the handling of parameters is complicated by allowing multiple handlers, each of which has its own fire count. There are several ways of dealing with this problem. One possibility is to have a buffer per attached handler and to subclass `AsyncEventHandler` so that methods that manipulate the fire count can be overridden.

11.9 Understanding Asynchronous Event Handlers

In order to appreciate and understand the limitations of the RTSJ event-handling model, it is necessary to consider how it might be implemented. The key challenge in implementing asynchronous event handlers is to

- limit the number of server real-time threads without jeopardizing the schedulability of the overall system

- have an implementation model that allows the deadlines of the handlers to be predicted.

This section considers sporadic and periodic event handlers; to have analysable aperiodic event handlers requires them to be implemented within the context of `Process-ingGroupParameters` (see Section 10.4.5). From a priority-based scheduling perspective, each sporadic or periodic handler has an inter-arrival time, a deadline and a priority. Here, it is assumed that the priorities have been set by the programmer, perhaps using a deadline monotonic priority assignment algorithm (see Section 10.1).

A thread per handler versus a single thread model

At one extreme of the continuum of possible implementation strategies is the approach that allocates a real-time thread for each handler and schedules the threads in competition with application-defined threads. While this is simple to implement and is adequate for systems with a small number of events, it is expensive for large numbers of events. Bound event handlers require a single thread per handler model.

At the other extreme, a single-server thread is used to execute all nonbound event handlers. This approach is illustrated in Figure 11.3.

There are two main issues associated with this approach:

- the order of the event handler queue
- the priority of the server thread.

To enable effective schedulability analysis and to give an appropriate response time to the handlers, the event handler queue should be priority ordered. Note that for each event firing, zero, one or more handlers may be added to a queue. The handlers might have different priorities. It is also necessary to check that the inter-arrival time of the release of the handlers has not been violated; however, this is not the concern here.

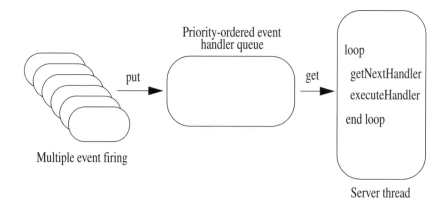

FIGURE 11.3. Handling Events via a Single Server

The priority of the server thread needs to reflect the priority of the handler it is executing. Hence, the server's priority must be dynamically changed. Furthermore, as an executing low-priority handler is not preemptible by a high-priority handler, it is necessary to implement a priority inheritance algorithm. The priority of the server thread can, therefore, be defined to be the maximum of the priority of the handler it is currently executing and the priority of the handler at the front of the event handler queue. Note that although the priority of the server is changing, it is still essentially a fixed priority system albeit with priority inheritance.

Unfortunately, there are some significant disadvantages with this approach.

Potentially unbounded priority inversion. The server thread causes priority inversion. A high-priority event handler will not be executed immediately. Instead it is blocked until the server thread finishes executing the current handler. Priority inheritance allows this blocking to be bounded, but only if the handlers themselves do not suspend (e.g., issue a `sleep` or `wait` method call). Multiple server threads are needed to avoid this problem.

No-heap event handlers. The RTSJ allows real-time threads and asynchronous event handlers to indicate that they will not access heap memory. This enables them to preempt the garbage collector safely. The single-server thread model presented above will fail when there is a mixture of heap and no-heap event handlers. For example, the server thread executing an event handler that uses the heap can inherit a no-heap event handler's priority. However, the thread is a real-time thread and, therefore, can still be preempted by the garbage collector. Consequently, the no-heap handler will be delayed when garbage collection occurs. The solution to this problem (when handlers do not block) is to have two server threads (a real-time thread and a no-heap real-time thread) and two priority ordered queues (one for real-time handlers and one for no-heap handlers).

Cost Enforcement: If cost enforcement is being implemented, the single-server thread model becomes very difficult to implement.

Multiple schedulers. If multiple schedulers are supported, then it will be necessary to have server threads for each scheduler.

Daemon handlers. If daemon handlers are introduced into the RTSJ, then further server threads will be needed.

Multiple servers

The RTSJ also allows an implementation of asynchronous event handlers to use more than one server thread and for there to be a dynamic association of handlers to threads. This general model has two main drawbacks:

- related handlers must now assume that there may be some contention for shared software resources

- the worst-case response times of the handlers are not dramatically improved as no knowledge of handler-to-server allocation can be assumed. The non-preemption time, say for a three-server thread system, is the minimum of the three maximum values of the lower-priority event handlers. To avoid this priority inversion, a new server thread could be created every time the priority of the handler at the head of the queue is greater that the priorities of the current servers. However, this more dynamic approach is more difficult to analyze.

The multiple-server approach has two main advantages over the single-server one:

- it has a better mapping for a multiprocessor system

- if a handler blocks waiting for I/O (or calls to the `sleep` and `wait` methods), other handlers may still be served. However, if all handlers block, significant priority inversion occurs.

Multiple queues and multiple handlers

A more flexible model can be obtained by having multiple queues of executable handlers, as depicted in Figure 11.4. Here, the scheduler is responsible for deciding which handler should be placed in which queue according to any feasibility analysis it can perform.

One possibility is to have a queue per priority level (Dibble, 2002b) where each queue has an associated server. If the handlers do not block, the analysis model is quite simple but pessimistic. To analyze the response time of a particular handler, it must be assumed that all other handlers at the same priority level are ahead of it in the queue. Again, to circumvent unbounded priority inversion when the handlers block, it is necessary to dynamically create new servers (or take them from a pool) as and when necessary.

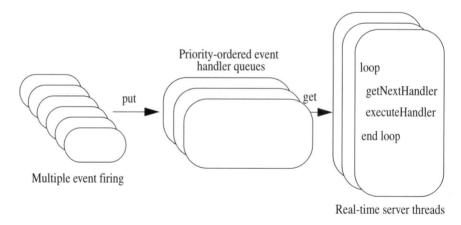

FIGURE 11.4. Multiple Queues and Multiple Servers

The main disadvantage of this general approach is that the application's programmer is not aware of the mapping; and consequently the application must still assume that there may be contention for shared resources between handlers.

11.10 Summary

Event-based systems are supported in the RTSJ by the `AsyncEvent` and `AsyncEventHandler` class hierarchies. Events can have many handlers, and a handler can handle many event occurrences. Events can also be associated with external happenings such as interrupts. If the real-time virtual machine is being implemented on top of a POSIX-compliant operating system, event handlers can be associated with the occurrence of a POSIX signal. Periodic, one-shot timers along with interrupt handlers are also supported.

Event handlers are schedulable entities and consequently can be given release and scheduling parameters. They compete with real-time threads for processor time according to their associated scheduler. They can be defined to be of the "no-heap" variety, in which case their execution can safely preempt garbage collection.

The RTSJ allows considerable freedom in the implementation of event handlers. This chapter has considered various models from the simple thread per handler model through to multiple server threads. Most models have their advantages and their drawbacks. Implementing the RTSJ event-handling model in an efficient and predictable manner is a major challenge for vendors; of particular concern is the implementation of cost enforcement and deadline monitoring.

Furthermore, if programmers are going to design efficient and analyzable event-based systems, they need to have a good understanding of how the model has been implemented. They will also need to have some control over the allocation of handlers to server threads.

12 Real-Time Threads

Introduction and chapter structure

For nontrivial real-time systems, it is necessary to model the activities in the controlled system with concurrent objects in the program. While conventional Java supports the notion of a thread that can be used for this purpose, in practice Java threads are both too general and yet not expressive enough to capture the properties of real-time activities. For example, most real-time activities have deadlines, yet there is no notion of a deadline in Java. Real-time activities are also usually characterized by their execution patterns: being periodic, sporadic or aperiodic. While all these patterns can be represented in Java, it can only be done by coding conventions in the program. Such conventions are error-prone and obscure the true nature of the application. For these reasons, the RTSJ introduces the notion of real-time threads. Although the classes that support real-time threads are presented as subclasses of the `Thread` class, this apparently simple relationship is a little misleading, as support for real-time threads (and some of the other RTSJ classes) require fundamental changes to the Java virtual machine. They are not just a library extension. Also, some of the methods that are provided by the `Thread` class are defined as final and, therefore, cannot be overridden, but have applicability to real-time threads; these have to be redefined; for example, `Thread.setPriority()`. Unfortunately, the notion of thread groups is not carried across very successfully to real-time threads.

This chapter discusses the `RealtimeThread` and `NoHeapRealtimeThread` classes and how they can be used with the `ReleaseParameters` class hierarchy to implement periodic, sporadic and aperiodic activities.

12.1 The Basic Model

The RTSJ defines two classes to support real-time threads: `RealtimeThread` and `NoHeapRealtimeThread`, the latter being a subclass of the former. Real-time threads are schedulable objects and, therefore, can have associated release, scheduling, memory and processing group parameters. A real-time thread can also have its memory area set.

Important
noteBy default, a real-time thread inherits the scheduling parameters of its parent (that is, the Java thread or schedulable object that created it). If the parent has no scheduling parameters (perhaps because it was a Java thread), the scheduler's default values are used. Other parameters default to those of the associated scheduler. See Section 10.3 for the default values for the priority scheduler.

The Real-timeThread class

The following defines the various constructors associated with the `RealtimeThread` class.

```
package javax.realtime;
public class RealtimeThread extends Thread
        implements Schedulable {

// constructors
public RealtimeThread();

// The following constructors throw:
// IllegalArgumentException if the parameters are not
//        compatible with the default scheduler;
// IllegalAssignmentError if there is a conflict in the
//        memory areas of the parameters and the new
//        RealtimeThread.
public RealtimeThread(SchedulingParameters scheduling);
public RealtimeThread(SchedulingParameters scheduling,
                       ReleaseParameters release);
public RealtimeThread(SchedulingParameters scheduling,
    ReleaseParameters release, MemoryParameters memory,
    MemoryArea area, ProcessingGroupParameters group,
    Runnable logic);

// Methods which implement the Schedulable interface
// see Section 10.2.
...
}
```

As the `RealtimeThread` class implements the schedulable interface, there is a set of methods for meeting its requirements. These methods have been described in Section 10.2.

The next set of methods deal with memory areas. As mentioned in Chapters 7 and 8, a real-time thread can enter into one or more memory areas. These areas are stacked, and the stack can be manipulated by the owning thread only (hence why the methods are declared as being static[1]). Only `getCurrentMemoryArea` can be called from a Java thread the others will throw a `ClassCastException`.

The `getCurrentMemoryArea` method gets the memory area that is currently being used for object allocation. The `getOuterMemoryArea` allows memory areas lower down the stack to be accessed. A real-time thread inherits a copy of the memory area stack of its parent. The `getInitialMemoryAreaIndex` method allows a thread to determine the depth of the stack that it was initially created with. Finally, `get-MemoryAreaStackDepth` allows the current depth of the stack to be determined.

In contrast, the `getMemoryArea` can be called by schedulable objects other than the owning real-time thread. It returns the default (initial) memory area used by the real-time thread. Memory allocation will occur from this area unless the real-time thread has entered into any new memory areas, or unless it explicitly requests allocation to occur elsewhere.

```
package javax.realtime;
public class RealtimeThread extends Thread
        implements Schedulable {
  ...
  public static MemoryArea getCurrentMemoryArea();

  // The following methods throw ClassCastException.
  public static MemoryArea getOuterMemoryArea(int index);
  public static int getInitialMemoryAreaIndex();
  public static int getMemoryAreaStackDepth();

  // The following method was added at Version 1.0.1
  public MemoryArea getMemoryArea();
  ...
}
```

Although `RealtimeThread` extends `Thread`, it only overrides, overloads or redefines a few of its methods. The `interrupt` method is redefined so that it can implement asynchronous transfer of control (see Chapter 13). Two new `sleep` methods are defined to interface with the new time and clock classes. The `start` method is also redefined so that it can record that any associated memory area has now become active. The real-time counterpart of `Thread.currentThread` is defined to allow the currently executing real-time thread to be identified. An exception is thrown if the currently executing thread is not a real-time thread (it may be, for example, a conventional Java

---

1. Note they can also be called by asynchronous event handlers as well—see Section 8.6.

thread)[2]. Finally, the redefined getPriority and setPriority methods are shown, which allow the expanded range of real-time priorities to be used.

```
package javax.realtime;
public class RealtimeThread extends Thread
        implements Schedulable {
  ...
  public void interrupt();

  public static void sleep(Clock clock,
          HighResolutionTime time)
          throws InterruptedException;
  public static void sleep(HighResolutionTime time)
          throws InterruptedException;

  public void start();

  public static RealtimeThread currentRealtimeThread();
    // Throws ClassCastException.

  // The following methods re-defined the methods in the
  // Thread class, they are given here for reference.

  public final int getPriority();
    // Equivalent to getSchedulingParameters().getPriority().

  public final void setPriority(int newPriority);
    // Equivalent to
    //     getSchedulingParameters().setPriority(newPriority).
  ...
}
```

The final set of methods are for the special case where the real-time thread has periodic release parameters. The waitForNextPeriod method suspends the thread until its next release time (unless the thread has missed its deadline – see below). The call returns true when the thread is next released. If the thread is not a periodic thread, an exception is thrown.

The deschedulePeriodic method will cause the associated thread to block at the end of its current release (when it next calls waitForNextPeriod). It will then remain blocked until schedulePeriodic is called. The thread now suspended is waiting for its next period to begin, when it is released again. Of course, if the associated thread is not a periodic thread, it will not call waitForNextPeriod and,

---

2. In this context, calling currentRealtimeThread from an event handler returns the server real-time thread currently executing that handler.

therefore, deschedulePeriodic and schedulePeriodic will have no effect. When a periodic thread is "rescheduled" in this manner, the scheduler is informed so that it can remove or add the thread to the list of schedulable objects it is managing.

```
package javax.realtime;
public class RealtimeThread extends Thread
     implements Schedulable {
  ...
  public static boolean waitForNextPeriod()
    // Throws IllegalThreadStateException;
  public static boolean WaitForNextPeriodInterruptible()
       throws InterruptedException;
    // Throws IllegalThreadStateException.
    // An interruptible version of waitForNextPeriod.
    // Added at version 1.0.1.
  public void deschedulePeriodic();
  public void schedulePeriodic();  ...
}
```

The waitForNextPeriodInteruptible method has the same semantics as waitForNextPeriod except that it throws the InterruptedException if the real-time thread is the target of an asynchronous transfer of control request while the thread is waiting for its next release to occur.

12.1.1 Cost overrun and deadline miss for periodic real-time threads

Recall from Section 10.4.1, the ReleaseParameters associated with a real-time thread can specify asynchronous event handlers that are released by the system if the associated real-time thread misses its deadline or overruns its cost allocation (budget). In version 1.0.1 of the RTSJ, the cost overrun and deadline miss model is underspecified, particularly for asynchronous event handlers (see Section 11.3) and for real-time threads with sporadic and aperiodic release parameters (see Section 12.3). The model is, however, coherent for real-time threads with periodic release parameters (called *periodic real-time threads* below).

Under the priority scheduler, a cost overrun results in the periodic real-time thread being immediately automatically descheduled (that is, it becomes not eligible for execution) and any cost overrun handler released. The real-time thread will not be rescheduled (made eligible for execution) until either its next release occurs (in which case its CPU budget is automatically replenished with the cost value) or its associated cost value is increased. In contrast, if the real-time thread misses its deadline, the thread is *not* immediately descheduled (unless it has also suffered a cost overrun). Any associated deadline miss handler is released at the point the deadline expires. If there is no associated handler at the point, the deadline miss occurs, a count (called deadlineMiss) of the number of missed deadlines is incremented.

The waitForNextPeriod (wFNP) (and waitForNextPeriodInterruptible) method (under the default priority scheduler) has the following semantics:

- When the deadlineMiss count is greater than zero and the previous call to wFNP returned *true*, wFNP decrements the deadlineMiss count and returns false immediately. This situation indicates that the *current* release has missed its deadline. *At this point, the current release is still active (this means the current budget is unaltered).*

- When the deadlineMiss count is greater than zero and the previous call to wFNP returned *false*, wFNP decrements the deadlineMiss count and returns false immediately. This situation indicates that the *next* release time has already passed and the next deadline has already been missed. *At this point, the current release has completed and the next release is active (and if it has not been allocated already, a new budget of cost is allocated).*

- When a deadline miss handler has been released and the deadlineMiss count equals zero and no call to the schedulePeriodic method has occurred since the deadline miss handler was released, wFNP deschedules the real-time thread until a call to the schedulePeriodic method occurs; wfNP then returns true at the point of the next release *after* the call to SchedulePeriodic. *At this point, the next release is active (and a new budget of cost is allocated).*

- When the deadlineMiss count equals zero and no deadline has been missed on the current release and the time for the next release has passed, wFNP returns true immediately. *At this point, the next release is active (and a new budget of cost is allocated).*

- When the deadlineMiss count equals zero and no deadline has been missed on the current release and the time for the next release has not passed, wFNP returns true at the next release time. *At which point, the next release is active (and a new budget of cost is allocated).*

A call to the schedulePeriod method sets the deadlineMiss count to zero Note that the fireCount for the deadlineMiss handler indicates the number of deadline overruns that have occurred.

1. If the programmer has set up the appropriate deadline miss handler, the RTSJ assumes that the handler will take some corrective action and then (if appropriate) reschedule the thread by calling the schedulePeriodic method. In this situation, waitForNextPeriod returns at the next release time *following* the call to schedulePeriodic. *All releases in between are lost.*

2. If the programmer has not set up the appropriate handler, the `waitForNext-Period` method will not deschedule the real-time thread in the event of a deadline miss. The RTSJ assumes that in this situation the thread itself will undertake some corrective action and then call `waitForNextPeriod` again. In this situation, the application may suffer a cost overrun if the time to handle the condition has not been accounted for in the cost parameter.

3. If a cost overrun occurs and no overrun handler is present, usually the only way for the periodic real-time thread to be rescheduled is when its next release occurs (unless some other event has occurred that implies that the real-time thread will overrun—in which case another schedulable object might increase the cost). This has the effect of giving it a new CPU budget of cost units. In this case, the periodic real-time thread will probably miss its deadline (particularly as the default priority scheduler requires that the deadline be less than or equal to the period).

4. Application-level calls to `deschedulePeriodic` take effect when the current release completes and all deadline misses have been accounted for (even if the next release has already occurred).

Example

Consider the following periodic real-time thread with deadline less than period illustrated in Figure 12.1

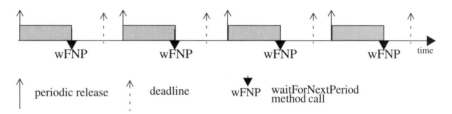

FIGURE 12.1. **The Release of a Periodic Real-time Thread**

Now consider the case where a deadline miss occurs as a result of a transient overload condition. The handler waits for the overload to subside and then reschedules the real-time thread. The time at which `schedulePeriodic` is called is marked with an **X** in Figure 12.2.

FIGURE 12.2. **The Release of a Periodic Real-time Thread with a Deadline Miss and a Deadline Miss Handler**

The case where there is no handler is illustrated in Figure 12.3. Here, the application repairs the situation and calls `waitForNextPeriod` again (assuming there is no cost overrun).

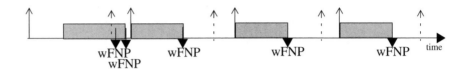

FIGURE 12.3. The Release of a Periodic Real-time Thread with a Deadline Miss and no Deadline Miss Handler

Deadline miss handlers can be dynamically added and removed while the real-time thread is executing. The RTSJ has two simple rules to ensure that the behavior of the `waitForNextPeriod` method is well defined. They are

1. when a deadline miss occurs and a handler is released, the `fireCount` of the handler is increased by the `deadlineMiss` count + 1, and the `deadlineMiss` count is set to zero;

2. the `waitForNextPeriod` method always returns immediately if the `deadlineMiss` count is greater than zero irrespective of whether a deadline miss handler is still active.

The programmer is responsible for handling any race conditions that might occur as a result of these dynamic changes.

12.2 The `NoHeapRealtimeThread` Class

One of the main weaknesses with Java, from a real-time perspective, is that threads can be arbitrarily delayed by the action of the garbage collector. The RTSJ has attacked this problem by allowing objects to be created in memory areas other than the heap. These areas are not subject to garbage collection. A nonheap real-time thread is a real-time thread that only ever accesses non-heap memory areas. Consequently, it can safely be executed even when garbage collection is occurring.

The constructors for the `NoHeapRealtimeThread` class all contain references to a memory area; all memory allocation performed by the thread will be from within this memory area. An unchecked exception is thrown if the HeapMemory area is passed. The start method is redefined; its goal is to check that the NoHeapReal-timeThread has not been allocated on the heap and that it has obtained no heap-allocated parameters. If either of these requirements has been violated, an unchecked exception is thrown.

```
package javax.realtime;
public class NoHeapRealtimeThread extends RealtimeThread {
   // constructors

   // The following constructors throw
   // IllegalArgumentException and IllegalAssigmentError.
   public NoHeapRealtimeThread(
       SchedulingParameters scheduling, MemoryArea area);
   public NoHeapRealtimeThread(
       SchedulingParameters scheduling,
       ReleaseParameters release, MemoryArea area);
   public NoHeapRealtimeThread(
       SchedulingParameters scheduling,
       ReleaseParameters release, MemoryParameters memory,
       MemoryArea area, ProcessingGroupParameters group,
       Runnable logic);

   // methods
   public void start();
       // Throws MemoryAccessError.
}
```

Important note

A no-heap real-time thread will only preempt the garbage collection if it has been given a priority higher than all heap-using real-time threads. Otherwise, garbage collection may occur on behalf of the high-priority real-time threads.

Warning

A no-heap real-time thread may require significant run-time checks to ensure that it does not reference the heap. Some of these checks may be omitted through static analysis if the compilation system is RTSJ-aware.

12.3 The Model of Periodic, Sporadic and Aperiodic Threads

Given that most real-time activities can be characterized as being either periodic, sporadic or aperiodic, it is crucial to have mechanisms in a real-time programming language that allow these abstractions to be represented easily. The RTSJ supports real-time threads and distinguishes between them in terms of their release parameters. However, there is no clean separation, as the real-time thread class has methods that support periodic activities only. Consequently, the structure for a periodic thread in RTSJ is given by (for example)

```
public class Periodic extends RealtimeThread {
  public Periodic(
      PriorityParameters pri, PeriodicParameters per) {
    super(pri, per);
  }
  public void run() {
    boolean noProblems = true;
    while(noProblems) {
      // Code to be run each period.
      ...
      noProblems = waitForNextPeriod();
    }
    // A deadline has been missed and there is no
    // event handler to schedule for recovery.
    ...
  }
}
```

Periodic threads are those real-time threads created with `PeriodicParameters`. The `start` method is called for the initial release of the thread (possibly with a time offset). Once the thread has executed, it calls `waitForNextPeriod` (or `waitForNextPeriodInterruptible`) to indicate to the scheduler that it should be made executable again when its next release period is due. Note that there needs to be a loop inside the `run` method.

The models for sporadic and aperiodic threads are not so clear. Unlike periodic threads, their release parameters have no start time, so they can be considered to be released as soon as they are started. However, there is no standard mechanism for them to indicate to the scheduler that they have completed their execution (other than by terminating) and no standard mechanism for them to be re-released.

Warning

There is no equivalent of `waitForNextPeriod` (contrast this with sporadic and asynchronous event handlers that have a `fire` method and a `handleAsyncEvent` method that is executed for each call of fire – see Chapter 11). Consequently, version 1.0.1 of the RTSJ supports only one-shot real-time threads with sporadic or aperiodic release parameters. Programmers must, therefore, provide their own support for this functionality if required.

One approach is to define an extension of the `RealtimeThread` class to provide the equivalent support of `waitForNextPeriod`. This is illustrated in Figure 12.4 below for aperiodic threads. An aperiodic thread is initially released by a call to the `start` method. When it wishes to wait for a new release, it calls the method `wait-ForNextRelease`. This returns false if the deadline from the last release has been missed. Subsequent releases occur by calls to the `release` method. In this example, the constructor assumes the priority scheduler is the default scheduler. It also assumes that calls to `release` are buffered and so requires the size of the buffer. *Note that this class is not part of the RTSJ.*

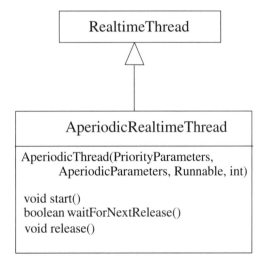

FIGURE 12.4. A User-defined Aperiodic Real-time Thread abstraction

The implementation of this AperiodicRealtimeThread class abstraction has the following simplification:

- For simplicity of illustration, deadline misses are not detected until the thread completes its execution and waits for its next release, and there is no provision for deadline miss event handlers;

- no overrun of the CPU cost is detected (the RTSJ has no primitive classes that would allow an applications programmer to monitor the CPU time consumed, although an implementation may provide such a facility as an extension to the Clock class);

- the aperiodic thread can only be released by software, there is no mechanism for allowing a hardware interrupt to release the thread (this situation is best catered for by the use of event handlers – see Chapter 11).

In order to detect a deadline miss, it is necessary to know the release time of the aperiodic thread. In general, there are several models that could be supported. The model implemented here is that the implementation of release (and start) uses the current value of the real-time clock. (An array is used to buffer the release calls.) Of course, the releaser could be preempted between it calling release and the clock being read, but this is acceptable as it could also have been preempted between its decision to call release and the actual call of release. The priority inheritance protocol is used during lock management of the object.

```
import javax.realtime.*;
public class AperiodicThread extends RealtimeThread {
  public AperiodicThread(PriorityParameters scheduling,
      AperiodicParameters release, int queueSize) {
    super(scheduling, release);
    releaseTimes = new AbsoluteTime[queueSize];
    first = queueSize -1;
    last = 0;
    size = queueSize;
    myClock = Clock.getRealtimeClock();
    myDeadline = release.getDeadline();
    MonitorControl.setMonitorControl(this,
        PriorityInheritance.instance());
  }
  public void start() {
    // Save the release time.
    synchronized(this) {
      releaseTimes[last] = myClock.getTime();
      last = (last + 1) % size;
    }
    super.start();
  }
```

```java
  public boolean waitForNextRelease() {
    synchronized(this) {
      first = (first + 1) % size;

      // Check for miss deadline.
      AbsoluteTime lastDeadline =
        releaseTimes[first].add(myDeadline);
      if(myClock.getTime().compareTo(lastDeadline) == 1)
        return false; // deadline miss
      try {
        while(((first + 1) % size) == last) wait();
        return true;
      } catch(Exception e) {
        return false;
      }
    }
  }
  public void release() {
    synchronized(this) {
      // Throws ResourceLimitError.
      if (first ==  last)
        throw new ResourceLimitError();
      releaseTimes[last] = myClock.getTime();
      last = (last + 1) % size;
      notify();
    }
  }

  private AbsoluteTime releaseTimes[];
  private int first, last, size;
  private Clock myClock;
  private RelativeTime myDeadline;
}
```

To use this class, it is necessary to extend it and override the run method to provide the functionality of the thread. For example,

```java
  public class MyAperiodic extends AperiodicThread {
    public void run() {
      boolean noProblems = true;
      while(noProblems) {
        myLogic.run();
        noProblems = waitForNextRelease();
      }
      // Deal with deadline overrun.
    }
  }
```

User-defined sporadic threads can be similarly implemented. Here, however, minimum inter-arrival time violations also need to be detected. This can be done in a similar manner to the model provided by sporadic event handlers.

Version 1.1 note User-implemented real-time threads with sporadic or aperiodic release parameters are severely limited in their ability to detect cost overruns. Consequently, it is likely that Version 1.1. of the RTSJ will provide the `waitForNextRelease` and `release` methods directly in the `RealtimeThread` class.

12.4 Monitoring Deadline Misses in Periodic Real-time Threads

In many soft real-time systems, applications will want to monitor any deadline misses, but take no action unless a certain threshold is reached. (For contrast, Section 13.8, gives an example where the asynchronous transfer of control facilities are used to inform the schedulable object immediately of any problems.)

Here, a health monitor object is assumed with the following interface:

```
import javax.realtime.*;
public class HealthMonitor {
  public void persistentDeadlineMiss(Schedulable s);
}
```

Now consider the following event handler for catching a missed deadline of a periodic real-time thread:

```
import javax.realtime.*;
class DeadlineMissHandler extends AsyncEventHandler {

  public DeadlineMissHandler(HealthMonitor mon,
                             int threshold) {
    super(new PriorityParameters(
             PriorityScheduler.MAX_PRIORITY),
          null, null, null, null, null);
    myHealthMonitor = mon;
    myThreshold = threshold;
  }
```

```
public void setThread(RealtimeThread rt)
{
  myrt = rt;
}
public void handleAsyncEvent()
{
  if(++missDeadlineCount < myThreshold)
    myrt.schedulePeriodic();
  else
    myHealthMonitor.persistentDeadlineMiss(myrt);
}
private RealtimeThread myrt;
private int missDeadlineCount = 0;
private HealthMonitor myHealthMonitor;
private final int myThreshold;
}
```

When the handler is executed, it increments the miss count and reschedules the thread. When the count reaches the threshold, it informs the health monitor and does not reschedule the thread.

Note that it is not possible to pass the real-time thread as a parameter to the constructor of the handler, as the handler itself is needed before the real-time thread can be constructed. Consequently, either the real-time thread must be created with a null handler and the handler set later or the handler class must allow the associated real-time thread to be set later. The latter approach is adopted here.

The following code sets up the real-time periodic thread:

```
{
  PriorityScheduler ps = (PriorityScheduler)Scheduler.
                       getDefaultScheduler();
  HealthMonitor healthMonitor = new HealthMonitor();
  DeadlineMissHandler missHandler = new
    DeadlineMissHandler(healthMonitor, 5);
  PriorityParameters pp1 = new
    PriorityParameters(ps.getMinPriority());

  PeriodicParameters release1 = new PeriodicParameters(
    new RelativeTime( 0,0),    // start,
    new RelativeTime(1000,0),  // period
    new RelativeTime( 100,0),  // cost
    new RelativeTime(500, 0),  // deadline
    null,                      // no overrun handler
    missHandler);              // miss handler
```

```
RealtimeThread rtt1 = new RealtimeThread(pp1,release1) {
    public void run() {
        // Code for thread.
    }
}
missHandler.setThread(rtt1);
rtt1.start();
}
```

Important note	Deadline miss handlers are schedulable objects. Consequently, they will compete for processor time with their associated schedulable objects according to their priorities. Hence, for the handler to have an impact on the (in this case) errant real-time thread, it must have a priority higher than the real-time thread. If the priority is lower, it will not run until the errant thread blocks.

12.5 Summary

The RTSJ supports the notion of schedulable objects with various types of release characteristics. This chapter has reviewed two types of schedulable objects: real-time threads and no-heap real-time threads. The chapter has illustrated that periodic activities are well catered for and has an integrated approach to handling cost overruns and deadline misses. The `waitForNextPeriod` (wFNP) method has the following semantics:

- When the `deadlineMiss` count is greater than zero and the previous call to wFNP returned *true*, wFNP decrements the `deadlineMiss` count and returns false immediately. This situation indicates that the *current* release has missed its deadline.

- When the `deadlineMiss` count is greater than zero and the previous call to wFNP returned *false*, wFNP decrements the `deadlineMiss` count and returns false immediately. This situation indicates that the *next* release time has already passed and the next deadline has already been missed.

- When a deadline miss handler has been released and the `deadlineMiss` count equals zero and no call to the `schedulePeriodic` method has occurred since the deadline miss handler was released, wFNP deschedules the real-time thread until a call to the `schedulePeriodic` method occurs; wFNP then returns true at the point of the next release *after* the call to `SchedulePeriodic`.

- When the `deadlineMiss` count equals zero and no deadline has been missed on the current release and the time for the next release has passed, `wFNP` returns true immediately.

- When the `deadlineMiss` count equals zero and no deadline has been missed on the current release and the time for the next release has not passed, `wFNP` returns true at the next release time.

Deadline miss handlers can be dynamically added and removed while the real-time thread is executing.

Unfortunately, support for aperiodic and sporadic activities is lacking. It is currently not possible for the RTSJ to detect either deadline miss or cost overruns for these activities, as there is no notion of a release event. Indeed, with Version 1.0.1 of the RTSJ, programmers are best advised to use event handlers to represent nonperiodic activities. It is likely that version 1.1. will provide the required support in this area.

13 Asynchronous Transfer of Control

Introduction and chapter structure

An asynchronous transfer of control (ATC) happens when the point of execution of one schedulable object (real-time thread or asynchronous event handler) is changed by the action of another schedulable object. Consequently, a schedulable object may be executing in one method and then suddenly, through no action of its own, find itself executing in another method. The inclusion of an ATC mechanism into any language is controversial (Burns and Wellings, 2001) and its introduction into the RTSJ is no exception (Brosgol, Robbins and Hassan, 2002). The primary reasons for this controversy are that ATC

- complicates the language's semantics,
- makes it difficult to write correct code as the code may be subject to interference,
- increases the complexity of the real-time JVM, and
- may slow down the execution of code that does not use the feature.

Despite all these disadvantages, ATC is an attempt to meet specific requirements of the real-time community. This chapter starts by reviewing the application-level requirements that motivated the inclusion of an ATC facility into the RTSJ. The basic model is then explored, and the notion of an asynchronously interrupted exception (AIE) is introduced along with its defining class.

Methods that allow ATCs to occur during their execution must explicitly indicate their permission by including AsynchronouslyInterruptedException in their throw clauses. All other methods are considered ATC-deferred; any ATC request targeted at a schedulable object while it is executing in an ATC-deferred method is held back until it can be delivered safely within a method allowing ATCs.

Following the discussion of the basic model, the Interruptible interface is introduced. This gives the programmer a high-level mechanism on which to build applications that use the ATC facilities. The problem of nested ATCs is considered in this context.

One particularly useful form of ATC is where the request for the transfer is caused by the passage of time. This is discussed, and an example of its use is given. The chapter concludes with three further examples. The first uses ATCs in conjunction with asynchronous event handlers to program recovery strategies for deadline misses. The second illustrates how user-level interrupts can be catered for. The final example shows how error handling between concurrent schedulable objects can be performed.

13.1 Application Requirements for Asynchronous Transfer of Control

The primary application-level requirement is to enable a schedulable object to respond *quickly* to a condition that has been detected by another schedulable object (or by the real-time virtual machine). The emphasis here is on a quick response; clearly a schedulable object can always respond to a condition by simply *polling* (as with the conventional Java interrupt mechanism and threads) or *waiting* for that condition. The notification of the condition can easily be mapped onto Java's monitor mechanisms. The handling schedulable object, when it is ready to receive the condition, simply issues the appropriate monitor call. Alternatively, the RTSJ event-handling mechanism can be used to schedule a handler.

Unfortunately, there are occasions when polling, waiting for conditions or scheduling event handlers is inadequate. These include the following (Burns and Wellings, 2001):

Error recovery between coordinated threads. Where several schedulable objects are collectively solving a problem, an error detected by one schedulable object may need to be quickly and safely communicated to the other schedulable objects. These types of activities are often called *atomic actions*. An error detected in one schedulable object requires all other schedulable objects to participate in the recovery. For example, a hardware fault detected by one real-time thread may mean that the other real-time threads will never finish their planned execution because the preconditions under which they started no longer hold; the real-time threads may never reach their polling point. Also, a timing fault might have occurred, which means that the real-time threads will no longer meet their deadline for the delivery of their service. In both these situations, the threads must be informed that an error has been detected and that they must undertake some error recovery as quickly as possible.

Mode changes. A real-time system often has several modes of operation. For example, a fly-by-wire civil aircraft may have a take-off mode, a cruising mode and a landing mode. On many occasions, changes between modes can be carefully managed and will occur at well-defined points in the system's execution, as in a normal flight plan for a civil aircraft. Unfortunately, in some application areas, mode changes are expected but cannot be planned. For example, a fault may lead to an aircraft abandoning its take-off and entering an emergency mode of operation; an accident in a manufacturing process may require an immediate mode change to ensure an orderly shutdown of the plant. In these situations, schedulable objects must be quickly and safely informed that the mode in which they were operating has changed, and that they now need to undertake a different set of actions.

Scheduling using partial/imprecise computations. There are many algorithms where the accuracy of the results depends on how much time can be allocated to their calculation. For example, numerical computations, statistical estimations and heuristic searches may all produce an initial estimation of the required result and then refine that result to a greater accuracy. At run-time, a certain amount of time can be allocated to an algorithm, and then, when that time has been used, the schedulable object must be interrupted, stopping further refinement of the result.

User interrupts. In an interactive environment, operators may wish to stop the current processing activity because they have detected an error condition and wish to initiate alternative actions.

One approach to ATC is to destroy the schedulable object and allow another schedulable object to perform some recovery. All operating systems and most concurrent programming languages provide such a facility for threads/processes. However, destroying a thread can be expensive and is often an extreme response to many error conditions. Furthermore, it may leave the system in an inconsistent state (for example, monitor locks may not be released). Consequently, some form of controlled ATC mechanism is required.

13.2 The Basic Model

The RTSJ model of asynchronous transfer of control brings together the Java exception handling model and an extension of thread interruption. Essentially the model is that when a real-time thread (or more generally a schedulable object) is interrupted, an asynchronous exception (`AsynchronouslyInterruptedException`) is delivered to the thread rather than the thread having to poll for the interruption as would be the case with conventional Java (see Section 3.5). `AsynchronouslyInterruptedException` is a checked exception.

The notion of an asynchronous exception is not new and has been explored in previous languages. The main problem with them is how to program safely in their presence. Most exception-handling mechanisms have exception propagation within a termination model. Consider a thread that has called method A, which has called method B, which has called method C. When an exception is raised within method C, if there is no local handler, the call to method C is terminated and a handler is sought in method B (the exception propagates up the call chain). If no handler is found in B, the exception is propagated to A. When a handler is found, it is executed, and the program continues to execute in the context in which the handler was found. *There is no return to the context where the original exception was thrown.* This model makes it difficult to write code that is tolerant of an asynchronous exception being thrown at it. Every method would need a handler for the root class of all asynchronous exceptions.

The RTSJ solution to this problem is to require that all methods (including constructors) that are prepared to allow the delivery of an asynchronous exception, place the exception in their throws lists; the RTSJ calls such methods *AI-methods* (*Asynchronously Interruptible*). If a method does not do this, then the asynchronous exception is not delivered but held pending until the schedulable object is in a method that has the asynchronous exception in its throw clause. Hence, code that has been written without being concerned with ATC can execute safely even in an environment where ATCs are being used. Furthermore, to ensure that ATC can be handled safely, the RTSJ requires that

1. ATCs are deferred during the execution of synchronized methods or statements and static initializers. This is to ensure that any shared data is left in a consistent state (however, see Section 13.4); the RTSJ calls these sections of code and the methods that are not AI methods collectively *ATC-deferred sections*.
2. An ATC can only be handled from within code that is an ATC-deferred section; this is to avoid the handler for one ATC being interrupted by another ATC being delivered.

Important note

An ATC-deferred section is defined in terms of the lexical scope of a method, statement or constructor. This is the textual region within the method, statement or constructor, and excludes any code within class declarations or the code within object creation expressions from anonymous classes. The lexical scope *does not* include the bodies of any methods or constructors called by the ATC-deferred section. For example,

```
void aiMethod() throws AsynchronouslyInterruptedException {
  Runnable  atcDeferred = new Runnable() {
    public void run() {
      // Code here is ATC-Deferred as run does not have a
      // throws AsynchronouslyInterruptedException.
    }};
  // Code here is asynchronously interruptible.
}
```

The RTSJ model is best explained in two stages. The first is the low-level support for the overall approach; the second is the use of the high-level support to provide a structured means for handling ATCs. Use of the low-level ATC facilities requires three activities:

- Declaring an AsynchronouslyInterruptedException (AIE)

- Identifying methods that can be interrupted by the ATC
- Signaling an `AsynchronouslyInterruptedException` to a schedulable object.

AIEs   AIEs are defined by the following class:

```
package javax.realtime;
public class AsynchronouslyInterruptedException extends
            InterruptedException {

  // constructor
  public AsynchronouslyInterruptedException();

  // methods
  public boolean enable();
  public boolean disable();
  public boolean isEnabled();
    // The above are only valid within a doInterruptible,
    // they return true if successful.

  public boolean doInterruptible (Interruptible logic);
    // Only one Interruptible per AIE object can be
    // running at any one time. Returns
    //    true, if the Interruptible is executed,
    //    false if one is already in progress.
    // Throws IllegalThreadStateException if called by a
    // a Java thread and IllegalArgumentException if
    // logic is null.

  public boolean fire();
    // Returns true, if enabled and a doInterruptible
    // is active and there is no outstanding fire request.
    // Returns false, otherwise.

  public boolean happened (boolean propagate);
    // Deprecated at version 1.0.1
    // Usually called from within an AIE handler.
    // Returns true, if this AIE is the current AIE.
    // Returns false, if propagate is false and this AIE
    // is not the current AIE (or if not called within
    // an AIE handler).
    // No return, if propagate is true and this AIE
    // is not the current AIE.
```

```
public static void propagate();
  // Deprecated at version 1.0.1
  // Propagate the current AIE.
  // No return if called within an AIE handler.

public boolean clear();
  // Atomically checks to see if this is the currently
  // pending exception. If it is, the pending state is
  // cleared, and true is returned. Otherwise, false is
  // returned.
  // Added at version 1.0.1.

public static AsynchronouslyInterruptedException
            getGeneric();
  // Returns the AsynchronouslyInterruptedException
  // that is generated when RealtimeThread.interrupt()
  // is invoked.
}
```

The methods will be explained in due course, but for now all that is required is to know that there is a system-wide generic AIE. This is generated when `Realtime-Thread.interrupt` is called[1] and can be made pending for *one or more* real-time threads.

To indicate that a method is interruptible requires `AsynchronouslyInter-ruptedException` to be placed in the `throws` list associated with the method. As this is a checked exception, any method calling the AI-method must itself be an AI-method, or it must have an appropriate handler. For example, consider the following class, which provides an interruptible service using a package that declares ATC-deferred services (that is, ones that do not have `throws` lists containing `Asynchro-nouslyInterruptedExceptions`).

```
import nonInterruptibleServices.*;
public class InterruptibleService {
  public boolean service()
        throws AsynchronouslyInterruptedException {
    // Code interspersed with calls to
    // NonInterruptibleServices.
  }
  ...
}
```

---

1. In this context, a call to `RealtimeThread.currentRealtimeThread()` from an asynchronous event handler can be considered to return an object representing the server real-time thread currently executing the event handler.

Now assume that a real-time thread `rtThread` has called an instance of this class to provide the `Service`:

```
// Code of real-time thread, rtThread.
InterruptibleService is = new InterruptibleService();

if(is.service()) { ... }
else { ... }
```

and that another thread interrupts `rtThread` by calling

```
rtThread.interrupt();
```

The consequences of this call depend on the current state of `rtThread` when the call is made.

- If `rtThread` is executing within an ATC-deferred section – that is, executing within the lexical scope of a synchronized method (or block), a static initializer or within a method that has *no* `AsynchronouslyInterruptedException` declared in its `throws` list (such as those in the package `nonInterruptibleServices`) – the AIE is marked as pending. The exception is delivered as soon as `rtThread` leaves the ATC-deferred region and is executing in a method with an `AsynchronouslyInterruptedException` declared in its `throws` list (such as the `service` method).

- If `rtThread` is executing within an AI-method (and it is not within a synchronized block), then the method's execution is interrupted, and control is transferred (propagated) up the calling chain until it finds a try block in an ATC-deferred region that has a catch clause naming `AsynchronouslyInterruptedException` (or a parent class). Any synchronized methods of statements that are terminated by this propagation have their monitor locks released (and their `finally` clauses executed). The handler is then executed.

- If `rtThread` is blocked inside a `sleep`, `join`, `MemoryArea.join` (or `joinAndEnter`) or `waitForNextPeriodInterruptible` method called from within an AI-method, `rtThread` is rescheduled and the `AsynchronouslyInterruptedException` is delivered.

- If `rtThread` is blocked inside a `wait`, `sleep`, `join`, `MemoryArea.join` (or `joinAndEnter`) or `waitForNextPeriodInterruptible` method called from within an ATC-deferred region, `rtThread` is rescheduled and the `AsynchronouslyInterruptedException` is thrown as a synchronous exception (it is a subclass of the `InterruptedException`) and it is also marked as pending. Even if the synchronous exception is handled, the asynchronous exception is redelivered as soon as `rtThread` enters an AI-method.

**Important
notes**

Although AIEs appear to have been integrated into the Java exception handling mechanism, the normal Java rules do not apply because

- Only the naming of the `AsynchronouslyInterruptedException` class in a `throw` clause indicates the schedulable object is interruptible. It is not possible to use the name of a subclass. This is to allow AI-methods to be readily identified in the source code and for the integration of the real-time thread interrupt semantics. Consequently, catch clauses for AIEs that name the class `AsynchronouslyInterruptedException` explicitly must exist even if catch clauses for subclasses are available.

- Handlers for `AsynchronouslyInterruptedExceptions` do not automatically `clear` the pending state of the AIE. It is necessary to call the `happened` or `clear` method in the `AsynchronouslyInterruptedException` class.

- Furthermore, as a result of the above, although catch clauses in ATC-deferred regions that name the `InterruptedException` or `Exception` classes *will handle* an `AsynchronouslyInterruptedException` they will *not* clear the pending state of the AIE.

- Although `AsynchronouslyInterruptedException` is a subclass of `InterruptedException`, which is a subclass of `Exception`, catch clauses that name these classes *in AI-methods* will not catch an `AsynchronouslyInterruptedException`.

- "Finally clauses" that are declared in AI-methods are not executed when an ATC is delivered. "Finally clauses" in ATC-deferred regions (including synchronized blocks or statements) are always executed.

- Where a normal Java exception is propagating into an AI-method, and there is a pending AIE, the normal exception is lost when the AIE is delivered.

From the above, it can be seen that the `happened` and `clear` methods declared in the `AsynchronouslyInterruptedException` class have an important role to play in the handling of ATCs. Essentially, when handling an ATC, it is necessary to ascertain whether the caught ATC is the one expected by the interrupted schedulable object. If it is, the exception can be handled and the pending state cleared. If it is not, the exception can be propagated to the calling method. The `happened` method is used for this purpose. Consider the following:

```
import NonInterruptibleServices.*;
public class InterruptibleService {
  public AsynchronouslyInterruptedException stopNow;

  ...

  public void useService() {
    stopNow =
        AsynchronouslyInterruptedException.getGeneric();
    try {
      // Code interspersed with calls to
      // InterruptibleServices.
    } catch (AsynchronouslyInterruptedException AIE) {
        if(stopNow.happened(true)) {
          // Handle the ATC.
        }
        // No else clause, the true parameter indicates
        // that if the current exception is not stopNow,
        // it is to be immediately propagated
        // to the calling method.
    }
  }
}
```

Here, when the AIE is fired, control is passed to the catch clause at the end of the try block. A handler is found for AsynchronouslyInterruptedException. In order to determine whether the current AIE is stopNow, a call is made to the stop-Now.happened method. This returns true if stopNow is the current AIE. If it is not the current AIE, then, as the parameter to happened is true, the exception is propagated. If the parameter were false, control would return to the catch statement with a false value. Now the called schedulable object might perform some cleanup routines before propagating the exception using the propagate method:

```
catch (AsynchronouslyInterruptedException AIE) {
  if(stopNow.happened(false)) {
    // Handle the AIE.
  } else {
    // Cleanup.
    AsynchronouslyInterruptedException.propagate();
  }
}
```

Note that even if `propagate` is not called the AIE (as a result of the `happened` method call) is still in the pending state, consequently when it again enters an AI-method, the AIE will be delivered.

Consider an `AsynchronouslyInterruptedException` object called `myAIE`. When the `myAIE.happened` method is called, the following rules apply:

- if `myAIE` is the current AIE, the current AIE is no longer pending; no propagation occurs and `true` is returned;

- if `myAIE` is not the current AIE and the parameter to `happened` is `true`, the current AIE is immediately propagated;

- if `myAIE` is not the current AIE and the parameter to `happened` is `false`, the current AIE remains pending and false is returned.

Warning

The `propagate` and `happen` methods have nonstandard Java semantics. They are not defined to be AI-methods and yet they have the effect of an AI-method. For this reason, they have been deprecated in version 1.0.1 of the RTSJ and the `clear` method introduced; `clear` simply resets the pending state if the AIE is current and returns true, indicating that the current AIE is now no longer pending. If the flag is not reset, the AIE will then be redelivered when control next enters an AI-method.

Using the `clear` method, the above example would be rewritten as

```
catch (AsynchronouslyInterruptedException AIE) {
  if(stopNow.clear()) {
      // Handle the AIE; stopNow is no longer pending.
  } else {
    // Cleanup and leave the current AIE still pending.
  }
}
```

13.3 Examples

To illustrate the above concepts, consider Figure 13.1. This shows a chain of method calls made by a real-time thread. Methods A, D and E are ATC-deferred regions, whereas B, C and F are AI-methods. Here, "Arbitrary" means some exception that is not an `AsynchronouslyInterruptedException` or an `Interrupted-Exception`.

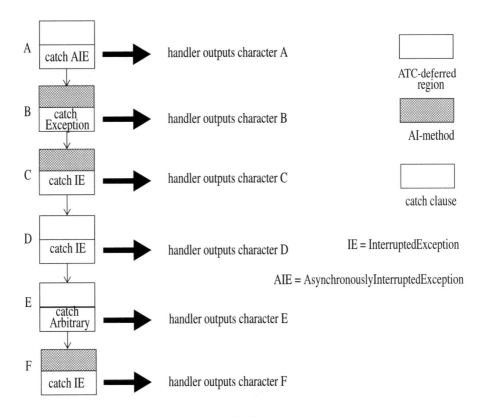

A — catch AIE → handler outputs character A

B — catch Exception → handler outputs character B

C — catch IE → handler outputs character C

D — catch IE → handler outputs character D

E — catch Arbitrary → handler outputs character E

F — catch IE → handler outputs character F

ATC-deferred region

AI-method

catch clause

IE = InterruptedException

AIE = AsynchronouslyInterruptedException

FIGURE 13.1. Example Method Call Chain

Now suppose that while executing in method F, the real-time thread is interrupted. As the thread is in an AI-method, the generic AIE is marked as pending and is immediately delivered and an appropriate handler is sought. The resulting transfer of control is

1. the method F is terminated (without executing any finally clauses);

2. E is an ATC-deferred region but it does not have an AIE handler, consequently the call to E is terminated (of course, it must have a throws `Exception` or throws `InterruptedException` clause); and any finally clauses are executed;

3. D is an ATC-deferred region and has a handler for the `InterruptedException` (a super class of the AIE); the handler executes (along with any finally clause), however, the AIE remains pending;

4. as soon as control returns to C, the AIE is again delivered and C is terminated (even though it has a catch clause for `InterruptedException` – no finally clauses are executed);

5. B is an AI-method so the exception propagates through the method (even though there is a catch clause for `Exception` – no finally clauses are executed) ;

6. Finally, control returns to A, which is an ATC-deferred region with an AIE catch clause; this executes; if A calls `clear` (or `happened`) on the current AIE, control will return to the point after the try block containing the catch AIE clause, and the AIE will have been handled and be no longer pending. If the handler for the AIE is for a different AIE, the current AIE will remain pending.

The output resulting from the ATC will, therefore, be the character 'D' followed by the character 'A'.

Now consider the example illustrated in Figure 13.2. This is very similar to the previous example except now the real-time thread is active in an ATC-deferred method when it is interrupted (this example assumes there are no finally clauses).

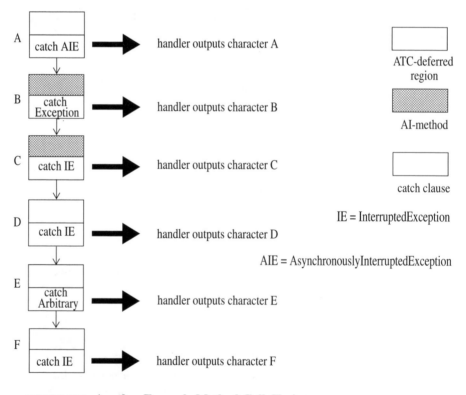

FIGURE 13.2. Another Example Method Call Chain

Suppose method F is a synchronized method when the real-time thread is interrupted. Now, the generic AIE is marked as pending. The AIE remains pending until control returns to C. The AIE is then delivered and the call to C is terminated as is the call to B. Finally, the handler in A is executed. The output is, therefore, just the character 'A'.

If method F had been blocked on a call to the `wait` method when the interrupt method was called, the generic AIE is marked as pending and is thrown immediately (as a regular Java exception). This would be handled by the local IE catch clause. However, the AIE is still marked as pending and will be delivered when control returns normally to method C (that is D and E will execute normally). When the AIE is delivered in C, the nearest valid handler is in A, so it is to there that control will be immediately transferred. In this example, the output will, therefore, be the characters 'F' and 'A'.

Finally, consider the case illustrated in Figure 13.3. Here, if the interrupt is called when a real-time thread is executing method F, the generic AIE is marked as pending; it is delivered when the thread returns to method E and control is immediately passed to the handler in D. If the handler in D is for a different AIE and it has requested propagation, the AIE is propagated immediately and control is passed to the handler in A (again, the example assumes no finally clauses).

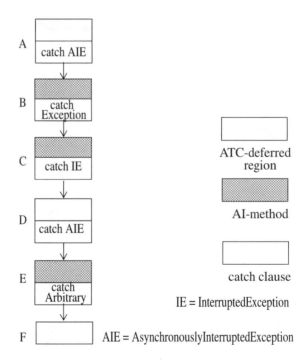

FIGURE 13.3. Example Method Call Chain with Propagation

13.4 Synchronized Methods and Statements

Although, a synchronized method or statement is ATC-deferred, it is still possible for it
to be terminated as a result of an AIE. Consider the following example:

```
void oneAIMethod() throws AsynchronouslyInterruptedException {
  ...
}
void anotherAIMethod()
       throws AsynchronouslyInterruptedException {
  synchronized(this) {
    oneAIMethod(); // call an AI-method
    // Code here will not be executed if an AIE is delivered
    // whilst the call to oneAIMethod() is in progress.
  }
}
```

The reason for this is that there is no try block in the ATC-deferred regions (in this case
the synchronized statement). Hence, the exception is propagated through the synchronized block looking for a try block (in the same way as a non-AIE exception would
propagate). The safe way to code this example is to encapsulate the call in a try block
with a finally clause

```
void oneAIMethod() throws AsynchronouslyInterruptedException {
  ....
}

void anotherAIMethod()
     throws AsynchronouslyInterruptedException {
  synchronized(this) {
    try {
      oneAIMethod(); // call an AI-method
    } finally {
      // Code here will be executed if an AIE is delivered
      // whilst the call to oneAIMethod() is in progress.
      // The AIE is held pending and will be re-delivered
      // when the synchronized block is finished.
    }
  }
}
```

Now, the propagation is stopped and the finally block executed. The AIE is redelivered
as soon as control returns to the AI method at the end of the synchronized statement.

A contradiction?

Consider now the following code fragment:

```
synchronized void method()
   throw AsynchronouslyInterruptedException {
   . . .
}
```

At first sight this seems a contradiction. A synchronized method is an ATC-deferred region, however, the programmer has indicated that it is an AI-method.

In conventional Java, a synchronized method is equivalent of a regular method encapsulating a synchronized statement (Gosling, Joy and Steele, 1996). Hence, the above example can be rewritten as

```
void method() throw AsynchronouslyInterruptedException {
   synchronized(this) {
      . . .
   }
}
```

Hence, the AIE can be delivered at the beginning and end of the method's execution but not in the middle.

13.5 The `Interruptible` Interface

The above discussion illustrates the basic mechanisms provided by the RTSJ for handling ATCs. To facilitate their structured use, the specification also provides an interface called `Interruptible`. Both real-time threads and asynchronous event handlers can use this facility.

```
package javax.realtime;
public interface Interruptible {
   public void interruptAction(
         AsynchronouslyInterruptedException exception);
   public void run(
         AsynchronouslyInterruptedException exception)
         throws AsynchronouslyInterruptedException;
}
```

An object that wishes to provide an interruptible method does so by implementing the `Interruptible` interface. The `run` method is the method that is interruptible; the `interruptAction` method is called by the system if the `run` method is interrupted during its execution.

When an object has implemented this interface, it can be passed as a parameter to the `doInterruptible` method in the `AsynchronouslyInterruptedException` class. The `doInterruptible` method then calls the `run` method of the `Interruptible`, passing the associated AIE as a parameter. A schedulable object executing the `run` method in this way can then be interrupted by calling the associated `fire` method. The system then calls the `interruptAction` method, passing the currently pending AIE as a parameter. The system also automatically clears the pending AIE when its associated `interruptAction` method has been called.

Further control over the AIE is given by the `disable`, `enable` and `isEnabled` methods. Note that only one `doInterruptible` method for a particular `AsynchronouslyInterruptedException` can be active at one time. If a call is outstanding, the method returns immediately with a `false` value.

Warning

> Note that the firing of an `AsynchronouslyInterruptedException` has no effect if there is no currently active `doInterruptible`. The firing is NOT persistent. Hence, care must be taken as there may be a race condition between one schedulable object calling a `doInterruptible` and another schedulable object calling `fire` on the same AIE. To help cope with this race condition, `fire` will return `false`, if there is no currently active `doInterruptible`.

Consider the case of a periodic real-time thread that has two modes of operation, A and B. Another real-time thread wishes to signal a mode change. When the mode change request occurs, the thread must abandon the operation being executed, undertake some housekeeping and then start its next period in the new mode. The functionality to be performed by the thread when in mode A is given by the following class that implements the `Interruptible` interface.

```
import javax.realtime.*;
public class ModeA implements Interruptible {

  public void run(AsynchronouslyInterruptedException aie)
    throws AsynchronouslyInterruptedException {
    // Operation performed in Mode A.
  }

  public void interruptAction(
        AsynchronouslyInterruptedException aie) {
    // Reset any internal state, so that when Mode A
    // again becomes current, it can continue.
  }
}
```

The functionality performed in mode B is structured in a similar manner.

The system's current mode and the mode change requests are encapsulated by the ModeChanger class, which extends the AsynchronouslyInterrupted-Exception class.

```java
import javax.realtime.*;
public enum Mode {MODE_A, MODE_B};
public class ModeChanger
        extends AsynchronouslyInterruptedException {
  public ModeChanger(Mode initial) {
    super();
    current = initial;
  }

  public synchronized int currentMode() {
    return current;
  }

  public synchronized void setMode(int nextMode) {
    current = nextMode;
  }

  public synchronized void toggleMode() {
    if(current == Mode.MODE_A) current = Mode.MODE_B;
    else current = Mode.MODE_A;

  }

  private Mode current;
}
```

The run method of the periodic thread now has the following structure.

```java
// assuming
ModeChanger modeChange = new ModeChanger(Mode.MODE_A);

public void run() {
  ModeA modeA = new ModeA();
  ModeB modeB = new ModeB();
  boolean ok = true;
  boolean result;
  while(ok) {
    if(modeChange.currentMode() == Mode.MODE_A)
      result = modeChange.doInterruptible(modeA);
      // Throw away result.
```

```
    else
      result = modeChange.doInterruptible(modeB);
      // Throw away result.
    ok = waitForNextPeriod();
  }
}
```

Finally, the signaler of the mode change undertakes the following:

```
modeChange.toggleMode();
boolean delivered = modeChange.fire();
```

Note that the signaler must set the new mode of operation (here, it simply toggles the mode). If the fire occurs while the thread is outside one of the doInterruptible calls, it is lost. However, as the thread reads the current mode at the beginning of each period, it will start the new period in the new mode. If the fire occurs during the execution of one of the doInterruptible calls, the current mode's operation is interrupted immediately (assuming it is not executing inside an ATC-deferred section). In the worst case, a mode change may arrive just after the call to currentMode but before the call to doInterruptible. This will not be acted upon until the next period.

An alternative approach would have the set and toggleMode methods call fire themselves. Hence, a signaler would only have to signal the new mode.

A persistent AIE

It is possible to extend the AIE class and build a persistent AIE. With this approach, a call to fire will be remembered if there is no outstanding call to doInterruptible. When the doInterruptible is finally called, the run method will not be executed. Instead, the interruptAction will be called straightaway. The following illustrates the approach (unfortunately, this suffers from a race condition).

```
import javax.realtime.*;
public class PersistentAIE
        extends AsynchronouslyInterruptedException {
        // first attempt
    public PersistentAIE() {
      super();
      outstandingAIE = false;
    }

    public boolean fire() {
      if(!super.fire()){
        // No currently active doInterruptible.
```

```
      outstandingAIE = true;
      return false;
    } else return true;
  }

  public boolean doInterruptible(Interruptible logic) {
    if(outstandingAIE) {
      // Outstanding fire, call interruptAction directly.
      outstandingAIE = false;
      logic.interruptAction(this);
      return true;
    } else {
      return super.doInterruptible(logic);
    }
  }

  private volatile boolean outstandingAIE;

}
```

Although the above illustrates the overall approach, it suffers from a race condition. In the overridden doInterruptible method, it is possible for a fire request to come in after the outstandingAIE flag has been tested but before **super**.doInterruptible has been called.

To remove these problems, it is necessary to make the doInterruptible method itself interruptible (Dibble, 2002a). This is illustrated below:

```
import javax.realtime.*;
public class PersistentAIE
      extends AsynchronouslyInterruptedException
      implements Interruptible {
  // The class now implements the Interruptible interface.
  public PersistentAIE() {
    super();
    outstandingAIE = false;
  }
  public boolean fire() {
    if(!super.fire()) {
      outstandingAIE = true;
      return false;
    } else return true;
  }
```

```
public boolean doInterruptible(Interruptible logic) {
  userLogic = logic; // save parameter
  // Call parent doInterruptible with this object
  // as a parameter.
  return super.doInterruptible(this);
}

public void run(AsynchronouslyInterruptedException aie)
      throws AsynchronouslyInterruptedException {
  if(outstandingAIE) {
    outstandingAIE = false;
    super.fire();
  } else {
    // Call original user's run method.
    userLogic.run(aie);
  }
}

public void interruptAction(
        AsynchronouslyInterruptedException aie) {
  // Call original user's interrupAction.
  userLogic.interruptAction(aie);
}
private volatile boolean outstandingAIE;
private Interruptible userLogic;
}
```

13.6 Multiple `AsynchronouslyInterruptedExceptions`

Given that `AsynchronouslyInterruptedException` can be deferred, it is possible for multiple ATC requests to be deferred. This can happen when the run method of one class (which implements the `Interruptible` interface) calls a doInterruptible method on an AIE. The associated run method may also call another doInterruptible method. Hence, it is possible for a thread to be executing nested doInterruptible method calls. Consider the following example illustrated in Figure 13.4. Here, a method has executed a doInterruptible method call on an `AsynchronouslyInterruptedException` object called AIE3. The run method of this has called doInterruptible on AIE2 whose run method has called doInterruptible on AIE1. The run method of the last `Interruptible` has called an ATC-deferred region.

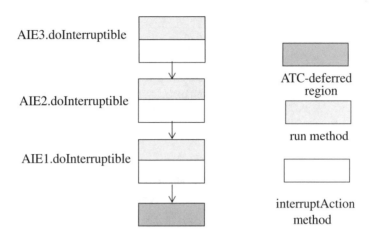

FIGURE 13.4. Nested Calls to the `doInterruptible` **Method**

Now suppose that while executing the ATC-deferred region a call to `AIE2.fire` occurs. This is held pending. If `AIE3.fire` now occurs, then `AIE2` is discarded as `AIE3` is at a higher level in the nesting. If `AIE1.fire` occurs, then `AIE1` is discarded (because it is at a lower level). Once the ATC-deferred region is exited, the currently pending AIE is delivered. Now this AIE will be caught by the `interruptAction` of the innermost nested AIE (`AIE1`) first. However, if this is not the currently pending AIE, the currently pending AIE remains pending. For example, the code for each call to a `doInterruptible` method might be structured as follows:

```
public class NestedATC {
  AsynchronouslyInterruptedException AIE1 = new
        AsynchronouslyInterruptedException();
  // Similarly for AIE2 and AIE 3.

  public void method1() {
   // ATC-deferred region.
  }

  public void method2()
        throws AsynchronouslyInterruptedException {
    AIE1.doInterruptible(new Interruptible() {
      public void run(
          AsynchronouslyInterruptedException aie)
            throws AsynchronouslyInterruptedException {
```

```
            // Interruptible code.
         method1();
      }

      public void interruptAction(
         AsynchronouslyInterruptedException aie) {
         // Recovery here.
      }
   } );
}
// Similarly for method3, whose run method calls method2,
// and for method4, whose run method calls method3.
```

Now suppose that a real-time thread rtThread has created an instance of Neste-dATC and has called method4, which has called method3, which has called method2, which has called method1, which is an ATC-deferred region. Assume that the thread is interrupted by a call to fire on one of the AIE objects. This is held pending. Any further fire calls are either discarded or replace the currently pending one (depending on the nesting). Once method1 has returned, the currently pending AIE is delivered. Method2's run method is immediately aborted and a call is made to its interruptAction. Recovery occurs. If AIE1 is the current AIE, the system clears the pending AIE. If it is not, the AIE is left pending. The result of this is that method3's run method is immediately aborted on its return from the doInterrupt-ible method call, and its interruptAction is called immediately, and so on.

Important note

If as a result of handling an AIE, the current AIE remains pending and control returns from the interruptAction (or catch clause) into an ATC-deferred region, execution will continue normally until control again enters an AI-method. Only at this point is the current AIE redelivered.

13.7 The Timed Class

A common use of ATC is to interrupt a real-time thread after a certain amount of time. Although this can be achieved by creating either

- a second thread that sleeps for the required period and then interrupts the first thread or
- an asynchronous event handler for a one-shot timer that interrupts the real-time thread.

The paradigm is so common that the RTSJ provides a special class for it. This is the Timed class given below.

```
package javax.realtime;
public class Timed
        extends AsynchronouslyInterruptedException {
  // constructors
  public Timed(HighResolutionTime time);
      // Throws IllegalArgumentException.

  // methods
  public boolean doInterruptible (Interruptible logic);
  public void resetTime(HighResolutionTime time);
}
```

The semantics of the Timed class are defined in terms of a timer whose handler fires the associated AIE. Consequently, when an instance of the Timed class is created, a timer is created and associated with the time value passed as a parameter. A null parameter results in the IllegalArgumentException being thrown.

The timer is started when the doInterruptible is called; if the time has passed, the AIE is fired immediately doInterruptible is called. The timer can be reset for the next call to doInterruptible by use of the resetTime method. Here, a null time parameter means that the time is not reset.

Imprecise computation example

As an example, consider using the Timed class to implement an imprecise algorithm. The algorithm consists of a compulsory part that computes an adequate, but imprecise, result. The optional part then iteratively refines the result. The optional part can be executed as part of a doInterruptible attached to a Timed object. The run method updates the result from within a synchronized statement so that it is not interrupted (in this example, as the result is an integer, it could be made volatile; however, for the general case, a synchronized statement is required).

First, the ImpreciseResult is defined. Here, there is also a boolean indicating whether the result is imprecise.

```
public class ImpreciseResult {
  public int value; // the result
  public boolean preciseResult;
    // Indicates if value is imprecise.
}
```

The class that implements the imprecise computation can now be given.

```java
import javax.realtime.*;
public class ImpreciseComputation {

  public ImpreciseComputation(HighResolutionTime T) {
    CompletionTime = T;  // Can be absolute or relative.
    iResult = new ImpreciseResult();
  }

  private int compulsoryPart() {
    // Function which computes the compulsory part.
  }

  public ImpreciseResult service() { // public service
    iResult.preciseResult = false;
    iResult.value = compulsoryPart();
      // Compute the compulsory part.

    Interruptible I = new Interruptible() {
        public void run(
            AsynchronouslyInterruptedException exception)
            throws AsynchronouslyInterruptedException {
          // This is the optional function which improves
          // on the compulsory part's value. It is called
          // when I is passed to the doInterruptible
          // method.
          boolean canBeImproved = true;
          while(canBeImproved) {
            // Improve result.
            synchronized(iResult) {
            // Write result, in an ATC-deferred region.
            }
          }
          iResult.preciseResult = true;
        }

        public void interruptAction(
            AsynchronouslyInterruptedException exception)
        { result.preciseResult = false; }
      };

    Timed t = new Timed(CompletionTime);
    boolean res = t.doInterruptible(I));
```

```
            // The above executes the optional part and
            // throws away the result of doInterruptible.
         return iResult; // return the impreciseResult
      }
      private HighResolutionTime CompletionTime;
      private ImpreciseResult iResult;
   }
```

Finally, a real-time thread can use the above classes:

```
new RealtimeThread(...)   {
      public void run() {
         ImpreciseComputation ic = new ImpreciseComputation(
             new RelativeTime(5000,0));
          ImpreciseResult pr = ic.service();
      }
   };
```

Fine detail note

The semantics of the Timed class are defined in terms of a timer. A typical implementation of Timed will, probably, create a Timer event, and the associated handler will fire the AIE. The goal of the Timed class is to interrupt a schedulable object after a certain time has expired. The RTSJ requires the delivery of the AIE to occur within a bounded execution time of the schedulable object being interrupted. One way of achieving this is for the implementation to run the Timer event handler at a priority just greater than the schedulable object.

13.8 Thread Deadline Miss Handlers Revisited

Chapter 12 discussed the mechanisms that the RTSJ provides for handling deadline misses and cost overruns of schedulable objects. The application can handle these misses and overruns by providing associated event handler objects. In some instances, these handlers will want to let the errant thread continue its execution. However, in other instances they will wish to terminate the current release of the thread. To do the latter in a controlled manner requires the use of the ATC facility. This section provides an example of how this can be achieved for a deadline miss. First, a new abstract periodic real-time thread class is created (called FlexibleRealtimeThread), which is defined to implement the interruptible interface (but does not provide the associated run and interruptAction methods). A class for handling the deadline miss is also needed (DeadlineMissHandler). Finally, a test class extends FlexibleRealtime-Thread. The relationship between the classes is shown in Figure 13.5.

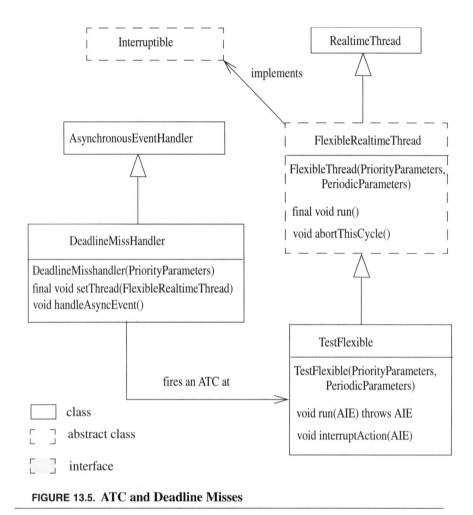

FIGURE 13.5. ATC and Deadline Misses

Consider first the code for the `FlexibleRealtimeThread`. The constructor creates a private persistent AIE object called `myAie`. If the `PeriodicParameters` associated with the thread include a deadline miss handler, then no further action is required. If there is no defined handler, a default one is created. The handler when scheduled will fire `myAie` and also call `schedulePeriodic` (to indicate that the deadline miss has been handled). `FlexibleRealtimeThread` also declares the `run` method necessary for the `RealtimeThread` class. In this example, the `run` method has an infinite loop that simply calls `myAie` passing itself as a parameter and then waits for the next period. Note that `FlexibleRealtimeThread` is an abstract class and therefore a subclass must be created before the constructor can be called. This subclass (`TestFlexible` in this example) will implement the `Interruptible` interface.

Finally, FlexibleRealtimeThread provides a public method to allow a user-defined handler to abort the current cycle.

```java
import javax.realtime.*;
public abstract class FlexibleRealtimeThread
        extends RealtimeThread implements Interruptible {

  protected FlexibleRealtimeThread(PriorityParameters pp,
                                   PeriodicParameters rp) {
    super(pp, rp);
    myRelease = rp;
    myAie = new PersistentAIE();
    handler = myRelease.getDeadlineMissHandler();
    if(handler == null) {
      // No handler, so create the default.
      handler = new AsyncEventHandler(
            new PriorityParameters(pp.getPriority() + 1),
            null, null, null, null, null) {
          public void handleAsyncEvent() {
            // Default handler actions.
            schedulePeriodic();
            myAie.fire();
          }
        };
        myRelease.setDeadlineMissHandler(handler);
    }
  }

  public void abortThisCycle() {
    myAie.fire();
  }

  public final void run() {
    // Run method for the RealtimeThread class.
    boolean ok = true;
    while(true) {
      // This code is executed each period, it calls the
      // doInterruptible method passing a reference to
      // itself.
      myAie.doInterruptible(this);
      ok = waitForNextPeriod();
    } // The loop does not terminate.
  }
  private PeriodicParameters myRelease;
  private AsyncEventHandler handler;
  private AsynchronouslyInterruptedException myAie;
}
```

Note that myAIE is a persistent AIE (see Section 13.5), this is because the real-time thread may not even reach the call to doInterruptible before it misses its deadline.

A TestFlexible class illustrates how the FlexibleRealtimeThread class is used.

```
import javax.realtime.*;
public class TestFlexible extends FlexibleRealtimeThread {

  public TestFlexible(PriorityParameters pp,
                      PeriodicParameters rp) {
    super(pp, rp);
  }

  public void run(AsynchronouslyInterruptedException aie)
        throws AsynchronouslyInterruptedException {
    // Code to be run each period, called from
    // doInterruptible.
  }

  public void interruptAction(
            AsynchronouslyInterruptedException aie) {
    // Action to be performed when interrupted.
  }
}
```

The DeadlineMissHandler class is given next. It extends the AsynchronousEventHandler class and overrides the handleAsyncEvent method. A subclass of this class can be declared by the application if it wants to provide augmented control when the deadline is missed. The default behavior is simply the same as the default handler provided by FlexibleRealtimeThread. The DeadlineMissHandler class also provides a method to set the thread to be interrupted.

```
import javax.realtime.*;
public class DeadlineMissHandler
      extends AsyncEventHandler {

  public DeadlineMissHandler(PriorityParameters pp) {
    super(pp, null, null, null, null, null);
  }

  public void setThread(FlexibleRealtimeThread frtt) {
    myThread = frtt;
  }
```

```
    public void handleAsyncEvent() {
      myThread.abortThisCycle();
      myThread.schedulePeriodic();
    }
    private FlexibleRealtimeThread myThread;
}
```

Finally, consider a main method that uses the above classes.

```
  public static void main(String [] args) {
    PriorityParameters priParams =
            new PriorityParameters (...);
    // If defining own handler use
    // DeadlineMissHandler handler =
    //      new DeadlineMissHandler(
    //      new PriorityParameters(
    //          priParams.getPriority() + 1));

    PeriodicParameters periodicParams =
        new PeriodicParameters(
      Clock.getRealtimeClock().getTime(),     // start
      new RelativeTime(10000,0),              // period
      new RelativeTime(1000,0),               // cost
      new RelativeTime(6000, 0),              // deadline
      null, null);
    TestFlexible ta = new TestFlexible(
                    priParams, periodicParams);
    // If defining own handler use handler.setThread(ta).
    ta.start();
  }
```

Warning

Note that it is essential that the deadline miss handler has a higher priority than the real-time thread it is to interrupt. Otherwise, it will not execute until the thread blocks.

To terminate the real-time thread completely, rather than just the current release, it is necessary to move the main while loop from the FlexibleRealTimeThread run method to inside the TestFlexible run method.

13.9 Further Examples

At the beginning of this chapter, several motivating examples for ATC were given. Two of these, mode changes and imprecise computations, have already been illustrated in previous sections. In this section, examples are given of user interrupts (via POSIX Signals) and error recovery between threads.

User Interrupts via POSIX signals

As discussed in Section 11.6, the RTSJ provides a class for interfacing with POSIX signals. This allows the RTSJ programmer to write an event handler that can catch one or more signals. This event handler can also fire an AIE if required. For example, consider the following class that attaches itself to the POSIX SIGINT signal and provides a handler. When the handler is executed, it fires an AIE (passed as a parameter on the class constructor).

```
import javax.realtime.*;
public class SigIntHandler extends AsyncEventHandler {
  public SigIntHandler(
     AsynchronouslyInterruptedException aie) {
    super();
    myAie = aie;
    POSIXSignalHandler.addHandler(
       POSIXSignalHandler.SIGINT, this);
  }

  public void handleAsyncEvent() {
    myAie.fire();
    int res = getAndClearPendingFireCount();
       // Throw away result.
  }
  private AsynchronouslyInterruptedException myAie;
}
```

An instance of this class can then be associated within a real-time thread to abort a long-running computation.

```
public void run() {
  Interruptible ie = new Interruptible() {

      public void run(
         AsynchronouslyInterruptedException aie)
         throws AsynchronouslyInterruptedException {
```

```
                   // Complex potentially non-terminating
                   // algorithm.
               }
           public void interruptAction(
                 AsynchronouslyInterruptedException aie) {
               System.out.println("Algorithm failed to
                                     terminate.");
           }
       };

   AsynchronouslyInterruptedException aie = new
           AsynchronouslyInterruptedException();
   AsyncEventHandler handler = new SigIntHandler(aie);
   PriorityScheduler ps = PriorityScheduler.instance();
   handler.setSchedulingParameters(
           new PriorityParameters(ps.getMaxPriority()));
   aie.doInterruptible(ie);
 }
```

In the above run method, an Interruptible is created, which undertakes a complex, potentially nonterminating algorithm. An AIE is created and passed as a parameter to the SIGINT signal handler. The handler is set to run at the highest real-time priority. The Interruptible is then passed as a parameter to the AIE. The user sitting at a terminal can now send the appropriate signal to the program. This will result in the handler firing the AIE and, thereby, terminating the complex algorithm.

Error handling between several threads

Where several real-time threads are working together on a problem, a situation may arise where one or more of them detects an error condition that must be handled by all of them. Alternatively, an event in the environment might mean that they all have to stop what they are doing immediately and perform an alternative action. Both these scenarios can be programmed using the RTSJ ATC and event-handling facilities.

Consider the following system as an example of where an event in the environment requires more than one real-time thread to take immediate action. Three tugboats are towing a disabled tanker carrying toxic chemicals. Each tugboat is connected to the tanker via a steel cable. A supervisor ship has an on-board computer that monitors the stress on the steel cables and sends control signals to the on-board computers on the three tugboats (via wireless communication devices). In the event of one of the cables being in danger of breaking, it is necessary to instruct all tugboats to immediately release their cables.

The control software on the supervisor ship executes on a single-processor embedded computer. An interrupt is generated when the stress on one (or more) of the cables is near breaking point. The real-time JVM associates the string "BreakingLimit" with this interrupt. The control software contains the following class for controlling the tugboats. The class implements the `Interruptible` interface as the control algorithm may need to be stopped at any point in time.

```
import javax.realtime.*;
public class TugControl implements Interruptible {
  public TugControl(int tid) {
    // tid is a Tug identifier
  }

  private void computeAndSendTugCableTension()
      throws AsynchronouslyInterruptedException {
    // Computationally complex periodic calculations
    // send communication to the appropriate tug's
    // on-board computer.
  }

  private void sendEmergencyRelease() {
    // Send a emergency command to the Tug to release
    // the cable.
  }

  public void run(
    AsynchronouslyInterruptedException aie)
    throws AsynchronouslyInterruptedException {
    computeAndSendTugCableTension();
  }

  public void interruptAction(
    AsynchronouslyInterruptedException aie) {
    sendEmergencyRelease();
  }
}
```

Each tugboat is represented in the control software by a real-time thread. Each thread simply executes its associated tug control software as part of a `doInterruptible`.

```
import javax.realtime.*;
public class TugThread extends RealtimeThread {
```

```
public TugThread(TugControl tc,
        AsynchronouslyInterruptedException aie) {
  super();
  myTug = tc;
  myAIE = aie;
}

public void run() {
  boolean OK;
  OK = myAIE.doInterruptible(myTug);
        // Throw away result.
}
private TugControl myTug;
private AsynchronouslyInterruptedException myAIE;
}
```

An asynchronous event handler handles the interrupt and sends an AIE to each tug task.

```
import javax.realtime.*;
public class EmergencyEventHandler
        extends AsyncEventHandler {
  AsynchronouslyInterruptedException ae1, ae2, ae3;

  public EmergencyEventHandler(
          AsynchronouslyInterruptedException aie1,
          AsynchronouslyInterruptedException aie2,
          AsynchronouslyInterruptedException aie3,
          AsyncEvent ae) {
    super();
    ae1 = aie1;
    ae2 = aie2;
    ae3 = aie3;
    ae.setHandler(this);
  }

  public void handleAsyncEvent() {
    ae1.fire();
    ae2.fire();
    ae3.fire();
  }
}
```

The relationship between the classes are illustrated in Figure 13.6.

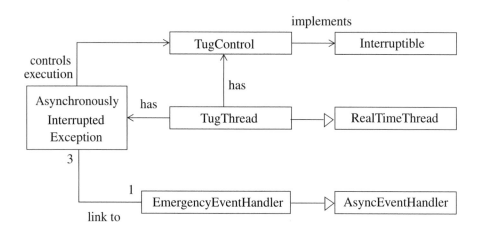

FIGURE 13.6. Relationship between Classes in Tug Control Example

A main program ties the software together; here, for clarity, all issues associated with scheduling have been ignored.

```
import javax.realtime.*;
public class tug {
  public static void main(String [] args) {
    boolean OK;

    AsynchronouslyInterruptedException emergencyStopTug1
        = new AsynchronouslyInterruptedException();
    AsynchronouslyInterruptedException emergencyStopTug2
        = new AsynchronouslyInterruptedException();
    AsynchronouslyInterruptedException emergencyStopTug3
        = new AsynchronouslyInterruptedException();

    AsyncEvent breakingPoint = new AsyncEvent();
    breakingPoint.bindTo("BreakingLimit");

    TugControl TC1 = new TugControl(1);
    TugControl TC2 = new TugControl(2);
    TugControl TC3 = new TugControl(3);
```

```
EmergencyEventHandler emergency =
    new EmergencyEventHandler(
        emergencyStopTug1, emergencyStopTug2,
        emergencyStopTug3, breakingPoint);
TugThread tt1 = new TugThread(TC1,
                    emergencyStopTug1);
TugThread tt2 = new TugThread(TC2,
                    emergencyStopTug2);
TugThread tt3 = new TugThread(TC3,
                    emergencyStopTug3);
tt1.start();
tt2.start();
tt3.start();
    }
}
```

Figure 13.7 illustrates the main object interactions.

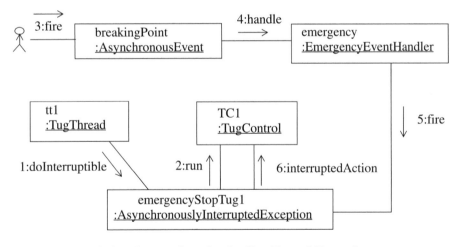

FIGURE 13.7. Object Interactions for the Tug Control Example

13.10 Summary

The ability to quickly gain the attention of a schedulable object, in an asynchronous manner, is a core requirement for the real-time community. The modern approach to meeting this requirement is via an asynchronous transfer of control (ATC) facility. The

RTSJ combines thread interruption with exception handling and introduces the notion of an asynchronously interrupted exception (AIE). The presence of a `throws AsynchronouslyInterruptedException` in a method's signature indicates that the method is prepared to allow asynchronous transfers of control. Such a method is termed an asynchronously interruptible method (AI-method).

The RTSJ requires that ATCs are deferred during the execution of synchronized methods or statements and that an ATC can only be handled from within code that is an ATC-deferred section.

Although AIEs appear to have been integrated into the Java exception handling mechanism, the normal Java rules do not apply because:

- Only the naming of the `AsynchronouslyInterruptedException` class in a `throw` clause indicates the schedulable object is interruptible. It is not possible to use the name of a subclass.

- Handlers for `AsynchronouslyInterruptedExceptions` do not automatically clear the pending state of the AIE. It is necessary to call the `happened` or `clear` method in the `AsynchronouslyInterruptedException` class.

- Although catch clauses in ATC-deferred regions that name the `InterruptedException` or `Exception` classes *will handle* an `AsynchronouslyInterruptedException`, they will *not* clear the pending state of the AIE.

- Although `AsynchronouslyInterruptedException` is a subclass of `InterruptedException`, which is a subclass of `Exception`, catch clauses, which name these classes *in AI-methods* will not catch an `AsynchronouslyInterruptedException`

- "Finally clauses" that are declared in AI-methods are not executed when an ATC is delivered. "Finally clauses" in ATC-deferred regions (including synchronized blocks or statements) are always executed.

- Where a normal exception is propagating into an AI-method and there is a pending AIE, the normal exception is lost when the AIE is delivered.

Note the firing of an `AsynchronouslyInterruptedException` has no effect if there is no currently active `doInterruptible`. The firing is not persistent.

14 Resource Sharing

Introduction and chapter structure

Although the RTSJ allows an implementation to support many different approaches to scheduling, the main focus is on priority-based scheduling. Over the last 25 years, much research has been undertaken on the analysis of timing properties in priority-based concurrent systems. One key aspect of this involves understanding the impact of communication and synchronization between different-priority schedulable objects.

In Java, communication and synchronization is based on mutually exclusive access to shared data via a monitor-like construct (see Chapter 3). Unfortunately, all synchronization mechanisms that are based on mutual exclusion suffer from *priority inversion*. An example of this is where a low-priority thread (schedulable object) enters into a mutual-exclusion zone (synchronized method or statement), which it shares with a high-priority thread. A medium-priority thread then becomes runnable, preempts the low-priority thread and performs a computationally intensive algorithm. At the start of this algorithm, a high-priority thread becomes runnable, preempts the medium-priority thread and tries to enter the mutual-exclusion zone. As the low-priority thread currently occupies the zone, the high-priority thread is blocked. The medium-priority thread then runs, thereby indirectly blocking the progression of the high-priority thread possibly for an unbounded period of time. It is this blocking that makes it very difficult to analyze the timing properties of schedulable objects.

There are two solutions to the priority inversion problem. The first is to use a *priority inheritance* algorithm; the second is to use nonblocking communication mechanisms. The RTSJ uses the former to limit the blocking between communicating schedulable objects, and the latter to facilitate communication between heap-using and non-heap-using threads/schedulable objects. This chapter considers these two approaches. First, the overall approach to priority inheritance is explained. Then, the details of the supporting RTSJ classes are described along with some examples of their use. This is followed by explanation of the need for nonblocking communication and the classes that provide this facility in the RTSJ.

14.1 Priority Inheritance

With *simple priority inheritance*, if a high-priority schedulable object attempts to enter a synchronized method (or statement), and the lock is held by a low-priority schedulable object, the low-priority schedulable object inherits (i.e. runs at) the priority of the high-priority schedulable object until it exits the synchronized method (or statement). If the low-priority schedulable object itself is also blocked, then the schedulable object that is blocking it also inherits the high priority (and so on).

With *priority ceiling emulation inheritance*, each object that can be locked (i.e. is a monitor) is given a *ceiling priority*. This priority is higher than (or equal to) the highest priority of all the schedulable objects that wish to synchronize on that lock. When a schedulable object obtains the lock, its priority is immediately raised to the ceiling priority. The execution profiles of three real-time threads (high priority, medium priority and low priority) are illustrated in Figure 14.1. Here, the high- and low-priority threads wish to share a lock.

In Figure 14.1(a), the low-priority thread (LP) is released, executes for a while and acquires the lock. When the medium-priority thread (MP) is released, it preempts LP and executes until the high-priority thread (HP) is released. When HP attempts to access the lock, it is blocked; MP runs to completion followed by LP running until it releases the lock. At this point, HP preempts and runs to completion. Finally, LP runs to completion. Figure 14.1(b) shows the same scenario, only this time with priority inheritance. Here, MP still preempts LP and, in turn, is preempted by HP. However, when HP attempts to get the lock, LP inherits HP's priority. Consequently, LP runs in preference to MP until it releases the lock, at which point LP's priority reverts back to its original priority, allowing HP to preempt it. Now HP runs to completion, followed by MP, followed by LP. Figure 14.1(c) shows the same scenario, only this time with priority ceiling emulation. Here, as soon as LP gets the lock, its priority is raised to one higher than HP and consequently, neither MP nor HP can preempt it until it releases the lock. At this point, its priority returns back to LP's original priority and MP preempts (which is later preempted by HP).

The advantage of priority ceiling emulation is that it is much easier to implement than priority inheritance. The disadvantage is that the programmer is required to have details of all the schedulable objects that can call the monitor. Also, the priority changes occur irrespective of whether there is any priority inversion happening.

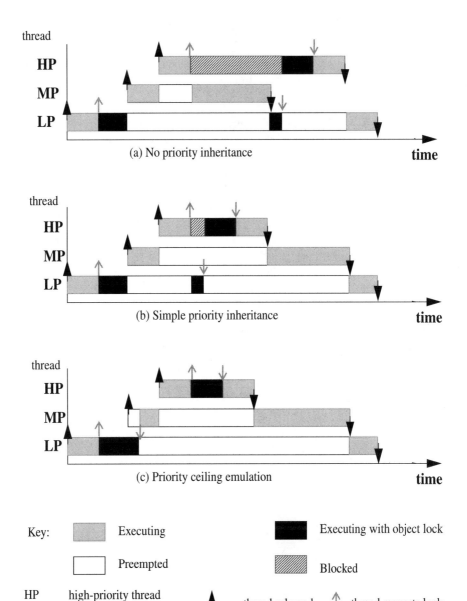

(a) No priority inheritance

(b) Simple priority inheritance

(c) Priority ceiling emulation

Key:
▨ Executing
☐ Preempted

■ Executing with object lock
▨ Blocked

HP high-priority thread
MP medium-priority thread
LP low-priority thread

▲ thread released
▼ thread finished

↑ thread requests lock
↓ thread releases lock

FIGURE 14.1. Priority Inversion and Priority Inheritance

14.2 The RTSJ and Priority Inheritance

Priority inversion can occur whenever a schedulable object is blocked waiting for a resource. In order to limit the length of time of that blocking, the RTSJ requires the following:

- All queues maintained by the real-time virtual machine must be priority ordered. So, for example, the queue of schedulable objects waiting for an object lock (as a result of a synchronized method call or the execution of a synchronized statement) must be priority ordered. Where there is more than one schedulable object in the queue at the same priority, the order between them is not defined (although it is usual for this to be first-in-first-out (FIFO)). Similarly, the queues resulting from calls to the `wait` methods in the `Object` class should be priority ordered.

- Facilities for the programmer to specify the use of different-priority inversion control algorithms. By default, the RTSJ requires priority inheritance to occur whenever a schedulable object is blocked waiting for a resource (for example, an object lock).

Monitor control

The programmer can change the default priority inversion control algorithm for individual objects (or for all objects) via the `MonitorControl` class hierarchy. At the root of this hierarchy is the following abstract class:

```
package javax.realtime;
public abstract class MonitorControl {
  // constructors
  protected MonitorControl();

  // methods
  public static MonitorControl getMonitorControl();
  public static MonitorControl getMonitorControl(
                             Object monitor);
   // Throws IllegalArgumentException if monitor is null.
  public static MonitorControl setMonitorControl(
    MonitorControl policy);
  public static MonitorControl setMonitorControl(
    Object monitor, MonitorControl policy);
   // Throws IllegalArgumentException if monitor is null.
}
```

The four static methods allow the getting/setting of the default policy and the getting/setting for an individual object (the methods return the old policy). The two RTSJ-defined policies are represented by subclasses. The default policy can be specified by passing an instance of the `PriorityInheritance` class:

```
package javax.realtime;
public class PriorityInheritance extends MonitorControl {
  // methods
  public static PriorityInheritance instance();
    // The instance is in immortal memory.
}
```

or an instance of the `PriorityCeilingEmulation` class:

```
package javax.realtime;
public class PriorityCeilingEmulation
            extends MonitorControl {

  // methods
  public int getCeiling();
    // Returns the current priority.
    // Added at version 1.0.1 replacing getDefaultCeiling
  public int getDefaultCeiling();
    // Returns the current priority.
    // Deprecated at 1.0.1 because of poor name.
  public static int getMaxCeiling();
    // Added at version 1.0.1
  public static PriorityCeilingEmulation instance(
            int ceiling);
    // Added at version 1.0.1.
    // Throws IllegalArgumentException if ceiling is
    // outside the permitted range.
}
```

Warning

The `PriorityCeilingEmulation` class has changed considerably since version 1.0. This is partly to make it more efficient but also because the interface was poor. In version 1.0.1, the `instance` method should be used to obtain an immutable object at the required ceiling priority. The returned object is held in immortal memory.

Changing the monitor control policy does not take place until the object is unlocked.

Warning and version 1.0 note

Changing the default priority inheritance algorithm takes effect immediately after the call to `setMonitor` is made. The initial default is priority inheritance. In version 1.0. of the RTSJ, it was not possible to change the initial default. Consequently, all monitors created before the `main` method was called had a priority inheritance control policy. Version 1.0.1 of the RTSJ encourages implementers to provide a mechanism by which the initial default value can be set. the programmer can retrieve this value via the `getInitialMonitorControl` method in the `RealtimeSystem` class (see Section 14.2.2).

Important note

The code used inside a synchronized method (or statement) should be kept as short as possible, as the time taken to execute this code will dictate the time a low-priority schedulable object can block a high-priority one. It is only possible to limit the blocking if the code does not contain

- unbounded loops,

- arbitrary-length blocking operations that hold the lock, for example, an arbitrary-length sleep request.

Fine detail note

If the code within the synchronized methods of a monitor contains no operations that suspend the calling schedulable object while holding the lock (for example, executing the `sleep` method), then it is possible for the real-time virtual machine (on a single-processor system) to optimize the implementation of the synchronized methods so that they do not require a lock. This is achieved by simply using the priority mechanism. If a schedulable object is

- executing within a synchronized method in a monitor at the ceiling priority, and

- preemptive priority-based scheduling is used with FIFO scheduling within priorities, and

- preempted schedulable objects are placed at the front of the run queue for their priority level, and

- the method does not suspend itself holding the monitor lock, then

on a single-processor system, no other schedulable object can issue a call to a synchronized method in the same monitor.

However, it is doubtful whether many implementation of the RTSJ will support this "no-lock" optimization.

14.2.1 Active and base priorities

In the presence of priority inheritance algorithms, each schedulable object has two associated priorities. The first is its *base priority*. This is the priority that the object is allocated as a result of its scheduling parameters. The second priority is its *active priority*. This is the priority at which the schedulable object is currently executing. It may be different from its base priority because of priority inheritance.

Important note

With priority-based scheduling, execution eligibility is based on active priority rather than base priority. Hence, the scheduler always chooses the schedulable object with the highest active priority for execution. Similarly, all queues are ordered according to active priority. However, it should be noted that a schedulable object that inherits a priority while inside a monitor will lose that priority when it calls the `Object.wait` method (because it has given up the monitor lock). Hence, it will be queued at the priority it had before it called the monitor.

Ceiling violations

Whenever a schedulable object calls a synchronized method (statement) in an object that has the `PriorityCeilingEmulation` policy in force, the real-time virtual machine will check the active priority of the caller. If the priority is greater than the ceiling priority, the unchecked `CeilingViolationException` is thrown.

Dynamic priorities

Both the base priority of a schedulable object and the ceiling priority of a monitor can be changed dynamically. In the later case, this is achieved by calling the `set-MonitorControl` method with a new `PriorityCeilingEmulation` object for the monitor. The change does not take place until the monitor becomes unlocked.

Warning

The semantics of priority changes can be quite complex. For example, consider what happens when the base priority or active priority of a schedulable object, `so1`, changes (as a result of the actions of another schedulable object, `so2`) while `so1` is active inside a monitor with a priority ceiling emulation policy. The problem is that `so1` may now violate a ceiling constraint but it cannot throw an exception. Given that `so1` already has the lock, then in the absence of any "no-lock" optimization, it is safe to allow `so1` to complete the synchronized call.

14.2.2 Tuning monitor locks

As well as allowing priority inversion to be avoided when using monitor locks, the RTSJ also

- allows the programmer to determine the initial default priority inversion avoidance algorithm, and

- gives the programmer the ability to get and set the number of concurrent locks that are/will be in use at any one time. The goal is to provide extra information to the real-time virtual machine so that it can make the mapping of objects to locks as efficient as possible.

The following mechanisms are available in the `RealtimeSystems` class.

```java
package javax.realtime;
public final class RealtimeSystem {
  ...
  public static int getConcurrentLocksUsed();
  public static int getMaximumConcurrentLocks();
  public static void setConcurrentLocksUsed(
                    int numLocks);
  public static void setMaximumConcurrentLocks(
                    int numLocks);

  // The following method was added at version 1.0.1
  public static MonitorControl getInitialMonitorControl();
  ...
}
```

14.2.3 Communication between heap-using and no-heap-using schedulable objects

One of the main driving forces behind the RTSJ is to make real-time Java applications more predictable. Hence, schedulable objects that need complete predictability can be defined not to reference the heap. This means that they can preempt any garbage collection that might be occurring when the schedulable objects are released.

Most large real-time systems will consist of a mixture of heap-using and no-heap schedulable objects. There will inevitably be occasions when they need to exchange information. To ensure that no-heap schedulable objects are not indirectly delayed by garbage collection requires

- all no-heap schedulable object should have priorities greater than heap-using schedulable objects,
- priority ceiling emulation should be used for all shared synchronized objects,
- all shared synchronized objects should have their memory requirements preallocated (or dynamically allocated from scoped or immortal memory areas), and
- objects passed in any communication should be primitive types passed by value (int, long, boolean, etc.) or be from scoped or immortal memory.

If these conditions are fulfilled, then there will be no unwanted interference from the garbage collector at inopportune moments. Note that if priority inheritance is used and shared objects are preallocated on the heap, it is possible that

- a Java thread, T1, enters into the monitor first (the schedulable object is currently not released),
- it is then preempted by a higher-priority Java thread, T2, whose operations cause garbage collection to occur,
- at this point, the schedulable object is released, preempts the garbage collector but cannot access the monitor
- priority inheritance occurs, but it is not safe for the Java thread, T1, to execute as memory compaction may be taking place.

With priority ceiling emulation, the above scenario cannot occur, as T1 will inherit a priority higher than all Java threads the moment it enters into the monitor. Hence, it cannot be preempted by T2.

14.3 Wait-Free Queues

The alternative to blocking communication based on synchronized objects is to use non-blocking (wait-free) communication. The RTSJ provides three classes that facilitate this form of communication. All are based on a queue.

- `WaitFreeWriteQueue` – this class is intended for situations where a no-heap real-time thread wishes to send data to one or more heap-using threads. However, it can be used by any thread. Essentially, the writer thread is never blocked when writing even when the queue is full (the write fails). Readers can be blocked when the queue is empty. The class assumes that multiple writers provide their own synchronization. If the queue is only accessed by a single reader and a single writer, that information can be provided by one of the constructors. This allows an implementation to optimize the access protocol.

```
package javax.realtime;
public class WaitFreeWriteQueue {
  // constructors

  // The constructors throw IllegalArgumentException if
  // maximum is less than or equal to zero and
  // MemoryScopeException if the MemoryArea parameter
  // results in a scoped memory assignment conflict.
  public WaitFreeWriteQueue(Thread writer
        Thread reader, int maximum, MemoryArea memory);
    // Where memory defines the memory area to hold the
    // actual queue.
```

```
  // The following have been added at version 1.0.1
  public WaitFreeWriteQueue(int maximum);
  public WaitFreeWriteQueue(int maximum,
                            MemoryArea memory);

  // methods

  public void clear();
    // Empty the queue.
  public boolean force(Object object);
    // Overwrite the last item in the queue.
    // Returns true, if last item over-written,
    // false otherwise.
    // Throws IllegalArgumentException if object is null
    // and MemoryScopeException if a memory access error
    // occurs.
  public boolean isEmpty();
  public boolean isFull();
  public Object read() throws InterruptedException;
  public int size(); // The current size.
  public boolean write(Object object);
    // Throws IllegalArgumentException if object is null
    // and MemoryScopeException if a memory access error
    // occurs.
    // Return true if write successful, false otherwise.
}
```

- WaitFreeReadQueue – this class is intended for situations where a no-heap real-time thread wishes to receive data from one or more heap-using threads. However, it can be used by any thread. Essentially, the reader thread is never blocked when reading even when the queue is empty (the read fails). Writers can be blocked when the queue is full. The class assumes that multiple readers provide their own synchronization.

```
package javax.realtime;
public class WaitFreeReadQueue {
  // constructors

  // The constructors throw IllegalArgumentException if
  // maximum is less than or equal to zero and
  // MemoryScopeException if the MemoryArea parameter
  // results in a scoped memory assignment conflict.
```

```
public WaitFreeReadQueue(Thread writer
        Thread reader, int maximum,
        MemoryArea memory);
public WaitFreeReadQueue(Thread writer
        Thread reader, int maximum,
        MemoryArea memory, boolean notify);
  // If notify is true, support the waitForData method

// The following have been added at version 1.0.1
public WaitFreeReadQueue(int maximum);
public WaitFreeReadQueue(int maximum,
                    MemoryArea memory, boolean notify);

// methods
public void clear();
public boolean isEmpty();
public boolean isFull();
public Object read();
  // Returns null, if the queue is empty.
public int size();
public void waitForData()
            throws InterruptedException;
  // Suspends the caller if the queue is empty.
  // Requires constructor with notify boolean.
  // Note, the writer is not suspended on the
  // waitFreeReadQueue object, so no priority
  // inheritance occurs.
public void write(Object object)
            throws InterruptedException;
  // Throws IllegalArgumentException if object is null
  // and MemoryScopeException if a memory access error
  // occurs.
}
```

- `WaitFreeDequeue` – this class is intended for situations where a wait-free read and wait-free write queue is needed. The class simply combines the two. It has been deprecated in version 1.0.1 because the semantics were not well defined and there was confusion between the two queues.

```
package javax.realtime;
public class WaitFreeDequeue {
  // constructors

  // The constructor throws IllegalArgumentException if
  // maximum is less than or equal to zero and
  // MemoryScopeException if the MemoryArea parameter
  // results in a scoped memory assignment conflict.
  public WaitFreeDequeue(Thread writer
          Thread reader, int maximum,
          MemoryArea memory);

  // methods
  public Object blockingRead();
     // Read from wait-free write queue.
  public void blockingWrite(Object object);
     // Throws IllegalArgumentException if object is null
     // and MemoryScopeException if a memory access error
     // occurs.
     // Write to the wait-free read queue.
  public boolean force (Object object);
     // Throws IllegalArgumentException if object is null
     // and MemoryScopeException if a memory access error
     // occurs.
     // Forced write on the wait free write queue.
  public Object nonBlockingRead();
     // Read on the wait-free read queue.
  public boolean nonBlockingWrite(
                  Object object);
     // Write on the wait-free write queue.
}
```

If a wait-free queue is being used to communicate between a no-heap schedulable object and a conventional Java thread, then

1. the queue must be in immortal memory as

   • a Java thread cannot enter scoped memory

   • immortal memory cannot point to scoped memory

   • a no-heap thread cannot access the heap

2. any objects passed must be in immortal memory, otherwise an exception will be thrown if

- a writer Java thread passes a heap object – the reader no-heap schedulable object will attempt to access the heap

- a writer no-heap schedulable object passes a scoped memory object – the reader Java thread will try to store a reference to a scoped memory object on the heap.

Under these circumstances, garbage collection will have no impact on the queue itself and the no-heap schedulable object never blocks waiting for the thread so it cannot be forced to wait for garbage collection.

If a wait-free queue is being used to communicate between a heap-using schedulable object and a no-heap using schedulable object, then

1. the queue can be in immortal or scoped memory
2. any objects passed must be in immortal and scoped memory

Under these circumstances, garbage collection will have no impact on the queue itself and the no-heap schedulable object never blocks waiting for the heap-using schedulable object so it cannot be forced to wait for garbage collection. Of course, exceptions can still be thrown if memory violations occur.

14.4 Summary

Limiting the impact of priority inversion is fundamental to any priority-based real-time system. There are two approaches to the problem. The first is to use a priority inheritance algorithm (the RTSJ supports both simple priority inheritance and priority ceiling emulation); the second is to use nonblocking communication mechanisms (the RTSJ provides wait-free read and write queues to facilitate communication between heap-using and no-heap threads).

15 Physical and Raw Memory

Introduction and chapter structure

Today's computers may have many different types of directly addressable memory available to them. Each type has its own characteristics (Barr, 2001) that determine whether it is

- *volatile* – whether it maintains its state when the power is turned off,

- *writable* – whether it can be written at all, written once or written many times and whether writing is under program control,

- *erasable at the byte level* – if the memory can be overwritten whether this is done at the byte level or whether whole sectors of the memory need to be erased,

- *fast to access* – both for reading and writing,

- *expensive* – in terms of cost per byte or power consumption.

Examples include dynamic and static random access memory (DRAM and SRAM), read-only memory (ROM and EPROM) and hybrid memory such as EEPROM (electrically erasable and programmable ROM) or FLASH memory. Memory may also be added and removed from the system dynamically. Furthermore, on-chip and off-chip caching may occur.

Individual computers are often targeted at a particular application domain, this domain will often dictate the cost and performance requirements, and therefore, the memory type used. For example, embedded computers targeted at, say, mass-produced consumer products will need to be cheap and, as a consequence, will only have a limited amount of fast (expensive) memory. In order to obtain maximum performance from the given computer, the programmer must make judicious use of the available memory. Placing a heavily used object in a slow memory area may seriously degrade the program's overall effectiveness, particularly if the system has a limited cache size or the cache has been turned off to ensure predictability.

As well as having different types of memory, many computers map input and output devices so that their registers can be accessed through memory location. Hence, some parts of the processor's address space will map to real memory and other parts will access devices. The situation may be further complicated because a Direct Memory Access (DMA) controller may access the real memory independently of the processor (although doing so may steal bus cycles from the processor).

For multiprocessor systems, the above complexities are compounded by the possibility of shared memory or dual ported memory. Figure 15.1 illustrates a multiprocessor system with shared memory and various classes of local memory and I/O devices.

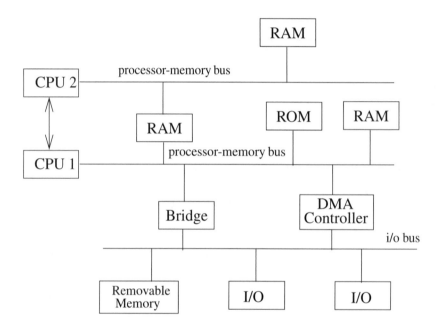

FIGURE 15.1. **A Dual-Processor Shared Memory System**

A possible physical memory map of CPU 1 in Figure 15.1 is illustrated in Figure 15.2.

Of course, the Java programmer is not concerned with any of these aspects and consequently the Java programming language provides no mechanisms to manipulate the different memory types or to interact with input and output devices (other than those that have a higher-level access model such as standard input/output or files). The programmer has to resort to using native methods if access to raw memory is required. The RTSJ, in contrast, is targeted toward the real-time and embedded programmer and, therefore, has to provide facilities that allow the programmer to exploit the underlying memory and I/O architecture.

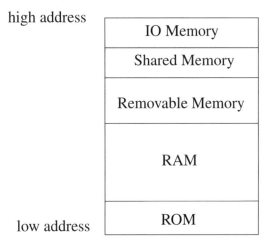

FIGURE 15.2. **An Example Physical Memory Map**

The memory used to implement all Java programs can be divided into three components:

- the method area – where the Java byte code is stored during interpretation,
- the stack – where local data is stored during method execution, and
- the heap – where an object's data is stored during its lifetime.

It is important to realize that the facilities described in this chapter can only be used to influence where the data associated with objects is stored. It is not possible, say, for the programmer to control the type of memory to be used for the method area.

15.1 The Basic Model

The RTSJ supports access to physical memory via a memory manager and one or more memory filters. The goal of the memory manager is to provide a single interface with which the programmer can interact in order to access memory with a particular characteristic. The role of a memory filter is to control access to a particular type of physical memory. Memory filters may be dynamically added and removed from the system, and there can only be a single filter for each memory type. The memory manager is unaware of the physical addresses of each type of memory. This is encapsulated by the filters. The filters also know the virtual memory characteristics that have been allocated to their memory type. For example, whether the memory is readable, writable or executable.

Each filter must implement the following interface.

```java
package javax.realtime;
public interface PhysicalMemoryTypeFilter {
  // Where the following methods have a base and a size,
  // parameter:
  // IllegalArgumentException is thrown if size
  //    is negative
  // OffsetOutOfBoundsException is thrown if base
  //    is negative
  // SizeOutOfBounds is thrown if the base + size is
  //    greater than the physical addressing range of the
  //    processor.
  public boolean contains(long base, long size);
    // Returns true, if the filter has some memory
    // in the physical address range,
    // returns false otherwise.

  public long find(long base, long size);
    // Starts from the base address and looks for a
    // memory area of the filter type of at least size
    // bytes and returns the start address;
    // returns -1, if no memory found of the filter type.

  public int getVMAttributes();
    // Returns any implementation-dependent access
    // attributes associated with the memory type.
    // This is intended for use with POSIX.
    // POSIX's mmap function maps the processor's memory
    // into the address space of a process. The memory can
    // be specified as having a combination of read, write
    // and execute permissions, or no access.

  public int getVMFlags();
    // Returns any implementation-dependent flags
    // associated with the memory type.
    // This is intended for use with POSIX.
    // POSIX's mmap function maps the processor's memory
    // into the address space of a process. The memory
    // can be specified as private or shared, and fixed at
    // a particular location.
```

```
public void initialize(
        long base, long vBase, long size);
    // Initializes the memory if required,
    // null operation otherwise.

public boolean isPresent(long base, long size);
    // Return true if the memory is present in the system
    // returns false otherwise;
    // Throws IllegalArgumentException if the memory range
    // is not covered by the filter.

public boolean isRemovable();
    // Returns true if the memory type is removable;
    // returns false otherwise.

public void onInsertion(long base, long size,
                        AsyncEventHandler aeh);
    // Associates an event handler with the insertion
    // of the memory into the system;
    // Throws IllegalArgumentException if the memory range
    // is not covered by the filter or aeh is null.

public void onInsertion(long base, long size,
                        AsyncEvent ae);
    // Associates an event with the insertion
    // of the memory into the system;
    // Throws IllegalArgumentException if the memory range
    // is not covered by the filter or ae is null.
    // Added at version 1.0.1.

public void onRemoval(long base, long size,
                      AsyncEventHandler aeh);
    // Associates an event handler with the removal
    // of the memory from the system;
    // Throws IllegalArgumentException if the memory range
    // is not covered by the filter or aeh is null.

public void onRemoval(long base, long size,
                      AsyncEvent ae);
    // Associates an event with the removal
    // of the memory from the system;
    // Throws IllegalArgumentException if the memory range
    // is not covered by the filter or ae is null.
    // Added at version 1.0.1.
```

```
public static void unregisterInsertionEvent(long base,
                    long size, AsyncEvent ae);
   // Unregister the specified insertion event.
   // If ae is null, all async events in the range
   // are unregistered.
   // Added at version 1.0.1.

public static void unregisterRemovalEvent(long base,
                    long size, AsyncEvent ae);
   // Unregister the specified insertion event.
   // If ae is null, all async events in the range
   // are unregistered.
   // Added at version 1.0.1.

public long vFind(long base, long size);
   // Searches the virtual memory for the memory type and
   // return its address or -1 if the memory is absent.
}
```

The physical memory manager is defined by a final class with only static fields and methods:

```
package javax.realtime;
public final class PhysicalMemoryManager {

   // fields, names for typical memory types, for example
   public static final Object ALIGNED;
   public static final Object BYTESWAP;
   public static final Object DMA;
   public static final Object IO_PAGE;
   public static final Object SHARED;

   // methods

   // Where the following methods have a base and a size,
   // parameter:
   // IllegalArgumentException is thrown if size
   //     is negative
   // OffsetOutOfBoundsException is thrown if base
   //     is negative
   // SizeOutOfBounds is thrown if the base + size is
   //     greater than the physical addressing range of the
   //     processor.
   public static boolean isRemovable(
         long address, long size);
      // Returns true if any part is removable.
```

```
public static boolean isRemoved(
        long address, long size);
// Returns true, if any part is currently removed.
public static void onInsertion(
        long base, long size, AsyncEventHandler aeh);
// Registers a handler to be run on insertion.
// Throws IllegalArgumentException if the memory range
// is not removable or aeh is null.
public static void onInsertion(
        long base, long size, AsyncEvent ae);
// Registers a handler to be run on insertion.
// Throws IllegalArgumentException if the memory range
// is not removable or ae is null.

public static void onRemoval(
        long base, long size, AsyncEventHandler aeh);
// Registers a handler to be run on removal.
// Throws IllegalArgumentException if the memory range
// is not removable or aeh is null.
public static void onRemoval(
        long base, long size, AsyncEvent ae);
// Registers a handler to be run on removal.
// Throws IllegalArgumentException if the memory range
// is not removable or ae is null.

public static final void registerFilter(Object name,
        PhysicalMemoryTypeFilter filter)
        throws DuplicateFilterException;
// Throws IllegalArgumentException if the name or
// the filter are not in immortal memory.
public static final void removeFilter(Object name);
public static void unregisterInsertionEvent(long base,
                long size, AsyncEvent ae);
// Unregister the specified insertion event.
// If ae is null, all async events in the range
// are unregistered.

public static void unregisterRemovalEvent(long base,
                long size, AsyncEvent ae);
// Unregister the specified insertion event.
// If ae is null, all async events in the range
// are unregistered.
}
```

Important
Note
The `PhysicalMemoryFilterType` interface and the `PhysicalMemory-Manager` class are not intended for the applications programmer. They are intended for use by the systems programmer who is providing the software necessary to host a particular implementation of the RTSJ on a particular hardware configuration with different memory types. However, the applications programmer will need access to the memory names defined by the static fields in the `PhysicalMemoryManager` class.

15.2 Creating Objects in Physical Memory

In order to create objects in physical memory, it is first necessary to create a memory area that defines the scope of the objects. The RTSJ views all physical memory as being nonheap memory. Hence, the following memory classes are supported:

- `ImmortalPhysicalMemory`
- `LTPhysicalMemory`
- `VTPhysicalMemory`

Immortal physical memory

Unlike regular immortal memory, which is accessed via a final class with a single instance, immortal physical memory access objects have to be created. Many areas of immortal physical memory can exist; each placed at a different location in physical memory and each with its own particular memory characteristic. The following class defines the interface. It consists of constructor methods only. Blocks of immortal physical memory can be allocated either with or without defining a base address:

```
package javax.realtime;
public class ImmortalPhysicalMemory extends MemoryArea {
    // All constructors throw the following unchecked exceptions:
    // IllegalArgumentException — size is zero or negative
    // MemoryTypeConflictException — incompatible memory
    // OutOfMemoryException — insufficient memory
    // SecurityException — no permissions
    // SizeOutOfBoundsException — extends to an invalid range
    // UnsupportedPhysicalMemoryException - memory not supported

    public ImmortalPhysicalMemory(Object type, long size);
        // Where type represents the type of memory required
        // (e.g., dma), and size is the size of the area in bytes.
```

```
  public ImmortalPhysicalMemory(
        Object type, long base, long size);
    // Parameters are as above, with base being the address of
    // the area; throws (as above with):
    // MemoryInUseException - the specified memory is already in
    // use.
  ...
}
```

The other constructors provide variations that use a sizeEstimator and have an associated Runnable.

```
package javax.realtime;
public class ImmortalPhysicalMemory extends MemoryArea {
  ...
  public ImmortalPhysicalMemory(
        Object type, SizeEstimator size);

  public ImmortalPhysicalMemory(
        Object type, long base, SizeEstimator size);
  public ImmortalPhysicalMemory(Object type, long size,
        Runnable logic);
    // Where logic contains the run method which will be
    // called whenever the memory area is entered.
  public ImmortalPhysicalMemory(Object type, long base,
        long size, Runnable logic);
   public ImmortalPhysicalMemory(Object type,
        SizeEstimator size,Runnable logic);

  public ImmortalPhysicalMemory(Object type, long base,
        SizeEstimator size, Runnable logic);
}
```

Linear time physical memory

The LTPhysicalMemory class is the physical memory counterpart to the regular LTMemory class. Its definition is given below.

```
package javax.realtime;
public class LTPhysicalMemory extends ScopedMemory {
  // All constructors throw the following unchecked exceptions:
  // IllegalArgumentException — size is zero or negative
  // MemoryTypeConflictException — incompatible memory
```

```
// OutOfMemoryException — insufficient memory
// SecurityException —  no permissions
// SizeOutOfBoundsException — extends to an invalid range
// UnsupportedPhysicalMemoryException - memory not supported
public LTPhysicalMemory(Object type, long size)
  // Where type represents the type of memory required
  // (e.g., dma), and size is the size of the area in bytes.
public LTPhysicalMemory(Object type, long base,
       long size);
  // Parameters are as above, with base being the address of
  // the area; throws (as above with):
  // MemoryInUseException - the specified memory is already in
  // use.
public LTPhysicalMemory(
       Object type, SizeEstimator size);
public LTPhysicalMemory(Object type,
       long base, SizeEstimator size);
public LTPhysicalMemory(Object type,
       long size, Runnable logic);
  // Where logic contains the run method which will be
  // called whenever the memory area is entered.
public LTPhysicalMemory(Object type,
       long base, long size, Runnable logic);
public LTPhysicalMemory(Object type,
       SizeEstimator size,Runnable logic);
public LTPhysicalMemory(Object type,
       long base, SizeEstimator size, Runnable logic);
public String toString();
}
```

Variable time physical memory

The VTPhysicalMemory class is the physical memory counterpart to the regular VTMemory class. Its definition is given below.

```
package javax.realtime;
public class VTPhysicalMemory extends ScopedMemory {
  // All constructors throw the following unchecked exceptions:
  // IllegalArgumentException — size is zero or negative
  // MemoryTypeConflictException — incompatible memory
```

```
// OutOfMemoryException — insufficient memory
// SecurityException —  no permissions
// SizeOutOfBoundsException — extends to an invalid range
// UnsupportedPhysicalMemoryException - memory not supported

public VTPhysicalMemory(Object type, long size);
  // Where type represents the type of memory required
  // (e.g., dma), and size is the size of the area in bytes.

public VTPhysicalMemory(Object type, long base,
                            long size);
  // Parameters are as above, with base being the address of
  // the area. Throws (as above with):
  // MemoryInUseException - the specified memory is already in
  // use.

public VTPhysicalMemory(Object type,
                            SizeEstimator size);

public VTPhysicalMemory(Object type,
        long base, SizeEstimator size);

public VTPhysicalMemory(Object type,
        long size, Runnable logic);
  // Where logic contains the run method which will be
  // called whenever the memory area is entered.

public VTPhysicalMemory(Object type,
          long base, long size, Runnable logic);

public VTPhysicalMemory(Object type,
        SizeEstimator size,Runnable logic);

public VTPhysicalMemory(Object type, long base,
        SizeEstimator size, Runnable logic);

public String toString();
}
```

Example   Consider a multiprocessor implementation of the Real-Time JVM. The multiprocessor has both memory that is shared between the processors and memory private to each processor. The Real-Time JVM uses the shared memory area by default. Furthermore, for predictability, each schedulable object is assigned to a processor when it is created. The schedulable object is then always executed by that processor. The PhysicalMemoryManager allows application threads to use the private memory by defining

public static final String PRIVATE;

An application schedulable object can then allocate objects from its processor's private memory by first creating an appropriate physical memory area and then allocating from that area:

```
{
  SizeEstimator needed = new SizeEstimator();
  needed.reserve(...);
  try {
    LTPhysicalMemory privateMemory =
              new ImmortalPhysicalMemory(
                  PhysicalMemoryManager.PRIVATE, needed);
    privateMemory.newInstance(someClass);
  } catch(Exception ex) {
      System.out.println("failed to get private memory
                          access; reason " +ex);
  }
}
```

15.3 Accessing Raw Memory

While the above physical memory classes allow the placement of objects to be controlled, the raw memory access classes allow memory to be accessed outside the object model (but under control of the physical memory manager). In real-time and embedded systems, this is necessary for two main reasons:

- The memory is being written by a process external to the Java application
- The memory is being used by a memory-mapped I/O device.

Clearly, accessing raw memory is very dangerous and it is the job of the physical memory manager to ensure that the integrity of the Java system is not undermined. For example, the physical memory manager should not allow the application to read and write raw memory that has been allocated to objects, say, via ImmortalPhysicalMemory. This is because the memory may contain references to Java objects that, if written to, would corrupt the system. Furthermore, again for security reasons, only primitive data types (byte, ints, longs, floats and doubles) can be read and written.

**Byte
ordering**

The RTSJ allows the byte ordering of the underlying hardware to be ascertained via the
RealtimeSystems class. The BYTE_ORDER constant indicates the current hardware's ordering. BIG_ENDIAN and LITTLE_ENDIAN are constants representing bit
number 0 as the most significant and least significant bit respectively.

```java
package javax.realtime;
public class RealtimeSystem {
  . . .
  public static final byte BIG_ENDIAN;
  public static final byte BYTE_ORDER;
  public static final byte LITTLE_ENDIAN;
  . . .
}
```

**Raw memory
access**

There are two classes: the RawMemoryAccess class and the RawMemory-
FloatAccessClass.

The RawMemoryAccess has two constructors: one that simply allocates a
chunk of memory and one that allocates it at a particular location:

```java
package javax.realtime;
public class RawMemoryAccess {
  // All constructors throw the following unchecked exceptions:
  // IllegalArgumentException - size is zero or negative
  // OutOfMemoryException - insufficient memory
  // SecurityException - no permissions
  // SizeOutOfBoundsException - extends to an invalid range
  // UnsupportedPhysicalMemoryException - memory not supported
  // constructors
  public RawMemoryAccess(Object type, long size);
    // Where type represents the type of memory required
    // (e.g., dma); size is the size of the area in bytes.
  public RawMemoryAccess(
    Object type, long base, long size);
    // Parameters are as above, with base being the address of
    // the area.

  . . .

}
```

There are methods that allow read and write operations on data (or arrays of data):

```
package javax.realtime;
public class RawMemoryAccess {
  // constructors
  ...
  // methods
  // All methods throw the following unchecked exceptions
  // SizeOutOfBoundsException — the object is not mapped, or
  // the item falls in an invalid address range,
  // OffsetOutOfBoundsException — the offset is negative or
  // greater than the size of the raw memory area.
  public byte getByte(long offset);

  public void getBytes(
      long offset, byte[] bytes, int low, int number);

  public int getInt(long offset);

  public void getInts(
      long offset, int[] ints, int low, int number);

  public long getLong(long offset);

  public void getLongs(
      long offset, long[] longs, int low, int number);

  public short getShort(long offset);

  public void getShorts(
      long offset, short[] shorts, int low, int number);
  public void setByte(long offset, byte value);

  public void setBytes(
      long offset, byte[] bytes, int low, int number);

  public void setInt(long offset, int value);

  public void setInts(
      long offset, int[] ints, int low, int number);

  public void setLong(long offset, long value);

  public void setLongs(
      long offset, long[] longs, int low, int number);

  public void setShort(long offset, short value);

  public void setShorts(
      long offset, short[] shorts, int low, int number);
  ...
}
```

Where the Real-Time JVM is hosted on a system that supports hardware memory management, the physical memory may be mapped to a particular virtual address. Raw memory access allows these addresses to be manipulated:

```
package javax.realtime;
public class RawMemoryAccess {
    // constructors
    ...
    // methods
    ...
    public long getMappedAddress();
    // Get the virtual address associated with the
    // raw memory object.
    public long map();
    // If the object is not mapped into the virtual memory,
    // map it and return the virtual address.
    public long map(long base);
    public long map(long base, long size);
    // As above, but the virtual address that is required is
    // given as a parameter.
    public void unmap();
    // Undo any mappings.
}
```

Raw memory access to floats

For completeness, the RTSJ allows raw memory to be accessed by reading and writing floating-point numbers. While this has limited use for memory-mapped I/O devices, it may be useful if the memory is shared with a process outside the Java system. However, care must be exercised, as it is essential that the process and JVM use the same floating-point format.

```
package javax.realtime;
public class RawMemoryFloatAccess extends RawMemoryAccess
{
    // All constructors throw the following unchecked exceptions:
    // IllegalArgumentException — size is zero or negative
    // OutOfMemoryException — insufficient memory
    // SecurityException —  no permissions
    // SizeOutOfBoundsException — extends to an invalid range
    // UnsupportedPhysicalMemoryException - memory not supported
    // constructors
```

```
public RawMemoryFloatAccess(Object type, long size);
  // Where type represents the type of memory required
  // (e.g., dma); size is the size of the area in bytes.
public RawMemoryFloatAccess(Object type, long base,
                            long size);
 // Parameters are as above, with base being the address of
 // the area.

// methods
// All methods throw the following unchecked exceptions
// SizeOutOfBoundsException —  the object is not mapped, or
// the item falls in an invalid address range,
// OffsetOutOfBoundsException — the offset is negative or
// greater than the size of the raw memory area.

public double getDouble(long offset);

public void getDoubles(long offset, double[] doubles,
                       int low, int number);

public float getFloat(long offset);

public void getFloats(
    long offset, float[] floats, int low, int number);

public void setDouble(long offset, double value);

public void setDoubles(
    long offset, double[] bytes, int low, int number);

public void setFloat(long offset, float value);
public void setFloats(
    long offset, float[] floats, int low, int number);
}
```

Important
note

The RTSJ does not require access to the primitive data types to be on address boundaries (for example, word boundaries for integers). Consequently, if the programmer tries to read/write to a primitive data type at an address, which is not on an appropriate boundary, the read/write operation may not be atomic. For example, writing a long on a byte boundary may require more than one read and write operation to memory.

Example

Consider the case where the applications programmer wishes to control access to an analogue-to-digital converter (ADC). Suppose that the device is accessed via two memory mapped IO registers: a control and status register, and a data buffer register. The control and status register resides at address 0x77FFE000 and is 16 bits long with the structure given in Figure 15.3:

Bits	Name	Meaning
0	Start	Set to 1 to start a conversion
6	Enable/Disable	Set to 1 to enable interrupts
7	Done	Set to 1 by device when conversion is complete
8-13	Channel	Indicates the required input (the converter has 64 analogue inputs)
15	Error	Set to 1 by the device when an error has occurred during conversion

FIGURE 15.3. **The Control and Status Register of an Analogue-to-Digital Converter**

When conversion is complete, the value is returned via a 16-bit data buffer register that resides at address 0x77FFE002.

To program the ADC, it is first necessary to produce a class that encapsulates the control and status register. The constructor of this class creates the raw memory access. Assume that the physical memory manager supports the IO_PAGE memory type.

```java
import javax.realtime.*;
public class AdcControlAndStatusRegister {
  public AdcControlAndStatusRegister(
        long base, short chan) {
    try {
      if(chan > 63) throw
       new IllegalArgumentException("channel > 63");
      rawMemory = new RawMemoryAccess(
          PhysicalMemoryManager.IO_PAGE, base, REG_SIZE);
      shadow = chan << 8;
    } catch(Exception e) {
        throw new
        IllegalArgumentException("illegal base address");
      }
  }
```

```
RawMemoryAccess rawMemory;
short shadow;
final long REG_SIZE = 2;
final short START = 01;
final short ENABLE = 040;
final short DONE = 0100;
final short ERROR = 04000;


  . . .

}
```

It is worth noting that on many machines more than one device register can be mapped to the same physical address in the memory map. Consequently, several variables may be mapped to the same location in memory. Furthermore, these registers are often read or write only. Care, therefore, must be taken when manipulating device registers. In the above example, if the control and status register is a pair of registers mapped to the same location, the control register will be write-only, and the status register read-only. The programmer's code that accesses the register pair may not have the desired effect. This is because to set a particular bit may require code to be generated, which reads the current value into the machine accumulator. As the control register is write-only, this would produce the value of the status register. It is advisable, therefore, to have other variables in a program, which represent device registers. These can be manipulated in the normal way. When the required register format has been constructed, it may then be assigned to the actual device register. Such variables are often called *shadow device registers.*

The remainder of the class provides methods to read and set the various bits:

```
import javax.realtime.*;
public class AdcControlAndStatusRegister {
  . . .

  public void startConversion() {
    shadow = shadow | START | ENABLE;
    rawMemory.setShort(0, shadow);
  }

  public boolean deviceError() {
    if((rawMemory.getShort(0) & ERROR) == ERROR)
      return true;
    else return false;
  }
```

```
public boolean conversionComplete() {
  if((rawMemory.getShort(0) & DONE) == DONE)
    return true;
  else return false;
}
}
```

Now the program can create the device registers at the required locations:

```
final long csrBaseAddress = 0x77FFE000;
final long dataBaseAddress = 0x77FFE002;
final long REG_SIZE = 2;
final short channel = 6;

myAdcReg = new AdcControlRegister(csrBaseAddress,
                                          channel);
dataBuffer = new RawMemoryAccess(
      PhysicalMemory.IO_PAGE, dataBaseAddress,REG_SIZE);
myAdcReg.startConversion();
```

To handle interrupts from the ADC device, it is necessary to attach an asynchronous event handler (see Section 11.1).

15.4 Summary

Normally, the Java programmer is not concerned with where the JVM stores the objects created during program execution. However, embedded systems may support different types of memory with different performance characteristics. Furthermore, I/O devices may be accessed via their memory locations. For these reasons, the RTSJ provide classes that allow

- memory areas to be created where the physical memory characteristics can be specified,
- memory locations to be read and written as primitive data types.

It is the job of the memory manager to ensure that these low-level uses of memory do not undermine the integrity of the Java program.

16 Case Study: Automobile Cruise Control System

Introduction and chapter structure

The automobile cruise control system (ACCS) case study has often been used by the real-time community over the years as it illustrates many of the differences between real-time embedded systems and traditional information processing systems. The requirements for the ACCS are presented first, followed by a discussion of the interactions between the system and its environment. The software design is then presented along with the RTSJ implementation.

16.1 ACCS Requirements

The overall goal of an automobile cruise control system is to maintain the speed of a vehicle automatically to a value set by the driver.[1] Commands to the system may be given explicitly or implicitly. The explicit commands are given by the driver's interface, which is a lever on the side of the steering wheel. The command lever has several positions that represent the following instructions to the system (the commands are only valid if the engine is turned on):

- **activate** – turn on the cruise control system if the car is in top gear, and maintain (and remember) the current speed

- **deactivate** – turn off the cruise control system

- **start accelerating** – accelerate the vehicle at a comfortable rate

- **stop accelerating** – stop accelerating and maintain (and remember) the current speed

- **resume** – return the car to the last remembered speed and maintain that speed.

---

1. The requirements for the system given in this section are based on those defined by (Hatley and Pirbhai, 1988).

Implicit commands are issued when the driver

- *changes gear* – the cruise control system is deactivated when the driver changes out of top gear

- *presses the brake pedal* – the cruise control system is deactivated whenever the drives brakes.

The speed of the car is measured by the ACCS via the rotation of the shaft that drives the back wheels. The shaft will generate an interrupt for each rotation. The system has a default setting for the number of interrupts that should be generated for each kilometer travelled.

The speed of the car depends on the throttle position. The throttle position is determined by two factors: the amount of depression of the accelerator pedal and the value supplied by the cruise control system. The throttle's cruise control component is controlled by varying the voltage to the throttle actuator. The values range from 0 (throttle fully closed) to 8 (throttle fully open). Voltages can be set in units of 0.1 volts. A voltage setting holds its value for 3 seconds. If it is not reset, then a default of 0 volts is used. It is assumed that the combining of the two throttle component values is performed outside the cruise control system.

Cruise control throttle settings are defined for "maintaining the current speed" and for "comfortable acceleration". The required settings are as follows:

Maintaining Speed. To maintain the desired speed, the following algorithm is used:

- if the desired speed minus the actual speed is greater than 2 kmph, the throttle is set to fully open

- if the actual speed minus the desired speed is greater than 2 kmph, the throttle is set to fully closed

- otherwise, the value of the throttle is set to $2(S_D - S_A + 2)$ volts where S_D is the desired speed and S_A is the actual speed.

More formally, if V is the voltage, then

$$V = \begin{cases} 8 & (S_D - S_A) > 2 \\ 2(S_D - S_A + 2) & -2 \le (S_D - S_A) \le 2 \\ 0 & -2 > (S_D - S_A) \end{cases}$$

Comfortable Acceleration. In order to avoid rapid changes in speed, the voltage to the throttle should not be changed by more than 0.1 in any one-second period.

16.2 System Interactions

All devices are memory mapped and have associated control and data registers. Sensors in the automobile detect state changes and generate appropriate interrupts to the control system, as illustrated in Figure 16.1. With each interrupt, the data register contains the event that caused the state change. The throttle actuator's data register takes a value between 0 and 800. This represents the requested voltage in units of 0.1 volts.

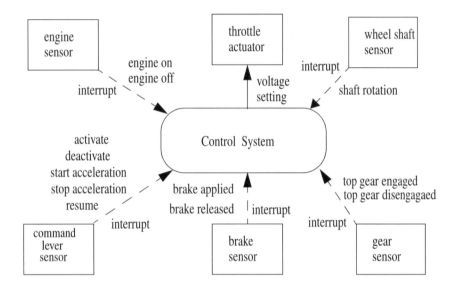

FIGURE 16.1. **Relationship between Devices and the Control System**

16.3 Software Design

The system consists of the following major components:

- Interrupt handlers for the command lever, brake, engine, wheel shaft and gear interrupts

- A periodic real-time thread to control the throttle

- A periodic thread to monitor the speed

- A cruise controller to coordinate the system.

The interaction between these components is represented by the object collaboration diagram given in Figure 16.2.

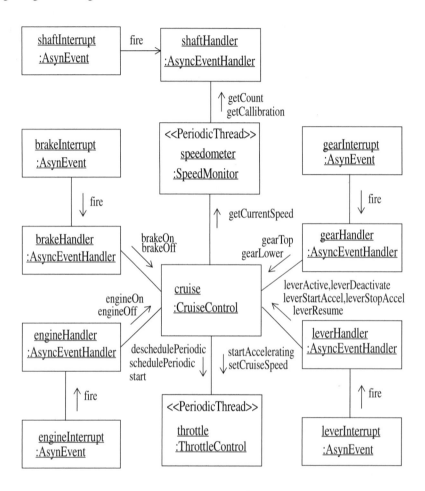

FIGURE 16.2. Cruise Control System: Object Collaboration Diagram

16.4 Implementation

Interrupts and their handlers

As mentioned in Chapter 10, interrupts in the RTSJ are represented by asynchronous events. Hence, for every interrupt there is an object of class `AsyncEvent` and an associated handler. Assume that the following class exists for interfacing to the device registers.

```java
import javax.realtime.*;
public class DeviceRegisterPair {
  public DeviceRegisterPair(
        long controlAddress, long dataAddress) {

    rawMemoryControl = new RawMemoryAccess(
        PhysicalMemoryManager.IO_PAGE,
        controlAddress, REG_SIZE);
    rawMemoryData = new RawMemoryAccess(
        PhysicalMemoryManager.IO_PAGE,
        dataAddress, REG_SIZE);
  }
  public void enableDevice() {
    shadow = ENABLE_DEVICE;
    rawMemoryControl.setShort(0, shadow);
  }
  public void setOperate() {
    shadow = ENABLE_DEVICE | SET_OPERATION;
    rawMemoryControl.setShort(0, shadow);
  }
  public void clearOperate() {
    shadow = ENABLE_DEVICE | SET_OPERATION;
    rawMemoryControl.setShort(0, shadow);
  }

  public int readDataRegister() {
    return rawMemoryData.getInt(0);
  }

  private RawMemoryAccess rawMemoryControl;
  private RawMemoryAccess rawMemoryData;
  private short shadow;
  private final long REG_SIZE = 2;
  private final short ENABLE_DEVICE = 01; // for example
  private final short SET_OPERATION = 02000; // for example
}
```

Now consider an example interrupt and its handler (for the cruise control lever). First, the interrupt handler is defined as a class that extends AsyncEventHandler. Its constructor takes a reference to the cruise control system and the device register pair that controls the interrupt. It also takes the parameters necessary for calling the parent class's constructor.

```
import javax.realtime.*;
public class Lever extends AsyncEventHandler {
  public Lever(CruiseControl cruise, DeviceRegisterPair reg
      PriorityParameters pri, ReleaseParameters rel) {
    super(pri, rel, null, null, null, null);
    myReg = reg;
    myCruise = cruise;
  }

  public void handleAsyncEvent() {
    int last = myReg.readDataRegister();
        // Get last event.
    switch(last) {
      case (CarEvent.LEVER_DEACTIVATE):
        myCruise.deactivate(); break;
      case (CarEvent.LEVER_RESUME):
        myCruise.resume(); break;
      case (CarEvent.LEVER_ACTIVATE):
        myCruise.activate(); break;
      case (CarEvent.LEVER_START_ACCELERATING):
        myCruise.startAcceleration(); break;
      case (CarEvent.LEVER_STOP_ACCELERATING):
        myCruise.stopAcceleration(); break;
      default:
        System.out.println("UNKNOWN LEVER INTERRUPT ");
    }
  }
  private CruiseControl myCruise;
  private DeviceRegisterPair myReg;
}
```

The interrupt handling code is given in the body of the handleAsyncEvent method. In this case, it reads the data register associated with the device to determine the cause of the interrupt. The case statement then undertakes the appropriate action. Here, it is assumed that the values returned in the data registers are unique across all interrupts and are defined as the enumeration class CarEvent.

The interrupt handler is associated with the interrupt and its device registers by the main program (the configuration constants for the device register pair address, the handler's minimum inter-arrival times and priority are assumed to be defined as constants elsewhere).

```
public static void main(String [] args) {
    ...
    // LEVER
    AsyncEvent leverInterrupt = new AsyncEvent();
    DeviceRegisterPair leverDevice = new
            DeviceRegisterPair(LEVER_CONTROL_REG_ADDRESS,
            LEVER_DATA_REG_ADDRESS);
    PriorityParameters leverHandlerPriority = new
            PriorityParameters(LEVER_HANDLER_PRIORITY);
    SporadicParameters leverHandlerRelease = new
            SporadicParameters(
                new RelativeTime(LEVER_HANDLER_ARRIVAL, 0));
    Lever leverHandler = new Lever(cruise, leverDevice,
            leverHandlerPriority, leverHandlerRelease);
    leverInterrupt.addHandler(leverHandler);
    ...

}
```

Similar structures can be defined for the other interrupts and their handlers. The shaft interrupt is slightly different in that it simply maintains a count of the number of rotations.

Periodic Real-time Threads

The system consists of two periodic activities: the speedometer and the throttle controller. Here, the SpeedMonitor class is presented. This extends the RealtimeThread class. The constructor saves the last count from the wheelShaft and determines the wheelShaft calibration. It also calculates the number of iterations that the thread will make in one hour. On every period of the thread, the current speed is approximated from the difference in the number of shaft rotations since its last period. The value is an approximation because of the variability of the thread's execution due to the nature of fixed priority scheduling.

```
import javax.realtime.*;
public class SpeedMonitor extends RealtimeThread {

    public SpeedMonitor(ShaftHandler wheelShaft,
                        PriorityParameters pri,
                        PeriodicParameters period) {
        super(pri, period);
        lastNumberRotations = wheelShaft.getCount();
```

```
      calibration = wheelShaft.getCallibration();
      iterationsInOneHour = (int)((1000 /
            period.getPeriod().getMilliseconds()) * 3600);
      shaft = wheelShaft;
}

public synchronized int getCurrentSpeed() {
    return currentSpeed;
}

public void run() {
    boolean ok = true;
    while(ok) {
        numberRotations = shaft.getCount();
        long difference = numberRotations -
                          lastNumberRotations;
        synchronized(this) {
            currentSpeed = (int) (
                (difference * calibration * iterationsInOneHour)/
                cmInKillometer);
        }
        lastNumberRotations = numberRotations;
        ok = waitForNextPeriod();
    }
    // ok should always be true, if it is not, there
    // is a serious problem and action must be taken here.
}

private WheelShaft shaft;
private long numberRotations, lastNumberRotations;
private final int calibration; // nearest centimetre
private int currentSpeed = 0; // nearest k.p.h
private final int iterationsInOneHour;
private final int cmInKillometer = 100000;
}
```

Associated with the speedometer thread is an event handler that is run when the system detects a deadline overrun. In general, the system can tolerate a missed deadline as the speed is only an approximation. However, the handler keeps track of the number missed and when it passes a threshold it informs the driver (via a light on the dashboard) that the system needs maintenance. The following class illustrates the approach.

```java
import javax.realtime.*;
public class SpeedDeadlineMissHandler
                extends AsyncEventHandler {
  public SpeedDeadlineMissHandler(PriorityParameters pri,
        ReleaseParameters rel, SpeedMonitor speedo) {
    super(pri, rel, null, null, null, null);
    mySpeedo = speedo;
  }

  public void handleAsyncEvent() {
    // Deadline has overrun.
    missedDeadlines = missedDeadlines++;
    if(missedDeadlines > THRESHOLD) {
      // Turn on light on dashboard to indicate
      // that the system needs maintenance.
    }
    mySpeedo.schedulePeriodic(); // reschedule the thread
  }

  private SpeedMonitor mySpeedo;
  private int missedDeadlines = 0;
  private final int THRESHOLD = 10;
}
```

The actual handler and thread are created and linked in the main program. Note that the handler is set after the thread object has been created.

```java
public static void main(String [] args) {
  ...
  // SPEEDO
  PriorityParameters speedPriority = new
      PriorityParameters(SPEEDOMETER_PRIORITY);
  PeriodicParameters speedRelease = new
      PeriodicParameters(
          SYSTEM_START_TIME,      // start
          SPEEDOMETER_PERIOD,     // period
          null,                   // cost
          SPEEDOMETER_DEADLINE,   // deadline
          null,                   // overrun
          speedoMissHandler);     // deadline miss
```

```
SpeedMonitor speedo = new SpeedMonitor(
        shaft, speedPriority, speedRelease);
PriorityParameters speedMissPriority = new
        PriorityParameters(SPEEDO_MISS_PRIORITY);
AperiodicParameters speedMissRelease = new
        AperiodicParameters();

SpeedDeadlineMissHandler speedoMissHandler = new
        SpeedDeadlineMissHandler(speedMissPriority,
                                speedMissRelease, speedo);
speedRelease.setDeadlineMissHandler(speedoMissHandler);
...

speedo.start();
}
```

**The cruise
control state
machine**

The final object presented is the object that coordinates the cruise control system. It is a
state machine. Figure 16.3 presents a state transition diagram for the object. When the
engine is switched on, the system goes into engine active mode. There are various
submodes within this and if the engine is turned off when the system is in one of these
submodes, the system returns to the engine off mode. The initial submode is the
running mode. When in the running mode, the system will change state as a result
of receiving one of the following events:

- ignition off – move back to the engine off mode
- engage top gear – move into the running in top gear mode
- engage brake – move into the braking in low gear mode.

All other events have no effect. Similarly for the other modes, any event not specified on
the diagram results in no transition.

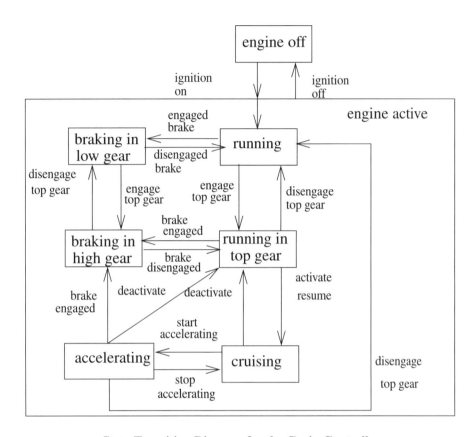

FIGURE 16.3. State Transition Diagram for the CruiseControllers

The code for this state machine is given below. First, consider the constructor, the `activate`, `deactivate` and `resume` events. The cruise controller needs to interact with the speedometer and the throttle controller. Hence, references to these objects are passed through the constructor. The approach adopted is that the first time the system goes into the `cruising` mode, the real-time thread controlling the throttle is started. If the system then comes out of the `cruising` mode, the thread is descheduled. This will cause it to block when it next executes its `waitForNextPeriod` method call. If the system enters the `cruising` mode again, the thread is simply rescheduled.

```
import javax.realtime.*;
public class CruiseControl {
  public CruiseControl(
         ThrottleController throttleControl,
         SpeedMonitor speedMon) {
```

```
      throttle = throttleControl;
      speed = speedMon;
  }
  public void activate() {
    if(engineActive & topGear & !braking) {
      cruising = true;
      throttle.setCruiseSpeed(speed.getCurrentSpeed());
      if(throttleStarted) throttle.schedulePeriodic();
      else {
        throttleStarted = true;
        throttle.start();
      }
    }
  }
  public void deactivate() {
    if (cruising){
      cruising = false;
      throttle.deschedulePeriodic();
    }
  }
  public void resume() {
    if(topGear & !braking & throttleStarted) {
      cruising = true;
      throttle.schedulePeriodic();
    }
  }
  ...
```

The code for the other events is given below:

```
public class CruiseControl {
  ...
  public void startAcceleration(){
    if(engineActive & topGear & !braking) {
      accelerating = true;
      if(throttleStarted) throttle.schedulePeriodic();
      else {
        throttleStarted = true;
        throttle.start();
      }
      throttle.accelerate();
    }
  }
```

```
public void stopAcceleration() {
  if(engineActive & topGear & !braking & accelerating) {
    accelerating = false;
    cruising = true;
    throttle.setCruiseSpeed(speed.getCurrentSpeed());
  }
}
public void ignitionOn() {
  engineActive = true;
  braking = false;
  topGear = false;
  cruising = false;
}
public void ignitionOff() {
  engineActive = false;
  braking = false;
  topGear = false;
  if(cruising) {
    cruising = false;
    throttle.deschedulePeriodic();
  }
}
public void topGearEngaged() {
  if(engineActive) topGear = true;
}
public void topGearDisengaged() {
  if(engineActive) {
    topGear = false;
    if(cruising){
      cruising = false;
      throttle.deschedulePeriodic();
    }
  }
}
public void brakeEngaged() {
  if(engineActive) {
    if(cruising){
      cruising = false;
      throttle.deschedulePeriodic();
    }
    braking = true;
  }
}
```

```
public void brakeDisengaged() {
  if(engineActive) {
    braking = false;
  }
}

private boolean engineActive = false;
private boolean topGear = false;
private boolean braking = false;
private boolean accelerating = false;
private boolean cruising = false;
private ThrottleController throttle;
private boolean throttleStarted = false;
private SpeedMonitor speed;
}
```

Finally, the main program creates an instance of the class.

```
public static void main(String [] args) {

  ...

  // CRUISE_CONTROL
  CruiseControl cruise = new
          CruiseControl(throttle, speedo);
  ...
}
```

16.5 Summary

The chapter has illustrated the design and implementation of a cruise control system. This demonstrates many of the facilities of the RTSJ – in particular, real-time threads, asynchronous events and their handlers, device register access and interrupt handling. The chapter assumes that real-time garbage collection performs adequately enough to cope with the memory demands of the system. No cost overrun detection has been performed.

17 High-Integrity Real-Time Systems

Introduction and chapter structure

Increasingly, software is being used in high-integrity systems; that is, systems where failure can cause loss of life, environmental harm, or significant financial loss. Here, it is essential for programs to be of the highest quality. In recognition of the demands placed on this "high-integrity software", there have been national and international standards agreed that give advice on how to develop high-integrity software components and present style guides on how to use particular programming languages. For example, the US Nuclear Regulatory Commission (NRC) has guidelines for the development of safe programs in languages like Ada 83, Ada 95, C and C++ (Hetch, Hetch and Graff, 1997). Most countries' safety-related industries also use guidelines on developing high-integrity software (DEF 055 in the UK and DO-178B in the US). Many of these standards either assume that systems are sequential and forbid the use of concurrency or recommend that concurrency be kept to a minimum.

To illustrate a typical standard's requirements, consider the NRC, which has developed a set of generic safe programming attributes. There are four top-level attributes (Hetch, Hetch and Graff, 1997):

- Reliability – defined as the "predictable and consistent performance of the software under conditions specified in its design". A key factor in obtaining reliability is to have predictability of the program's execution, in particular, predictability of control and data flow, predictability of memory utilization and predictability of response times.

- Robustness – defined as "the capability of the safety system software to operate in an acceptable manner under abnormal conditions or events". Often called fault tolerance or survivability, this attribute requires the system to cope with both anticipated and unexpected faults. Techniques such as using replication, diversity and exception handling are commonly used (Burns and Wellings, 2001).

- Traceability – relates to "the feasibility of reviewing and identifying the source code and library component origin and development processes", thus facilitating verification and validation techniques which are essential aids to ensuring program correctness.

- Maintainability – relates to "the means by which the source code reduces the likelihood that faults will be introduced during changes made after delivery". All the standard software engineering issues apply here such as good readability, use of appropriate abstraction techniques, strong cohesion and loose coupling of components, and portability of software components between compilers and platforms (Sommerville, 2000).

For many people, Java is the antithesis of a high-integrity programming language. Ironically, many of the features that have led to its success as a programming language for general applications are problematic when used in high-integrity systems. Its combination of object-oriented programming features, lack of any mechanisms for memory reclaiming (thereby necessitating the virtual machine to undertake garbage collection) and its poor support for real-time multithreading are all seen as particular drawbacks. The RTSJ has introduced many new features that help in the real-time domain. However, the expressive power of these features means that very complex programming models can be created, necessitating complexity in the supporting real-time virtual machine. Consequently, Java, with the real-time extensions as they stand, is too complex for confident use in high-integrity systems.

Ada is one of the most important programming languages for the high-integrity systems application domain. As with Java, full Ada is not appropriate for high-integrity programming. However, the SPARK subset of Ada (Barnes, 1997) (which removes many of the language's complicated or advanced features such as tasking, exceptions, overloading, etc.) allows programs to be proven correct mathematically. In recent years, advances in real-time systems research, particularly in the area of schedulability analysis, mean that it is now possible to show mathematically that a concurrent program will meet its deadlines. Of course, constraints must be placed on the particular concurrency mechanisms used to ensure predictability. However, it is no longer axiomatic that concurrency should be forbidden or even discouraged. To encourage the use of concurrency in high-integrity real-time systems, the Ada community has developed a subset of the Ada tasking model (including the Real-Time Annex) called the Ravenscar Profile (or just Ravenscar) (Burns, Dobbings and Romanski, 1998). The main aims of the subset are to support a predictable computational model and to enable a small, efficient and predictable run-time support system to be produced. The Ravenscar Profile has attracted support from users and compiler (and run-time) vendors, and has become a de facto standard in the high-integrity systems domain. It has recently been incorporated into the Ada language standard.

The goal of this chapter is to discuss a Ravenscar-inspired subset for Java and the RTSJ extensions. The discussion builds on the work of (Puschner and Wellings, 2001), (Kwon, Wellings and King, 2002, 2003).

17.1 The Ravenscar Computational Model

The main goal of Ravenscar is to define a computational model for application programs so that they can be analyzed for their timing properties on single-processor systems (using standard feasibility analysis techniques such as Response Time Analysis (Audsley et al, 1993; Burns and Wellings, 2001)). Hence, it addresses the "reliability" aspects of the NRC's top-level attributes rather than the "robustness" aspects. Ravenscar is silent on issues like exception handling, which it considers to be part of the sequential language and, therefore, outside its scope. For high-integrity systems, an application might also impose other nonconcurrency-related restrictions.

The model classifies concurrent entities as being either periodic or sporadic. The use of these terms in Ravenscar is consistent with their use in the RTSJ. That is, periodic entities are released on a regular basis (they are usually time triggered) and sporadic entities are released on an irregular basis (albeit with a minimum separation between releases – they are usually event triggered). Aperiodic entities are not encouraged in Ravenscar as they are, by definition, unpredictable[1].

A Ravenscar program consists of a fixed number of concurrent entities that are created immediately after the program begins its execution. A program is considered to have

- an initialization phase – where all the concurrent entities (and all other permanent objects) are created; typically there are no hard time constraints associated with this phase of execution,

- an execution phase – where all concurrent entities execute under time constraints.

Concurrent entities, in Ravenscar, do not terminate and, hence, the program does not terminate. All concurrent entities have unique fixed priorities and they are executed using preemptive priority-based scheduling. Sporadic entities are usually released by a single event that can be either software generated or hardware generated (by an interrupt).

Communication between concurrent entities is via shared data. Where data cannot be accessed atomically, it is encapsulated by procedures that enforce mutual exclusion. Ceiling priority inheritance (called priority ceiling emulation by the RTSJ) is used to bound the time that a high-priority entity can be blocked by a low-priority entity accessing shared data. Concurrent entities that access shared data must not suspend themselves while holding a mutual exclusion lock.

Although Ravenscar says little about memory management issues, it is targeted at static real-time systems. Hence, no dynamic creation of concurrent entities is allowed. For the purpose of this chapter, it will be assumed that there is an implicit requirement

---

1. It is possible to bound the impact of aperiodic activities using server technologies (for example, sporadic or deferrable servers, see Section 10.4.5). However, these are not supported by the Ravenscar profile.

that all memory management is predictable. This is in keeping with the guidelines given by other standards; furthermore, without predictable memory management, it would not be possible to analyze Ravenscar-compliant programs. The profile is also silent on control flow issues, although, again, there is an implicit assumption that they are statically analyzable.

Although the Ravenscar model is very simple, it is reasonably expressive. User experience with the model has shown up some "ease of use" problems, however, in general, the experience has been positive (Brach, 2002; Michell, 2002).

17.2 Java, the RTSJ and Ravenscar

In recent years, the scope of Java has been extended to address the demands of small-scale embedded systems and consumer electronics. The Java 2 Platform Micro Edition has been introduced (J2ME) (Sun Microsystems, 2000). In essence, this consists of a three-layered architecture:

- a virtual machine layer (usually implemented on top of a host operating system);

- a configuration layer that defines the set of Java language features, a minimum set of virtual machine features and the available class libraries that can be supported by a particular implementation platform (for example, a mobile phone);

- a profile layer that defines a minimum set of Application Programmers Interfaces (APIs) targeted at a particular application domain.

More than one profile may be supported by the same configuration layer, and different configuration layers may support the same profile. A configuration layer, called Connected, Limited Device Configuration (CLDC) has been defined for small, resource-constrained mobile devices (mobile phones, pagers, personal organizers, etc.) typically with a memory capacity of up to 512 kb. The K (kilo bytes) virtual machine (KVM) is a specifically designed virtual machine to support the CLDC. The restrictions imposed on the Java language and this virtual machine include (Topley, 2002): no support for floating point operations, no support for native interfaces, no user-defined class loaders, no thread groups or daemon threads, no object finalization, etc. The main motivation for these restrictions is to reduce the size of memory required to implement the virtual machine.

It is clear that the overheads of implementing the RTSJ make it unsuitable for the CLDC configuration and consequently RTSJ, as it stands, is probably best targeted at Java 2 Standard Edition (J2SE) or the CDC – Connected Device Configuration – within the J2ME framework. However, a subset of the RTSJ along the lines of the Ravenscar model would be appropriate for J2ME CLDC, and it is possible to imagine a Ravenscar virtual machine and a Ravenscar CLDC along with one or more profiles.

17.3 The Ravenscar-Java Profile

The Ravenscar profile for Java, augmented by the RTSJ (Ravenscar-Java), focusses on the "reliability" attribute of high-integrity programming. The attributes can be summarized under the following headings:

- predictability of memory utilization
- predictability of response times
- predictability of control and data flow.

Although restrictions on the use of Java and the RTSJ will be specified, *there is an underlying requirement that the resulting Ravenscar-Java programs are valid RTSJ programs and will execute on a standard RTSJ platform with the same functional results* (although not necessarily with the same response times).

17.3.1 Predictability of memory utilization

Initialization and mission phases

An overriding concern of a Ravenscar-Java program is to avoid garbage collection (it is assumed that the underlying virtual machine does not even support it). However, with the current RTSJ definition it is not possible to write a program that does not use the heap at all. All Java programs begin with the execution of a main method. Any objects created by this method will be allocated from the heap. This problem is compounded by the RTSJ rule that only schedulable objects can enter into a memory area. Hence, to obtain predictable memory usage, the main method of a Ravenscar-Java program should be structured to construct a high-priority real-time thread whose run method executes in immortal memory.[2] Its function is to perform the initialization phase of the program. The following illustrates the approach.

```
import javax.realtime.*;
class Main implements Runnable {
  public static void main(String [] args) {
    RealtimeThread initializer =
      new RealtimeThread( new PriorityParameters(
          PriorityScheduler.MAX_PRIORITY), null, null,
      ImmortalMemory.instance(), null, new Main()));
    initializer.start();
  }
  public void run() {
    // Initialization phase of the program.
  }
}
```

---

2. In the absence of garbage collection, heap memory is equivalent to immortal memory. However, to be compatible with non-Ravenscar RTSJ implementations, immortal memory is explicitly used.

Note that the initializing thread has no release parameters, no memory parameters and no processing group parameters. In the context of a J2ME profile, the initializer thread might be predefined as an extension of the `RealtimeThread` class that sets up its own parameters, as illustrated below:

```
package javax.ravenscar;
public class Initializer extends RealtimeThread {
  public Initializer() {
    super( new PriorityParameters(
        PriorityScheduler.MAX_PRIORITY),
        ImmortalMemory.instance());
  }
}
import javax.ravenscar.*;
class Main extends Initializer {
  public static void main(String [] args) {
    Initializer initializer = new Main();
    initializer.start();
  }
  public void run() {
    // Initialization phase of the program.
  }
}
```

Use of immortal and scoped memory areas

Objects that are needed for the lifetime of the program must be created by the initializer in immortal memory (this includes all periodic threads and sporadic event handlers). Objects required for the lifetime of a periodic or sporadic activity must be created by the constructors for the classes. Objects required for each release of an activity can be created in a scoped memory area that can be entered as and when required. All scoped memory areas must be created by the initializer (or by constructors) in immortal memory.

Only the `LTMemory` class is defined by Ravenscar-Java, as it gives predictable memory allocation. The set of methods in the `MemoryArea` class that deal with joining a scoped memory area are absent from the Ravenscar-Java specification, as these potentially block the calling schedulable object.

The `MemoryArea` class hierarchy is defined below. First, the base class is illustrated.

```
package javax.ravenscar;
public abstract class MemoryArea {
  protected MemoryArea(long size);
  protected MemoryArea(SizeEstimator size);
  public void enter(Runnable logic);
```

```
   public static MemoryArea getMemoryArea(Object object);
   public long memoryConsumed();
   public long memoryRemaining();
   public Object newArray(Class type, int number);
   public Object newInstance(Class type)
     throws IllegalAccessException, InstantiationException;
   public Object newInstance(
         reflect.Constructor c, Object[] args)
     throws IllegalAccessException, InstantiationException;
   public long size();
 }
```

The MemoryArea class has been significantly simplified compared to its RTSJ counterpart. Note also that for predictability any high-integrity profile will probably impose restrictions on the use of java.lang.reflect. Also static analysis applied to the application program will require memory sizes to be accurately determined. Hence, no OutOfMemoryError exception should be thrown.

Further restrictions can be imposed to reduce the complexity of the underlying run-time support. For example, run-time support will be significantly reduced by disallowing nested scoped memory areas and allowing only one schedulable object to be active in a single scoped memory area.

The remainder of the MemoryArea class hierarchy can now be given.

```
package javax.ravenscar;
public final class ImmortalMemory extends MemoryArea {
  public static ImmortalMemory instance();
}
package javax.ravenscar;
public abstract class ScopedMemory extends MemoryArea {
  public ScopedMemory(long size);
  public ScopedMemory(SizeEstimator size);

  public void enter(Runnable logic);
  public int getReferenceCount(); // returns 0 or 1
}
package javax.ravenscar;
public class LTMemory extends ScopedMemory {
  public LTMemory(long size);
  public LTMemory(SizeEstimator size);
}
```

The timing characteristics of LTMemory allocation must be documented. Furthermore, if object finalizers are allowed, the implementation of Ravenscar-Java must document when objects created in LTMemory are finalized. One possibility is that finalization should be executed by the thread that, on leaving the memory area, causes the reference count to become zero. The thread should not return from the enter method until the finalization is completed and the memory reclaimed. Finalization should be performed at the same priority as the thread.

17.3.2 Predictability of response times

Ravenscar-Java requires all concurrent entities to be either periodic or sporadic. In RTSJ there are two vehicles for creating concurrent entities: real-time threads and asynchronous event handlers. Threads with sporadic release parameters are not very well-defined in RTSJ (see Section 12.3); consequently, in Ravenscar-Java, this requirement is interpreted to be that

- all threads other than the initializing thread must not require access to the heap and have periodic release parameters
- all event handlers must be statically bound to a thread with no heap requirements and have sporadic release parameters; each handler must be attached to a single asynchronous event and each asynchronous event can only have one handler.

Use of the scheduler and on-line schedulability analysis

In Ravenscar, all schedulability (feasibility) analysis is performed off-line. Fixed priority scheduling is assumed. Consequently, the following APIs are defined in Ravenscar-Java. Firstly, the Schedulable interface is a null interface. It is not possible for application threads to interface with the default scheduler.

```
package javax.ravenscar;
public interface Schedulable extends Runnable { }
```

The Scheduler and the PriorityScheduler class are essentially redundant for Ravenscar-Java (as no on-line analysis is allowed and priorities are, essentially, static). However, it is necessary to have access to the maximum and minimum priorities that the scheduler supports. Hence, the following classes are defined:

```
package javax.ravenscar;
public abstract class Scheduler { }

package javax.ravenscar;
public class PriorityScheduler extends Scheduler {
  public static int getMaxPriority();
  public static int getMinPriority();
}
```

Furthermore, it is necessary to have restricted `PriorityParameters` that allow the priority to be set and queried but not changed:

```
package javax.ravenscar;
public class PriorityParameters {
  public PriorityParameters(int priority);
  public int getPriority();
}
```

There is no `ImportanceParameters` class.

Use of release parameters

Given that it is assumed that schedulability analysis is performed off-line and that the on-line environment is predictable, Ravenscar provides no mechanisms for coping with overruns or deadline misses. Consequently, in Ravenscar-Java, the support for these mechanisms is removed. This is reflected in the `ReleaseParameters` class hierarchy. Note also the absence of an `AperiodicParameters` class.

```
package javax.ravenscar;
public class ReleaseParameters {
  protected ReleaseParameters();
}
package javax.ravenscar;
public class PeriodicParameters extends ReleaseParameters
{
  public PeriodicParameters(AbsoluteTime startTime,
                            RelativeTime period);

  protected AbsoluteTime getStartTime();
  protected RelativeTime getPeriod();
}
package javax.ravenscar;
public class SporadicParameters extends ReleaseParameters
{
  public SporadicParameters(
          RelativeTime minInterarrival);
  protected RelativeTime getMinInterarrival();
}
```

There is no `ProcessingGroupParameters` class in Ravenscar-Java.

Use of threads

Given that Ravenscar-Java only supports periodic threads, the API for Ravenscar-Java thread classes will be very restricted. For example, a restricted version of `java.lang.Thread` for a high-integrity J2ME profile might be simply

```
package java.lang;
public class Thread implements Runnable {
  protected Thread();
  protected Thread(String name);

  protected void start();
}
```

The goal here is to restrict application programmers so that they cannot create Java threads, yet at the same time allow the classes in the `ravenscar` package to extend from the thread class (to be compatible with the RTSJ). Unfortunately, Java does not allow this fine level of control unless the `Thread` class is in the `ravenscar` package as well. Here, it is assumed that static analysis has shown that no attempt has been made to create a non-real-time thread.

The Ravenscar-Java `RealtimeThread` and `NoHeapRealtimeThread` are equally simple.

```
package javax.ravenscar;
public class RealtimeThread extends Thread
              implements Schedulable {
  // Constructors only callable within the same package.
  RealtimeThread(PriorityParameters pp,
        PeriodicParameters p, MemoryArea mem);
  RealtimeThread(PriorityParameters pp,
    PeriodicParameters p, MemoryArea mem, Runnable run);

  public static RealtimeThread currentRealtimeThread();
  public static MemoryArea getCurrentMemoryArea();

  // The following methods are only callable
  // within the same package.
  void start();
  static boolean waitForNextPeriod();
}
```

```
package javax.ravenscar;
public class NoHeapRealtimeThread extends RealtimeThread {
  NoRealtimeThread(PriorityParameters pp,
        PeriodicParameters p, MemoryArea ma);

  void start();
}
```

There is very little that can be done with the above class. Indeed, the programmer cannot create objects of these classes as there is no valid constructor available. Instead, the programmer must use the PeriodicThread abstraction:

```
package javax.ravenscar;
public class PeriodicThread extends NoHeapRealtimeThread
{
  public PeriodicThread(PriorityParameters pp,
        PeriodicParameters p, Runnable logic);

  public final void run();
  public void start();
}
```

In the above, the logic (passed as a parameter to the constructor) is the code to be called each period. The implementation of the PeriodicThread class might be structured as follows. Note the class assumes that the default memory area is immortal. The Runnable logic can enter any appropriate scoped memory area as required.

```
package javax.ravenscar;
public class PeriodicThread extends NoHeapRealtimeThread {
  public PeriodicThread(PriorityParameters pp,
        PeriodicParameters p, Runnable logic) {
    super(pp, p, ImmortalMemory.instance());
    applicationLogic = logic;
  }

  public void run()  {
    boolean noProblems = true;
    while(noProblems) {
      applicationLogic.run();
      noProblems = waitForNextPeriod();
    }
```

```
    // A simple extension to Ravenscar-Java would allow
    // waitForNextPeriod to return false if a deadline has
    // been missed. In which case, recovery occurs here.
  }
  public void start() {
    super.start();
  }
  private Runnable applicationLogic;
}
```

Use of sporadic events and their handlers

Sporadic activities are represented in Ravenscar-Java by using the RTSJ asynchronous event-handling mechanisms. In keeping with the approach outlined above for threads, events and their handlers have equally simple APIs. First, the AsyncEvent class is given:

```
package javax.ravenscar;
public class AsyncEvent {
  AsyncEvent();
  void addHandler(AsyncEventHandler handler);
  void fire();
  void bindTo(String happening);
}
```

Ravenscar-Java distinguishes between software-generated sporadic events and hardware-generated events. The following classes are defined:

```
package javax.ravenscar;
public class SporadicEvent extends AsyncEvent {
  public SporadicEvent(SporadicEventHandler handler);
  public void fire();
}

public class SporadicInterrupt extends AsyncEvent {
  public SporadicInterrupt(SporadicEventHandler handler,
                           String happening);
}
```

All events must have their handlers bound to them when they are created. This binding is permanent.

The handler hierarchy is given below:

```
package javax.ravenscar;
public class AsyncEventHandler implements Schedulable {

  AsyncEventHandler(PriorityParameters pp,
        ReleaseParameters p);
  AsyncEventHandler(PriorityParameters pp,
        ReleaseParameters p, Runnable logic);

  void handleAsyncEvent();
  public final void run();
}

public class BoundAsyncEventHandler
              extends AsyncEventHandler {
  BoundAsyncEventHandler(PriorityParameters pp,
        ReleaseParameters p);
  BoundAsyncEventHandler(PriorityParameters pp,
        ReleaseParameters p, Runnable logic);

  void handleAsyncEvent();
}
```

Again, there is little that a programmer can do with these classes, instead they should use the following class:

```
package javax.ravenscar;
public class SporadicEventHandler
        extends BoundAsyncEventHandler {
  public SporadicEventHandler(PriorityParameters pri,
                              SporadicParameters spor);
  public SporadicEventHandler(PriorityParameters pri,
                              SporadicParameters spor,
                              Runnable);

  public void handleAsyncEvent();
}
```

This handler will automatically be created so that its default memory area is immortal memory (it can enter any scoped memory area as and when required).

The implementation must document the model for mapping bound event handlers to no-heap real-time threads. RTSJ requires the handler to be bound permanently to a thread and each thread should have only a single handler bound it.

Use of priority ceiling inheritance

Ravenscar requires the use of priority ceiling emulation. The appropriate RTSJ classes are

```
package javax.ravenscar;
public abstract class MonitorControl {
  public static void setMonitorControl(
        Object monitor, MonitorControl monCtl);
   // throws IllegalMonitorStateException
  public static MonitorControl getMonitorControl(
        Object monitor);
}
```

```
package javax.ravenscar;
package javax.realtime;
public class PriorityCeilingEmulation
        extends MonitorControl {
  // methods
  public static int getMaxCeiling();
  public static PriorityCeilingEmulation instance(
        int ceiling);
}
```

Ceiling priorities should be static; hence, a call to `setMonitorControl` throws an exception if the ceiling priority has already been set. The intention is that Ravenscar-Java should facilitate the no-lock implementation of synchronized methods and statements (see Section 14.2).

Other RTSJ restrictions

The following RTSJ classes/interfaces are not available in the Ravenscar-Java profile:

- `Timer` and its subclasses – only periodic threads can be released by time events.

- `AsynchronouslyInterruptedException`, `Interruptible` and `Timed` – no asynchronous transfer of control is allowed.

17.3.3 Predictability of control and data flow

It is beyond the scope of this chapter to consider restrictions that might be applied to the whole Java language in order to obtain predictability of control and data flow (see (Kwon, Wellings and King, 2002) for a detailed analysis). However, it is worth noting that any class loading is only performed during the initialization phase of the program execution, and there are no user-defined class loaders. If further controls are placed on the use of class paths by the development and execution environment, static analysis tools can determine which classes will be loaded.

The other major impact on control and data flow predictability is that all nonstatic and nonprivate method calls in Java are virtual (that is, they may require a run-time look-up mechanism to determine which method to call). In Ravenscar-Java all classes and interfaces are known statically and hence it is possible to determine the set of methods that can be called (given a complete program). This means that it is possible to predict the feasible control and data flows.

All forms of schedulability analysis require that the worst-case execution time (WCET) of schedulable objects be known. With Ravenscar, the values must be known statically. The restrictions mentioned above allow the worst case flow through a schedulable object to be determined. However, without programmer annotations, these WCET values may be very pessimistic. Consequently, it is normal practice to add some annotation to the code to aid the analysis. Of course, for high-integrity systems, it must be possible to show that the annotation correctly represents the control flows through the program. See (Puschner and Burns, 2000) for a full discussion on worst-case execution time analysis and (Hu, Bernat and Wellings, 2002) for details on potential Java annotations.

17.4 Summary of Ravenscar-Java Profile

Figure 17.1 summarizes the main classes in Ravenscar-Java that have been discussed in this chapter. Other classes associated with physical and raw memory access are assumed to extend the Ravenscar-Java `ScopedMemory` class hierarchy.

17.5 An Extended Example—A Mine Control System

The example that has been chosen here is based on one that commonly appears in the literature. It concerns the software necessary to manage a simplified pump control system for a mining environment; it possesses many of the characteristics that typify embedded real-time systems. The software design is based on that given by Burns and Wellings (2001). It is assumed that the system will be implemented on a single processor with a simple memory-mapped I/O architecture.

The system is used to pump mine water, which collects in a sump at the bottom of a shaft, to the surface. The main safety requirement is that the pump should not be operated when the level of methane gas in the mine reaches a high value, because of the risk of explosion. A simple schematic diagram of the system is given in Figure 17.2 (taken from (Burns and Wellings, 2001)).

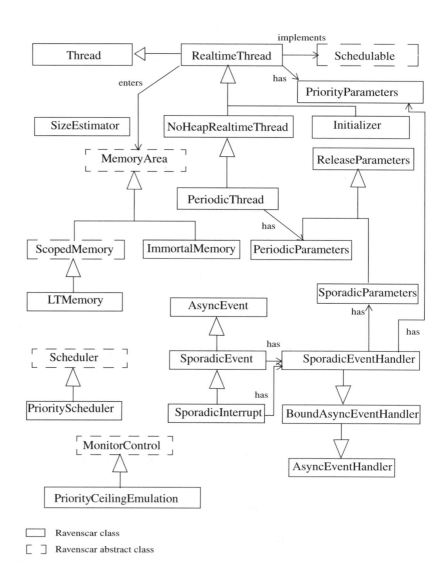

FIGURE 17.1. The Main Classes in Ravenscar-Java

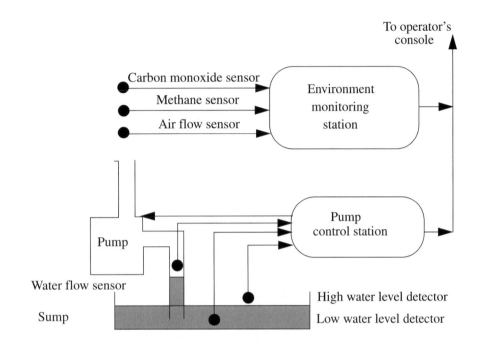

FIGURE 17.2. A Mine Drainage Control Systems (Burns and Wellings, 2001)

The relationship between the control system and the external devices is shown in Figure 17.3. Note that only the high and low water sensors communicate via interrupts (indicated by dashed arrows); all the other devices are either polled or directly controlled.

17.5.1 Functional requirements

The functional specification of the system (given by Burns and Wellings) is divided into four components: pump operation, environment monitoring, operator interaction, and system monitoring.

Pump operation. The required behavior of the pump controller is that it monitors the water levels in the sump. When the water reaches a high level (or when requested by the operator), the pump is turned on and the sump is drained until the water reaches the low level. At this point (or when requested by the operator), the pump is turned off. A flow of water in the pipes can be detected if required. The pump should only be allowed to operate if the methane level in the mine is below a critical level.

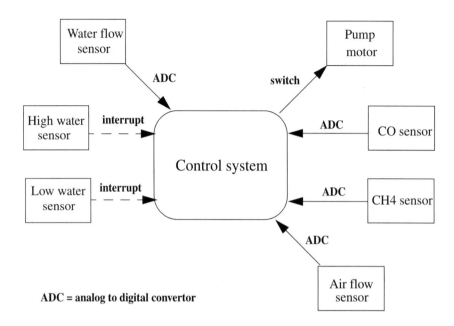

FIGURE 17.3. External Devices and the Control System (Burns and Wellings, 2001)

Environment monitoring. The environment must be monitored to detect the level of methane in the air; there is a level beyond which it is not safe to cut coal or operate the pump. The monitoring also measures the level of carbon monoxide in the mine and detects whether there is an adequate flow of air. Alarms must be signaled if gas levels or air-flow become critical.

Operator interaction. The system is controlled from the surface via an operator's console. The operator is informed of all critical events.

System monitoring. All the system events are to be stored in an archival database, and may be retrieved and displayed upon request.

17.5.2 Nonfunctional requirements

The nonfunctional requirements are divided (by Burns and Wellings) into three components: timing, dependability and security. This case study is mainly concerned with timing requirements and consequently, dependability and security will not be addressed. There are several requirements that relate to the timeliness of system actions (Burns and Wellings, 2001).

Monitoring periods

The maximum periods for reading the environment sensors may be dictated by health and safety legislation. For the purpose of this example, it is assumed that these periods are the same for all sensors, namely 100 ms. In the case of methane, there may be a more stringent requirement based on the proximity of the pump and the need to ensure that it never operates when the methane level is critically high. This is discussed below.

The CH4 and CO sensors when polled each require 40 ms in order for a reading to become available (via an analog-to-digital converter). Hence, they require a deadline of 60 ms.[3] The water flow object executes periodically and has two roles. While the pump is operational, it checks that there is a water flow; but while the pump is off (or disabled) it also checks that the water has stopped flowing. This latter check is used as confirmation that the pump has indeed been stopped. Because of a time lag in the flow of water, this object is given a period of 1 second, and it uses the results of two consecutive readings to determine the actual state of the pump. To make sure that two consecutive readings are actually one second apart (approximately), the object is given a tight deadline of 40 ms (that is, two reading will be at least 960 ms, but no more than 1040 ms, apart).

It is assumed that the water-level detectors are event driven and that the system should respond within 200 ms. The physics of the application indicate that there must be at least 6 seconds between interrupts from the two water level indicators.

Shut-down deadline

To avoid explosions, there is a deadline within which the pump must be switched off once the methane level exceeds a critical threshold. This deadline is related to the methane-sampling period, to the rate at which methane can accumulate, and to the margin of safety between the level of methane regarded as critical and the level at which it explodes. With a direct reading of the sensor, the relationship can be expressed by the inequality:

$$R(T + D) < M$$

where
    R is the rate at which methane can accumulate
    T is the sampling period
    D is the shut-down deadline
    M is the safety margin.

---

3. This is because the reading will be initiated at the end of one period so that data will be available at the start of the next.

In this example, it is assumed that the presence of methane pockets may cause levels to rise rapidly, and therefore a deadline requirement (from methane going high to the pump being disabled) of 200 ms is assumed. This can be met by setting the rate for the methane sensor at 80 ms, with a deadline of 30 ms. Note this level will ensure that correct readings are taken from the sensor (that is, the displacement between two readings is at least 50 ms).

Operator information deadline

The operator must be informed: within 1 second of detection of critically high methane or carbon monoxide readings, within 2 seconds of a critically low air-flow reading and within 3 seconds of a failure in the operation of the pump. These requirements are easily met when compared to the other timing requirements.

In summary, Figure 17.4 defines the periods, or minimum inter-arrival times and deadlines (in milliseconds) for the sensors.

	Periodic/Sporadic	Period/Interarrival time (ms)	Deadline (ms)
CH4 sensor	Periodic	80	30
CO Sensor	Periodic	100	60
Air flow sensor	Periodic	100	100
Water flow sensor	Periodic	1000	40
High water interrupt	Sporadic	6000	200
Low water interrupt	Sporadic	6000	200

FIGURE 17.4. The Attributes of Periodic and Sporadic Entities

17.5.3 Software Design

The main components of the software design are illustrated in Figure 17.5. Here, the boxes represent instances of classes (X :Xclass is object X of class Xclass), and the arrows shows the collaboration between the objects.

Consider one of the sensors, the `ch4Sensor`. This is a periodic activity and must, therefore, be represented by an instance of the `PeriodicThread` class. The sensor needs to access a device. In this example, the device is an analog-to-digital converter accessed through shared memory-based device registers (an example of which is given in Section 15.3). The converter supports 64 channels.

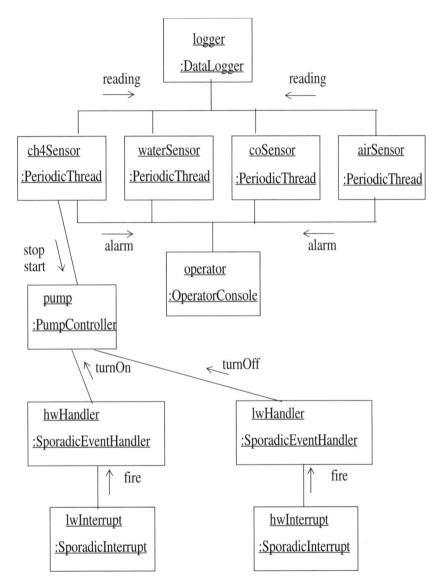

FIGURE 17.5. Object Interaction Diagram for Mine Control Software

The Ravenscar-Java code for the function to be executed each period is given below. This class is called `CoSensorFunction`. The ADC converter requires time to settle. The sensor, therefore, initiates a read on the converter just before it waits-for-next-period. The deadline of the sensor has been set so that the time between the deadline and the earliest next release of the thread is such that the converter will have produced a result.

```java
import javax.realtime.*;
public class Ch4SensorFunction implements Runnable {
  public Ch4SensorFunction(PumpController pump,
          OperatorConsole operator, DataLogger logger)
{
    myPump = pump;
    myOperator = operator;
    myLogger = logger;

    myAdcReg = new AdcControlRegister(
                    csrBaseAddress, channel);
    dataBuffer = new RawMemoryAccess(
                    PhysicalMemory.IO_PAGE,
                    dataBaseAddress,REG_SIZE);
    myAdcReg.startConversion();
  }

  PumpController myPump; OperatorConsole myOperator;
  DataLogger myLogger;
  final long csrBaseAddress = 01400;
  final long dataBaseAddress = 01402;
  final short channel = 6;
  final long REG_SIZE = 2;
  final short CH4_HIGH = 01000;
  AdcControlRegister myAdcReg;
  RawMemoryAccess dataBuffer;

  public void run() {
   if(!myAdcReg.conversionComplete())
     myOperator.activateAlarm(
            AlarmEvent.CH4_DEVICE_ERROR);
   else {
     short reading = dataBuffer.getShort(0);
     if(reading >= CH4_HIGH) {
       myPump.stop();
       myOperator.activateAlarm(
              AlarmEvents.CH4_PRESENT);
     } else {
       myPump.start();
       myLogger.ch4_log(reading);
     }
   }
   myAdcReg.startConversion();
  }
}
```

The other periodic sensors are similar in structure, although they do not involve calls to the pump.

The sensor function algorithms are very simple. However, one could imagine a more complex algorithm that needed to create temporary objects during its processing. For example, suppose the methane level needed to be computed from several samples in order to determine whether the level was dangerously high. Assume that the following class implements an appropriate algorithm:

```
public class ComputeMethaneLevel implements Runnable {
  public ComputeMethaneLevel(int numberOfSamples) {
    samples = new int[numberOfSamples];
    methaneHigh = false;
  }
  private int[] samples;
  public boolean methaneHigh;
  public void run() {
    // Complex algorithm requiring
    // temporary objects to be created.
    methaneHigh = true; // or false
  }
  public void latestReading(int reading) {
    // Save latest reading.
  }
}
```

Now, an object of this class can be created and the run method executed from within a scoped memory area. This will ensure that any temporary objects are reclaimed when the run method exits. The new Ch4SensorFunction would become

```
public class Ch4SensorFunction implements Runnable {

  public Ch4SensorFunction(PumpController pump) {
    compute = new ComputeMethaneLevel(1000);
    scratchMemory = new LTMemory(10000);
                   // reserve appropriate size
    ... // As before.
  }
  LTMemory scratchMemory;
  ComputeMethaneLevel compute;
  ... // As before.
```

```
    public void run() {
        ... // As before.
        compute.latestReading(reading);
                // Inform compute engine of the latest reading.
        scratchMemory.enter(compute); // compute
        // As before, with compute.methaneHigh.
    }
}
```

The two interrupt handlers are identical in structure. First, a class that implements
Runnable is defined. This can then be directly associated with the Ravenscar-Java
SporadicEventHandler class during initialization.

```
import ravenscar.*;
public class LWInterruptHandler implements Runnable {
    public LWInterruptHandler(PumpController pump) {
        myPump = pump;
    }
    PumpController myPump;
    public void run() {
        myPump.turnOff();
    }
}
```

The pump controller class is illustrated next: it is a simple state machine. The motor is
switched on if the water is high and if the methane level is low. This is represented by
the variables pumpOn and pumpOperational. The variable pumpOn is true if the
water is high; pumpOperational is true if the methane level is low. The motor is on
whenever both these variables are true.

```
public class PumpController {
    public PumpController() {
        pumpOn = false;
        pumpOperational = false;
        myDevice = new DeviceRegister(csrBaseAddress);
    }
    public synchronized void turnOn() {
        pumpOn = true;
        if(pumpOperational) myDevice.setOperate();
    }
```

```
    public synchronized void turnOff() {
      pumpOn = false;
      myDevice.clearOperate();
    }

    public synchronized void start() {
      pumpOperational = true;
      if(pumpOn) myDevice.setOperate();
    }

    public synchronized void stop() {
      myDevice.clearOperate();
      pumpOperational = false;
    }

    boolean pumpOn;
    boolean pumpOperational;
    DeviceRegister myDevice;
    final long csrBaseAddress = 01300;
  }
```

The structure of the initialization phase is shown below. The MineControl class extends the Ravenscar-Java Initializer real-time thread class. It sets up the no-heap real-time threads and asynchronous event handlers.

```
import ravenscar.*;
public class MineControl extends Initializer {
  // Priority settings.
  public final int CH4_PRIORITY = 10;
    // similarly for other sensors
  public final int HLW_HANDLER = 6;
  public final int MOTOR = 11;

  // Arrival times.
  public final RelativeTime CH4_PERIOD =
      new RelativeTime (800,0);
  public final RelativeTime HLW_ARRIVAL =
      new RelativeTime (6000,0);
    // Similarly for other schedulable objects.

  // Interrupt happening.
  public final String HW_HAPPENING = "HW_INTERRUPT";
```

```
public final int INIT_TIME = 500;
   // Allow 0.5 seconds to initialize.
public AbsoluteTime epoch;

public void run() {
  epoch = new AbsoluteTime(
          Clock.getRealtimeClock().getTime());
  epoch.set(epoch.getMilliseconds() + INIT_TIME, 0);

  PumpController pump = new PumpController();
  MonitorControl.setMonitorControl(pump,
          PriorityCeilingEmulation.instance(MOTOR));

  PriorityParameters ch4Priority = new
           PriorityParameters(CH4_PRIORITY);
  PeriodicParameters ch4Period =
      new PeriodicParameters(epoch, CH4_PERIOD);
  Ch4SensorFunction ch4Function =
      new Ch4SensorFunction(pump);
  PeriodicThread ch4Sensor = new PeriodicThread(
      ch4Priority, ch4Period, ch4Function);
    // Similarly for other sensors.

  PriorityParameters hlwPriority =
    new PriorityParameters(HLW_HANDLER);
  LWInterruptHandler lwHandler =
    new LWInterruptHandler(pump);
  SporadicEventHandler lw =
    new SporadicEventHandler(hlwPriority,
      new SporadicParameters(HLW_ARRIVAL,1), lwHandler);
  SporadicInterrupt lwInterrupt = new SporadicInterrupt(
        lw,LW_HAPPENING);
  // Similarly for hw interrupt.

  ch4Sensor.start();

  // Start other periodic threads.
  }
public static void main(String [] args) {
  Initializer init = new MineControl();
  init.start();
  }
}
```

17.6 Summary

Java's combination of object-oriented programming features, its use of garbage collection and its poor support for real-time multithreading are all seen as particular impediments to using the language for implementing high-integrity systems. The RTSJ has introduced many new features that help address the real-time problems. However, the expressive power of these features means that very complex programming models can be created, necessitating complexity in the supporting real-time virtual machine. Consequently, Java, with the real-time extensions as they stand, is too complex for confident use in high-integrity systems.

This chapter has discussed a profile of Java (Ravenscar-Java) and the RTSJ that is in line with the J2ME architecture. The goal of the profile is to support the construction of analyzable real-time Java programs that can be hosted on top of a small, predictable real-time virtual machine.

18 Conclusions

Introduction and chapter structure

Although there is little doubt that the Java language has been immensely successful in a wide range of application areas, it has yet to establish itself completely in the real-time and embedded markets. This market is huge and growing all the time. It has been estimated that 100 time more processors are destined for embedded systems than for the desktop (Eggermont, 2002). These systems are mainly small (for example, mobile phones) but can sometimes be extremely large (for example, air traffic control systems). For small embedded applications, sequential languages like C and C++ reign supreme. For the larger real-time high integrity systems, Ada is still important.

The introduction of a Real-Time Specification for Java could dramatically alter the status quo. The provision of real-time programming abstractions along with the promise of a predictable real-time Java Virtual Machine has the potential to add fuel to the already raging Java fire. However, there are still obstacles to be overcome before Java can replace its main competitors in these important application areas. This chapter reviews some of the challenges facing the real-time Java community over the next few years. Meeting these challenges will allow the language to compete with the currently preferred implementation technologies. The main challenges are in the following areas:

- *Specification* – to produce a consistent and unambiguous Real-Time Specification for Java along with well-defined profiles for particular real-time application domains;
- *Implementation* – to generate efficient implementations of real-time virtual machines (both open source and proprietary ones) for the full specification and the profiles;
- *Maintaining Momentum* – to stimulate evolution of the specification in a controlled and sustained manner to add new functionality and to address new architectures.

Concurrency is an integral part of most real-time embedded systems. Here, progress has been made with the introduction of Java 1.5. The revamping of the Java Memory Model allows more precise semantics to be given to concurrent Java programs. The provision of a full set of concurrency utilities should ease the difficult task of constructing correct multithreaded programs.

18.1 Specification Challenges

Developing real-time extensions to the Java platform must have been a daunting task for the Real-Time for Java Expert Group when it started its work in late 1998. It is a credit to the group that they have managed to change people's expectations on the feasibility of achieving "real-time Java". Before their work, the phrase "real-time Java" was considered by many to be an oxymoron. Now the real-time community argues over issues such as whether no-heap real-time threads are really necessary or whether real-time garbage collection combined with static analysis techniques can provide predictable response times in a hard real-time environment. There is little doubt that the real-time landscape has been irrevocably altered in the last five years.

Specification problems and inconsistencies

The Real-Time Specification for Java, however, is not without its problems. A preliminary version was released in June 2000 in parallel with the development of a "reference implementation" (RI). Inevitably, the completion of the RI showed up errors and inconsistencies in the specification. Many of these have been removed in the 1.0.1 version that was released in August 2004 (Belliardi *et al.*, 2004)[1]. However, some outstanding issues whose resolution may require more significant changes have been addressed in this book and are likely to be addressed in a 1.1 version. These issues are outlined below.

Schedulable objects. The RTSJ has made a good attempt to generalize real-time activities away from real-time threads toward the notion of schedulable objects. In the current specification, both real-time threads and asynchronous event handlers are considered schedulable objects. Unfortunately, the operations that can be performed on a schedulable object are not consistently defined. For example, a schedulable object can create and enter into one or more scoped memory areas. The methods for manipulating the resulting scoped memory stack can be found partly in the `RealtimeThread` class and partly in the `AsyncEventHandler` class. Ideally, all operations associated with schedulable objects should be defined either in the `Schedulable` interface or in the class defining the associated functionality. In this example, the methods would be better defined either in the `Schedulable` interface or in the `MemoryArea` class.

Aperiodic and sporadic real-time threads. Although the RTSJ supports `Aperiodic-Parameters` and `SporadicParameters` they can only successfully be used with asynchronous event handlers. There is no notion of a release event for an aperiodic (or sporadic) thread and consequently it is difficult to see how an implementation can detect deadline miss or cost overrun. The resolution of this problem is tied closely to the resolution of the following issue.

---

1. This book is conformant to that specification.

The WaitForNextPeriod *method.* This method is defined in the Realtime-Thread class. However, it is only applicable to real-time threads with periodic release parameters. Ideally, the RealtimeThread class should contain a waitForNext-Release method rather than a waitForNextPeriod method. A release method would also be needed. For real-time threads with periodic parameters, this method would be called by the implementation (although to be consistent with periodic event, any schedulable object would also be able to call it). This approach would also solve the previous problem with aperiodic threads, and provide a level of consistency between asynchronous event handlers and real-time threads (particularly in their approach to cost enforcement and deadline monitoring).

Profiles   Chapter 17 has already commented on the need to consider profiles of RTSJ in the context of J2ME and, in particular, to produce a profile for use in high-integrity (and possibly safety-critical) systems. The Ravenscar-Java profile is perhaps the first step along this road. At the time of writing (June, 2004), the Open Group is in the process of creating a Java Specification Request to address this important application domain.

18.2 Implementation Challenges

One of the key and immediate challenges facing the real-time Java community is to produce predictable and efficient implementations of the RTSJ. Three areas give particular cause for concern.

Memory management. The RTSJ has established a new memory management model (via the introduction of memory areas) to facilitate more predictable memory allocation and deallocation. The result is that there are assignment rules that must be obeyed by the programmer and that, consequently, must be checked by the implementation. Furthermore, the ability to nest memory areas means that illegal nestings must be prohibited. While it is clear that static analysis of programs can eliminate many of the run-time checks, this requires special RTSJ-aware compilers or tools. The availability of these, along with efficient run-time implementations of the overall model, may well determine the eventual impact and take up of the RTSJ.

Asynchronous Transfer of Control. Introducing facilities for the management of ATC into Java was always going to be controversial. However, there is an undeniable real-time application requirement for such a facility. It is a major challenge to keep the resulting overheads in the JVM small and predictable, and to ensure that code not using this facility suffers minimal impact.

Asynchronous Event Handling. The goal for asynchronous event handlers is to have a lightweight concurrency mechanism. Some implementations will, however, simply map an event handler to a real-time thread, and the original motivations for event handlers will be lost. It is a major challenge to provide effective implementations that can cope with heap-using and no-heap handlers, blocking and nonblocking handlers, daemon and nondaemon handlers, multiple schedulers, cost enforcement and deadline monitoring.

18.3 Maintaining Momentum

With the introduction of any new technology, there is a tension between producing a stable standard base that users can depend on, and providing a dynamic product that continues to evolve and address new application needs. So far, Java has caught the imagination of the user community, produced stable releases and maintained momentum for its evolution. If the RTSJ is to survive, it is important that it keeps pace with more general Java development and also that it develops its own momentum. Two areas can be identified to help produce this momentum.

Increased functionality. Although the RTSJ provides a framework within which implementors can provide increased functionality, it is inevitable that there will be a need to standardize on the different approaches. The following topics can be recognized.

- *New standard schedulers* – Currently only a fixed priority scheduler has been defined, other schedulers such as earliest-deadline-first or value-based schedulers are needed.

- *Multiple schedulers* – While the RTSJ does not rule out multiple schedulers, there is little in the specification that addresses the problems they introduce.

- *Multiple criticalities* – The notion of importance parameters has been introduced as a subclass of scheduling parameters. However, there is no support for, say, executing safety-critical and non-safety-critical schedulable objects within the same real-time virtual machine (except via the `NoHeapRealtimeThread` class). Better support for appropriate temporal and spatial fire walls is needed. Some early work has now begun in this area (Cai and Wellings, 2004), inspired by the current work on the Application Isolation API Specification (Java Community Process, JSR 121, 2001).

- *Multiple clocks* – Currently only the real-time clock is supported. There is a need for other clocks such as one that measures the execution time consumed by a schedulable object.

- *Alternative interrupt handling models* – currently interrupt handlers are viewed as schedulable objects. For many systems, the overheads introduced by this model are prohibitive. Alternative models, therefore, need to be introduced.

- *Real-time concurrency utilities* – concurrency utilities that have predictable and analyzable timing properties are needed (probably based on the ones which have now been incorporated in Java 1.5). For example, a reusable event with parameter class is needed, along the lines outlined in Section 11.8. Furthermore, there is now some overlap between the facilities proposed by Java 1.5 and the RTSJ (for example, in the area of high-resolution time types). There is a need to remove any duplicate functionality.

Multiprocessor and distributed systems. Although the RTSJ attempts not to preclude multiprocessor implementations, it provides no direct support. Furthermore, little, if any, consideration has been given to the RTSJ in a distributed real-time environment. The latter is beginning to be addressed in JSR 50 (Java Community Process, JSR 50, 2000) but as yet no definitive specification has been produced – although some initial ideas have been published (Wellings, Clark, Jenson, and Wells, 2002). A similar activity needs to be started on multiprocessor systems.

18.4 Finally...

For any new technology to be accepted, it is essential to have supporting material to instruct users on how to apply that technology. Again, this is an area in which Java has excelled. There are many excellent books that teach all aspects of Java from basic introductions to programming through to the application of Java to large-scale enterprises. It is hoped that this book can provide a valuable addition to the literature on *Concurrent and Real-time Programming in Java*.

Appendix: **Java Class and Interface Specifications**

This appendix summarizes the main classes and interfaces used in this book. Only checked exceptions are shown in the throw clauses.

A.1 `AbsoluteTime`

```
package javax.realtime;
public class AbsoluteTime extends HighResolutionTime {

  // constructors
  public AbsoluteTime();
  public AbsoluteTime(AbsoluteTime time);
  public AbsoluteTime¹(AbsoluteTime time, Clock clock);
  public AbsoluteTime¹(Clock clock);
  public AbsoluteTime(java.util.Date date);
  public AbsoluteTime¹(java.util.Date date, Clock clock);
  public AbsoluteTime(long millis, int nanos);
  public AbsoluteTime¹(long millis, int nanos, Clock clock);

  // methods
  public AbsoluteTime absolute(Clock clock);
  public AbsoluteTime absolute(Clock clock,
                               AbsoluteTime destination);
  public AbsoluteTime add(long millis, int nanos);
  public AbsoluteTime add(long millis, int nanos,
                          AbsoluteTime destination);
  public AbsoluteTime add(RelativeTime time);
  public AbsoluteTime add(RelativeTime time,
                          AbsoluteTime destination);
  public java.util.Date getDate();
  public RelativeTime relative(Clock clock);
  public RelativeTime relative(Clock clock,
                               RelativeTime destination);
  public void set(java.util.Date date);
  public RelativeTime subtract(AbsoluteTime time);
```

```
        public RelativeTime subtract(AbsoluteTime time,
                              RelativeTime destination);
        public AbsoluteTime subtract(RelativeTime time);
        public AbsoluteTime subtract(RelativeTime time,
                                       AbsoluteTime destination);
        public String toString();
    }
```

A.2 AperiodicParameters

```
        package javax.realtime;
        public class AperiodicParameters extends ReleaseParameters {
        // fields
        public static final string arrivalTimeQueueOverflowExcept[2];
        public static final string arrivalTimeQueueOverflowIgnore[2];
        public static final string arrivalTimeQueueOverflowReplace[2];
        public static final string arrivalTimeQueueOverflowSave[2];

        // constructors

        public AperiodicParameters[1]();
        public AperiodicParameters(RelativeTime cost,
             RelativeTime deadline, AsyncEventHandler overrunHandler,
             AsyncEventHandler missHandler);

        // The following constructor may be added at Version 1.1
        protected AperiodicParameters(RelativeTime cost,
             RelativeTime deadline, RelativeTime blockingTerm,
             AsyncEventHandler overrunHandler,
             AsyncEventHandler missHandler);

        // methods
        public String getArrivalTimeQueueOverflowBehaviour[1]();
        public int getInitialArrivalTimeQueueLength[1]();
        public void setArrivalTimeQueueOverflowBehaviour([1]String);
        public boolean setIfFeasible(RelativeTime cost,
                                 RelativeTime deadline);
        public void setInitialArrivalTimeQueueLength[1](int initial);
    }
```

A.3 ArrivalTimeQueueOverflowException

```
        package javax.realtime;
        public class ArrivalTimeQueueOverflowException extends
              RuntimeException {

        // constructors
        public ArrivalTimeQueueOverflowException();
        public ArrivalTimeQueueOverflowException(String description);
    }
```

A.4 `AsyncEvent`

```
package javax.realtime;
public class AsyncEvent {
  // constructors
  public AsyncEvent();

  // methods
  public void addHandler(AsyncEventHandler handler);
  public void bindTo(String happening);
  public ReleaseParameters createReleaseParameters();
  public void fire();
  public boolean handledBy(AsyncEventHandler handler);
  public void removeHandler(AsyncEventHandler handler);
  public void setHandler(AsyncEventHandler handler);
  public void unbindTo(String happening);
}
```

A.5 `AsyncEventHandler`

```
package javax.realtime;
public class AsyncEventHandler implements Schedulable {
  // constructors

  public AsyncEventHandler();
  public AsyncEventHandler(boolean nonheap);
  public AsyncEventHandler(boolean nonheap, Runnable logic);
  public AsyncEventHandler(Runnable logic);
  public AsyncEventHandler(SchedulingParameters scheduling,
          ReleaseParameters release, MemoryParameters memory,
          MemoryArea area, ProcessingGroupParameters group,
          boolean nonheap);
  public AsyncEventHandler(SchedulingParameters scheduling,
          ReleaseParameters release, MemoryParameters memory,
          MemoryArea area, ProcessingGroupParameters group,
          boolean nonheap, Runnable logic);
  public AsyncEventHandler(SchedulingParameters scheduling,
          ReleaseParameters release, MemoryParameters memory,
          MemoryArea area, ProcessingGroupParameters group,
          Runnable logic);

  // methods
  public boolean addIfFeasibility();
  public boolean addToFeasibility();
  protected int getAndClearPendingFireCount();
  protected int getAndDecrementPendingFireCount();
  protected int getAndIncrementPendingFireCount();
  public MemoryArea getMemoryArea();
  public MemoryParameters getMemoryParameters();
```

```
protected int getPendingFireCount();
public ProcessingGroupParameters getProcessingGroupParameters();
public ReleaseParameters getReleaseParameters();
public Scheduler getScheduler();
public SchedulingParameters getSchedulingParameters();
public void handleAsyncEvent();
public final boolean isDaemon¹();
public boolean removeFromFeasibility();
public final void run();
public final void setDaemon¹(boolean on);
public boolean setIfFeasible(ReleaseParameters release,
                             MemoryParameters memory);
public boolean setIfFeasible(ReleaseParameters release,
    MemoryParameters memory, ProcessingGroupParameters group);
public boolean setIfFeasible(ReleaseParameters release,
                             ProcessingGroupParameters group);
public boolean setIfFeasible(SchedulingParameters sched,
                             ReleaseParameters release,
                             MemoryParameters memory);
public boolean setIfFeasible(SchedulingParameters sched,
               ReleaseParameters release, MemoryParameters memory,
               ProcessingGroupParameters group);
public void setMemoryParameters(MemoryParameters memory);
public boolean setMemoryParametersIfFeasible(
                             MemoryParameters memory);
public void setProcessingGroupParameters(
               ProcessingGroupParameters group);
public boolean setProcessingGroupParametersIfFeasible(
               ProcessingGroupParameters group);
public void setReleaseParameters(ReleaseParameters release);
public boolean setReleaseParametersIfFeasible(
                             ReleaseParameters release);
public void setScheduler(Scheduler scheduler);
public void setScheduler(Scheduler scheduler,
    SchedulingParameters scheduling, ReleaseParameters release,
    MemoryParameters memory, ProcessingGroupParameters group);
public void setSchedulingParameters(
                             SchedulingParameters scheduling);
public boolean setSchedulingParametersIfFeasible(
               SchedulingParameters scheduling);
}
```

A.6 AsynchronouslyInterruptedException

```
package javax.realtime;
public class AsynchronouslyInterruptedException
          extends InterruptedException {
```

```
        // constructors
        public AsynchronouslyInterruptedException();
        // methods
        public boolean clear¹();
        public boolean disable();
        public boolean doInterruptible(Interruptible logic);
        public boolean enable();
        public boolean fire();
        public static AsynchronouslyInterruptedException getGeneric();
        public boolean happened³(boolean propagate);
        public boolean isEnabled();
        public static void propagate³();
    }
```

A.7 BoundAsyncEventHandler

```
        package javax.realtime;
        public class BoundAsyncEventHandler extends AsyncEventHandler {
          // constructors
          public BoundAsyncEventHandler();
          public BoundAsyncEventHandler(SchedulingParameters scheduling,
                ReleaseParameters release, MemoryParameters memory,
                MemoryArea area, ProcessingGroupParameters group,
                boolean nonheap, Runnable logic);
        }
```

A.8 CeilingViolationException

```
        package javax.realtime;
        public class CeilingViolationException¹
                    extends IllegalThreadStateException {
          // methods
          public int getCallerPriority();
          public int getCeiling();
        }
```

A.9 Clock

```
        package javax.realtime;
        public abstract class Clock {
          // constructors
          public Clock();
          // methods
          public abstract RelativeTime getEpochOffset¹();
```

```
    public static Clock getRealtimeClock();
    public abstract RelativeTime getResolution();
    public abstract AbsoluteTime getTime();
    public abstract AbsoluteTime getTime⁴(AbsoluteTime time);
    public abstract void setResolution(RelativeTime resolution);
}
```

A.10 DuplicateFilterException

```
    package javax.realtime;
    public class DuplicateFilterException
        extends Exception {

    // constructors
    public DuplicateFilterException();
    public DuplicateFilterException(String description);
}
```

A.11 GarbageCollector

```
    package javax.realtime;
    public abstract class GarbageCollector {

    // constructors
    public GarbageCollector³();

     // methods
    public abstract RelativeTime getPreemptionLatency();
}
```

A.12 HeapMemory

```
    package javax.realtime;
    public final class HeapMemory extends MemoryArea {

    // methods
    public static HeapMemory instance();
}
```

A.13 HighResolutionTime

```
    package javax.realtime;
    public abstract class HighResolutionTime
        implements Comparable, Cloneable {

    // methods
    public abstract AbsoluteTime absolute(Clock clock);
    public abstract AbsoluteTime absolute(Clock clock,
                                      AbsoluteTime destination);
```

```
        public Object clone¹();
        public int compareTo(HighResolutionTime time);
        public int compareTo(Object object);
        public boolean equals(HighResolutionTime time);
        public boolean equals(Object object);
        public Clock getClock¹();
        public final long getMilliseconds();
        public final int getNanoseconds();
        public int hashCode();
        public abstract RelativeTime relative(Clock clock);
        public abstract RelativeTime relative(Clock clock,
                                RelativeTime destination);
        public void set⁵(HighResolutionTime time);
        public void set(long millis);
        public void set(long millis, int nanos);
        public static void waitForObject(Object target,
                HighResolutionTime time) throws InterruptedException;
}
```

A.14 IllegalAssignmentError

```
        package javax.realtime;
        public class IllegalAssignmentError
                    extends Error {

          // constructors
          public IllegalAssignmentError();
          public IllegalAssignmentError(String description);
}
```

A.15 ImmortalMemory

```
        package javax.realtime;
        public final class ImmortalMemory extends MemoryArea {

          // methods
          public static ImmortalMemory instance();
}
```

A.16 ImmortalPhysicalMemory

```
        package javax.realtime;
        public class ImmortalPhysicalMemory extends MemoryArea {

          // constructors
          public ImmortalPhysicalMemory(Object type, long size);
          public ImmortalPhysicalMemory(Object type, long base, long size);
```

```
      public ImmortalPhysicalMemory(Object type, long base,long size,
                                    Runnable logic);
      public ImmortalPhysicalMemory(Object type, long size,
                                    Runnable logic);
      public ImmortalPhysicalMemory(Object type, long base,
                                    SizeEstimator size);
      public ImmortalPhysicalMemory(Object type, long base,
                                SizeEstimator size, Runnable logic);
      public ImmortalPhysicalMemory(Object type, SizeEstimator size);
      public ImmortalPhysicalMemory(Object type, SizeEstimator size,
                                    Runnable logic);
}
```

A.17 ImportanceParameters

```
package javax.realtime;
public class ImportanceParameters extends PriorityParameters {
   // constructors
   public ImportanceParameters(int priority, int importance);

   // methods
   public int getImportance();
   public void setImportance(int importance);
   public String toString();
}
```

A.18 InaccessibleAreaException

```
package javax.realtime;
public class InaccessibleAreaException extends RuntimeException {
   // constructors
   public InaccessibleAreaException();
   public InaccessibleAreaException(String description);
}
```

A.19 java.lang.InheritableThreadLocal

```
package java.lang;
public class InheritableThreadLocal extends ThreadLocal {
   public InheritableThreadLocal();
   protected Object childValue(Object parentValue);
}
```

A.20 Interruptible

```
package javax.realtime;
public interface Interruptible {
```

```
        public void interruptAction(
                  AsynchronouslyInterruptedException exception);
        public void run(AsynchronouslyInterruptedException exception)
            throws AsynchronouslyInterruptedException;
}
```

A.21 LTMemory

```
        package javax.realtime;
        public class LTMemory extends ScopedMemory {

          // constructors
          public LTMemory(long initial, long maximum);
          public LTMemory(long initial, long maximum,Runnable logic);
          public LTMemory¹(long size); // in bytes
          public LTMemory¹(long size, Runnable logic);
          public LTMemory(SizeEstimator initial, SizeEstimator maximum);
          public LTMemory(SizeEstimator initial, SizeEstimator maximum,
                          Runnable logic);
          public LTMemory¹(SizeEstimator size);
          public LTMemory¹(SizeEstimator size, Runnable logic);

          // methods
          public String toString();
}
```

A.22 LTPhysicalMemory

```
        package javax.realtime;
        public class LTPhysicalMemory extends ScopedMemory {

          // constructors
          public LTPhysicalMemory(Object type, long size);
          public LTPhysicalMemory(Object type, long base, long size);
          public LTPhysicalMemory(Object type, long base, long size,
                                    Runnable logic);
          public LTPhysicalMemory(Object type, long size,
                                    Runnable logic);
          public LTPhysicalMemory(Object type, long base,
                                    SizeEstimator size);
          public LTPhysicalMemory(Object type, long base,
                              SizeEstimator size, Runnable logic);
          public LTPhysicalMemory(Object type, SizeEstimator size);
          public LTPhysicalMemory(Object type, SizeEstimator size,
                                    Runnable logic);
          public String toString();
}
```

A.23 **MemoryAccessError**

```
package javax.realtime;
public class MemoryAccessError extends Error {
  // constructors
  public MemoryAccessError();
  public MemoryAccessError(String description);
}
```

A.24 **MemoryArea**

```
package javax.realtime;
public abstract class MemoryArea {

  // constructors
  protected MemoryArea(long size);
  protected MemoryArea(long size, Runnable logic);
  protected MemoryArea(SizeEstimator size);
  protected MemoryArea(SizeEstimator size, Runnable logic);
  // methods
  public void enter();
  public void enter(Runnable logic);
  public void executeInArea(Runnable logic);
  public static MemoryArea getMemoryArea(Object object);
  public long memoryConsumed();
  public long memoryRemaining();
  public Object newArray(Class type, int number);
  public Object newInstance(Class type)
          throws IllegalAccessException, InstantiationException;
  public Object newInstance(reflect.Constructor c,
                            Object [] args)
          throws IllegalAccessException, InstantiationException,
          reflect.InvocationTargetException;
  public long size();
}
```

A.25 **MemoryInUseException**

```
package javax.realtime;
public class MemoryInUseException extends RuntimeException {
  // constructors
  public MemoryInUseException();
  public MemoryInUseException(String description);
}
```

A.26 `MemoryParameters`

```
package javax.realtime;
public class MemoryParameters implements Cloneable {
  // fields
  public static final long NO_MAX;

  // constructors
  public MemoryParameters(long maxMemoryArea, long maxImmortal);
  public MemoryParameters(long maxMemoryArea, long maxImmortal,
                          long allocationRate);

  // methods
  public Object clone1();
  public long getAllocationRate();
  public long getMaxImmortal();
  public long getMaxMemoryArea();
  public void setAllocationRate(long rate);
  public boolean setAllocationRateIfFeasible(long rate);
  public boolean setMaxImmortalIfFeasible(long maximum);
  public boolean setMaxMemoryAreaIfFeasible(long maximum);
}
```

A.27 `MemoryScopeException`

```
package javax.realtime;
public class MemoryScopeException extends RuntimeException {
  // constructors
  public MemoryScopeException();
  public MemoryScopeException(String description);
}
```

A.28 `MemoryTypeConflictException`

```
package javax.realtime;
public class MemoryTypeConflictException extends RuntimeException {
  // constructors
  public MemoryTypeConflictException();
  public MemoryTypeConflictException(String description);
}
```

A.29 `MITViolationException`

```
package javax.realtime;
public class MITViolationException extends RuntimeException {
```

```
    // constructors
    public MITViolationException();
    public MITViolationException(String description);
}
```

A.30 MonitorControl

```
package javax.realtime;
public abstract class MonitorControl {

  // constructors
  protected MonitorControl();

  // methods
  public static MonitorControl getMonitorControl();
  public static MonitorControl getMonitorControl(
                            Object monitor);
  public static MonitorControl setMonitorControl⁴(
                            MonitorControl policy);
  public static MonitorControl setMonitorControl⁴(Object monitor,
                            MonitorControl policy);
}
```

A.31 NoHeapRealtimeThread

```
package javax.realtime;
public class NoHeapRealtimeThread extends RealtimeThread {
  // constructors
  public NoHeapRealtimeThread(SchedulingParameters scheduling,
                            MemoryArea area);
  public NoHeapRealtimeThread(SchedulingParameters scheduling,
        ReleaseParameters release, MemoryArea area);
  public NoHeapRealtimeThread(SchedulingParameters scheduling,
        ReleaseParameters release, MemoryParameters memory,
        MemoryArea area, ProcessingGroupParameters group,
        Runnable logic);
  // methods
  public void start();
}
```

A.32 java.lang.Object

```
package java.lang;
public class Object {
  // constructors
  public Object();
```

```
                  // methods
                  protected Object clone() throws CloneNotSupportedException;
                  public boolean equals(Object obj;
                  protected void finalize() throws Throwable;
                  public int hashCode();
                  public final Class getClass();
                  public final void notify();
                  public final void notifyAll(;
                  public String toString();
                  public final void wait() throws InterruptedException;
                  public final void wait(long timeout)
                          throws InterruptedException;
                  public final void wait(long timeout, int nanos)
                          throws InterruptedException;
                }
```

A.33 OffsetOutOfBoundsException

```
                  package javax.realtime;
                  public class OffsetOutOfBoundsException extends RuntimeException {
                    // constructors
                    public OffsetOutOfBoundsException();
                    public OffsetOutOfBoundsException(String description);
                  }
```

A.34 OneShotTimer

```
                  package javax.realtime;
                  public class OneShotTimer extends Timer {

                    // constructors
                    public OneShotTimer(HighResolutionTime fireTime,
                                   AsyncEventHandler handler);
                    public OneShotTimer(HighResolutionTime fireTime, Clock clock,
                                   AsyncEventHandler handler);
                  }
```

A.35 PeriodicParameters

```
                  package javax.realtime;
                  public class PeriodicParameters extends ReleaseParameters {

                    // constructors
                    public PeriodicParameters[1](HighResolutionTime start
                         RelativeTime period);
                    public PeriodicParameters(HighResolutionTime start
                         RelativeTime period, RelativeTime cost,
```

```
            RelativeTime deadline, AsyncEventHandler overrunHandler,
            AsyncEventHandler missHandler);
    public PeriodicParameters¹ (RelativeTime period);
    // The following constructor may be added in Version 1.1
    public PeriodicParameters(HighResolutionTime start
            RelativeTime period, RelativeTime cost,
            RelativeTime deadline, RelativeTime blockingTerm,
            AsyncEventHandler overrunHandler,
            AsyncEventHandler missHandler);
    // methods
    public RelativeTime getPeriod();
    public HighResolutionTime getStart();
    public boolean setIfFeasible(RelativeTime period,
                RelativeTime cost, RelativeTime deadline);
    public void setPeriod(RelativeTime period);
    public void setStart(HighResolutionTime start);
    // The following methods may be added at Version 1.1
    public boolean setIfFeasible(RelativeTime period,
                RelativeTime cost, RelativeTime deadline,
                RelativeTime blockingTerm);
}
```

A.36 `PeriodicTimer`

```
    package javax.realtime;
    public class PeriodicTimer extends Timer {
    // constructors
    public PeriodicTimer(HighResolutionTime start,
            RelativeTime interval, AsyncEventHandler handler);
    public PeriodicTimer(HighResolutionTime start,
            RelativeTime interval, Clock clock,
            AsyncEventHandler handler);
    // methods
    public ReleaseParameters createReleaseParameters();
    public AbsoluteTime getFireTime();
    public RelativeTime getInterval();
    public void setInterval(RelativeTime interval);
}
```

A.37 `PhysicalMemoryManager`

```
    package javax.realtime;
    public final class PhysicalMemoryManager {
    // Example fields
    public static final Object ALIGNED⁶;
    public static final Object BYTESWAP⁶;
```

```
        public static final Object DMA6;
        public static final Object IO_PAGE1,6;
        public static final Object SHARED6;
        // methods
        public static boolean isRemovable(long base, long size);
        public static boolean isRemoved(long base, long size);
        public static void onInsertion1(long base, long size,
                                        AsyncEvent ae);
        public static void onInsertion3(long base, long size,
                                        AsyncEventHandler aeh);
        public static void onRemoval1(long base, long size,
                                        AsyncEvent ae);
        public static void onRemoval3(long base, long size,
                                        AsyncEventHandler aeh);
        public static final void registerFilter(Object name,
                                        PhysicalMemoryTypeFilter filter)
            throws DuplicateFilterException;
        public static final void removeFilter(Object name);
        public static void unregisterInsertionEvent1(long base,
                        long size, AsyncEvent ae);
        public static void unregisterRemovalEvent1(long base,
                        long size, AsyncEvent ae);
    }
```

A.38 `PhysicalMemoryTypeFilter`

```
    package javax.realtime;
    public interface PhysicalMemoryTypeFilter {
      public boolean contains(long base, long size);
      public long find(long base, long size);
      public int getVMAttributes();
      public int getVMFlags();
      public void initialize(long base, long vBase, long size);
      public boolean isPresent(long base, long size);
      public boolean isRemovable();
      public static void onInsertion1(long base, long size,
                                      AsyncEvent aeh);
      public static void onInsertion3(long base, long size,
                                      AsyncEventHandler aeh);
      public static void onRemoval1(long base, long size,
                                      AsyncEvent aeh);
      public static void onRemoval3(long base, long size,
                                      AsyncEventHandler aeh);
```

```
                   public static void unregisterInsertionEvent[1](long base,
                                 long size, AsyncEvent aeh);
                   public static void unregisterRemovalEvent[1](long base,
                                 long size, AsyncEvent aeh);
                   public long vFind(long base, long size);
               }
```

A.39 `POSIXSignalHandler`

```
           package javax.realtime;
           public final class POSIXSignalHandler {

           //fields
           public static final int SIGABRT;
           public static final int SIGALRM;
           public static final int SIGBUS;
           public static final int SIGCANCEL[3];
           public static final int SIGCHLD;
           public static final int SIGCLD;
           public static final int SIGCONT;
           public static final int SIGEMPT;
           public static final int SIGFPE;
           public static final int SIGFREEZE[3];
           public static final int SIGHUP;
           public static final int SIGILL;
           public static final int SIGINT;
           public static final int SIGIO[3];
           public static final int SIGIOT;
           public static final int SIGKILL;
           public static final int SIGLOST[3];
           public static final int SIGLWP[3];
           public static final int SIGPIPE;
           public static final int SIGPOLL[3];
           public static final int SIGPROF[3];
           public static final int SIGPWR[3];
           public static final int SIGQUIT;
           public static final int SIGSEGV;
           public static final int SIGSTOP;
           public static final int SIGSYS;
           public static final int SIGTERM;
           public static final int SIGTHAW[3];
           public static final int SIGTRAP;
           public static final int SIGTSTP;
           public static final int SIGTTIN;
           public static final int SIGTTOU;
           public static final int SIGURG[3];
```

```
                 public static final int SIGUSR1;
                 public static final int SIGUSR2;
                 public static final int SIGVTALRM³;
                 public static final int SIGWAITING³;
                 public static final int SIGWINCH³;
                 public static final int SIGXCPU³;
                 public static final int SIGXFSZ³;

                 // methods
                 public static void addHandler(int signal,
                                               AsyncEventHandler handler);
                 public static void removeHandler(int signal,
                                                  AsyncEventHandler handler);
                 public static void setHandler(int signal,
                                               AsyncEventHandler handler);
             }
```

A.40 PriorityCeilingEmulation

```
             package javax.realtime;
             public class PriorityCeilingEmulation extends MonitorControl {

                 // methods
                 public int getCeiling¹();
                 public int getDefaultCeiling²();
                 public static int getMaxCeiling²();
                 public static PriorityCeilingEmulation instance¹(int ceiling);
             }
```

A.41 PriorityInheritance

```
             package javax.realtime;
             public class PriorityInheritance extends MonitorControl {

                 // methods
                 public static PriorityInheritance instance();
             }
```

A.42 PriorityParameters

```
             package javax.realtime;
             public class PriorityParameters extends SchedulingParameters {

                 // constructors
                 public PriorityParameters(int priority);
```

```
    // methods
    public int getPriority();
    public void setPriority(int priority);
    public String toString();
}
```

A.43 PriorityScheduler

```
package javax.realtime;
public class PriorityScheduler extends Scheduler {

    // fields
    public static int MAX_PRIORITY³;
    public static int MIN_PRIORITY¹

    // constructors
    protected PriorityScheduler() ;

    // methods

    protected boolean addToFeasibility¹(Schedulable schedulable);
    public void fireSchedulable(Schedulable schedulable);
    public int getMaxPriority();
    public static int getMaxPriority(Thread thread);
    public int getMinPriority();
    public static int getMinPriority(Thread thread);
    public int getNormPriority();
    public static int getNormPriority(Thread thread);
    public String getPolicyName();
    public static PriorityScheduler instance();
    public boolean isFeasible();
    protected boolean removeFromFeasibility(Schedulable schedulable);
    public boolean setIfFeasible(Schedulable schedulable,
            ReleaseParameters release, MemoryParameters memory);
    public boolean setIfFeasible(Schedulable schedulable,
            ReleaseParameters release, MemoryParameters memory,
            ProcessingGroupParameters group);

    // The following method may be added in Version 1.1
    public boolean setIfFeasible(Schedulable schedulable,
            PriorityParameters priority,
            ReleaseParameters release, MemoryParameters memory,
            ProcessingGroupParameters group);
}
```

A.44 Process

```
package java.lang;
public abstract class Process {
```

```
                // constructors
                public Process();

                  // methods
                public abstract void destroy();
                public abstract int exitValue();
                public abstract java.io.InputStream getErrorStream();
                public abstract java.io.InputStream getInputStream();
                public abstract java.io.OutputStream getOutputStream();
                public abstract int waitFor() throws InterruptedException;
                }
```

A.45 `ProcessingGroupParameters`

```
                package javax.realtime;
                public class ProcessingGroupParameters implements Cloneable{

                // constructors
                public ProcessingGroupParameters(HighResolutionTime start,
                        RelativeTime period, RelativeTime cost,
                        RelativeTime deadline, AsyncEventHandler overrunHandler,
                        AsyncEventHandler missHandler);

                // The following constructor may be added in Version 1.1
                public ProcessingGroupParameters(HighResolutionTime start,
                        RelativeTime period, RelativeTime cost,
                        RelativeTime blockingTerm, RelativeTime deadline,
                        AsyncEventHandler overrunHandler,
                        AsyncEventHandler missHandler);

                // methods
                public Object clone[1]();
                public RelativeTime getCost();
                public AsyncEventHandler getCostOverrunHandler();
                public RelativeTime getDeadline();
                public AsyncEventHandler getDeadlineMissHandler();
                public RelativeTime getPeriod();
                public HighResolutionTime getStart();
                public void setCost(RelativeTime cost);
                public void setCostOverrunHandler(AsyncEventHandler handler);
                public void setDeadline(RelativeTime deadline);
                public void setDeadlineMissHandler(AsyncEventHandler handler);
                public boolean setIfFeasible(RelativeTime period,
                        RelativeTime cost, RelativeTime deadline,
                public void setPeriod(RelativeTime period);
                public void setStart(HighResolutionTime start);

                // The following methods may be added in Version 1.1
                public RelativeTime getBlockingTerm();
                public void setBlockingTerm(RelativeTime deadline);
```

```
    public boolean setIfFeasible(RelativeTime period,
            RelativeTime cost, RelativeTime blockingTerm
            RelativeTime deadline,
}
```

A.46 `RationalTime`

```
package javax.realtime;
public class RationalTime extends RelativeTime {
    // This class has been deprecated at Version 1.0.1

    // constructors
    public RationalTime(int frequency);
    public RationalTime(int frequency, long millis, int nanos);
    public RationalTime(int frequency, RelativeTime interval);

    // methods
    public AbsoluteTime absolute(Clock clock,
                                    AbsoluteTime destination);
    public void addInterarrivalTo(AbsoluteTime destination);
    public int getFrequency();
    public RelativeTime getInterarrivalTime();
    public RelativeTime getInterarrivalTime(
                                    RelativeTime destination);
    public void set(long millis, int nanos);
    public void setFrequency(int frequency);
}
```

A.47 `RawMemoryAccess`

```
package javax.realtime;
public class RawMemoryAccess {

    // constructors
    public RawMemoryAccess(Object type, long size);
    public RawMemoryAccess(Object type, long base, long size);

    // methods
    public byte getByte(long offset);
    public void getBytes(long offset, byte[] bytes, int low,
                            int number);
    public int getInt(long offset);
    public void getInts(long offset, int[] ints, int low, int number);
    public long getLong(long offset);
    public void getLongs(long offset, long[] longs, int low,
                            int number);
    public long getMappedAddress();
    public short getShort(long offset);
    public void getShorts(long offset, short[] shorts, int low,
                            int number);
```

```
        public long map();
        public long map(long base);
        public long map(long base, long size);
        public void setByte(long offset, byte value);
        public void setBytes(long offset, byte[] bytes, int low,
                             int number);
        public void setInt(long offset, int value);
        public void setInts(long offset, int[] ints, int low,
                            int number);
        public void setLong(long offset, long value);
        public void setLongs(long offset, long[] longs, int low,
                             int number);
        public void setShort(long offset, short value);
        public void setShorts(long offset, short[] shorts, int low,
                              int number;
        public void unmap();
    }
```

A.48 RawMemoryFloatAccess

```
    package javax.realtime;
    public class RawMemoryFloatAccess extends RawMemoryAccess {
      // constructors
      public RawMemoryFloatAccess(Object type, long size);
      public RawMemoryFloatAccess(Object type, long base, long size);

      // methods
      public double getDouble(long offset);
      public void getDoubles(long offset, double[] doubles,
                             int low, int number);
      public float getFloat(long offset);
      public void getFloats(long offset, float[] floats, int low,
                            int number);
      public void setDouble(long offset, double value);
      public void setDoubles(long offset, double[] bytes, int low,
                             int number);
      public void setFloat(long offset, float value);
      public void setFloats(long offset, float[] ints, int low,
                            int number);
    }
```

A.49 RealtimeSecurity

```
    package javax.realtime;
    public class RealtimeSecurity {
      // constructors
      public RealtimeSecurity();

      // methods
      public void checkAccessPhysical();
```

```
  public void checkAccessPhysicalRange(long base, long size);
  public void checkAEHSetDaemon[1]();
  public void checkSetFilter();
  public void checkSetMonitorControl[1] (MonitorControl policy);
  public void checkSetScheduler();
}
```

A.50 RealtimeSystem

```
package javax.realtime;
public class RealtimeSystem {

  // fields
  public static final byte BIG_ENDIAN;
  public static final byte BYTE_ORDER;
  public static final byte LITTLE_ENDIAN;

  // methods
  public static GarbageCollector currentGC();
  public static int getConcurrentLocksUsed();
  public static MonitorControl getInitialMonitorControl[1]();
  public static int getMaximumConcurrentLocks();
  public static RealtimeSecurity getSecurityManager();
  public static void setMaximumConcurrentLocks(int number);
  public static void setMaximumConcurrentLocks(int number,
                                               boolean hard);
  public static void setSecurityManager(
              RealtimeSecurity manager);
}
```

A.51 RealtimeThread

```
package javax.realtime;
public class RealtimeThread extends Thread implements Schedulable
{
  // constructors
  public RealtimeThread();
  public RealtimeThread(SchedulingParameters scheduling);
  public RealtimeThread(SchedulingParameters scheduling,
                        ReleaseParameters release);
  public RealtimeThread(SchedulingParameters scheduling,
        ReleaseParameters release, MemoryParameters memory,
        MemoryArea area, ProcessingGroupParameters group,
        Runnable logic);

  // methods
  public boolean addIfFeasibility();
  public boolean addToFeasibility();
```

```
public static RealtimeThread currentRealtimeThread();
public void deschedulePeriodic();
public static MemoryArea getCurrentMemoryArea();
public static int getInitialMemoryAreaIndex();
public MemoryArea getMemoryArea¹();
public static int getMemoryAreaStackDepth();
public MemoryParameters getMemoryParameters();
public static MemoryArea getOuterMemoryArea(int index);
public ProcessingGroupParameters
                                getProcessingGroupParameters();
public ReleaseParameters getReleaseParameters();
public Scheduler getScheduler();
public SchedulingParameters getSchedulingParameters();
public void interrupt();
public boolean removeFromFeasibility();
public void schedulePeriodic();
public boolean setIfFeasible(ReleaseParameters release,
                                MemoryParameters memory);
public boolean setIfFeasible(ReleaseParameters release,
                                MemoryParameters memory,
                                ProcessingGroupParameters group);
public boolean setIfFeasible(ReleaseParameters release,
                                ProcessingGroupParameters group);
public boolean setIfFeasible¹(SchedulingParameters sched,
        ReleaseParameters release, MemoryParameters memory);
public boolean setIfFeasible¹(SchedulingParameters sched,
        ReleaseParameters release, MemoryParameters memory,
        ProcessingGroupParameters group);
public void setMemoryParameters(MemoryParameters memory);
public boolean setMemoryParametersIfFeasible(
                                MemoryParameters memory);
public void setProcessingGroupParameters(
                                ProcessingGroupParameters group);
public boolean setProcessingGroupParametersIfFeasible(
                                ProcessingGroupParameters group);
public void setReleaseParameters(ReleaseParameters parameters);
public boolean setReleaseParametersIfFeasible(
                                ReleaseParameters release);
public void setScheduler(Scheduler scheduler);
public void setScheduler(Scheduler scheduler,
    SchedulingParameters scheduling, ReleaseParameters release,
    MemoryParameters memory, ProcessingGroupParameters group);
public void setSchedulingParameters(
                                SchedulingParameters scheduling);
public void setSchedulingParametersIfFeasible(
                                SchedulingParameters scheduling);
```

```java
public static void sleep(Clock clock, HighResolutionTime time)
       throws InterruptedException;
public static void sleep(HighResolutionTime time)
       throws InterruptedException;
public void start();
public static boolean waitForNextPeriod[7]();
public static boolean waitForNextPeriodInterruptible[1]()
       throws InterruptedException;

}
```

A.52 RelativeTime

```java
package javax.realtime;
public class RelativeTime extends HighResolutionTime {
  // constructors

  public RelativeTime();
  public RelativeTime[1](Clock clock);
  public RelativeTime(long millis, int nanos);
  public RelativeTime[1](long millis, int nanos, Clock clock);
  public RelativeTime(RelativeTime time);
  public RelativeTime[1](RelativeTime time, Clock clock);

  // methods
  public AbsoluteTime absolute(Clock clock);
  public AbsoluteTime absolute(Clock clock,
                               AbsoluteTime destination);
  public RelativeTime add(long millis, int nanos);
  public RelativeTime add(long millis, int nanos,
                          RelativeTime destination);
  public RelativeTime add(RelativeTime time);
  public RelativeTime add(RelativeTime time,
                          RelativeTime destination);
  public void addInterarrivalTo[3](AbsoluteTime destination);
  public RelativeTime getInterarrivalTime[1]();
  public RelativeTime getInterarrivalTime[1](
                      RelativeTime destination);
  public RelativeTime relative(Clock clock);
  public RelativeTine relative(Clock clock,
                               RelativeTime destination);
  public RelativeTime subtract(RelativeTime time);
  public RelativeTime subtract(RelativeTime time,
                               RelativeTime destination);
  public String toString();
}
```

A.53 ReleaseParameters

```
package javax.realtime;
public class ReleaseParameters implements Cloneable{

  // constructors
  protected ReleaseParameters();
  protected ReleaseParameters(RelativeTime cost,
          RelativeTime deadline, AsyncEventHandler overrunHandler,
          AsyncEventHandler missHandler);

  // The following constructor may be added at Version 1.1
  protected ReleaseParameters(RelativeTime cost,
          RelativeTime deadline, RelativeTime blockingTerm,
          AsyncEventHandler overrunHandler,
          AsyncEventHandler missHandler);

  // methods
  public Object clone¹();
  public RelativeTime getCost();
  public AsyncEventHandler getCostOverrunHandler();
  public RelativeTime getDeadline();
  public AsyncEventHandler getDeadlineMissHandler();
  public void setCost(RelativeTime cost);
  public void setCostOverrunHandler(AsyncEventHandler handler);
  public void setDeadline(RelativeTime deadline);
  public void setDeadlineMissHandler(AsyncEventHandler handler);
  public boolean setIfFeasible(RelativeTime cost,
                  RelativeTime deadline);

  // The following methods may be added at Version 1.1
  public RelativeTime getBlockingTerm();
  public void setBlockingTerm(RelativeTime deadline);
  public boolean setIfFeasible(RelativeTime cost,
                  RelativeTime deadline, RelativeTime blockingTerm);
}
```

A.54 ResourceLimitError

```
package javax.realtime;
public class ResourceLimitError extends Error {

  // constructors
  public ResourceLimitError()
  public ResourceLimitError(String description)
}
```

A.55 `java.lang.Runnable`

```
package java.lang;
public interface Runnable {
  public void run();
}
```

A.56 `java.lang.Runtime`

```
package java.lang;
public class Runtime {

  // methods
  public void addShutdownHook(Thread hook);
  public int availableProcessors();
  public Process exec(String[] cmdarray) throws IOException;
  public Process exec(String command) throws IOException;
  public Process exec(String command, String[] envp)
          throws IOException;
  public Process exec(String[] cmdarray, String[] envp)
          throws IOException;
  public Process exec(String cmd, String[] envp,
                      java.io.File dir) throws IOException;
  public Process exec(String[] command, String[] envp,
                      java.io.File dir) throws IOException;
  public void exit(int status);
  public long freeMemory();
  public void gc();
  public static Runtime getRuntime();
  public void halt(int status);
  public void load(String filename);
  public void loadLibrary(String libname);
  public long maxMemory();
  public boolean removeShutdownHook(Thread hook);
  public void runFinalizers();
  public long totalMemory();
  public void traceInstructions(boolean on);
  public void traceMethodCalls(boolean on);
}
```

A.57 `Schedulable`

```
package javax.realtime;
public interface Schedulable extends Runnable {
  public boolean addIfFeasibility();
  public boolean addToFeasibility();
  public MemoryParameters getMemoryParameters();
```

```
      public ProcessingGroupParameters getProcessingGroupParameters();
      public ReleaseParameters getReleaseParameters();
      public Scheduler getScheduler();
      public SchedulingParameters getSchedulingParameters();
      public boolean removeFromFeasibility();
      public boolean setIfFeasible¹(ReleaseParameters release,
                                 MemoryParameters memory);
      public boolean setIfFeasible¹(ReleaseParameters release,
            MemoryParameters memory, ProcessingGroupParameters group);
      public boolean setIfFeasible¹(ReleaseParameters release,
                                 ProcessingGroupParameters group);
      public boolean setIfFeasible¹(SchedulingParameters sched,
            ReleaseParameters release, MemoryParameters memory);
      public boolean setIfFeasible¹(SchedulingParameters sched,
            ReleaseParameters release, MemoryParameters memory,
            ProcessingGroupParameters group);
      public void setMemoryParameters(MemoryParameters memory);
      public boolean setMemoryParametersIfFeasible(
                                       MemoryParameters memory);
      public void setProcessingGroupParameters
                          (ProcessingGroupParameters parameters);
      public boolean setProcessingGroupParametersIfFeasible(
                    ProcessingGroupParameters group);
      public void setReleaseParameters(ReleaseParameters release);
      public boolean setReleaseParametersIfFeasible(
                                       ReleaseParameters release);
      public void setScheduler(Scheduler scheduler);
      public void setScheduler(Scheduler scheduler,
            SchedulingParameters scheduling, ReleaseParameters release,
            MemoryParameters memory, ProcessingGroupParameters group);
      public void setSchedulingParameters(
                                 SchedulingParameters scheduling);
      public void setSchedulingParametersIfFeasible(
                                 SchedulingParameters scheduling);
   }
```

A.58 Scheduler

```
      package javax.realtime;
      public abstract class Scheduler {
        // constructors
        protected Scheduler();

        // methods
        protected abstract void addToFeasibility(
                                       Schedulable schedulable);
        public abstract void fireSchedulable();
```

```
public static Scheduler getDefaultScheduler();
public abstract String getPolicyName();
public abstract boolean isFeasible();
protected abstract void removeFromFeasibility(
                                    Schedulable schedulable);
public static void setDefaultScheduler(Scheduler scheduler);
public abstract boolean setIfFeasible(Schedulable schedulable,
        ReleaseParameters release, MemoryParameters memory);
public abstract boolean setIfFeasible(Schedulable schedulable,
        ReleaseParameters release, MemoryParameters memory,
        ProcessingGroupParameters group);
}
```

A.59 SchedulingParameters

```
package javax.realtime;
public abstract class SchedulingParameters implements Cloneable{
    // constructors
    public SchedulingParameters();
    // methods
    public Object clone¹();
}
```

A.60 ScopedCycleException

```
package javax.realtime;
public class ScopedCycleException extends RuntimeException {
    // constructors
    public ScopedCycleException();
    public ScopedCycleException(String description);
}
```

A.61 ScopedMemory

```
package javax.realtime;
public abstract class ScopedMemory extends MemoryArea {
    // constructors
    public ScopedMemory(long size);
    public ScopedMemory(long size, Runnable logic);
    public ScopedMemory(SizeEstimator size);
    public ScopedMemory(SizeEstimator size, Runnable logic);
    // methods
    public void enter();
    public void enter(Runnable logic);
    public void executeInArea(Runnable logic);
    public long getMaximumSize();
```

```
      public Object getPortal();
      public int getReferenceCount();
      public void join() throws InterruptedException;
      public void join(HighResolutionTime time)
            throws InterruptedException;
      public void joinAndEnter() throws InterruptedException;
      public void joinAndEnter(HighResolutionTime time)
            throws InterruptedException;
      public void joinAndEnter(Runnable logic)
            throws InterruptedException;
      public void joinAndEnter(Runnable logic, HighResolutionTime time)
            throws InterruptedException;
      public Object newArray(Class type, int number);
      public Object newInstance(Class type)
            throws IllegalAccessException, InstantiationException;
      public Object newInstance(reflect.Constructor c,
                                Object [] args)
            throws IllegalAccessException, InstantiationException;
      public void setPortal(Object object);
      public String toString();
}
```

A.62 SizeEstimator

```
package javax.realtime;
public final class SizeEstimator {
  // constructor
  public SizeEstimator();
  // methods
  public long getEstimate();
  public void reserve(Class c, int number);
  public void reserve(SizeEstimator size);
  public void reserve(SizeEstimator size, int number);
  public void reserveArray[1](int dimension);
  public void reserveArray[1](int dimension, Class type);
}
```

A.63 SizeOutOfBoundsException

```
package javax.realtime;
public class SizeOutOfBoundsException extends RuntimeException {
  // constructors
  public SizeOutOfBoundsException();
  public SizeOutOfBoundsException(String description);
}
```

A.64 `SporadicParameters`

```
package javax.realtime;
public class SporadicParameters extends AperiodicParameters {
  // fields
  public static final string mitViolationExcept;
  public static final string mitViolationIgnore;
  public static final string mitViolationReplace;
  public static final string mitViolationSave;

  // constructors
  public SporadicParameters[1](RelativeTime minInterarrival);
  public SporadicParameters(RelativeTime minInterarrival,
        RelativeTime cost, RelativeTime deadline,
        AsyncEventHandler overrunHandler,
        AsyncEventHandler missHandler);

  // The following constructor may be added at Version 1.1
  protected SporadicParameters(RelativeTime minInterarrival,
        RelativeTime cost, RelativeTime deadline,
        RelativeTime blockingTerm,
        AsyncEventHandler overrunHandler,
        AsyncEventHandler missHandler);

  // methods

  public RelativeTime getMinimumInterarrival();
  public String getMitViolationBehaviour();
  public boolean setIfFeasible(RelativeTime interarrival,
         RelativeTime cost, RelativeTime deadline);
  public void setMinimumInterarrival(RelativeTime minimum);
  public void setMitViolationBehaviour(String behavior);

  // The following method may be added at Version 1.1
  public boolean setIfFeasible(RelativeTime interarrival,
             RelativeTime cost, RelativeTime deadline,
             RelativeTime blockingTerm);
}
```

A.65 `java.lang.Thread`

```
package java.lang;
public class Thread extends Object implements Runnable {
  //nested classes
  public static final enum State[8]{BLOCKED, NEW, RUNNABLE,
               TERMINATED, TIMED_WAITING, WAITING);
  public static interface UncaughtExceptionHandler[8]{
```

```
      public void uncaughtException(Thread t, Throwable e);
};


// fields
public static int MAX_PRIORITY;
public static int MIN_PRIORITY;
public static int NORM_PRIORITY;

// constructors
public Thread();
public Thread(String name);
public Thread(Runnable target);
public Thread(Runnable target, String name);
public Thread(ThreadGroup group, String name);
public Thread(ThreadGroup group, Runnable target);
public Thread(ThreadGroup group, Runnable target, String name);
public Thread(ThreadGroup group, Runnable target, String name,
              long stackSize)

// methods
public static int activeCount();
public void checkAccess();
public int countStackFrames();
public static Thread currentThread();
public void destroy(); // DEPRECATED
public static void dumpStack();
public static int enumerate(Thread[] tarray);
public static java.util.Map<Thread,StackTraceElement[]>
              getAllStackTraces8();
public ClassLoader getContextClassLoader();
public static UncaughtExceptionHandler
      getDefaultUncaughtExceptionHandler1();
public long getId8();
public String getName();
public int getPriority();   //redfined by RealtimeThread
public StackTraceElement[] getStackTrace8();
public State getState8();
public ThreadGroup getThreadGroup();
public UncaughtExceptionHandler
        getUncaughtExceptionHandler8();
public static boolean holdsLock(Object obj);
public void interrupt();
public static boolean interrupted();
public final boolean isAlive();
public final boolean isDaemon();
```

```java
        public boolean isInterrupted();
        public final void join() throws InterruptedException;
        public final void join(long millis) throws InterruptedException;
        public final void join(long millis, int nanos)
                throws InterruptedException;
        public void resume(); //DEPRECATED
        public void run();
        public void setContextClassLoader(ClassLoader cl);
        public final void setDaemon();
        public static setDefaultUncaughtExceptionHandler¹(
                   UncaughtExceptionHandler eh);
        public void setName(String name);
        public void setPriority(int newPriority);
                   //redfined by RealtimeThread
        public void setUncaughtExceptionHandler¹(
                   UncaughtExceptionHandler);
        public static void sleep(long millis)
                throws InterruptedException;
        public static void sleep(long millis, int nanos)
                throws InterruptedException;
        public void start();
        public final void stop(); // DEPRECATED
        public final void stop(Throwable o); // DEPRECATED
        public void suspend();   // DEPRECATED
        public String toString();
        public static void yield();
    }
```

A.66 `java.lang.ThreadGroup`

```java
        package java.lang;
        public class ThreadGroup implements UncaughtExceptionHandler⁹{
          // constructors
          public ThreadGroup(String name);
          public ThreadGroup(ThreadGroup parent, String name);

          // methods
          public int activeCount();
          public int activeGroupCount();
          public boolean allowThreadSuspension(boolean b); // DEPRECATED
          public final void checkAccess();
          public final void destroy();
          public int enumerate(Thread[] list);
          public int enumerate(Thread[] list, boolean recurse);
          public int enumerate(ThreadGroup[] list);
          public int enumerate(ThreadGroup[] list, boolean recurse);
```

```
            public int getMaxPriority();
            public String getName();
            public final ThreadGroup getParent();
            public void interrupt();
            public final boolean isDaemon();
            public synchronized boolean isDestroyed();
            public void list()
            public final boolean parentOf(ThreadGroup g);
            public void resume(); // DEPRECATED
            public final void setDaemon(boolean daemon);
            public void setMaxPriority(int pri);
            public final void stop();  // DEPRECATED
            public void suspend(); // DEPRECATED
            public String toString();
            public void uncaughtException(Thread t, Throwable e)
        }
```

A.67 `java.lang.ThreadLocal`

```
        package java.lang;
        public class ThreadLocal<T>[10] {

          // constructor
          public ThreadLocal();

          // methods
          public T get();
          public void set(T value);
          protected T initialValue();
          public void remove[8]();
        }
```

A.68 `ThrowBoundaryError`

```
        package javax.realtime;
        public class ThrowBoundaryError extends Error {

          // constructors
          public ThrowBoundaryError();
          public ThrowBoundaryError(String description);
        }
```

A.69 `Timed`

```
        package javax.realtime;
        public class Timed extends AsynchronouslyInterruptedException {
          // constructors
          public Timed(HighResolutionTime time);
```

```
// methods
public boolean doInterruptible(Interruptible logic);
public void resetTime(HighResolutionTime time);
}
```

A.70 Timer

```
package javax.realtime;
public abstract class Timer extends AsyncEvent {
    // constructors
    protected Timer(HighResolutionTime time, Clock clock,
                    AsyncEventHandler handler);

    // methods
    public ReleaseParameters createReleaseParameters();
    public void destroy();
    public void disable();
    public void enable();
    public void fire1(); // Always throws UnsupportedOperationException
    public Clock getClock();
    public AbsoluteTime getFireTime();
    public boolean isRunning();
    public void reschedule(HighResolutionTime time);
    public void start();
    public void start1(boolean disabled);
    public boolean stop();
}
```

A.71 java.util.Timer

```
package java.util;
public class Timer {
    // constructors
    public Timer();
    public Timer(boolean isDaemon);

    // methods
    public void cancel();
    public void schedule(TimerTask task, long delay);
    public void schedule(TimerTask task, Data time);
    public void schedule(TimerTask task, Data firstTime,
                         long period);
    public void schedule(TimerTask task, long delay, long period);
    public void scheduleAtFixedRate(TimerTask task,
                                    Date firstTime, long period);
    public void scheduleAtFixedRate(TimerTask task, long delay,
                                    long period);
}
```

A.72 `java.util.TimerTask`

```
package java.util;
public abstract class TimerTask implements Runnable {

  // constructors
  protected TimerTask();

  // methods
  public boolean cancel();
  public abstract void run();
  public long scheduledExecutionTime();
}
```

A.73 UnknownHappeningException

```
package javax.realtime;
public class UnknownHappeningException extends RuntimeException {

 // constructors
 public UnknownHappeningException();
 public UnknownHappeningException(String description);
}
```

A.74 UnsupportedPhysicalMemoryException

```
package javax.realtime;
public class UnsupportedPhysicalMemoryException
            extends RuntimeException {

  // constructors
  public UnsupportedPhysicalMemoryException();
  public UnsupportedPhysicalMemoryException(String description);
}
```

A.75 VTMemory

```
package javax.realtime;
public class VTMemory extends ScopedMemory {

  // constructors
  public VTMemory(long initial, long maximum);
  public VTMemory(long initial, long maximum,Runnable logic);
  public VTMemory(long size); // in bytes
  public VTMemory(long size, Runnable logic);
  public VTMemory(SizeEstimator initial, SizeEstimator maximum);
  public VTMemory(SizeEstimator initial, SizeEstimator maximum,
                  Runnable logic);
```

```
public VTMemory(SizeEstimator size);
public VTMemory(SizeEstimator size, Runnable logic);

// methods
public String toString();
}
```

A.76 `VTPhysicalMemory`

```
package javax.realtime;
public class VTPhysicalMemory extends ScopedMemory {

  // constructors
  public VTPhysicalMemory(Object type, long size);
  public VTPhysicalMemory(Object type, long base, long size);
  public VTPhysicalMemory(Object type, long base, long size,
                          Runnable logic);
  public VTPhysicalMemory(Object type, long size, Runnable logic);
  public VTPhysicalMemory(Object type, SizeEstimator size);
  public VTPhysicalMemory(Object type, long base,
                          SizeEstimator size);
  public VTPhysicalMemory(Object type, long base,
                    SizeEstimator size, Runnable logic);
  public VTPhysicalMemory(Object type, SizeEstimator size,
                          Runnable logic);

}
```

A.77 `WaitFreeDequeue`

```
package javax.realtime;
public class WaitFreeDequeue {
 // This class has been deprecated in 1.0.1.

  // constructors
  public WaitFreeDequeue(Thread writer, Thread reader,
                         int maximum, MemoryArea memory);

  // methods
  public Object blockingRead();
  public void blockingWrite(Object object)
  public boolean force (Object object);
  public Object nonBlockingRead();
  public boolean nonBlockingWrite(Object object);
}
```

A.78 `WaitFreeReadQueue`

```
package javax.realtime;
public class WaitFreeReadQueue {
```

```
    // constructors
public WaitFreeReadQueue¹(int maximum, boolean notify);
public WaitFreeReadQueue¹(int maximum, MemoryArea memory,
                    boolean notify);
public WaitFreeReadQueue(Thread writer, Thread reader,
                    int maximum, MemoryArea memory);
public WaitFreeReadQueue(Thread writer, Thread reader,
                    int maximum, MemoryArea memory,
                    boolean notify);

    // methods
public void clear();
public boolean isEmpty();
public boolean isFull();
public Object read();
public int size();
public void waitForData¹¹() throws InterruptedException;
public void write¹¹,¹²(Object object)
            throws InterruptedException;
}
```

A.79 `WaitFreeWriteQueue`

```
package javax.realtime;
public class WaitFreeWriteQueue
{

    // constructors

public WaitFreeWriteQueue¹ (int maximum);
public WaitFreeWriteQueue¹ (int maximum, MemoryArea memory);
public WaitFreeWriteQueue(Thread writer, Thread reader,
                    int maximum, MemoryArea memory);

    // methods
public void clear();
public boolean force(Object object);
public boolean isEmpty();
public boolean isFull();
public Object read¹() throws InterruptedException;
public int size();
public boolean write(Object object);
}
```

Footnotes

1. Added at version 1.0.1 of the RTSJ

2. These fields and methods have been moved from the `SporadicParameters` class at verson 1.0.1 of the RTSJ.

3. Deprecated at version 1.0.1 of the RTSJ.

4. In version 1.0. of the RTSJ, this method returned void.

5. The semantics of this method has changed between versions 1.0. and 1.0.1 of the RTSJ.

6. In version 1.0. of the RTSJ, this field was of type `String`.

7. This method has been made static at version 1.0.1 of the RTSJ.

8. This has been added at Java 1.5.

9. This implementation clause has been added at Java 1.5.

10. This class was made generic at Java 1.5.

11. Throws `InterruptedException` has been added at version 1.0.1 of the RTSJ.

12. In version 1.0. of the RTSJ, this method returned boolean.

References

Aldea Rivas, M., and González Harbour, M. (2002), "POSIX-Compatible Application-Defined Scheduling in MaRTE OS", *Proceedings of 14th Euromicro Conference on Real-Time Systems*, Vienna, Austria, IEEE Computer Society Press, pp. 67–75.

Audsley, N.C., Burns, A., Richardson, M., Tindell, K. and Wellings, A.J. (1993), "Applying New Scheduling Theory to Static Priority Pre-emptive Scheduling", *Software Engineering Journal*, 8(5), pp. 284–292.

Bacon, D.F, Cheng, P., and Rajan, V.T. (2003), "A Real-Time Garbage Collector with Low Overhead and Consistent Utilization", *Proceedings of the 30th ACM SIGPLAN-SIGACT Symposium on Principles of Programming Languages*, pp. 285–298.

Barnes, J.G.P. (1997), *High Integrity Ada: The SPARK Approach*, Addison-Wesley.

Barr, M. (2001), "Memory Types", *Embedded Systems Programming*, pp. 103–104.

Belliardi, R., Brosgol, B., Dibble, P., D. Holmes and A.J. Wellings, (2004), *The Real-Time Specification for Java*, Version 1.0.1, 2nd edition Addison-Wesley.

Benowitz, E. and Niessner, A. (2003), "A Pattern Catalog for RTSJ Software Designs", *Workshop on Java Technologies for Real-Time and Embedded Systems, Lecture Notes in Computer Science,* Volume 2889, pp. 497-507.

Bloch, J. (2001), *Effective Java: Programing Language Guide*, Addison-Wesley.

Bollella, G., Brosgol, B., Dibble, P., Furr, S., Gosling, J., Hardin, D., and Turnbull, M. (2000), *The Real-Time Specification for Java*, Addison-Wesley.

Borg, A. (2004), "One the Development of Dynamic Real-Time Applications in the RTSJ - A Model for Expressing Dynamic Memory Requirements", *Technical Report YCS 379*, Department of Computer Science University of York, UK, www.cs.york.ac.uk/ftpdir/reports/YCS-2004-379.pdf

Borg, A. and Wellings, A.J. (2003), "Reference Objects for RTSJ Scoped Memory Areas", *Workshop on Java Technologies for Real-Time and Embedded Systems, Lecture Notes in Computer Science,* Volume 2889, pp. 397-410.

Brach, D. (2002), "User Experiences with the Aonix Object Ada RAVEN Ravenscar Profile Implementation", *Proceedings of the 11th International Real-Time Ada Workshop, Ada Letters*, XXII(4), 10–21.

Briot, J. Guerraoui, R., and Lohn, K. (1998), "Concurrency and Distribution in Object-Oriented Programming", *ACM Computing Surveys*, 30(3), 291–329.

Brosgol, B.M., Robbins, S., and Hassan, R.J. (2002), "Asynchronous Transfer of Control in the Real-Time Specification for Java", *Proceedings of the 5th IEEE International Symposium on Object-Oriented Real-Time Distributed Computing ISORC 2002*, IEEE Computer Society, pp. 101–108.

Burns, A. (2002), "Real-Time Systems", *Encyclopedia of Physical Science and Technology*, Vol. 14, Academic Press, pp. 45–54.

Burns, A., Dobbing, B., and Romanski, G. (1998), "The Ravenscar Tasking Profile for High Integrity Real-Time Programs", *Proceedings of Ada Europe-Europe '98*, LNCS, Vol. 1411, Springer-Verlag, pp. 263–275.

Burns, A., and Wellings, A.J. (1998), *Concurrency in Ada*, 2nd Edition, Cambridge University Press.

Burns, A., and Wellings, A.J. (2001), *Real-Time Systems and Programming Languages*, 3rd Edition, Addison-Wesley.

Burns, A., and Wellings, A.J. (2003), "Processing Group Parameters and the Real-Time Specification for Java", *JTRES 2003, Workshop on Java Technologies for Real-Time and Embedded Systems*, Lecture Notes in Computer Science, LNCS 2889, pp. 360–370.

Butenhoff, D.R. (1997), *Programming with POSIX Threads*, Addison-Wesley.

Cai, H. and Wellings, A.J. (2004), "A Real-Time Isolate Specification for Ravenscar-Java", *Proceedings of the 7th IEEE International Symposium on Object-Oriented Real-Time Distributed Computing ISORC 2004*, pp. 325-328.

Carnahan, L., and Ruark, M. (Eds) (1999), "Requirements for Real-time Extensions for the Java Platform", NIST Publication 5000-243, http://www.nist.gov/rt-java, last accessed 20/8/2002.

Dibble, P. (2002a), Private Communication.

Dibble, P. (2002b), Real-Time Java Platform Programming, Sun Microsystems Press.

Eggermont, L.D.J. (Ed) (2002), *Embedded Systems Roadmap 2002*, Technology Foundation (STW), STW-2002, ISBN: 90-73461-30-8.

Gosling, J., and McGilton, H. (1996), "The Java Language Environment: A White Paper", *http://java.sun.com/doc/language_environment*.

Gosling, J., Joy, B., and Steele, G. (1996), *The Java Language Specification*, Addison-Wesley.

Hately, D.J., and Pirbhai, I.A. (1988), *Strategies for Real-Time Specifications*, Dorset Hourse.

Henriksson, R. (1998), "Scheduling Garbage Collection in Embedded Systems", PhD Thesis, Department of Computer Science, Lund University, Sweden.

Hetcht, H., Hetch, M. and Graff, S. (1997), *Review Guidelines for Software Languages for Use in Nuclear Power Plant System*, NUREG/CR-643, U.S. Nuclear Regulatory Commission, 1997, available at http://fermi.sohar.com/J1030/index.htm, last accessed 20/8/2002.

Hu, E.Y-S., Bernat, G., and Wellings, A.J. (2002), "Addressing Dynamic Dispatching Issues in WCET Analysis for Object-Oriented Hard Real-Time Systems", *Proceedings of the 5th IEEE International Symposium on Object-Oriented Real-Time Distributed Computing ISORC 2002*, pp. 109–116.

Java Community Process, JSR50 (2000), "JSR 50: Distributed Real-Time Specification", http://www.jcp.org/jsr/detail/50.jsp, last accessed 20/8/2002.

Java Community Process, JSR121 (2001), "JSR 121: Application Isolation API Specification", http://www.jcp.org/jsr/detail/121.jsp, last accessed 20/8/2002.

Java Community Process, JSR133 (2001), "JSR 133: Java Memory Model and Thread Specification Revision", http://www.jcp.org/jsr/detail/133.jsp, last accessed 20/8/2002.

Java Community Process, JSR166 (2002), "JSR 166: Concurrency Utililities", http://www.jcp.org/jsr/detail/166.jsp, last accessed 7/7/2003.

J-Consortium (2000), "Realtime Core Extensions", Revision 1.0.14, http://www.j-consortium.org/rtjwg/index.html, last accessed 20/8/2002.

Karaorman, M., and Bruno, J. (1993), "Introducing Concurrency in a Sequential Language", *Communications of the ACM*, 36(9), 103–116.

Kim, T., Chang, N., Kim, N. and Shin, H.. (1999), "Scheduling Garbage Collection for Embedded Real-Time Systems", *ACM Workshop on Language, Compilers and Tools for Embedded Systems (LCTES '99)*, pp. 55–64.

Kopetz, H. (1997), *Real-time Systems: Design Principles for Distributed Embedded Applications*, Kluwer International Series in Engineering and Computer Science, Kluwer.

Kwon, J., Wellings, A.J., and King, S. (2002), "Ravenscar-Java: A High-Integrity Profile for Real-Time Java", *Proceedings of the Joint Java Grande ISCOPE 2002 Conferences*, pp. 131–140.

Kwon, J., Wellings, A.J., and King, S. (2003), "Predictable Memory Utilzation in Ravenscar-Java", *Proceedings of the 6th IEEE International Symposium on Object-Oriented Real-Time Distributed Computing, ISOORC 2003*, pp. 267–276.

Lea, D. (1999), *Concurrent Programming in Java: Design Principles and Patterns*, 2nd Edition, Addison-Wesley.

Lea, D. (2004), "JSR 166 API Snapshot", http://gee.cs.oswego.edu/dl/concurrent/dist/docs/index.html, last accessed 19/5/2004.

Lehoczky, J.P., Sha, L., and Strosnider, J.K. (1987), "Enhanced Aperiodic Responsiveness in a Hard Real-Time Environment", *Proceedings of the IEEE Real-Time Systems Symposium*, pp. 261–270.

Manson, J., and Pugh, W. (2001), "Semantics of Multi-Threaded Java Programs", *Proceeding of ACM Java Grande Conference*, pp. 29–38.

Meyer, B. (1993), "Systematic Concurrent Object-Oriented Programming", *Communications of the ACM*, 36(9), 56–80.

Michell, A (2002), "Practical Implementations of Embedded Software Using the Ravenscar Profile", *Proceedings of the 11th International Real-Time Ada Workshop, Ada Letters*, XXII(4), 28–36.

OMG (2002), "Enhanced View of Time Specification", V1.1, http://www.omg.org/ci-bin/doc?formal/02-05-07, last accessed 31/5/2004.

OMG (2003), "Real-time Corba Version 2.0", OMG Document formal/03-11-01, http://www.omg.org/docs/formal/03-11-01.pdf, last accessed 26/5/2004.

Ousterhout, J. (1996), "Why Threads are a Bad Idea (for most purposes)", *USENIX Technical Conference*, San Diego, CA, also available at http://www.home.pacbell.net/ouster/thread.ppt, last accessed 20/8/2002.

Pizlo, F., Fox, J., Holmes, D. and Vitek, J. (2004), "Real-Time Java Scoped Memory: Design Patterns and Semantics", *Proceedings of the Seventh IEEE Symposium on Object-Oriented Real-Time Distributed Computing, ISORC*, pp. 101-110.

Pugh, W. (1999), "Fixing the Java Memory Model", *Proceeding of ACM Java Grande Conference*, pp. 89–98.

Pugh., W. (2000), "The Double-Checked Locking is Broken Declaration", http://www.cs.umd.edu/users/pugh/java/memoryModel/DoubleCheckedLocking.html, last accessed 20/8/2002.

Pugh, W. (2004), "JSR133 - Java Memory Model and Thread Specification", http://www.cs.umd.edu/users/pugh/java/memoryModel/jsr133.pdf, last accessed 18/4/2004.

Puscher, P., and Burns, A. (2000), "A Review of Worst-Case Execution Time Analysis", *Real-Time Systems*, 18(2/3), 115–127.

Puschner, P., and Wellings, A.J. (2001), "A Profile for High Integrity Real-Time Java Programs", *Proceedings of the 4th IEEE Symposium on Object-Oriented Real-Time Distributed Computing, ISORC*, pp. 15–22.

Schmidt, D.C., and Harrison, T. (1997), "Double-Checked Locking", in *Pattern Languages of Program Design*, Robert Martin, Frank Bruschmann and Dirk Riehle (eds), Addison-Wesley.

Siebert, F. (1999), "Real-Time Garbage Collection in Multi-Threaded Systems on a Single Micro-processor", *IEEE Real-Time Systems Symposium*, pp. 277–278.

Siebert, F. (2004), "The Impact of Real-Time Garbage Collection on Realtime Java Program-ming", *Proceedings of the Seventh International Symposium on Object-Oriented Real-time Distributed Computing ISORC 2004*, pp. 33-44.

Sommerville, I. (2000), *Software Engineering*, 6th Edition, Addison-Wesley.

Stankovic, J.A., Ramamritham, K. and Spuri, M. (1998), *Deadline Scheduling for Real-Time Systems: EDF and Related Algorithms*, Kluwer Academic.

Sun Microsystems (2000), "Java 2 Platform Micro Edition (J2ME) Technology for Creating Mobile Devices", http://www.java.sun.com/products/cldc/wp/KVMwp/pdf, last accessed 20/8/2002.

Toply, K. (2002), *J2ME in a Nutshell*, O'Reilly.

van Renesse, R. (1998), "Goal-oriented Programming, or Composition using Events, Threads, considered Harmful", *Proceedings of the Eighth ACM SIGOPS European Workshop*, also available at http://www.cs.cornell.edu/Info/People/rvr/papers/event/event.ps, last accessed 20/8/2002.

Wellings, A.J., Clark, R., Jenson, D., and Wells, D. (2002), "A Framework for Integrating the Real-Time Specification for Java and Java's Remote Method Invocation", *Proceedings of the Fifth International Symposium on Object-Oriented Real-time Distributed Computing ISORC 2002*, pp. 13–23.

Index